ELEMENTARY CLASSROOM MANAGEMENT

LESSONS FROM RESEARCH AND PRACTICE

ELEMENTARY CLASSROOM MANAGEMENT

LESSONS FROM RESEARCH AND PRACTICE

SECOND EDITION

Carol Simon Weinstein
Rutgers Graduate School of Education

Andrew J. Mignano, Jr.
Highland Park Public Schools

THE McGRAW-HILL COMPANIES, INC.

New York   St. Louis   San Francisco   Auckland   Bogotá
Caracas   Lisbon   London   Madrid   Mexico City   Milan   Montreal
New Dehli   San Juan   Singapore   Sydney   Tokyo   Toronto

McGraw-Hill

A Division of The **McGraw·Hill** Companies

This book was developed by Lane Akers, Inc.

This book was set in Times Roman by Graphic World, Inc.
The editor was Lane Akers;
the production supervisor was Louise Karam.
The cover was designed by Joseph Gillians.
Project supervision was done by Tage Publishing Service, Inc.
R. R. Donnelley & Sons Company was printer and binder.
The photographer was Suzanne Karp Krebs.

ELEMENTARY CLASSROOM MANAGEMENT
Lessons from Research and Practice

This book is printed on acid-free paper.

1 2 3 4 5 6 7 8 9 0 DOC DOC 9 0 9 8 7 6

ISBN 0-07-069129-0

Library of Congress Cataloging-in-Publication Data

Weinstein, Carol Simon.
     Elementary classroom management : lessons from research and
 practice / Carol Simon Weinstein, Andrew J. Mignano, Jr.
          p.   cm.
     Includes bibliographical references and index.
     ISBN 0-07-069129-0
     1. Classroom management—United States—Case studies.
 2. Education, Elementary—United States—Case studies.   3. Home and
 school—United States.   4. Handicapped children—Education—United
 States.   I. Mignano, Andrew J.   II. Title.
 LB3013.W45   1997
 372.11′024—dc20   96-23788

ABOUT
THE AUTHORS

CAROL SIMON WEINSTEIN is professor of elementary education at Rutgers, the State University of New Jersey. She received her doctorate from Harvard Graduate School of Education in 1975, where she first became interested in the impact of classroom design on students' behavior and attitudes. Her fascination with this topic has resulted in numerous journal articles and an edited book (with Tom David), *Spaces for Children: Child Development and the Built Environment.* Her current interests focus on teacher education and the process of learning to teach. Dr. Weinstein has been one of the leaders in Rutgers' redesign of its teacher education programs and is active in a professional development school established collaboratively with New Brunswick Public Schools. She is the author of *Secondary Classroom Management* (McGraw Hill, 1996).

ANDREW J. MIGNANO, JR. is principal of Irving Primary School in Highland Park, New Jersey. He received his bachelor's degree in elementary education from Rutgers College in 1974 and his master's degree in educational psychology from Kean College in 1981. During his 15 years as a teacher, he taught all levels from kindergarten to grade five, including 1 year teaching a special education class. His tenure as a principal has been characterized by the implementation of new programs in early literacy, cooperative learning, learning styles, and other developmentally appropriate practices. A firm believer in professional development and teacher preparation, Mr. Mignano has worked closely with the Rutgers Office of Teacher Education. He has welcomed Rutgers' student teachers and pre-student teachers to his school and has also served as an adjunct professor for the seminar that accompanies student teaching.

To Barbara, Garnetta,
Ken, and Viviana

CONTENTS IN BRIEF

CONTENTS

PREFACE

Although the first edition of *Elementary Classroom Management* was published just a few years ago, rapid changes have occurred in elementary education. We have seen a move away from classrooms that are teacher-centered toward those that are more learner-centered. Educators speak less frequently about "direct instruction" and more frequently of learning as an active process in which students work to construct their own meanings and understandings. Professional development workshops increasingly focus on cooperative learning, multiple intelligences, and diverse learning styles. Teachers are urged to implement "integrated thematic instruction," mathematics activities based on the standards published by the National Council of Teachers of Mathematics, and "whole language" approaches to literacy (although in this case there is already sign of a backlash).

The changes in curriculum and instruction have been accompanied by unparalleled increases in the diversity of our student population. In many schools, children who need instruction in basic skills attend classes with those who are considered "gifted and talented"; children with severe disabilities, previously sent out of district, are educated with their nondisabled peers in regular classrooms; and children from Mexico, Nicaragua, the Dominican Republic, El Salvador, and Colombia sit next to children from Vietnam, Cambodia, Taiwan, Korea, Japan, Iran, India, Russia, and Israel.

In addition to being more diverse, classrooms contain a greater number of children from impoverished families—children who are growing up without adequate shelter, nutrition, or medical care and who are vulnerable to developmental delays, health problems, and school failure. Teachers are filing an increasing number of child abuse and neglect reports, and they witness the fear of violence with which too many children are living.

Obviously, all of these changes make managing today's classrooms far more challenging than ever before. This fact was made clear to us by the four teachers whose experiences are described here—Barbara Broggi, Garnetta Chain, Ken Kowalski, and Viviana Love. When we met one year ago to discuss the idea of doing a second edition, they enthusiastically urged us on. They described the changes in curriculum and instruction that were taking place, shared stories of increasing poverty and growing numbers of dysfunctional families, and reminisced about the days when gum chewing typified the behavior problems that teachers faced. They pointed out topics that needed to be included or expanded in a new edition—topics such as the management of learning centers and student-centered discussions, ways of helping children from chemically dependent families, full inclusion, peer mediation and conflict resolution, and strategies for communicating with troubled children.

Having confirmed the need for a second edition, Garnetta, Ken, Viviana, and Barbara had no choice but to allow us back into their classrooms—and they did so graciously. Once again, they reflected aloud on their experiences, patiently answered our questions, and read drafts of every chapter. The subtitle of our book reads "Lessons from Research and Practice," and it is largely the practices of these four teachers from which we derive the lessons. We hope that readers will come to "know" them—to see the ways they apply the principles of classroom management and to understand the reasoning behind their behavior. We do not mean to convey the impression that their ways are the only ways (or even the best ways) of managing classrooms, but we think that novice teachers can learn from "seeing" and "hearing" four masterful teachers in action. Clearly, *Elementary Classroom Management* would not have been possible without Ken, Viviana, Barbara, and Garnetta. With gratitude, we dedicate this edition to these four devoted, caring teachers.

Two points about the structure and format of the book should be made explicit. First, this edition integrates our observations and discussions from 1991–1992 with those conducted in 1994–1995. In other words, we have created a composite picture of each teacher by portraying incidents that occurred in different years with different students as though they had all occurred in the same academic year with the same class. We have sacrificed absolute verity, but we have gained simplicity and coherence.

Second, *Elementary Classroom Management* parallels *Secondary Classroom Management* (Weinstein, 1996) as much as possible, so that instructors teaching courses for prospective elementary and secondary teachers can use both books as a package. The structure and format of the two books are the same (except for one extra chapter in the elementary book), and the same language has been used wherever appropriate. The major difference, obviously, is that the "Lessons from Research and Practice" described in the secondary book are largely based on studies conducted in junior- and senior-high classrooms and on the practices of four secondary teachers. We hope that we will hear from faculty using both books, so we can learn if they do, in fact, work well together. (Electronic mail users can contact Weinstein at csw@rci.rutgers.edu.)

We wish to acknowledge the debt we owe to the numerous individuals who contributed to the making of this edition. We thank Peter Bastardo, Superintendent of Schools in Highland Park, Ronald Larkin, Superintendent of Schools in New Brunswick, and Willa Spicer, Assistant Superintendent in South Brunswick, for allowing us to work in their districts and for taking the time to read and respond to the manuscript. We are grateful to Tonia Moore in Highland Park, Leslie Lillian in South Brunswick, and Marilyn Green in New Brunswick for providing information on programs for students with special problems. We also thank Bridget DiMartini for obtaining permission to reprint copyrighted material. We appreciate the willingness of student teachers and beginning teachers to share their experiences and their journal entries with us; in addition to Jeanne Barnes, Cynthia Szumowski, and Mary Porcelli, we particularly thank Karen Boose, Mary Callahan, Mary Custy, and Terri Ann Fleischman. To Suzanne Krebs, our photographer, we express our continuing gratitude; no matter how poor the lighting or how fidgety the students, she still manages to create incredible photographs. Thanks also to Neil, Laura, and Rachel for not complaining about all the take-out suppers. Finally, we thank our editor, Lane Akers; like a good classroom manager, he knows when to be flexible and when to stand firm.

Carol S. Weinstein
Andew J. Mignano, Jr.

PART I

INTRODUCTION

Chapter One

The Elementary Classroom Environment: Crowded, Complex, and Potentially Chaotic

For many prospective and beginning teachers, entering an elementary classroom is like returning home after a long absence. So much is familiar: bulletin boards still display "Good Work" studded with A's, stars, and smiling faces; bells and buzzers still interrupt lessons to announce fire drills; the dusty odor of chalk still permeates the air. The familiarity of these sights, sounds, and smells makes us feel comfortable and at ease; in fact, it may lead us to think that the transition from student to teacher will be relatively easy. Yet, ironically, this very familiarity can be a trap; it can make it difficult to appreciate what a curious and demanding place the elementary classroom really is. Looking at the classroom as if we have never seen one before can help us recognize some of its strange characteristics and contradictions.

Viewed from a fresh perspective, the classroom turns out to be an extremely crowded place. It is more likely a subway or a bus than a place designed for learning. In fact, it is difficult to think of another setting, except prison, where such large groups of individuals are packed so closely together for so many hours. Amid this crowdedness, however, students are often not allowed to interact. As Philip Jackson (1968) has noted,

> . . . students must try to behave as if they were in solitude, when in point of fact they are not. . . . in the early grades it is not uncommon to find students facing each other around a table while at the same time being required not to communicate with each other. These young people, if they are to become successful students, must learn how to be alone in a crowd. (p. 16)

There are other contradictions in this curious place. Children are expected to work together in harmony, yet they may be strangers—even rivals—and may come from very different cultural backgrounds. Students are urged to cooperate, to share, and to help one another, but they are also told to keep their eyes on their own papers, and they often compete for grades and special privileges. They are lectured about being independent and responsible, yet they are also expected to show com-

3

plete, unquestioning obedience to the teacher's dictates. (This peculiar situation is captured in the cartoon that appears in Figure 1-1.)

In addition to these contradictions, Walter Doyle (1986) has pointed out six features of the classroom setting that make it even more complex. First, classrooms are characterized by *multidimensionality*. Unlike a post office or a restaurant, places devoted to a single activity, the classroom is the setting for a broad range of events. Within its boundaries, students read, write, and discuss. They form friendships, argue, celebrate birthdays, and play games. Teachers not only instruct, they also collect milk money, take attendance, and settle disputes. They counsel students with problems and meet with parents to discuss students' progress. Somehow, the classroom environment must be able to accommodate all these activities.

Second, many of these activities take place at the same time. This *simultaneity* makes the elementary classroom a bit like a three-ring circus. It is not uncommon to see a cluster of students discussing a story with the teacher, individuals writing at their desks, pairs of students practicing multiplication facts with flash cards, and a small group working on a social studies mural. Still other students may be passing notes about yesterday's soccer game. It is this simultaneity—this three-ring circus quality—that makes having "eyes in the back of your head" so valuable to teachers.

FIGURE 1-1
Students are urged to be independent and responsible, yet they are also expected to show complete obedience to the teacher.

"*I expect you all to be independent, innovative, critical thinkers who will do exactly as I say.*"

A third characteristic of classrooms is the rapid pace at which things happen. Classroom events occur with an *immediacy* that makes it impossible to think through every action ahead of time. A squabble erupts over the ownership of an action figure; a student complains that a neighbor is copying; a normally silent child makes a serious, but irrelevant, comment during a group discussion. Each of these incidents requires a quick response, an on-the-spot decision about how to proceed. Furthermore, classroom events like these cannot always be anticipated, despite the most careful planning. This *unpredictability* is a fourth characteristic of classrooms. It ensures that being a teacher is rarely boring, but unpredictability can also be exhausting.

A fifth characteristic of classrooms is the *lack of privacy*. Classrooms are remarkably public places. Within their four walls, each person's behavior can be observed by many others. Teachers talk of feeling as though they are always "on stage" or living in a "fishbowl" (Lortie, 1975). Their feelings are understandable. With 20 or 30 pairs of eyes watching, it is difficult to find a moment for a private chuckle or an unobserved groan. But the scrutiny goes two ways: teachers constantly monitor students' behavior as well. And in response to this sometimes unwelcome surveillance, students develop an "active underlife" (Hatch, 1986) in which to pursue their own personal agendas. With skills that increase as they progress from grade to grade, students learn to pass notes, comb their hair, read comic books, and doodle, all—they hope   without the teacher's ever noticing. Yet, even if they avoid the teacher's eyes, there are always peers watching. It is difficult for students to have a private interaction with the teacher, to conceal a grade on a test, or to make a mistake without someone noticing.

Finally, over the course of the academic year, classes construct a joint *history.* This sixth characteristic means that classes, like families, remember past events— both positive and negative. They remember who got yelled at, who was chosen to be the paper monitor, and what the teacher said about homework assignments. They remember who was going to have only "one more chance" before getting detention, and if the teacher didn't follow through, they remember that too. The class memory means that what happens today affects what happens tomorrow. It also means that teachers must work to shape a history that will support, rather than frustrate, future activities.

Crowded, competitive, contradictory, multidimensional, simultaneous, unpredictable, public—this portrait of the classroom highlights characteristics that we often overlook. We have begun the book with this portrait because we believe that *effective organization and management require an understanding of the unique features of the classroom.* Many of the management problems experienced by beginning teachers can be traced to their lack of understanding of the complex setting in which they work.

Past experiences with children may also mislead beginning teachers. For example, you may have tutored an individual student who was having academic difficulties, or perhaps you have been a camp counselor or a swim-club instructor. Although these are valuable experiences, they are very different from teaching in classrooms. Teachers do not work one-on-one with students in a private room; they seldom lead recreational activities that children have themselves selected. Teachers do not even work with youngsters who have chosen to be present. (See Figure 1-2 for Calvin's perspective on compulsory attendance.) Instead, *teachers work with captive groups of students, on academic agendas that students have not always helped to set, in a crowded, public setting.* Within this setting, teachers must gain the cooperation of students and foster their involvement in educational activities. This is not a simple task, and the difficulty is exacerbated if we are not sensitive to students' needs and interests. As Tracy Kidder (1989) notes, in far too many classrooms it seems "as if a secret committee, now lost to history, had made a study of children and, having figured out what the greatest number were least disposed to do, declared that all of them should do it" (p. 115). But it doesn't have to be like this.

The purpose of this book is to help prospective and beginning teachers understand the special characteristics of the classroom setting and their implications for organization and management. We hope to provide concepts and principles that you can use to think about the managerial tasks you will encounter as a teacher. For example, once you recognize that students are a captive audience, you are better able to see why it's necessary to stimulate interest in lessons. If you are aware of the crowded, public nature of classrooms, you can minimize congestion and provide needed privacy through the careful arrangement of your classroom furnishings. A group of strangers can become a cohesive learning community if you know how to foster an atmosphere of caring and mutual support. Simultaneity of classroom events is manageable if you teach students what to do when you are busy elsewhere—and if you hold them accountable for doing it.

GUIDING ASSUMPTIONS

Five underlying assumptions have guided the content and organization of this book. First, *we assume that most problems of disorder in classrooms can be*

FIGURE 1-2
Calvin is captive. (Calvin and Hobbes © *Watterson. Dist. by Universal Press Syndicate. Reprinted with permission. All rights reserved.)*

CALVIN AND HOBBES   **By BILL WATTERSON**

avoided if teachers use good preventive management strategies. Thus, we emphasize the prevention of misbehavior, rather than strategies for coping with misbehavior. This emphasis is consistent with classroom management research conducted within the last 25 years. In a now classic study, Jacob Kounin (1970) set out to explain the differences between orderly and disorderly classes by examining how teachers responded to misconduct. To his surprise, he found that the reactions of effective and ineffective managers were quite similar. What accounted then for the differences in order? Kounin eventually determined that the orderly classes were more the result of a teacher's ability to *manage the activities of the group* than of particular ways of handling student misconduct. Kounin's research changed the way in which we think about classroom management. The focus is no longer on ways of disciplining students, but rather on ways of creating and maintaining a classroom environment that supports learning (Evertson and Randolph, 1995).

Our second assumption is that the way teachers think about management strongly influences how they behave. Research has provided some fascinating examples of the relationship between teachers' beliefs about management and their behavior. Consider, Sarah, for example, a first-year teacher who was having difficulties managing her class (Ulerick and Tobin, 1989). Sarah's behavior in the classroom seemed to reflect her belief that effective teachers should use "charm and humor" to engage students in learning and gain their cooperation. In short, her thinking about management reflected a metaphor of "teacher as comedian." Eventually, Sarah reconceptualized the role of teacher, discarding the comedian metaphor and adopting a metaphor of teacher as "social director." As "social director," the teacher's job was to "invite students to appropriate, interesting, and meaningful learning activities" (p. 12), and to assist students in directing their own learning activities. This change in Sarah's thinking about classroom management led to changes in her behavior and dramatic improvements in the atmosphere of her classes.

In a similar study, Carter (1985) reviewed narrative descriptions of life in the classrooms of an effective and an ineffective classroom manager. Carter's analysis of the descriptions led her to conclude that the two teachers thought about classroom management in very different ways. She concluded that the effective manager saw her managerial role as "a driver navigating a complex and often treacherous route" (p. 89). From this perspective, her responsibility was to guide classroom events smoothly and efficiently; she emphasized the academic tasks that students needed to accomplish and did not allow minor misbehavior and interruptions to get her off course. In contrast, the ineffective manager seemed to see her role as "defender of a territory." Constantly vigilant for threats to order, she was careful to catch all misbehavior whenever they occurred and used reprimands and appeals to authority in order to control inappropriate behavior.

Taken together, these studies suggest that teachers who view classroom management as a process of guiding and structuring classroom events tend to be more effective than teachers who stress their disciplinary role or who see classroom management as a product of personal charm (Brophy, 1988). This perspective on classroom management is also consistent with an emphasis on prevention.

A third assumption of this book is that the concern for order must not supersede the need for meaningful instruction. Current educational reform efforts share a vision of students as active learners engaged in meaningful, complex tasks, problem-solving and critical thinking, collaboration and cooperative groupwork. This means that classrooms will be noisier and more active than in the past—more "a bee-hive of activity" than "a well-oiled machine" (Evertson and Randolph, 1995). Certainly, learning and teaching cannot take place in an environment that is chaotic and disorderly. On the other hand, excessive concerns about quiet and uniformity can *hinder* this kind of learning and teaching (Doyle, 1986). For example, a teacher may wish to divide the class into small groups for a hands-on science experiment, believing that her students will learn better by "doing" rather than by simply watching. Yet her anxiety about the noise level and her fear that students may not cooperate could make her abandon the small group project and substitute a teacher demonstration and an individual workbook assignment. In one respect this teacher is correct: a collaborative science experiment will not only be more intellectually and socially challenging, it will also be more challenging from a managerial perspective. Nonetheless, it is crucial that teachers not sacrifice opportunities to learn in order to achieve a quiet classroom. As Doyle (1985) comments, "A well-run lesson that teaches nothing is just as useless as a chaotic lesson in which no academic work is possible" (p. 33). The solution is to anticipate the specific managerial "hazards" that can arise in different situations (Carter, 1985) and try to prevent them from occurring.

Our fourth assumption is that classroom management varies across different classroom situations. Ecological psychologists remind us that the classroom is not a "homogenized glob" (Kounin and Sherman, 1979, p. 150). Rather, it is composed of distinct "subsettings"—reading groups, whole class discussions, transition times, cooperative groups—and what constitutes order may be different in each of these subsettings. For example, "calling out" may be a problem during a teacher-directed question-and-answer session (often referred to as "recitation"), but it may be perfectly acceptable in a more student-centered discussion. Similarly, students may be prohibited from helping one another during a weekly quiz, but they may be encouraged to work together during a cooperative learning activity. Students have the right to know what is expected of them in these different classroom situations. This means that teachers must think about the behavior that is appropriate in each classroom subsetting and make a point of teaching students how they need to behave. In order to assist in this task, *Elementary Classroom Management* devotes separate chapters to seatwork, groupwork, and recitations and discussions.

Our final assumption is that managing classrooms is a decision-making process. Despite numerous books that provide "101 guaranteed ways of creating classroom order," classroom management cannot be reduced to a set of recipes or a list of "how to's." As we have seen, the classroom environment is crowded, complex, and potentially chaotic. Pat answers won't work. Teachers must be able to anticipate problems, analyze situations, generate solutions, and make decisions—sometimes within seconds. And they must become familiar with relevant research that can help to inform these decisions.

PLAN OF THE BOOK

Elementary Classroom Management focuses first on "beginning-of-the-year" tasks, such as designing the physical environment of the classroom and developing rules and routines for behavior. We then move to longer term issues—for example, gaining students' cooperation, using time wisely, and managing various subsettings of the classroom. Next, we examine issues that extend beyond the classroom environment; we discuss ways of working with families and the special programs and resources that are available for children with special needs. Finally, we consider some of the very difficult problems that teachers encounter, such as substance abuse, aggression and violence, and child abuse and neglect.

Throughout the book, we weave together concepts and principles derived from research with wisdom gleaned from classroom experience. Instead of using vignettes collected from many different teachers to make our points, the book tells the stories of four real elementary teachers. These teachers share their thinking about the challenges of classroom management. You learn about the composition of their classes and the physical constraints of their rooms; you hear them reflect on their rules and routines and watch as they teach them to students. You listen as they talk about motivating students and fostering cooperation, and as they think about appropriate ways to deal with misbehavior. In sum, *the book focuses on real decisions made by real teachers as they manage the complex environment of the elementary classroom.* By sharing these stories, we do not mean to suggest that their ways of managing classrooms are the only effective ways; rather, we mean to illustrate how four reflective, caring, and very different individuals approach the tasks involved in classroom management.

And now, let's meet the teachers.

SUMMARY

In this chapter, we examined some of the contradictions and special characteristics of classrooms. We argued that effective management requires an understanding of the unique features of the classroom environment and stressed the fact that teachers work with captive groups of students on academic agendas that students have not always helped to set. We then discussed five assumptions that guided the content and organization of the book.

Contradictions of the Classroom Environment

- Classrooms are crowded, yet students are often not allowed to interact.
- Children are expected to work together harmoniously, yet they may not know or like each other.

- Students are urged to cooperate, yet they often work in individual or competitive situations.
- Students are encouraged to be independent, yet they are also expected to conform to the teacher's dictates.

Characteristics of the Classroom Environment

- Multidimensionality
- Simultaneity
- Immediacy
- Unpredictability
- Lack of privacy
- History

Guiding Assumptions of the Book

- Most problems of disorder can be avoided if teachers use good preventive management strategies.
- The way teachers think about management influences the way they behave.
- The concern for order must not supersede the need for meaningful instruction.
- Behavioral expectations vary across different subsettings of the classroom.
- Managing classrooms is a decision-making process that should be informed by relevant research.

In an effort to illustrate various ways of managing classrooms effectively, the book focuses on real decisions made by real teachers as they manage the complex environment of the elementary classroom.

REFERENCES

Brophy, J. (1988). Educating teachers about managing classrooms and students. *Teaching and Teacher Education, 4*(1), 1–18.

Carter, K. (March-April 1985). Teacher comprehension of classroom processes: An emerging direction in classroom management research. Paper presented at the annual meeting of the American Educational Research Association, Chicago.

Doyle, W. (1985). Recent research on classroom management: Implications for teacher preparation. *Journal of Teacher Education, 36*(3), 31–35.

Doyle, W. (1986). Classroom organization and management. In M. C. Wittrock (Ed.), *Handbook of research on teaching.* New York: Macmillan, pp. 392-431.

Evertson, C. M., and Randolph, C. H. (1995). Classroom management in the learning-centered classroom. In A. C. Ornstein (Ed.), *Teaching: Theory and practice.* Boston: Allyn & Bacon, pp. 118–131.

Hatch, J. A. (March 1986). Alone in a crowd: Analysis of covert interactions in a kindergarten. Presented at the annual meeting of the American Educational Research Association, San Francisco. ERIC Document Reproduction Service No. 272 278.

Jackson, P. (1968). *Life in classrooms.* New York: Holt, Rinehart & Winston.

Kidder, T. (1989). *Among schoolchildren.* Boston: Houghton Mifflin.

Kounin, J. S. (1970). *Discipline and group management in classrooms.* New York: Holt, Rinehart & Winston.

Kounin, J. S., & Sherman, L. (1979). School environments as behavior settings. *Theory into Practice, 14,* 145–151.

Lortie, D. (1975). *Schoolteacher.* Chicago: University of Chicago Press.

Ulerick, S. L., and Tobin, K. (March 1989). The influence of a teacher's beliefs on classroom management. Paper presented at the annual meeting of the American Educational Research Association, San Francisco.

Chapter Two ⸻⸻⸻⸻⸻⸻⸻

Meeting the Teachers

Two of our teachers work in New Brunswick, a relatively small urban district in central New Jersey. Here, *Viviana Love* teaches first grade, and *Garnetta Chain* teaches third grade. Across the Raritan River from New Brunswick is Highland Park, where *Barbara Broggi* is a fourth-grade teacher. Finally, *Ken Kowalski* teaches sixth grade in nearby South Brunswick. This chapter introduces all four teachers and briefly describes the districts within which they work. We begin with New Brunswick.

Of the 4,448 students who attend this district's ten schools, 50 percent are African-American and 44 percent are Hispanic. Many of the children come from families who live in poverty, evidenced by the fact that 82 percent of the students qualify for the federal free lunch program. The poverty breeds other problems typical of urban areas—drugs, a high drop-out rate, transiency, homelessness, teenage pregnancy, physical abuse.

About fifteen years ago, after receiving some of the lowest scores in New Jersey on a statewide standardized test, New Brunswick instituted a highly structured curriculum. Objectives were developed for every subject at every grade level, along with timelines for teaching each objective. Teachers must submit plan books and grade books to building principals, who closely monitor when each objective is taught and evaluated and how students are progressing.

Critics argue that the new curriculum restricts creativity and burdens teachers with unnecessary paperwork, but academic achievement has steadily increased in the last decade. Nonetheless, a sizable number of students still have difficulty passing the High School Proficiency Test that New Jersey requires for graduation. Fall 1994 results indicate that 59.8 percent of eleventh graders passed the reading portion of the test; 58.3 percent passed the math portion; and 72.3 percent passed the writing portion. Although these percentages seem low, they compare favorably with other urban school districts in the state, and teachers and administrators are convinced that New Brunswick is moving in the right direction. Financial support from local corporations (in particular, Johnson & Johnson, whose world headquarters is located in the city) and collaborative projects with Rutgers, the state university, have also aided the district's quest for improvement.

VIVIANA LOVE 1st grade

Roosevelt School is in the heart of downtown New Brunswick, surrounded by single- and multi-family dwellings. It is an old, but well-cared for building with a capacity for 700 students. On the first floor, in a spacious, carpeted room next to the office, we find Viviana Love, a first-grade bilingual teacher.

Viviana was born in a small town in Puerto Rico. Although her parents had only a third-grade education, they instilled in Viviana a desire to learn and a strong ambition to succeed. Her mother taught her to read and write, and with these skills Viviana began her teaching career at the age of seven. She tutored neighborhood children, and much to her delight, she sometimes received a quarter for her services! From the very beginning, Viviana knew teaching felt right.

Viviana Love.

An image of her first-grade teacher, Mrs. Hernandez, is as strong today as it was 50 years ago:

> She wore a lot of bracelets and when she went to the board . . . oh, those bracelets! I loved the chiming of the bracelets. I used to just look at them and say to myself that the first thing I'll do when I am a teacher is buy a lot of shiny bracelets—and I did. The bracelets, for me, were a glamorous symbol of high social status. I couldn't wait to write on the board with my shining bracelets.

Viviana began her professional teaching career in Puerto Rico, before she even completed college. She taught for seven years in a small two-room schoolhouse while pursuing her bachelor's degree; she then moved to the island of St. Croix where she taught Spanish for half a year. In 1970, she arrived in New Jersey. She has taught in New Brunswick ever since—a total of 34 years of teaching.

With no children of her own, Viviana "adopts" her students: "They are my children," she says. "I will do anything for them, just like mothers do for their own children. I want them to be the best." Sometimes she feels like taking them home with her, so she can give them the love and stability some of them lack. Above all, she seeks to stimulate her students' desire to learn.

Viviana's commitment to her students is evident in her first-grade bilingual classroom. With an energy level that is rare, she motivates, prods, instructs, models, praises, and captivates her students. Most instruction is delivered to the whole class, as required by the district. The pace is brisk, and Viviana clearly has a flair for the dramatic; she uses music, props, gestures, facial expressions, and shifts in voice tone to communicate the material.

Viviana's 25 students have all emigrated from the Dominican Republic, Mexico, Puerto Rico, and Honduras. Eighteen attended kindergarten here; seven are "port-of-entry" (POE) children who have just arrived in this country. Early in the school year, Viviana instructs primarily in Spanish. She moves to English as soon as possible, however, using Spanish whenever she perceives problems in comprehension. Viviana is vehement about not wanting her children segregated or labeled as disadvantaged because they are not fluent in English. She uses every available minute for instruction, even turning interruptions or unexpected events into "teachable moments." When a visitor comes to her classroom, for example, she asks her students to use English to describe the person's clothing, hair color, and height. Her efforts pay off: although her children begin the year speaking little or no English, they leave in June generally having achieved the normal first-grade objectives for New Brunswick.

Knowing that her children come from poor families, Viviana provides all the materials they need to complete class assignments. "My children cannot say they couldn't complete a project because they didn't have a magazine or scissors. I give them what they need so that there is no excuse for failure." Some people say that Viviana is strict and demands too much of first-grade students, but her students don't seem daunted by her high expectations. They look enthusiastic and speak proudly about their accomplishments.

Viviana also sets high standards for herself. A firm believer in continuing professional development, she has a master's degree in urban education and additional credit hours in bilingual education. She frequently serves as a cooperating teacher for student teachers and regularly attends workshops and courses. She is part of the Rutgers-New Brunswick Math Project, a program that emphasizes the importance of mathematical problem-solving and the use of manipulative materials. She recently volunteered to participate in another Rutgers-New Brunswick collaboration on literacy. When we comment on her continuing efforts to improve her teaching, she shrugs: "Teachers have to keep current. . . . Education changes because students change. Our teaching must reflect the changes of the world around us." Viviana's success in the classroom and her commitment to her profession have been acknowledged by the district and the state: in 1990, she received the Governor's Teacher Recognition Award.

Viviana is also valued and appreciated by the parents of the children she teaches. On the first day of school, she talks openly with the parents who have accompanied their children to school: "At home, *you're* the parents. . . . but at school, *I'm* the mother. We're all family, one big family, all Hispanic, and we all help each other." She communicates frequently with parents, not simply to discuss children's progress in school, but also to counsel parents on discipline, guide them in their search for employment, and suggest ways they can help their children learn.

Despite having lived here for 26 years, Viviana maintains strong ties with her parents who are still in Puerto Rico. She is grateful for the love of learning and the drive to succeed that they stimulated in her. She hopes to share these same gifts with her students and their families.

GARNETTA CHAIN 3rd grade

We move now to the outskirts of New Brunswick, where McKinley School sits amid low-income housing projects and worn-looking factories. In a brand new addition to the building, we meet third-grade teacher Garnetta Chain. Garnetta's classroom belies the stereotype of the urban school. The blue-gray carpeting that covers two-thirds of the classroom creates a feeling of warmth and homeyness, while the linoleum on the other third provides a suitable flooring for messy activities. From the back wall, next to the sink, juts a peninsula of shelving and cabinets. Two aquariums with long-haired guinea pigs sit on the formica countertop, and math manipulatives of all sizes and colors fill the shelves. Brightly colored posters suggest the topics the class will be studying—the solar system, "exploring emotions," the cursive alphabet. In one corner is a library center; on the opposite wall is a collection of board games.

Garnetta, a mother of three children, has been teaching for 25 years, two of which were spent as director of a day care center in New York. Although she began college intending to become a biochemist, she soon realized she'd much rather work with children than with test tubes and changed her major to education. Her family supported this decision, especially her grandmother, a teacher herself for 30 years. Garnetta eventually received a master's degree in elementary education; she has taught third grade for the last 13 years. This year her class is small, only 15 stu-

Garnetta Chain.

dents; three are Hispanic and 12 are African-American. It's quite a change from last year, when she had a class of 39 children and had to teach in the library, since no classroom was large enough!

Garnetta speaks candidly of the difficulties her students face. Too many of them have been victims of physical and sexual abuse. Drugs, teenage pregnancy, and violence plague the community in which they live. It is no wonder that Garnetta feels that her main goals as a teacher are to impart moral values, give plenty of love and attention, and teach her students to feel good about themselves and to enjoy learning.

She also aims to offer a secure and safe environment. Class rules are clearly posted in her room. Garnetta feels that her children live with so much uncertainty in their lives that they need to know there is one place they can count on consistency. She tells us: "They need to know that a no or yes answer will remain that way, whether it's Monday or Friday. They have to have limits; there need to be consequences for their behaviors so that they'll develop responsibility for their actions."

Along with limits, Garnetta provides praise and affection. We watch her calm an angry child with a soft word and prevent a disruption with a hand on a shoulder, and it's easy to see why her students come to respect and trust her. She offers so many of the qualities they lack in their personal lives. It's not unusual for students to return to her classrooms years after they've moved on, just to chat or to discuss a problem.

Garnetta's caring, like Viviana's, goes well beyond the classroom walls. This fact was strongly impressed upon us one day in April as we sat watching her teach. Suddenly, a little boy appeared outside her window, his face pressed against the glass. The child had been in Garnetta's class, but a social service agency had removed him from his foster home and placed him with his father in a neighboring town. Although Garnetta had strongly opposed the move, she had not been able to convince the authorities that he was better off where he was.

On that April day, Garnetta invited him in. He found his old chair and a sweatshirt he had left behind. The children accepted him, and you could tell by the smile on his face that he felt at home. Once again, Garnetta tried to intervene. She had heard the boy wasn't attending his new school regularly and was seen out late at night unsupervised. She immediately got on the telephone with the boy's caseworker. Suggesting he return to McKinley, Garnetta even volunteered to pick him up at his new address and drive him each day. It didn't work. Garnetta gave him all the love she could that day and then gently told him he had to return to his new school.

When we asked Garnetta how she maintains her optimism and enthusiasm for teaching, she replied:

> I always hope that there's somebody out there that I will reach and that I'll make a difference. I know society has a strong hold on my students and I may fail, but if someone makes something of themselves, and I've had a role in making a difference, then it's all worthwhile. I have to believe this.

If making a difference depends on energy and enthusiasm, then Garnetta will surely succeed. She's a veritable whirlwind. She not only participates in the Rutgers-New Brunswick Math Project, she's also one of three McKinley teachers involved in New Jersey's "Statewide Systemic Initiative," designed to upgrade mathematics and science education. Her classroom also participates in "Project 2000," in which Merrill-Lynch executives serve as teaching assistants and role models one day per week, and "Family Science," a program that invites families to come to school and participate in science activities with their children. In addition, Garnetta regularly supervises student teachers and coordinates several extracurricular programs—the yearly bazaar, the African-American History Week program, and holiday dessert night. One of her favorite projects is "career week," when students learn about vocational opportunities. (On "aerospace day," she even had a helicopter pilot land his helicopter in the school yard!) Garnetta also spends a lot of time on the phone, trying to generate parent support. It's not easy; most families are caught up in their own lives and have difficulty maintaining contact with the school. But she keeps after them.

In class, Garnetta never sits down. She is everywhere, all at once, making sure that her students are actively involved. When they learn about liquid measurement, she gives them water and containers for pouring and measuring. Sometimes she has them work in pairs, interviewing each other and then describing their partners in oral reports to the class. When they begin the fearsome topic of long division, they work with Unifix™ cubes, and it's suddenly not so scary. When they read about bread-baking in their reading books, they make bread in class. Although Garnetta is required to present new concepts and skills to the whole class, she frequently uses small groups for reinforcement and enrichment. She strongly believes in the value of students teaching each other and stresses the importance of their learning to work together.

Garnetta is hopeful that all her extra efforts will pay off and that a potential drop-out will become a high school graduate. She tries to serve as a model for her students, and she wants them to see the pride she has in herself and her career. She tells us, "I want them to see that teaching is as great as being a doctor or lawyer."

BARBARA BROGGI 4th grade

The tree-lined borough of Highland Park lies on the other side of the Raritan River from New Brunswick. The population of this small community is extremely diverse. The district's three schools serve children who live in homes valued at $500,000 as well as those from low-income apartment complexes. The student population of 1,450 is 61 percent white, 17 percent African-American, 12 percent Hispanic, and 10 percent Asian-American. About 10 percent of the children qualify for the federal free lunch program. HSPT results from Fall 1994 indicates that 90 percent of the eleventh graders passed the reading portion of the test; 91.4 percent passed the math portion; and 98.6 percent passed the writing portion. These results reinforce Highland Park's reputation as a district that works hard to promote excellence, no mean accomplishment in the face of recent budget problems and changing demographics. In fact, the January 1996 issue of *Money* magazine ranked Highland Park in the top 100 school districts in the nation that offer academic excellence in a community with reasonably priced housing.

Barbara Broggi.

Barbara Broggi, also a mother of three children, is a product of the Highland Park school system. She currently teaches fourth grade at Bartle School, the district's intermediate school. Bartle houses 450 students in grades three through six. This year, Barbara has 27 students. Like Highland Park itself, her class is diverse in terms of racial/ethnic composition: 17 of her students are white, five are African-American, three are Hispanic, and two are Asian-American. The class is also heterogeneous in terms of academic ability and achievement: six students qualify for enrichment; three students have been classified as having learning disabilities; three children receive extra "basic skills instruction"; and one boy has autism. His inclusion in Barbara's classroom exemplifies the district's policy of educating students with disabilities in neighborhood schools instead of sending them to special schools out of the district. (We will discuss the topic of "full inclusion" in Chapter 12.)

Barbara never thought of becoming anything but a teacher. Her mother taught high school in Highland Park, and Barbara grew up with an insider's view of the profession. She was present when students dropped by to talk with her mother or to ask for extra help, and it was this close personal connection with people that first attracted Barbara to teaching. Even now, after 18 years in the classroom, it's the relationship with students that means the most to her:

> Everyday contact with my students is what makes teaching so special for me. I want to get to know them as *people*—not just names on a seating chart. I want them to know *me,* to see that I'm a person with strengths and needs just like them. If I cry when I'm reading them a sad passage from a novel, they see that I have feelings and that I'm not afraid to express them. And they learn that it's okay to express *their* feelings as well. I tell my students, "We're in this together. We're going to learn, work, and play together. And our common goal is to get the most out of every single day."

For the last several years, Barbara has participated in a program called "Creating an Original Opera," sponsored by the Metropolitan Opera Guild. Teachers in this program learn how to act as facilitators who help children produce their own opera. Not only do the students decide on the theme and thesis of the story, they also write the actual dialogue, the music, and the lyrics. In addition, they do every other task involved in staging an opera except the directing: sets, lighting, props, costumes, makeup, public relations, advertising, and, of course, performing. According to Barbara, participation in the opera project has had an impact on the way she teaches all areas of the curriculum:

> Philosophically, I've always believed that classrooms should be student-centered. But this project has given my teaching definition and direction. It has taught me so much about how to turn over ownership of learning to kids, and how much kids can do when they're given the chance. When you see children functioning really well as carpenters and set designers, it makes you more aware of their talents. For some kids, it's the first time that someone's found out what they're good at. You begin to honor those talents and to think: How can we use these talents in the classroom?

Barbara's classroom reflects her belief in the importance of creative expression and active participation. Students' work covers the walls and hangs from the ceiling. Science experiments are always in progress, and illustrations of novels enliven a bulletin board. Three computers remain on all day so students can write and edit.

Barbara is given quite a bit of latitude in the materials and teaching strategies she uses. Nine years ago, for example, she stopped using basal readers and is now an avid supporter of literature-based reading instruction. She selects novels that touch her, *Bridge to Terabithia* (Paterson, 1977), *The War with Grandpa* (Smith, 1984), *Sarah, Plain and Tall* (MacLachlan, 1985)—novels that will be meaningful to her students: "During literature discussions, I can tap into a whole range of student feelings on a wide variety of subjects. And as we share ideas, we grow closer together." Barbara also uses children's literature as a springboard for teaching vocabulary, grammar, writing, and spelling.

Barbara enjoys living in the town where she teaches. She likes being able to run into parents at the local food store, at a soccer game, or in the sports collectibles card shop that she and her husband own. This accessibility is appreciated by parents, and the informality of their encounters helps Barbara to establish a partnership with them. She is on a first-name basis with the parents of her students—an indication of their open, easy relationship.

Barbara volunteers for many district committees and plays a very active role on them. She says it's out of nosiness, but it's clear that she is seriously committed to educational improvement. Always seeking better and more interesting ways to teach, she frequently participates in professional development activities. She regularly supervises student teachers and conducts workshops on learning styles and cooperative learning for her colleagues and teachers from other districts.

Each afternoon when the dismissal bell has sounded, students of all ages cluster around the door to Barbara's classroom. They come to share some news, to complain about a perceived injustice, or simply to see what's going on in her room. It was the promise of close personal relationships with children that lured Barbara into teaching. Now, as we watch Barbara surrounded by her present and former students, it's clear that the promise has been realized.

KEN KOWALSKI 6th grade

Not far from New Brunswick is the community of South Brunswick. The school district has a reputation for innovation. Indeed, a 1989 issue of *Newsweek* magazine featured South Brunswick's initiatives in early childhood education. Recently, with a substantial grant from the R. J. R. Nabisco Foundation, the district has also begun to explore new ways to assist at-risk children. And locally, South Brunswick is known for its commitment to "whole language," in which the language arts—reading, writing, speaking, and listening—are integrated with one another and with other areas of the curriculum.

This well-regarded school district currently has about 5,000 students and is gaining more than 200 a year. The student population is becoming increasingly diverse; it is now 69 percent white, 15 percent Asian-American, 11 percent African-American, and 6 percent Hispanic. Over 100 children—representing about 60 different languages—require instruction in English as a second language, and like Highland

Park, the socioeconomic range is striking. Although many people think of South Brunswick as a middle- or upper-middle class community, a sizable number of its children live in low-cost mobile home parks. About 10 percent are eligible for the federal free lunch program. The HSPT results from Fall 1994 show that 92.1 percent of the eleventh graders passed the reading portion of the test; 89.8 percent passed the math; and 92.5 percent passed the writing.

At first glance, Brunswick Acres School looks as if it's situated in the middle of a park. It's surrounded by woods and grassy fields; a wooden foot bridge spans a creek flowing nearby. Built in 1975, the school serves 542 students from kindergarten through sixth grade. A new addition was recently completed, and a gym is currently being transformed into classrooms to accommodate the growing population in this area.

Brunswick Acres is an "open space" building. The main instructional area is a huge space that can accommodate at least ten "classrooms." There are few permanent interior walls; instead classroom boundaries are delineated by folding walls, file cabinets, bulletin boards, shelves, and cubbies. As we walk through the "hallways," on our way to Ken Kowalski's teaching area, we can see what's happening in various classes. We watch students traveling from one area to another, constructing models, discussing a story, and working in the media center.

Ken Kowalski.

Ken, who has a ten-year-old daughter, is a sixth-grade teacher. He came to teaching in a roundabout way. After graduating from college with a degree in sociology, he became a writer. He began working in an after-school program in New Brunswick to supplement his income. As he came to know the children in his charge, he realized that they needed more than arts and crafts, but he wasn't sure how to help them:

> I had gone to a parochial school as a kid, and there were 50 to 60 students in a class. The nuns were just overwhelmed by that many students; they had little time for individuals. I couldn't draw on my own personal experiences to help "my kids," and I didn't know intuitively what to do. If teaching is an art, then I came into it with no colors on my palette.

Ken decided to enroll in a teacher certification program so he could "do something" for his at-risk students. He soon had children playing word games and dropping by his house to talk or listen to stories. His career in teaching had begun.

Sometimes, Ken regrets that his route to teaching was indirect: "Too many people 'end up' teaching—and it seems so much less noble than knowing from the very start that you want to be a teacher." Despite the serendipitous way he entered teaching, Ken has a strong commitment to the profession and a deep attachment to his colleagues. He constantly questions what he does in the classroom, searching for the best ways to help his students grow. He received a master's degree in reading, and regularly participates in inservice courses. Over the years, he has achieved a reputation as a master teacher. Like Viviana, Garnetta, and Barbara, Ken frequently serves as a cooperating teacher and is active on district committees.

This year, Ken has 22 students in his class. The ethnic and racial diversity is striking: there are five Asian-Americans, three Hispanics, two African-Americans, and twelve whites. Eleven of the children come from families that emigrated from Mexico, Puerto Rico, Sri Lanka, India, Turkey, Korea, and the Philippines. Six of these students need instruction in English as a second language.

Many of Ken's students were in his fifth-grade class the year before, so the relationship between them is easy and familiar from the very beginning. Since he knows his students, Ken can "pick up" from the previous year and develop plans that he knows will be intellectually challenging. His students will continue to do "process writing"—they will write first drafts, discuss them with peers, revise, edit, and finally "publish" their work. Using a National Geographic Society computer network, they will link up with other schools to identify acid rain patterns around the world. During social studies, they will do two simulation games focusing on the first half of the 1800s: first they will live as mountain men hunting for animal skins, then as pioneers heading west to stake their claims during the Gold Rush.

Ken is also very concerned about his students' social and emotional development. He wants them to feel good about themselves and to develop life skills:

> Geometry is an exciting, necessary lesson, but to say that geometry is more important than sitting with kids and dealing with issues like teasing and humiliation is a mistake. If the kids sit there feeling miserable, then school is a sham—a place to come and feel terrible while you're trying to learn. Instead, school should be a place where you come

to deal with the most important problems—which are how do you deal with people—and then you're ready to learn some geometry. Geometry can be fun when kids don't have to worry about other things.

Ken works hard to create an atmosphere of understanding, responsibility, and mutual respect. During class, he appears relaxed and patient. When students speak to him, he listens intently. His students know that they can confide in him; they often use their daily journals as an opportunity to tell him about concerns. Ken knows that writing offers a privacy that's difficult to achieve in the classroom, and he always writes back.

Most instruction occurs in small groups, with lots of cooperative learning and opportunities for student decision-making. Whether students are in clusters working out a math problem, conferencing about their writing, or discussing a recently read novel, Ken pushes them to think critically, to reason, and to solve problems. His emphasis on critical thinking even extends to outdoor activities. He is a firm believer in daily physical exercise and takes his class outside every day. But here, too, Ken stresses the importance of *strategy*. And as always, he's in the middle of it all—running and dodging, coaching and exhorting.

Ken may have begun teaching with no colors on his palette, but he has certainly become a master of even the most subtle hues.

CONCLUDING COMMENTS

Viviana, Garnetta, Barbara, and Ken teach in very different settings. Grade levels range from Viviana's first grade to Ken's sixth grade. The racial composition of the four classes differs dramatically: Barbara's and Ken's classes are extremely heterogeneous, Viviana's children are all Hispanic, and Garnetta's class is predominantly African-American. Viviana and Garnetta work in a district where 80 percent of the children are eligible for free lunch, compared with the 10 percent figure in Barbara's and Ken's districts. And while Viviana and Garnetta must follow a carefully prescribed curriculum, Ken and Barbara are given a great deal of freedom. In order to be effective, our four teachers must be sensitive and responsive to these differences in age, race, culture, socioeconomic conditions, and district policy.

Despite these differences, Viviana, Garnetta, Barbara, and Ken are alike in many ways. Obvious similarities emerge when they talk about the tasks of classroom management. In Chapter 1, we discussed our assumption that the way teachers think about management strongly influences how they behave. We cited research suggesting that teachers who view classroom management as a process of guiding and structuring classroom events tend to be more effective than teachers who stress their disciplinary role. Interestingly, when Viviana, Garnetta, Barbara, and Ken speak about classroom management, they rarely use the words "discipline" or "punishment," "confrontation" or "penalty." Instead, they stress the need to develop a "caring community," in which all children are contributing, valued members (Schaps and Solomon, 1990); they speak about involving students and helping them to achieve; they talk about the importance of being organized and well-prepared.

These views are captured in the metaphors they hold for classroom management. Viviana's metaphor is "mothering"—just as mothers teach their children how to behave in various situations, so must teachers. Barbara speaks of "gardening," and Ken talks about "coaching." For Garnetta, management is "choreography": "You're setting the stage for the dance, helping everyone to do the right steps, to make one big beautiful dance together. . . ." These metaphors reveal the difficulty the teachers have separating classroom management from instruction. To them, it's "all of a piece."

It's important to remember that Viviana, Garnetta, Barbara, and Ken are real human beings working in the complex, uncertain environment of the elementary classroom. Although they are intelligent, skillful teachers who are extremely effective at preventing misbehavior, their classrooms are not free of problems. (In fact, Chapter 6 focuses specifically on the ways they deal with misbehavior.) Like all of us, they make mistakes; they become frustrated and impatient; they sometimes fail to live up to their image of the "ideal" teacher. By their own testimony, they are all still learning how to run more effective classrooms.

It is also important to remember that these four teachers do not follow recipes or prescriptions for classroom management, so their ways of interacting with children often look very different. Nonetheless, underlying the differences in behavior, we often detected the same guiding principles. In the chapters that follow, we will try to convey the ways these four excellent teachers tailor the principles to fit their own particular contexts.

Finally, it is necessary to point out that these teachers do not work in schools where conditions are so bad that classes have to be held in stairwells or storage closets, where windows remain broken for years, and where 40 students in a class have to share a handful of books. Nor do they teach in schools that have installed metal detectors or where students regularly carry weapons. In recent years, New Brunswick, Highland Park, and South Brunswick have all experienced a frightening increase in the number of serious problems—even at the elementary level—but serious acts of violence are not an everyday occurrence. Whether the strategies discussed here are generalizable to severely troubled schools is not clear. Nevertheless, we hope that *Elementary Classroom Management* will prove to be a useful starting point for teachers everywhere.

REFERENCES

MacLachlan, P. (1985). *Sarah, plain and tall.* New York: Harper & Row Junior Books.

Paterson, K. (1977). *Bridge to Terabithia.* New York: Harper & Row Publishers.

Schaps, E., and Solomon, D. (1990). Schools and classrooms as caring communities. *Educational Leadership, 48*(3), 38–42.

Smith, R. K. (1984). *The war with grandpa.* New York: Dell Publishing Co.

PART II

ESTABLISHING AND MAINTAINING AN ENVIRONMENT FOR LEARNING

Chapter Three

Designing the Physical Environment

Discussions of organization and management often neglect the physical character-istics of the classroom. Unless it becomes too hot, too cold, too crowded, or too noisy, we tend to think of the classroom setting as merely an unimportant backdrop for interaction. Yet, *this setting can influence the way teachers and students feel, think, and behave.* Careful planning of the physical environment is an integral part of good classroom management.

Environmental psychologists point out that the effects of the classroom environ-ment can be both *direct* and *indirect* (Proshansky and Wolfe, 1974). For example, if students seated in straight rows are unable to carry on a class discussion because they can't hear one another, the *environment is directly hindering their participation.* Stu-dents might also be affected *indirectly,* if they infer from the seating arrangement that the teacher does not really want them to interact. In this case, the arrangement of the desks is sending a message to the students about how they are supposed to behave. Their reading of this message would be accurate if the teacher had deliberately arranged the seats to inhibit discussion. More likely, however, the teacher genuinely desires class participation, but has simply not thought about the link between class-room environment and student behavior.

This chapter is intended to help you develop "environmental competence" (Steele, 1973)—awareness of the physical environment and its impact and the ability to use that environment to meet your goals. Teachers who are environ-mentally competent can plan spatial arrangements that support their instructional plans. They are sensitive to the messages communicated by the physical set-ting. They know how to evaluate the effectiveness of a classroom environment. They are alert to instances when physical factors might be contributing to be-havioral problems, and they can modify the classroom environment when the need arises.

As you read this chapter, keep in mind our discussion of classroom manage-ment in Chapter 1. (You might find it helpful to refer back to the section on

"Guiding Assumptions.") From our perspective, classroom management is not simply a matter of dealing with misbehavior. Instead, effective management means *gaining students' cooperation and promoting their involvement in educational activities.* Our discussion of the classroom environment reflects this perspective: We are concerned not only with reducing distraction or minimizing congestion through good environmental design, but also with ways the environment can foster children's security, increase their comfort, and stimulate their interest in learning tasks.

Throughout this chapter, we will illustrate our major points with examples from the classrooms of the teachers you have just met. At the end of the chapter, we will revisit Barbara's classroom and listen to her reflect on the ways her classroom environment helps her to achieve her goals.

SIX FUNCTIONS OF THE CLASSROOM SETTING

In Chapter 1, we talked about the wide variety of activities that occur in classrooms. Although we normally think of the classroom as a place for instruction, it is also a place for Halloween parties and making friends, for collecting book club money and passing notes. It is a setting for social interaction; for trying out new roles; and for developing trust, confidence, and a sense of personal identity. Fred Steele (1973) has suggested that physical settings serve *six basic functions:* security and shelter, social contact, symbolic identification, task instrumentality, pleasure, and growth. These six functions provide a useful framework for thinking about the physical environment of the elementary classroom.

Security and Shelter

This is the most fundamental function of all built environments. Like homes, office buildings, and stores, classrooms should provide protection from bad weather, noise, extreme heat or cold, and noxious odors. Sadly, even this most basic function is sometimes not fulfilled, and teachers and students must battle highway noise, broken windows, and leaky roofs. In situations like this, it is difficult for any of the other functions to be met. Physical security is a *precondition* that must be satisfied, at least to some extent, before the environment can serve students' and teachers' other, higher level needs.

Physical security is a particularly important issue in classes like science and art, where students may come into contact with potentially dangerous supplies and equipment. It is essential that teachers of these subjects know about their state's safety guidelines regarding proper handling, storage, and labeling. The art teacher in Viviana's school, for example, is careful to store supplies according to state specifications. She also keeps informed about regulations regarding the kinds of materials she can order; pointed scissors and rubber cement are definitely out!

Often, schools provide *physical* security, but fail to offer *psychological* security— the feeling that this is a safe, comfortable place to be. Psychological security is becoming increasingly crucial as more and more children live in impoverished, unstable, and sometimes unsafe home environments. For them, in particular, schools must serve as a haven. Psychological security is also particularly important in open-space settings, like Ken's, where background noise and large interior spaces can be unsettling.

One way of enhancing psychological security is to make sure your classroom contains some "softness." Many classrooms are examples of "hard architecture" (Sommer, 1974). With their linoleum floors, concrete block walls, and formica surfaces, they are designed to be "strong and resistant to human imprint" (p. 2). But children (and adults) tend to feel more secure and comfortable in environments that contain items that are soft or responsive to their touch. In Garnetta's classroom, we find guinea pigs to hold and beanbag chairs in which to relax; Viviana's room contains a leather couch, two armchairs, and pillows to sit on while reading. Other soft elements that teachers can use are plants, fish tanks, and stuffed animals. Warm colors, bright accents, and varying textures (e.g., burlap, wood, and felt) can also help to create an atmosphere of security and comfort.

Another way of increasing psychological security is to arrange classroom space so that students have as much freedom from interference as possible. In the crowded environment of the classroom, it is easy to become distracted. You need to make sure that students' desks are not too near areas of heavy traffic (e.g., the pencil sharpener, the sink, a learning center), and that noisy activities are separated from quiet ones (e.g., block play from the literacy center).

It's also helpful to create cozy corners with pillows and a rug where students can retreat when things get too hectic. Low partitions will allow children to feel separated and private, but still enable you to see what's going on. In addition, you might set up a few study carrels or "private offices" where children who want more enclosure can work alone, or provide folding cardboard dividers (three pieces of heavy cardboard bound together) that they can place on their desks. All of us need to "get away from it all" at times, but research suggests that opportunities for privacy are particularly important for children who are distractible and for those who have difficulty relating to their peers (Weinstein, 1982). Barbara recognizes this need for privacy when she tells us:

> I always arrange the desks in clusters because I use a lot of small group activities, but I've had kids who ask to sit all alone, and I allow them that opportunity. What I've found is that they usually want to be back in the group after a while. I've never put a child by him- or herself, because then that child can't be part of the activities I plan—for example, with your table group, write a couplet that describes what happened in this chapter; or write a math riddle that another table will solve. I want the kid to be part of the cluster, but have the right to buy out when he or she can't handle it. If I see a kid having trouble at a table, I might say, "Look, if you would like to go work by yourself, go ahead, but you can't ruin this for everyone." Or the kid might ask me to go work alone. He or she can move their desk to a corner or find a little enclosed place on the floor. . . .

Freedom from distraction is especially crucial for children with Attention Deficit Disorder (ADD) or Attention Deficit Hyperactivity Disorder (ADHD), neurobiological disabilities that interfere with an individual's ability to sustain attention. (See Chapter 12 for a fuller discussion.) Children with ADD have difficulty focusing attention, concentrating, listening, following instructions, and organizing tasks. Children with ADHD not only have attentional problems, they also exhibit behaviors associated with hyperactivity—difficulty staying seated, fidgeting, impulsivity, lack of self-control. You can help ADD/ADHD children by seating them away from noisy areas, near well-focused students, and as close to you as possible so that it's easy to make eye contact. For these children, study carrels, folding dividers, and retreat spaces are especially important.

Social Contact

Interaction Among Students   As you plan the arrangement of students' desks, you need to think very carefully about how much interaction among students you want there to be. Clusters of desks promote social contact since children are close together and can have direct eye contact with those across from them. In clusters, children can work together on activities, share materials, have small group discussions, and help each other with assignments. This arrangement is most appropriate if you plan to emphasize cooperative learning activities. But it is unwise—even inhumane—to seat children in clusters and never allow them to interact. If you do that, students receive two contradictory messages: the seating arrangement is communicating that it's okay to interact, while your verbal message is just the opposite!

As a beginning teacher, you may want to place desks in rows until you are confident about your ability as a classroom manager. Rows of desks reduce interaction among students and make it easier for them to concentrate on individual assignments (Axelrod, Hall, and Tams, 1979; Bennett and Blundell, 1983; Wheldall, Morris, Vaughan, and Ng, 1981). Rows also direct students' attention toward the teacher, so they are particularly appropriate for teacher-centered instruction. If you feel more comfortable with rows of desks, but your room has been equipped with tables, you may want to try trading furniture with another teacher. If you keep the tables, think very carefully about the behavior you will expect from your students, and make sure that your expectations are both reasonable and clear.

You might also consider putting desks in horizontal rows. (See Figure 3-1.) This arrangement still orients students toward the teacher, but provides them with close "neighbors" on each side.

Figures 3-2 to 3-4 illustrate the way Viviana, Garnetta, and Ken have arranged their classrooms. As you can see, Viviana uses a horseshoe arrangement. This layout is consistent with the teacher-directed nature of her instructional program, but it also allows students to work easily with the individuals sitting on either side. Viviana explains this choice of layout:

> I like the desks in a horseshoe because this way everyone can see what's going on in the front of the room. They can see the work on the board or demonstrations at the small round table. But it's also a good arrangement for working with a partner. The horseshoe also lets me see everybody and to get close to them.

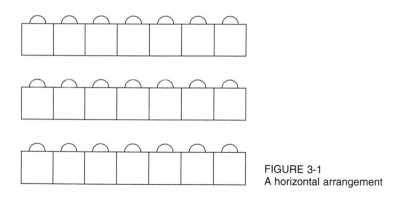

FIGURE 3-1
A horizontal arrangement

Garnetta also used to arrange desks in a horseshoe, but this year she has created three clusters of five desks each. The change was instigated by McKinley's adoption of a new reading series that promotes "integrated" language arts instruction and encourages peer interaction. By arranging the desks in clusters, Garnetta has organized the physical environment to support the new approach.

While Garnetta is teaching in a brand new classroom that is far more spacious than the classrooms she has had in previous years, Ken's classroom space this year is much

FIGURE 3-2
Viviana's room arrangement

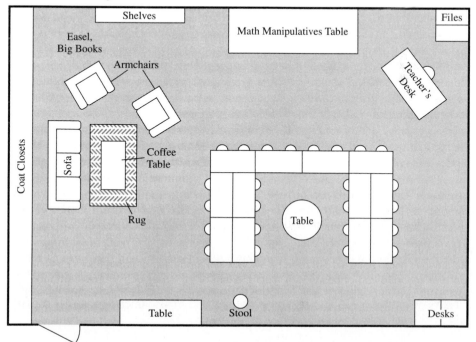

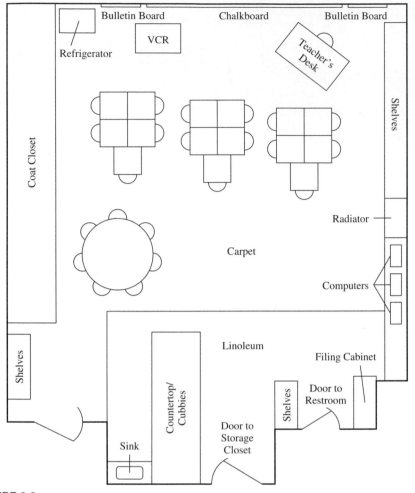

FIGURE 3-3
Garnetta's room arrangement

smaller than the spaces he used to have. His classroom has also been moved from the building's perimeter to the center of the school (in what used to be part of the school library). This means that Ken's classroom has no windows, no permanent walls, and no ready access to the outdoors. Noise from surrounding areas easily flows over the six-foot-high bookshelves and dividers that create the classroom's portable walls.

The reason for the change in size and location is the increase in enrollment at Brunswick Acres; to accommodate the additional students, walls had to be shifted to create extra classrooms. Given the cramped space—and five new computers— Ken has decided to put individual desks into clusters. Fortunately, this arrangement is also compatible with his teaching strategies and goals, since he emphasizes co-operative small group activities:

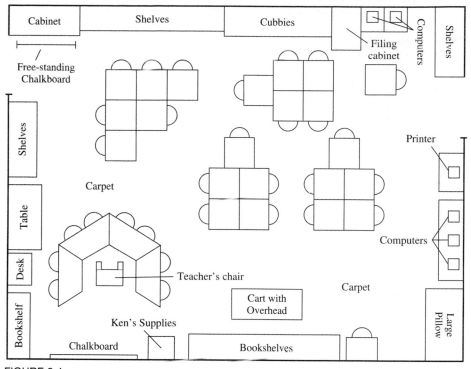

FIGURE 3-4
Ken's room arrangement

By pushing the desks together, I not only save space, I also create areas that are appropriate for small group work and provide a nice big surface for artwork. I've oriented the desks so that practically no one has to turn completely around to face the front of the room. It's real easy for them to communicate with one another, yet they can still see presentations that are done with the overhead.

Interaction Between the Teacher and the Students   The way students are arranged can also affect interaction between the teacher and the students. A number of studies have found that in classrooms where desks are arranged in rows, the teacher interacts mostly with students seated in the front and center of the classroom. Students in this "action zone" (Adams and Biddle, 1970) participate more in class discussions and initiate more questions and comments.

Educational researchers have tried to tease out the reasons for this phenomenon. Do students who are more interested and more eager to participate select seats in the front, or does a front seating position somehow produce these attitudes and behaviors? This issue has not yet been fully resolved, but the weight of the evidence indicates that a front-center seat does encourage participation, while a seat in the back makes it more difficult to participate and easier to "tune out."

Although research on the action zone has only examined row arrangements, it is easy to imagine that the same phenomenon would occur whenever teachers direct most of their comments and questions to the students who are closest to them. Keep this in mind and take steps to ensure that the action zone encompasses your whole class. Some suggestions are to: (1) move around the room whenever possible; (2) establish eye contact with students seated farther away from you; (3) direct comments to students seated in the rear and on the sides; and (4) periodically change students' seats so that all students have an opportunity to be up front.

Symbolic Identification

This intimidating term simply refers to the information provided by a setting about the people who spend time there. The key questions are: What does this classroom tell us about the students—their interests, activities, backgrounds, accomplishments, and preferences? And what does the classroom tell us about the teacher's goals, values, and beliefs about education?

Too often classrooms resemble motel rooms. They are pleasant but impersonal, revealing nothing about the people who use the space. Yet it is not difficult to "personalize" a classroom setting, and by doing so you communicate to children that they are important and special. Barbara describes an introductory activity she does on the first day of school:

> The first thing I do with kids is a writing activity and an art activity. They write a piece about why they're unique (for example, maybe somebody's a ballerina or likes computers). Then we turn that into a banner made out of felt. Each person has a banner, even me. We put our names on the banners with puff paint and hang them all around the edge of the classroom. Then we take the essays and hang them on the writing bulletin board. The banners stay up all year long.

There are lots of ways to personalize classroom space: you can post children's photographs, artwork and projects, the stories they dictate or write, and charts listing heights, weights or birthdays. You can decorate your room with silhouettes of the children or with life-size bodies traced on large paper. You can set aside a bulletin board for the "student of the week." You can display children's best work. One idea we especially like is to allow each child to select his or her own best piece of work each week. In this way, you encourage children to be self-evaluative, and you avoid the danger of continually posting the work of only a few children.

You can also personalize space by displaying materials that reflect the cultural backgrounds of the children in your class. For example, you might post a map of the world highlighting students' countries of origin. At the beginning of the year, you could create a welcome sign written in the different languages spoken by your students or their families. You might exhibit photographs of children from around the world, list accomplishments of notable people from your children's native countries, or hang posters showing art from different cultures. In Viviana's room, colorful, fabric parrots from Puerto Rico hang from the ceiling; bulletin board displays are labelled in both English and Spanish; and paper flags of the Dominican

Republic, Nicaragua, Mexico, Ecuador, Puerto Rico, Cuba, Peru, Honduras, and Colombia decorate one wall. Displays like these communicate respect for your students' diverse cultural backgrounds.

In addition, consider ways you can use the environment to communicate something about your *own* cultural background, experiences, and idiosyncrasies. You might want to hang your favorite art prints, display pictures of your family, or exhibit your collections of "precious objects." We've seen hippopotamuses of all sizes, paperweights, kaleidoscopes—even hubcaps. In Barbara's classroom, giraffes sit on her desk and perch on the top of cabinets. Not only do they encourage students to take risks and to "stick their necks out," they allow students to see that Mrs. Broggi is a real person.

Task Instrumentality

This function concerns the many ways the environment helps us to carry out the tasks we need to accomplish. Think about the tasks and activities that will be carried out in your classroom. Will students work alone at their desks on seatwork assignments? Will they work cooperatively on activities and projects? Will you instruct the whole class from the chalkboard? Will you work with small reading groups? Will students do research using encyclopedias and trade books? Will they work at learning centers around the room? Will they engage in dramatic play, block play, arts and crafts, science experiments?

For each of these tasks, you need to consider the physical design requirements. For example, if you plan to meet with small reading groups, you have to think carefully about where to locate the small group area. Do you want it near a chalkboard or a bulletin board? In any case, its location should not be distracting to students working independently. You also want to be able to monitor the rest of the students while you are working with the small group.

A relatively new addition to the classroom environment is the microcomputer. Computers can provide opportunities for students to complete practice exercises, to engage in problem-solving and exploration through games and simulations, and to experience the writing process—to compose, edit, revise, and publish (Weinstein, 1991). This year, Ken is lucky enough to have five computers in his room, and Barbara and Garnetta each have three. This is substantially better than having only one computer per classroom (or none), a situation that exists in many schools, but it still means that the computer is a scarce but precious resource. This increases the need to think carefully about location. If students are going to work at the computer in pairs or in small groups, place it in an area where clusters of students can gather around without creating traffic congestion and distraction. Also keep in mind that the computer is often "a social event" (Genishi, 1988); the upright position of the screen invites comment and inquiry from students walking past or sitting nearby, at least until the novelty wears off. How you feel about this spontaneous interaction should be a factor in your decision about the computer's location.

Whatever tasks will occur in your classroom, there are a few general guidelines you need to keep in mind.

Frequently used classroom materials should be accessible to students.   Materials like crayons, pencils, paper, dictionaries, rulers, and staplers should be easy to reach. This will minimize the time spent preparing for activities and cleaning up. Decide which materials will be kept in students' desks and which will be kept on shelves.

Shelves and storage areas should be well-organized so that it is clear where materials and equipment belong.   It is useful to label shelves so that everyone knows where things go. (For very young children, you can use picture labels.) This will make it easier to obtain materials and to return them. You should also have some sort of a system for the distribution and collection of students' work (e.g., in-out boxes or individual student mailboxes).

Pathways throughout the room should be designed carefully to avoid congestion and distraction.   Paths to the water fountain, pencil sharpener, coat closet, and trash can should be clearly visible and unobstructed. These high traffic areas should be as far from students' desks as possible. Make sure that your pathways don't go through work areas. For example, you don't want children to have to walk through a library corner in order to get something from the coat closet. Children shouldn't have to walk behind the small group reading area in order to get a needed dictionary.

The seating arrangement should allow students to have a clear view of instructional presentations.   If possible, students should be able to see instructional presentations without turning their desks or chairs around.

Students should have a place to keep their belongings (lunch boxes, backpacks, skateboards, etc.).   This is especially important if your classroom doesn't have desks with storage space.

The location of the teacher's desk depends on where you will be spending your time.   If you will be constantly moving about the room, your desk can be out of the way, in a corner perhaps. If you will use your desk as a conference area or work station, then it needs to be more centrally located. But be careful: With a central location, you may be tempted to remain at your desk for long periods of time, and this cuts down your ability to monitor students' work and behavior. All four of our teachers have their desks off in a corner or in the back of the room.

Incompatible activities should be separated.   If you plan to set aside spaces for particular activities, think carefully about their relative locations. Make sure to separate activities that don't go well together: noisy-quiet, messy-neat, and wet-dry (e.g., the computers should be far away from the sink!).

Pleasure

The important question here is whether students and teachers find the classroom attractive and pleasing. To the already overworked teacher preoccupied with covering the curriculum, raising test scores, and maintaining order, aesthetic concerns may seem irrelevant and insignificant (at least until parent conferences draw near). Yet given the amount of time that you and your students spend in your classroom, it is worth thinking about ways to create a pleasing environment. It is sad when students associate education with sterile, uncomfortable, unpleasant places.

The classic study on environmental attractiveness was conducted by Maslow and Mintz (1956). These experimenters compared interviews that took place in an "ugly" room with those that took place in a "beautiful" room. Neither the interviewer nor the subject knew that the real purpose of the study was to assess the impact of the environment on their behavior. Maslow and Mintz found that interviewers assigned to the ugly room complained of headaches, fatigue, and discomfort. Furthermore, the interviews *finished more quickly* in the ugly rooms. Apparently, people in the ugly room tried to finish their task as quickly as possible in order to escape from the unpleasant setting.

Subsequent studies have also demonstrated that aesthetically pleasing environments can influence behavior. For example, primary-grade children in rooms decorated with "happy" pictures showed more persistence at tasks than those in rooms with sad or neutral pictures (Santrock, 1976). Two college-level studies have indicated that attractive classrooms have a positive effect on attendance and feelings of group cohesion (Horowitz and Otto, 1973) and on participation in class discussions (Sommer and Olsen, 1980). The classrooms in these college studies had specially designed seating, soft lighting, and carpeting, hardly the kinds of aesthetic improvements that can be implemented by most elementary teachers. Nonetheless, it is worth thinking about the kinds of environmental modifications that are possible—for example, plants, mobiles, banners, bulletin board displays. In Garnetta's room, plants line the windowsill; Barbara uses large pieces of boldly patterned wrapping paper to cover bulletin boards; and Viviana's colorful parrots create a festive air.

Identifying specific characteristics that everyone considers pleasing has been difficult. It may be trite, but it appears to be true that "beauty is in the eye of the beholder." Nonetheless, there are some principles to keep in mind when thinking about ways to create an attractive classroom. In general, people seem to respond positively to the presence of *variation*. In other words, they seem to enjoy being in environments that contain both warm colors and cool colors; open, spacious areas and small, cozy corners; hard surfaces and soft surfaces; textures that are smooth and those that are rough (Olds, 1987). However, it is important that this variation be *moderate* and *orderly*. A lack of stimulus variation can lead to monotony, but too much variation can produce feelings of anxiety and chaos, especially if it lacks patterning or predictability.

Growth

Steele's last function is particularly relevant to classrooms, since they are settings specifically intended to promote children's development. This function is also the most difficult to pin down, however. While it's easy to see that environments should be functional and attractive, it's less obvious that they can be designed to foster growth. Furthermore, growth can refer to any number of areas—learning to tie one's shoes; increasing your self-confidence; learning to cooperate. For simplicity, we will restrict our discussion to ways in which the environment can promote children's *cognitive development*.

Psychologists have found that the opportunity to explore rich, stimulating environments is related to cognitive growth. Your classroom should be more than a place where children listen to instruction, complete workbook pages, and demonstrate mastery of skills. It should be a setting that *invites children to explore, observe, investigate, test, and discover.* This means that in addition to the standard readers, dictionaries, and workbooks, your classroom should contain a wide variety of materials such as puzzles, brainteasers, math manipulatives, science equipment, and art supplies.

When stocking your classroom, it is useful to think about materials that are "open"—water, paint, clay—and those that are "closed"—puzzles, workbooks, tracing patterns (Jones and Prescott, 1978). Location on an open-closed continuum describes the extent to which a material or object dictates *one right answer.* For example, children have many options when creating with clay, but there is only one right way to complete a wooden puzzle. Materials like blocks, Lego™, and Tinkertoys™ lie somewhere in the middle of the continuum: although these materials impose some restrictions on what can be done with them, they still invite experimentation and improvisation. Analyzing materials in terms of openness can help you to structure a setting that promotes creativity and divergent thinking.

The environment can also foster children's growth by stimulating their interest in books. Studies suggest that students spend little classroom time actually reading (as opposed to doing phonics worksheets or answering questions at the end of the story)—as little as seven or eight minutes per day at the primary level and 15 minutes per day at the middle school level (Dishaw, 1977, cited in Guthrie and Greaney, 1991). Moreover, children appear to devote little time *outside* of school to leisure reading (Guthrie and Greaney, 1991). Fielding, Wilson, and Anderson (1986), for example, found that 50 percent of the fifth-grade children in their study read books for an average of four minutes per day or less, while 30 percent read two minutes per day or less.

To promote an interest in books, educators (e.g., Morrow, in press) encourage teachers to provide children with the opportunity to have pleasurable experiences with literature: to read daily to children, to discuss the stories, to schedule recreational reading periods, and to integrate literature with other areas of the curriculum. An appealing, well-organized literacy center can support these literature activities. Viviana, for example, has created a "mini-living room" in her classroom, complete with a leather-upholstered sofa and armchairs (salvaged from a school storage closet). A coffee table overflows with newspapers, books, and magazines, and a small rug and pillows allow children to sit comfortably on the floor. Viviana tells us why she has provided this center:

> For many of my children, the only thing they do in the living room is watch television. I want them to realize that you can sit in the living room and read a good book. Every day I sit on the sofa and have them sit around me on chairs and pillows. I read a story or an article from the day's newspaper (which I bring in). Then I let someone take the newspaper home. The kids love our "living room," and I feel so good when I see them curled up on the sofa with a book.

Viviana reads a story to her class in the library corner.

Here are a few simple guidelines to keep in mind if you decide to include a literacy center in your classroom (Morrow and Weinstein, 1982, 1986).

Locate your literacy center in a quiet area of the room.   Use low partitions that provide protection from distraction and intrusion, but that still permit you to see what's going on.

Display at least some of the books so that the covers are clearly visible.   In this way, children can see the illustrations on the front. The spine of a book rarely contains more than the title, and this is often hard to read unless you crane your neck sideways.

Include some element of softness in the literacy center.   For example, use pillows, beanbag chairs, rockers, plants to provide a comfortable, cozy feeling.

Stock the center with a wide variety of magazines, newspapers, and books.   Use novels, reference books, poetry, catalogs, cookbooks, biographies, travel books, appliance manuals, picture books, etc., on a wide variety of reading levels. If possible, include audiotapes of books that children can listen to and read along with.

Include literature props.   You may want to consider felt-board stories, roll movies, and puppets, as well as materials that children can use to make their own books (e.g., paper, staplers, cardboard, markers, pencils). If particular books are as-

The Literacy Corner	Yes	No
1 Children participate in some phase of the library corner design (develop rules, select a name for the area, develop materials, etc.).	___	___
2 The area is placed in a quiet section of the room.	___	___
3 The area is visually and physically accessible.	___	___
4 Part of the area is partitioned off from the rest of the room.	___	___
5 There is an organizational system for shelving books (e.g., color coding for topic).	___	___
6 Bookshelves are available for displaying featured books with covers facing outward.	___	___
7 Five to eight books are available per child.	___	___
8 Many books are available representing three to four grade levels and of the following types:	___	___
picture books	___	___
picture storybooks	___	___
traditional literature	___	___
poetry	___	___
realistic literature	___	___
informational books	___	___
biographies	___	___
novels	___	___
easy-to-read books	___	___
riddle and puzzle books	___	___
participation books	___	___
series books	___	___
TV-related books	___	___
newspapers	___	___
magazines	___	___
9 New books are circulated every two weeks.	___	___
10 There is a check-out/check-in system for children to check out books daily.	___	___
11 There is a rug, throw pillows, rocking chair, or beanbag chair.	___	___

FIGURE 3-5
A Checklist for Evaluating and Improving the Literacy Environment
(adapted from Morrow, in press)

sociated with specific activities that could be carried out in the classroom, include the materials children will need. For example, a book about magnets might be displayed next to a tray with magnets, paper clips, nails, and tacks (Loughlin and Martin, 1987). You could also include paper on which children can record the results of their investigations.

Place a bulletin board in the literacy center.   Post children's book reviews, the jackets of featured books, and sign-up charts for students who want to read aloud to classmates or to children in younger grades.

	Yes	No
The Literacy Corner—cont'd		
12 There are head sets and taped stories.	___	___
13 There are posters encouraging children to read.	___	___
14 There are stuffed animals.	___	___
15 The area is labeled with a name selected by the class.	___	___
16 There is a felt board with story characters and the related books and other story manipulatives (roll movies, puppets, etc.).	___	___
17 There is a system for recording books read.	___	___
18 The area occupies about 10 percent of the classroom space.	___	___
The Writing Center Portion of the Literacy Center		
19 There are a table and chairs.	___	___
20 There are writing posters and bulletin boards on which children can display their writing by themselves.	___	___
21 There are writing utensils (pens, pencils, crayons, markers, colored pencils).	___	___
22 There is writing paper (many varieties of paper in all sizes, booklets, pads).	___	___
23 There is a message board for children to post messages for the teacher and other members of the class.	___	___
24 There is a place to store "Very Own Words."	___	___
25 There are folders for children to place samples of their writing.	___	___
26 There are materials to make books.	___	___
27 There is a typewriter and/or computer.	___	___
Literacy Rich Environment for the Rest of the Classroom		
28 There is environmental print, such as signs related to themes studied, directions, rules, functional messages.	___	___
29 There is a calendar.	___	___
30 There is a current events board.	___	___
31 There are content area centers.	___	___
32 There are appropriate books, magazines, and newspapers in all centers.	___	___
33 There are writing utensils and varied types of paper in all centers.	___	___
34 There is print representative of multicultural groups.	___	___

FIGURE 3-5—cont'd

Plan set times for students to use the literacy center. Too many teachers design and equip literacy centers and then don't provide opportunities for children to use them. Some teachers allow children to go to the center only if they are finished with their "real work." This means that children who work slowly may never get to use the center. It also conveys the message that the activities done in the literacy center are not considered so important or valuable as those done at desks under the teacher's direct supervision.

Figure 3-5 contains a checklist you can use to evaluate and improve the literacy environment of your classroom (Morrow, in press).

THE TEACHER AS ENVIRONMENTAL DESIGNER

Steele's six functions give you a way of thinking about the environment, but they don't provide you with an architectural blueprint. If you think about the various roles that settings play, you will realize that the functions not only overlap, they may actually conflict. Seating that is good for social contact may be bad for testing. Room arrangements that provide children with privacy may be poor for monitoring and maintaining order. As you think about your room and your own priorities, you will have to determine which functions will take precedence over others.

In this section of the chapter, we describe a process you can follow as you design your classroom.

Think About the Activities the Room Will Accommodate

The first step in designing a classroom is to decide on the activities your room is to accommodate. For example, if you are teaching a kindergarten or primary classroom, you may wish to create areas for sharing time, reading aloud, small group reading instruction, whole group math instruction, blocks, housekeeping, and arts and crafts. An intermediate-grade teacher might want to accommodate whole group literature discussions, small group work, media presentations, hands-on projects, and testing. List these activities in a column and next to each activity, note if it poses any special physical requirements (e.g., art and science areas should be near a sink; the library corner should be in a quiet area of the room; computers need to be near electrical outlets and away from chalkboards to avoid chalk dust).

Draw a Floor Plan

Before actually moving any furniture, draw a number of different floor plans and select the one that seems most workable. (Figure 3-6 depicts symbols that may be

FIGURE 3-6
Drawing a floor plan: some useful symbols

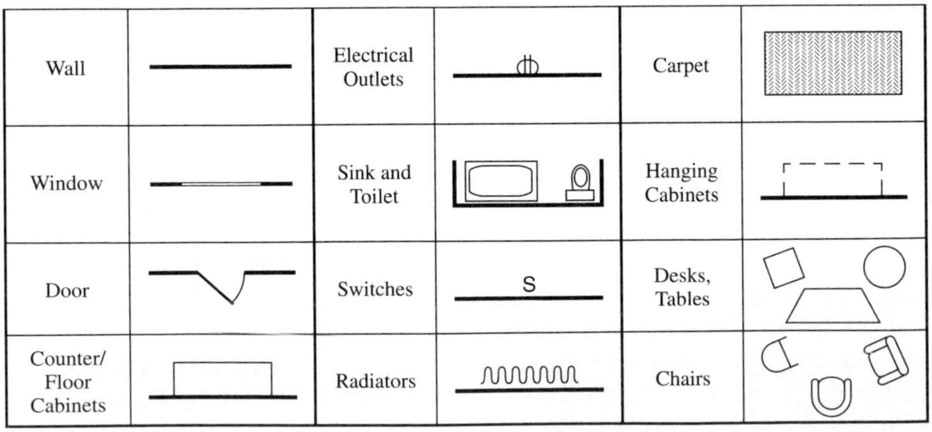

Wall	———————	Electrical Outlets		Carpet	
Window	———————	Sink and Toilet		Hanging Cabinets	
Door		Switches	S	Desks, Tables	
Counter/ Floor Cabinets		Radiators	∿∿∿∿∿	Chairs	

useful.) As you decide where to place furniture and equipment, consider the special requirements noted on your list of activities, as well as the room's "givens"—the location of the outlets, the chalkboard, the windows, and the built-in shelves. Also keep in mind our discussion of psychological security, social contact, and task instrumentality.

It may be helpful to begin by deciding where you will conduct whole group instruction (if at all) and the way students will be seated during this time. Think about where the teacher's desk should be; if frequently used materials are stored on shelves or in cabinets that are accessible to you and your students; and if pathways are clear. Remember, there is no one right way to design your classroom. The important thing is to make sure that your spatial arrangement supports the teaching strategies you will use and the kinds of behaviors you want from your students.

Involve Students in Environmental Planning

Although a great deal can be done before the start of school, it is a good idea to leave some things undone, so your students can be involved in the design process. David (1979) found that elementary children from very different school settings express the same, basic concerns: they want a stimulating environment, adequate room, "a place of my own where I can keep my things," and private places. In addition, they appreciate the opportunity to help decide on the room arrangement.

Although students' suggestions are occasionally beyond the means of the normal public school—planetarium-type ceilings, rope ladders, child-scale doorways (Hill, 1968)—most of their ideas are reasonable. Listen to Arthur, a student at an inner-city junior high, speaking of his ideal classroom (Coles, 1969):

> I'd like comfortable chairs, like ones that had cushions so your back doesn't hurt and your bottom either. I'd like us sitting around—you know, looking at each other, not in a line, not lined up. I'd like a sink, where you could get some water to drink, and you wouldn't have to ask the teacher to go down the hall. . . . There'd be a table and it would be a lot nicer homeroom than it is now. . . . (pp. 49-51)

It's obviously impossible to involve everyone in all environmental decisions; however, you might solicit children's ideas for room design and then select those that seem most feasible. You might also rotate responsibility for some aspect of the environment among small groups of students (e.g., each group could have an opportunity to design a bulletin board display). Inviting children to participate in environmental decision-making not only helps to create more responsive physical arrangements, it also prepares students for their roles as active, involved citizens who possess environmental competence.

Try the New Arrangement, Evaluate, and Redesign

Use Steele's six functions of the environment as a framework for evaluating your classroom design. For example, does the classroom provide opportunities for retreat and privacy? Does the desk arrangement facilitate or hinder social contact among students? Do displays communicate information about the students and their work? Are frequently used materials accessible to students? Does the room provide pleasure? Does it contain materials that invite children to explore and to extend their interests and abilities?

As you evaluate the effectiveness of the classroom setting, stay alert for behavioral problems that might be caused by the physical arrangement. For example, if a small cluster of students suddenly becomes inattentive when their desks are moved next to the hamster cage, it is likely that an environmental change is in order, rather than detention. If students rarely demonstrate interest in reading during free-choice time, it may be due to the way the books are displayed. If the classroom floor is constantly littered despite your appeals for neatness, the underlying problem may be an inadequate number of trash cans.

Improving your room does not have to be tedious and time-consuming. In fact, small modifications can bring about gratifying changes in behavior. This was demonstrated by Krantz and Risley (1972), who found that when kindergartners crowded around a teacher who was reading a story, they were inattentive and disruptive. Just spreading the children out in a semi-circle markedly improved their attentiveness. In fact, this simple environmental modification was as successful as a complicated system of rewards and privileges that the experimenters had devised!

DESIGNING A FOURTH-GRADE CLASSROOM

This chapter has tried to provide you with a way of thinking about classroom environments and an outline of the design process. Now we'll take a closer look at Barbara's fourth-grade classroom (see Figure 3-7). As you can see, she has arranged the desks in clusters of four or five. Her own desk is in the rear of the classroom, out of the way and adjacent to the library area. The class computers are placed along one side wall.

As Barbara planned her room at the beginning of the school year, she shared her thoughts with us. The following transcript illustrates the way one teacher thinks through the process of designing the classroom environment.

> The first thing I think about is what has to stay where it is (like the bulletin boards), where the outlets are located, and other kinds of constraints (for example, my room has a folding wall, which means that you can't have any noisy activities along that wall). Then I decide where the main instructional area will be—where I'll do whole group instruction, lead a discussion, show a video. The lab table is there; it houses all kinds of science materials underneath and provides me with a high demonstration area that everyone can see. The stool is where I sit if I'm going to sit—for example, when I read to the class.

> After that I go on to the things that I personally find important for my teaching style. This year, I'm involved in a cooperative learning science project, and my students have to sit in groups of four or five. I don't want to change the seating every day just for science, so I designed the room with that need in mind. The one exception is Joey's desk [the child with autism]. Because he's easily distracted and has difficulty in social situations, his desk has to be toward the outside edge of the room and with his back to a window. He'll move it in whenever we have science. I'm hoping that eventually he'll be able to sit in a cluster all day, just like everyone else.

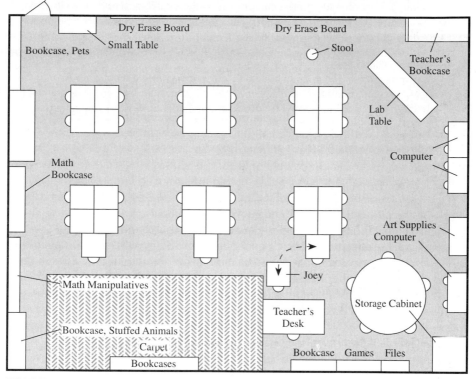

FIGURE 3-7
Barbara's classroom arrangement

I also know that I need a library area, a place for the three computers (with room so that kids can work in clusters around the computers), and a research or resource center. I also think about where to put storage for things that kids will need. For example, I've set out all the art supplies on a bookcase in front of the folding wall, so that kids can have easy access to markers, paper, glue, etc. I want the kids to be independent and feel that they have control over their needs. A kid shouldn't have to come to me and ask if he can get into the closet for a marker. I've found that you can't have everything the kids need in the same place, because then you have too many kids in the same place at the same time. It becomes chaotic. So I spread supplies around: paper is over here, art supplies over there. I also have three pencil sharpeners (one by the door and one on top of a bookshelf, and a battery-operated one on my desk).

I've put the library corner on the other side of the room. There's a bookcase there filled with stuffed animals that kids have given me that go along with pieces of literature that we've read—lots of penguins for *Mr. Popper's Penguins!* There's also a collection of books that I've built up over my years in fourth grade. Next to that I've put a bookcase of math manipulatives and games, because my math class plays the games on the rug. Although people also play board games on the rug, I've stored them on the other side of the room so kids don't have to climb over other kids in order to get a game.

I plan to use the large table next to the math bookcase for science displays and experiments, with the chalkboard above it for illustrations. Suppose I'm teaching about plants and talking about root structure. I can draw it on the chalkboard and leave it. Then the next day, I can start on the stem and draw that part. Kids are pulled out of science for basic skills class, and if you miss the notes, it's tough. This way the notes and illustrations can remain up there for a week, and the kids won't miss it. Next to the science table I've stored the resource books—encyclopedias and dictionaries, thesaurus, etc. And on the top of the bookcase is the aquarium with our chameleons. (They're great pets—they don't bite, nobody's allergic to them, they're neat to watch, and you can use them to teach about habitat. They're the best pets I've ever had—but I won't touch them.)

I've arranged the computers differently this year. One computer and printer are off by themselves this year. That one's reserved only for writing. The other two can be used not only for writing but also for games (e.g., during free time). One has CD-ROM, and there's a modem on another.

We'll start off the year with this arrangement, but of course, we'll have to see how it works and we'll probably change things around. I try to give the kids a say in how things are arranged. We have a deal: sometimes I make the final decision, and sometimes they do. Whichever, we agree to live with the arrangement for a designated period of time. Then if we don't like it, we can change it. Last year my class decided they wanted the round table in the center of the room with the desks in a horseshoe around it. I hated this, but I lived with it for a month. Then I told them exactly why I didn't like it: I had no privacy, and all the noise faced the front of the room. So together we changed the arrangement.

I think a lot about the way the room looks. I hate dull, boring classrooms. Rooms need to be filled with children's work and to reflect your own personal touch. I decorate with wrapping paper. On one bulletin board I put bright yellow paper with flowers of purple and red. Then I put black paper on the bulletin boards on either side and made flowers to match the center paper. One of those areas will be for displays related to the opera we create; one other will be for children's own personal writing; and the third will be for activities that we do with literature. When you put up bulletin boards, they need to be neat and attractive because that shows the children that you took time and effort, and they need to do the same thing. I don't think we should expect more from kids than we're willing to give. We're models of what we expect from them.

I tend not to be the neatest person in the world, and unfortunately my kids model *that* behavior too. So there comes a time when we have to say, "Okay, let's clean up. Dump your desk and let's make a clean start." It's wonderful if you can be neat, but I'm not. In an elementary classroom, you go from activity to activity, and if you use a lot of materials, you tend to end up with a mess. But I don't want to forego an activity because it makes a mess.

One very annoying constraint I have is a lack of running water in the room. I usually leave two buckets of clean water under the table by the door just in case I need it. Kids can wash hands in one bucket, and get water (e.g., for watercolors) out of the other bucket. I also keep paper towels there. The custodians are not wild about it, but it's nice not to have to run down the hall every time someone spills juice. I usually change the water at lunch time because I need water in the afternoon for science.

I've tried to create a room that's flexible and that can adapt to our changing needs at different times of the year; a room that's inviting and attractive and personal; a room that encourages kids to work together but that also provides them with an opportunity to be alone; a room that helps them to be independent. Now we'll just have to wait and see what happens.

SUMMARY

In this chapter we discussed how the physical environment of the classroom influences the way teachers and students feel, think, and behave. We stressed the need for teachers to be aware of the *direct* and *indirect* effects of the physical environment. This awareness is the first step to developing "environmental competence." We suggested ways to design a classroom that will support your instructional goals, using Steele's six functions of the environment as a framework for discussion.

Security and Shelter

- Add elements of softness.
- Arrange space for freedom from interference.
- Create a "retreat" area.

Social Contact

- Consider how much interaction among students you want there to be.
- Think about whether you are making contact with *all* of your students.

Symbolic Identification

- Personalize your classroom space so that it communicates information about you and your students.

Task Instrumentality

- Make sure frequently used materials are accessible to students.
- Make it clear where things belong.
- Plan pathways to avoid congestion and distraction.
- Arrange seats for a clear view of presentations.
- Offer students a personal space in which to keep belongings.
- Locate your desk in an appropriate place (off to the side helps to ensure that you will circulate).
- Separate incompatible activities.

Pleasure

- Use a variety of colors and textures to create an aesthetically pleasing environment.

Growth

- Stock your room with a variety of activities, both "open" and "closed."
- Create a literacy center.

Careful planning of the physical environment is an integral part of good class-room management. When you begin to design your room, think about the activities it will accommodate and invite your students to participate in the planning process. Try your arrangement, evaluate it, and redesign as necessary.

ACTIVITIES

The following activities are intended to help you think about classroom physical environments. The activities are appropriate for inservice teachers with their own classrooms, as well as preservice teachers engaged in pre-student teaching field experiences or student teaching.

1 Visit an elementary classroom, draw a classroom map, and evaluate the physical layout in terms of Steele's six functions of the environment. The following questions, adapted from Bruther (1991), may be helpful.

Security and Shelter

1 Does the classroom feel like a safe, comfortable place to be?
2 Does it contain furnishings and materials that are soft and responsive to touch?
3 Do children have freedom from intrusion and interference?
4 Is there any opportunity for retreat or privacy?

Social Contact

5 Does desk arrangement facilitate or hinder social contact among students? Is this compatible with the explicit objectives?

Symbolic Identification

6 Are there displays of students' work throughout the room?
7 Is there evidence of the students themselves displayed throughout the room (e.g., name tags, photographs, silhouettes, brown paper bodies, multicultural materials, "star of the week" bulletin board, etc.)?

Task Instrumentality

8 Are frequently used classroom materials accessible to students?
9 Are shelves and cabinets well-organized so that it is clear where materials/equipment are stored?
10 Are pathways clearly visible?
11 Do pathways allow easy access in and out of all areas?
12 Does the seating arrangement allow students to see instructional presentations without difficulty?

Pleasure

13 Does the room make people feel good?

14 Does the room contain some type of softness (e.g., carpeting, pillows, bean-bag chairs, cushions, rocking chair)?

15 Are there any amenities present (e.g., plants, aquarium, etc.)?

16 Is the classroom colorful and brightly decorated?

Growth

17 Does the classroom contain a wide selection of supplemental reading materials?

18 Are the books displayed in a way that encourages students to engage in voluntary reading?

19 Does the classroom contain a variety of materials and equipment (e.g., science materials, art materials, puzzles, computers, etc.)?

2 Have students compose a "wish poem" (Sanoff, 1979) by responding to the phrase "I wish my classroom . . ." This is an excerpt from one written by the kindergartners of a student teacher who tried this activity (with the original spellings and translations):

I wish my classroom had a firv truk (a fire truck).
I wish my classroom had a gold fish.
I wish my clasroom wasn't hot and I wish my clasroom was quiet.
I wus my classroom wus nis (was nice).
I wish my classroom it cmptr (had a computer).

3 Consider the following seating arrangements. For each one, think about the types of instructional strategies for which it is appropriate or inappropriate. The first one has been done as an example.

Arrangement	Instructional strategies for which this arrangement is appropriate	Instructional strategies for which this arrangement is inappropriate
Rows	teacher or student presentations; audio-visual presentations; testing	student-centered discussions; small group work
Horizontal rows		
Horseshoe		
Small clusters		
Circle		

4 Scrutinize the floor plan of a first-grade room where the teacher is experiencing difficulty with classroom management. (See Figure 3-8). According to the teacher, there are four primary problems: (1) children in the small group reading area are frequently distracted; (2) clean-ups and transitions between activities take too long; (3) there is conflict between children in the literacy center and those playing with puzzles and

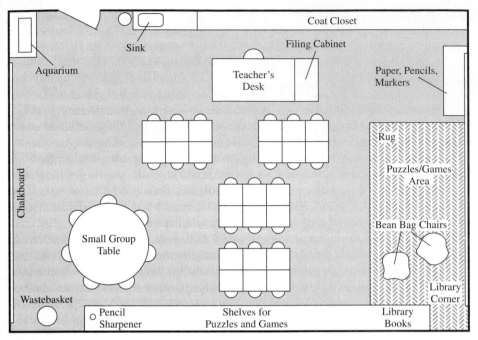

FIGURE 3-8
Floor plan of a first-grade room

games; and (4) when the teacher is working with a small group, the children who are not in the group have difficulty staying on task.

Think about the ways in which the environment might be contributing to the problems. How would you rearrange the room?

REFERENCES

Adams, R. S., and Biddle, B. J. (1970). *Realities of teaching: Explorations with video tape.* New York: Holt, Rinehart, & Winston.

Axelrod, D., Hall, R. V., and Tams, A. (1979). Comparison of two common classroom seating arrangements. *Academic Therapy, 15,* 29–36.

Bennett, N., and Blundell, D. (1983). Quantity and quality of work in rows and classroom groups. *Educational Psychology, 3,* 93–105.

Bruther, M. (1991). Factors influencing teachers' decisions about their classroom physical environments. Unpublished doctoral dissertation, Rutgers Graduate School of Education.

Coles, R. (1969). Those places they call schools. *Harvard Educational Review: Architecture and Education, 39*(4), 46–57.

David, T. G. (1979). Students' and teachers' reactions to classroom environments. Unpublished doctoral dissertation, University of Chicago.

Dishaw, M. (1977). *Description of allocated time to content areas for the A-B period.* (Beginning Teacher Evaluation Study Tech. Note IV-11a). San Francisco: Far West Regional Laboratory for Educational Research and Development.

Fielding, L., Wilson, P., and Anderson, R. (1986). A new focus on free reading: The role of trade books in reading instruction. In T. Raphael and R. Reynolds (Eds.), *The contexts of school-based literacy.* New York: Random House, pp. 149–160.

Genishi, C. (1988). Kindergartners and computers: A case study of six children. *Elementary School Journal, 89,* 185–201.

Guthrie, J. T., and Greaney, V. (1991). Literacy acts. In R. Barr, M. L. Kamil, P. Mosenthal, and P. D. Pearson (Eds.), *Handbook of reading research, volume 2.* New York: Longman, pp. 68–96.

Hill, W. (1968). Using students as school design consultants. *School Management,* November, 81–86.

Horowitz, P., and Otto, D. (1973). *The teaching effectiveness of an alternate teaching facility.* Alberta, Canada: University of Alberta. ERIC Document Reproduction Service No. ED 083 242.

Jones, E., and Prescott, E. (1978). *Dimensions of teaching learning environments. II: Focus on day care.* Pasadena, CA: Pacific Oaks College.

Krantz, P. J., and Risley, T. R. (September, 1972). The organization of group care environments: Behavioral ecology in the classroom. Paper presented at the Annual Convention of the American Psychological Association, Honolulu. ERIC Document Reproduction Service No. ED 078 915.

Loughlin, C. E., and Martin, M. D. (1987). *Supporting literacy: Developing effective learning environments.* New York: Teachers College Press.

Maslow, A. H., and Mintz, N. L. (1956). The effects of esthetic surroundings: I. *Journal of Psychology, 41,* 247–254.

Morrow, L. M. (in press). *Literacy Development in the early years: Helping children read and write* (3rd edition). Boston: Allyn & Bacon.

Morrow, L. M., and Weinstein, C. S. (1982). Increasing children's literature use through program and physical design changes. *Elementary School Journal, 83*(2), 131–137.

Morrow, L. M., and Weinstein, C. S. (1986). Encouraging voluntary reading: The impact of a literature program on children's use of library centers. *Reading Research Quarterly, 21*(3), 330–346.

Olds, A. R. (1987). Designing settings for infants and toddlers. In C. S. Weinstein and T. G. David (Eds.), *Spaces for children: The built environment and child development.* New York: Plenum Press, pp. 117–138.

Proshansky, E., and Wolfe, M. (1974). The physical setting and open education. *School Review, 82,* 557–574.

Sanoff, H. (1979). *Design games.* Los Altos, CA: William Kaufmann, Inc.

Santrock, J. W. (1976). Affect and facilitative self-control: Influence of ecological setting, cognition, and social agent. *Journal of Educational Psychology, 68*(5), 529–535.

Sommer, R. (1974). *Tight spaces: Hard architecture and how to humanize it.* Englewood Cliffs, NJ: Prentice-Hall.

Sommer, R., and Olsen, H. (1980). The soft classroom. *Environment & Behavior, 12*(1), 3–16.

Steele, F. I. (1973). *Physical settings and organization development.* Reading, MA: Addison-Wesley.

Weinstein, C. S. (1982). Privacy-seeking behavior in an elementary classroom. *Journal of Environmental Psychology, 2,* 23–35.

Weinstein, C. S. (1991). The classroom as a social context for learning. *Annual Review, 42,* 493–525.

Wheldall, K., Morris, M., Vaughn, P., and Ng, Y. (1981). Rows versus tables: An example of the use of behavioral ecology in two classes of eleven-year-old children. *Educational Psychology, 1*(2), 171–184.

FOR FURTHER READING

Hannah, G. G. (1982). *Classroom spaces and places: Sixty-five projects for improving your class-room.* Belmont, CA: Fearon Teacher Aids, a division of Pitman Learning, Inc.

Loughlin, C., and Suina, J. H. (1982). *The learning environment: An instructional strategy.* New York: Teachers College Press.

Loughlin, C. E., and Martin, M. D. (1987). *Supporting literacy: Developing effective learning environments.* New York: Teachers College Press.

Weinstein, C.S. (1981). Classroom design as an external condition for learning. *Educational Technology, 21*(8), 12–19.

Weinstein, C. S., and David, T. G. (1987). *Spaces for children: The built environment and child development.* New York: Plenum Press.

Chapter Four

Developing and Teaching Rules and Routines

The first day of a new academic year can be scary, even for students who have been in school several years. There are so many unknowns: What will the teacher be like? Who will be in my class? Will I be able to find my room? And, of course, there are all those "what if" questions—What if I have to go to the bathroom? What if my pencil point breaks? What if the teacher asks me a question and I don't know the answer?

Beginning teachers have their *own* set of "what ifs": What if the kids don't listen to me? What if I forget what I was going to say? What if a student asks me a question and I don't know the answer? Nonetheless, as adults, we may underestimate the intensity of students' September anxieties. To understand what students are feeling, try to recall a time when your unfamiliarity with societal norms and customs made you uncomfortable and insecure. Perhaps you visited a shop in a foreign country and weren't certain whether it was appropriate to bargain with a vendor. Maybe you attended a service in a church of a different faith and wondered whether to kneel with the rest of the congregation. Or perhaps you had dinner in an unusually elegant restaurant and felt unsure about proper table etiquette.

In each of these situations, *not knowing what was expected* caused insecurity, discomfort, and self-consciousness. All of us feel more competent when we understand the norms for appropriate behavior, and elementary students are no exception. Indeed, a recent study on motivation in the classroom provides research support for this common-sense notion. Skinner and Belmont (1993) hypothesized that clearly structured classroom environments (i.e., those that provided information about how to achieve desired outcomes) would satisfy children's need for competence. Consistent with this hypothesis, they found that third, fourth, and fifth graders were more likely to work harder and to be more persistent when they perceived their teachers as providing clear expectations. The message is clear: *Well-defined classroom rules and routines can help to dispel the "what ifs" and to create an environment that is comprehensible and predictable.*

Rules and routines have another major benefit. As we have emphasized in earlier chapters, classes are crowded, complex settings in which individuals engage in a wide variety of activities. *Clear rules and routines decrease the complexity of the classroom.* They minimize confusion and prevent the loss of instructional time. They enable you to carry out "housekeeping" tasks, like taking attendance, distributing materials, and cleaning up, smoothly and efficiently—almost automatically. They free you and your students to concentrate on the real tasks of teaching and learning.

In this chapter we describe research that demonstrates the importance of rules and routines. We then discuss some principles to guide you in establishing rules for your own classrooms. We'll also learn how Viviana, Garnetta, Barbara, and Ken introduce rules and routines to their students and what they think about this central task of classroom management.

RESEARCH ON EFFECTIVE CLASSROOM MANAGEMENT

Until recently, teacher preparation programs could offer only limited advice about classroom management to beginning teachers. Teacher educators shared useful "tricks of the trade" (e.g., flick the lights for quiet), stressed the importance of firmness and consistency, and warned prospective teachers not to smile until Christmas. But research identifying the behaviors of effective managers was unavailable, and it was simply not clear why some classrooms function smoothly while others are chaotic.

That situation changed in 1970, with the publication of Jacob Kounin's study of orderly and disorderly classrooms. You may recall from Chapter 1 that Kounin set out to compare teachers' methods of responding to misbehavior. To his surprise, he found that the reactions of good classroom managers were not substantially different from the reactions of poor classroom managers. What *did* differ were the strategies that teachers used to *prevent* misbehavior. Effective classroom managers constantly monitored students' behavior. They displayed what Kounin called "withitness": they were aware of what was happening in all parts of the room, and they communicated this awareness to students. They also exhibited an ability to "overlap"—to do more than one thing at a time—certainly a desirable skill in a setting where so many events occur simultaneously! Furthermore, effective managers kept lessons moving at a brisk pace, so that there was little opportunity for students to become inattentive and disruptive.

Kounin's work led researchers to wonder how effective managers began the school year. In the late 1970s, a series of studies was launched at the Research and Development Center for Teacher Education, located at the University of Texas at Austin. One project (Emmer, Evertson, and Anderson, 1980) involved observations of 27 self-contained, third-grade classrooms in an urban district. During the first three weeks of school, researchers observed extensively in each classroom and kept detailed records of what occurred. Observations were then stopped, but were resumed in November and continued until the end of the school year. On the basis of the November through May data, the researchers identified more effective and less effective managers. They then went back to the information collected at the beginning of the year and compared what the teachers had done during the first three weeks of school. Striking differences were apparent—even on the very first day of school!

Among the major differences documented by Emmer, Evertson, and Anderson was the way teachers handled rules and routines. *Effective managers had clear rules for general conduct* (e.g., "Be prepared for class"), *as well as procedures or routines for carrying out specific tasks* (e.g., going to the restroom). Furthermore, effective managers spent much of the first few days teaching these rules and procedures to students—as carefully as they taught academic content—and they continued to review during the first three weeks of school.

In contrast, the ineffective teachers did not have well-defined rules or procedures. One new teacher, for example, had no routines for going to the restrooms, using the pencil sharpener, or getting a drink of water. As a result, children wandered about, coming and going as they pleased. Although ineffective managers did have rules, the rules were often vague ("Be in the right place at the right time") and were not clearly explained. Ineffective managers frequently introduced rules casually, neglecting to teach them to students in a careful, deliberate way.

The research conducted by Emmer, Evertson, and their colleagues has helped to clarify what effective managers do to create order in their classrooms. This work underscores the importance of *(1) deciding how you want your students to behave and (2) making these expectations absolutely clear to students.* Let's look at each of these steps separately.

DEFINING YOUR EXPECTATIONS FOR BEHAVIOR

Before the first child enters your classroom, you need to think about how you expect your students to behave. Not only do you need to decide on *rules for students' general conduct,* you also need to identify the *behavioral routines or procedures* you and your students will follow in specific situations. For example, when students arrive in the morning, are they to hang up their coats, go immediately to their desks, and take out a book? Or may they chat quietly with neighbors, sharpen pencils, and play games? When students need paper for an assignment, will they get it themselves, will you have a "paper monitor," or will you distribute it yourself? When students have to use the bathroom, are they to ask permission or simply get a pass and leave? When students are working at their seats, may they help one another or must they work individually?

Because these seem like such trivial, mundane isssues, it is easy to underestimate their contribution to classroom order. But lessons can fall apart while you try to decide how to distribute paper, and students feel anxious if they're unsure whether answering a classmate's question during seatwork is helping or cheating. As we will see, rules and routines may vary from class to class, but no class can function smoothly without them.

Planning Rules for General Conduct

Emmer, Evertson, and their colleagues found that effective managers typically have three to six general rules of conduct. These rules describe the behaviors that are necessary if your classroom is to be a good place in which to live and work—for example, "respect other people's property," "keep your hands to yourself," and "follow directions." In Garnetta's classroom, she and the children decided upon the following rules:

> Be respectful.
> Raise your hand to talk.
> Don't fight; settle disagreements peacefully.
> Listen when someone is talking.
> Think before you do something.

As you reflect on rules for your own classroom, there are four principles to keep in mind. (These are summarized in Table 4-1.) First, *rules should be reasonable and necessary.* Think about the age and characteristics of the children you are teaching, and ask yourself: What rules are appropriate for them? For example, it is unreasonable to require kindergartners to "sit quietly at your desks at all times." Given young children's irresistible need to move, establishing such a rule will only result in squirming, fidgeting, and frustration.

Also ask yourself whether each rule is necessary. Is there a compelling reason for it? Will it make the classroom a more pleasant place to be? Will it increase children's opportunity to learn? A second-grade teacher we know established a strict "no talking" rule during snack time (while children sat at four-person clusters of desks). It was difficult for students (and for us!) to understand why they should be

TABLE 4-1
FOUR PRINCIPLES FOR PLANNING CLASSROOM RULES

Principle	Questions to think about
1. Rules should be reasonable and necessary.	What rules are appropriate for this grade level? Is there a good reason for this rule?
2. Rules need to be clear and understandable.	Is the rule too abstract for students to comprehend? To what extent do I want my students to participate in the decision-making process?
3. Rules should be consistent with instructional goals and with what we know about how people learn.	Will this rule facilitate or hinder my students' learning?
4. Classroom rules need to be consistent with school rules.	What are the school rules? Are particular behaviors required in the halls, during assemblies, in the cafeteria, etc.?

forbidden to talk quietly while eating. Although the teacher was able to enforce the rule, her class perceived it as arbitrary and unfair.

Second, *rules need to be clear and understandable.* Because rules are often stated in very general terms ("be polite"), they may be too abstract for children to comprehend. When planning your rules, you need to think of specific examples to discuss with students. For example, Barbara's most basic rule for general conduct is "be courteous." She makes sure that "courtesy" is spelled out in terms of real behaviors: "When you play with someone who's being left out." "When you listen politely when someone's speaking." "When you don't tease." "When you don't call people names." "When you say 'please' and 'thank you.'"

Some teachers believe that rules are more understandable and more meaningful when students are allowed to participate in the decision-making process. Participation, especially at higher grade levels, may increase students' willingness to "buy into" the rules, may make them more invested in seeing that rules are followed, and may help to prepare students for adult life (Solomon, Watson, Delucchi, Shaps, and Battistich, 1988). Ken advocates this position, but instead of deciding on a set of rules, his sixth graders draft a "Bill of Rights." According to Ken, "The bill of rights changes the way kids think about classroom behavior. I hear kids say to other kids, 'This place is different; we have rights here.' If kids get teased, they're empowered to say, 'This shouldn't happen. I shouldn't be made fun of, people shouldn't tease me. It's not just a rule; it's my right.'" (We return to Ken's Bill-of-Rights approach later in the chapter.)

If you decide to include students in the process of deciding on rules, be prepared to receive some suggestions that are silly and overly harsh ("Students who forget homework have to copy 100 pages from the dictionary"). Don't be afraid to veto inappropriate rules, but make sure your reason for rejecting a seriously made suggestion is clear to students.

As a beginning teacher, you may feel more comfortable presenting rules you have developed yourself, or perhaps presenting a few rules and having students suggest some additional ones. Emmer, Evertson, and their associates found that many effective teachers did not allow students to participate in the decision-making process. They did, however, discuss the rationale for the rules they had established, and they solicited examples from students.

A third principle to keep in mind is that *rules should be consistent with instructional goals and with what we know about how people learn.* In the first chapter, we discussed the assumptions underlying this book. One assumption stated that the need for order should not supersede the need for meaningful instruction. As you develop rules for your classroom, think about whether they will *facilitate or hinder the learning process.* For example, a second-grade teacher we know had a "no erasures" rule for written work done in class. Her reason was clear: children tended to create holes in their papers when they erased, and the results were messy and difficult to read. Unfortunately, not being allowed to erase created a good deal of anxiety; some students actually became more focused on not making mistakes than on what they were writing. Although the rule was well-intended, it interfered with children's learning.

In the pursuit of order, teachers sometimes prohibit talking during seatwork assignments. Or they may refrain from using cooperative learning activities for fear that students will be too rowdy. Obviously, such restrictions are necessary at times, but it is sad if they become the status quo. Educational psychologists who study the ways children learn stress the importance of children's interaction. Much of this thinking is based on the work of the Soviet psychologist, Lev Vygotsky, who believed that children's intellectual growth is fostered through collaboration with adults who serve as coaches and tutors and with more capable peers (Wertsch, 1985). Interestingly, recent research on the use of small groups indicates that these interactions benefit the *tutor* as well as the person being tutored. Noreen Webb (1985), for example, has found that children who provide explanations for their peers also show increased achievement. Given the important role that interaction plays in children's learning and cognitive development, it seems sensible not to eliminate interaction, but to spend considerable time teaching children how to behave in these situations. (We will address this topic more fully in Chapter 9.)

Finally, *classroom rules need to be consistent with school rules.* For example, some schools require students to possess a pass when they leave the classroom; if this is the case, you need to establish the same rule. Your school may hold an orientation meeting for new teachers where school rules and procedures are explained. If not, see if there is a school handbook and consult with office staff and other teachers. In particular, find out about behaviors that are expected during assemblies, in the cafeteria and library, and on the playground. You also need to know about any administrative procedures for which you are responsible (e.g., taking attendance, collecting lunch money, supervising fire drills, communicating with parents).

Planning Routines for Specific Situations

So many different activities occur in classrooms that trying to define behavior for specific situations can be daunting. Researchers at the Learning Research and Development Center at the University of Pittsburgh have observed the behavior of effective classroom managers and have categorized the routines they use (Leinhardt, Weidman, and Hammond, 1987). We have adapted their three-category system to provide you with a way of thinking about routines for your own classroom.

Class-Running Routines   These are *nonacademic routines that enable you to keep the classroom running smoothly.* This category of routines includes *administrative duties* (taking attendance; recording the number of students who are buying lunch each day; distributing school notices), *procedures for student movement* (entering the room at the beginning of the day; leaving the room at the end of the day; leaving the room to go to the bathroom, the nurse, the library, or lockers; lining up to go to "specials" such as art, music, and physical education; fire drills; moving around the room to sharpen pencils, use learning centers, or get materials), and *housekeeping routines* (cleaning chalkboards; watering plants; storing personal items such as book bags and coats; cleaning out desks; maintaining storage for materials used by everyone).

Without clear, specific class-running routines, these activities can consume a significant part of the school day. Reserach on the way time is used in second-grade classrooms has indicated that, on the average, noninstructional activities (transition, waiting, housekeeping) consume almost 20 percent of the time spent in the classroom—more than the amount of time spent in mathematics instruction (Rosenshine, 1980). This figure is undoubtedly higher in classrooms that are not well managed.

By defining how children are to behave in these specific situations, you can save precious minutes for instruction. You also enable children to carry out many of these routines without your direct supervision, freeing you to concentrate on instruction. For example, Barbara allows her students to take a laminated cardboard pass and go to the bathroom without asking permission—as long as the class is not in the middle of a lesson. Having a single pass means that only one child can be out of the room at a time and, of course, Barbara makes sure that no one leaves the room an unreasonable number of times. With these safeguards in place, the routine runs smoothly and saves Barbara from innumerable interruptions.

Lesson-Running Routines   These routines *directly support instruction by specifying the behaviors that are necessary for teaching and learning to take place.* They allow lessons to proceed briskly and eliminate the need for students to ask questions like "Do I hafta use pen?" "Should we number from 1 to 20?" and "What do I do if I'm finished?"

Lesson-running routines describe what items students are to have on hand when a lesson begins, how materials are to be distributed and collected, what kind of paper or writing instrument is to be used, and what should be done with the paper (folded into eight boxes; numbered from 1 to 10 along the left margin; headed with name, date, and subject). In addition, lesson-running routines specify the behaviors that students are to engage in at the beginning of the lesson (e.g., have books open to the relevant page, with your partner, read the directions for the assignment) and what they are to do if they finish early or if they are unable to finish the assignment by the end of the time period. Homework procedures can also be considered lesson-running routines, since the pace and content of lesson often depends on whether students have done their homework assigments. You need to establish routines for determining quickly which students have their homework and which do not, as well as routines for checking and collecting assignments.

Interaction Routines   These routines refer to the *rules for talk*—talk between teachers and students and talk among students themselves. Interaction routines specify *when talk is permitted and how it is to occur.* For example, during a whole class discussion, students need to know what to do if they want to respond to a question or contribute a comment. All four of our teachers, like many others, usually require students to raise their hands and wait to be called on, rather than simply calling out. In this way, the teachers can distribute opportunities to participate throughout the class and can ensure that the conversation is not dominated by a few overly eager individuals. The teachers can also check on how well the class understands the lesson by calling on students who do not raise their hands.

Sometimes it's hard to keep track of which students have had an opportunity to speak. In order to avoid this problem, Ken uses "the cup system"—a coffee mug containing slips of paper with students' names. He shakes the cup, pulls out a name, and then places the slip of paper on the side until he's worked his way through the whole class.

During some lessons, you may want students to respond chorally rather than individually (e.g., a flash card drill on addition facts). A simple signal can be used to indicate that the rules for talk have changed. Viviana, for example, uses hand gestures. When she wants students to raise their hands, she shoots her arm into the air as she asks the question. When she wants a choral response, she reaches out both hands, palms up, in a clear invitation to respond.

Barbara also suspends the normal rules for talk at times. For example, during a "great books discussion," she encourages her students to respond directly to one another. It's amazing how difficult they find this to be, at least at first; students repeatedly seek her permission to talk, despite her frequent reminders that they can comment without first being called on.

Interaction routines also include *procedures that students and teachers use to gain each other's attention.* For example, if students are busy working, and you need to give additional instructions, how will you signal that you want their attention? Will you say, "Excuse me," as Garnetta does, or will you clap your hands, flick the lights, or ring a bell? Conversely, if you are busy working with a small group or an individual, and students need your assistance, how will they communicate that to you? Will they be allowed to call your name or leave their seats and approach you? Will they turn over a "help" sign at their desks, or perhaps raise a red flag?

Finally, you need to think about the rules that will govern *talk among students.* When 20 to 30 students sit so close to one another, it's only natural for them to talk. You must decide when it's all right for students to talk about the television show they saw last night (e.g., during recess and free time) and when their talk must be about academic work (e.g., during cooperative learning activities). You also need to think about times when students may talk quietly (e.g., during seatwork), and when you need to have absolute silence (e.g., when you are giving instructions or during a test).

Table 4-2 summarizes the three types of routines we have just discussed.

THE FIRST FEW DAYS OF SCHOOL: TEACHING STUDENTS HOW TO BEHAVE

Learning how to behave in school is not always easy. Too often, students have to guess the rules for appropriate behavior from teachers' indirect statements like "I see someone whose hands are not folded" [translation: students' hands should be folded now] (Shuy, 1988) or "I don't see any hands" [translation: students should raise their hands if they wish to speak] (Gumperz, 1981). Students must also be sen-

TABLE 4-2
SUMMARY OF CLASSROOM ROUTINES

CLASS-RUNNING ROUTINES: Nonacademic routines that enable the classroom to run smoothly

Administrative routines
    Taking attendance
    Recording lunch orders
    Distributing school notices

Routines for student movement
    Entering the room at the beginning of the day
    Leaving the room at the end of the day
    Going to the restroom
    Going to the nurse
    Going to the library
    Going to "specials"
    Fire drills
    Sharpening pencils
    Using learning centers
    Getting materials

Housekeeping routines
    Cleaning chalkboards
    Watering plants
    Storing personal items (book bags, coats)
    Cleaning desks
    Maintaining common storage areas

LESSON-RUNNING ROUTINES: Routines that directly support instruction by specifying the behaviors that are necessary for teaching and learning to take place

    What to bring to the lesson
    Collecting homework
    Recording who has done homework
    Returning homework
    Distributing materials
    Preparing paper for assignment (heading, margins, type of writing instrument)
    Collecting in-class assignments
    What to do when assignments have been completed

INTERACTION ROUTINES: Routines that specify when talk is permitted and how it is to occur

Talk between teacher and students:
    During whole-class lessons
    When the teacher is working with a small group
    When the teacher needs the class' attention
    When students need the teacher's attention

Talk among students:
    During seatwork
    During free time
    During transitions
    During loudspeaker announcements
    When a visitor comes to speak with the teacher

---

sitive to cues provided by nonverbal behavior, like voice tone and pitch, posture, tempo and rhythm of speech, and facial expression. Sometimes students "misbehave" simply because they have incorrectly interpreted these subtle cues!

In order to minimize confusion, you need to teach students rules and routines as deliberately and thoroughly as you would teach academic content. As we indicated earlier in this chapter, Emmer, Evertson, and Anderson (1980) found that effective managers spent a large portion of the first few days of school teaching rules and procedures and then reviewed and reinforced them during the first three weeks. More recent research has confirmed this finding. In fact, Leinhardt, Weidman, and Hammond (1987) found that during days one through four, teachers and students spent *more time on management issues than on academic content.* This may seem like an unreasonable amount of time to invest in rules and routines, but your investment should pay off later when your class runs smoothly.

Teaching Rules for General Conduct

It's not enough to state rules for general conduct and expect sudents to understand or remember them. Instead, you need to *define terms* as clearly as possible, *discuss rationales,* and *provide examples.* Let's see what this looks like in action. On the morning of the first day of school, Barbara taught students her most basic rule: "Be courteous." During this discussion, she also explained the difference between "talking quietly" and "being silent." Notice how she solicits examples, explains why certain behaviors are necessary, comments on students' attentiveness, and checks to see that students understand how to whisper.

BARBARA: I guess it's time now to talk about fourth grade. This is a big step for you. People have a lot of expectations of fourth graders. Let's discuss some of those expectations. I expect you to *be courteous.* What does that mean? What are some examples of being courteous?

STUDENT: Not being rude.

BARBARA: That's right, but give me an example of not being rude.

STUDENT: Not slamming the door on somebody.

BARBARA: Good. What's another example?

STUDENT: Listen to people when they're talking.

BARBARA: Yes. I can see that you people don't have any problem with that, because you're listening now as we're talking. Another example of being courteous? [Students can't think of any.] Let's say we're having a lesson and someone walks in to talk to me. What could you do to be courteous?

STUDENT: Sit quietly.

STUDENT: Whisper quietly.

BARBARA: Good. It's important for you to know that it's all right with me if you whisper quietly. But I need to know that you know what whispering quietly means. So go ahead and do that. [Students whisper.] All right, I can live with that. That was fine. Okay, so you can *sit silently,* or you can *whisper quietly.* What else?

STUDENT: You can read a book.

BARBARA: Yes, that's a good idea. Do you think you could get up and walk around? [Students murmur no and shake their heads.] Right, because as soon as the person leaves we'll resume the lesson, and we'll lose time if you're all around the room. Is there anything else you could do when I'm speaking with someone?

STUDENT: Continue working on our work.

BARBARA: Absolutely. Let's talk some more about what courtesy means. Let's suppose I'm teaching a lesson and your pencil point breaks. What will you do?

STUDENT: Take out another pencil.

BARBARA: Wonderful solution. What else?

STUDENT: Ask if we can sharpen our pencil.

BARBARA: Okay. When someone's talking, it's impolite to just get up and sharpen a pencil. As long as we're talking about sharpening pencils, let me give you another example of courtesy: if the pencil sharpener drops and makes a mess, I don't go crazy, but I do expect you to clean it up. That's being courteous.

    You know, we're going to be living here together all day long, and we're going to be friends. We're going to be like a family. So we have to treat each other courteously and learn to care about one another.

Later in the morning, Barbara came back to her theme about "quiet" and "silence."

BARBARA: Most of the time I want the class to be quiet when we're working. To me, being quiet is different from being absolutely silent. Can someone tell me the difference?

STUDENT: When you're quiet you can whisper, but when you're silent, you can't even whisper.

BARBARA: Absolutely. Now, there are certain times when you'll be working that I'll ask for silence, but most of the time I expect you to be quiet. That means that you can talk quietly. When might you need to talk as you're doing your work?

STUDENT: When we're helping someone with a problem.

STUDENT: When we ask someone for help.

BARBARA: Right. Is this the time you arrange whose house you're visiting after school?

CLASS: No-o-o-o.

BARBARA: Good. There are different times for different kinds of conversations, and conversations about visiting or what you did over the weekend should take place during lunch or recess or before school begins.

    As this example illustrates, teaching students rules of conduct doesn't have to be unpleasant or oppressive. Interestingly, Barbara doesn't even use the word "rule" as she discusses her expectations for students' behavior. Nor does she post rules on a bulletin board, although many effective managers do. When we asked her about this, she explained her reasoning:

Even if a rule is stated positively, the word "rule" itself has a negative connotation. From a child's perspective, rules are made up by adults to tell kids, "These are the things you can't do, and these are the things you have to do, and if you don't follow the rules you get punished." I also think that children think the rules are only for *them,* not for the teacher. I much prefer to talk about the way we all need to treat each other. When I talk about the need for courtesy, I try to make it clear that *I* need to be courteous too, not just the children. I also want to communicate that there is no question in my mind that we will all be courteous, so I don't talk about penalties or punishments, or what will happen if people *aren't* courteous.

Viviana also prefers not to use the word "rule" or to post rules. Nonetheless, she clearly communicates her expectations to her first graders by giving explicit directions, reinforcing appropriate behavior, and correcting inappropriate behavior. During one interview, she shared her thinking with us:

> Sure I have rules —listen when someone is talking, follow directions—but I don't tell the children "This is a rule." I teach the rules as the need arises. For example, with talking, if I'm talking and someone talks, then I say, "Wait a minute, I'm talking and you're not listening. How will you know what to do? You won't hear the directions." Everyone hears what I say, and they get the message, "I'm not supposed to talk when she talks." I also tell them how pleased I am when they're being quiet and how that way everyone can hear the directions. I don't post rules or talk about rules. I don't think that would be meaningful for my children. Instead I explain what to do when the opportunity comes up. Then it has an impact.

Teaching Specific Routines

Teaching students how to carry out behavioral routines is much like teaching them how to add or subtract. Emmer, Evertson, and Anderson (1980) found that effective classroom managers *explained and demonstrated* procedures, allowed students to *practice* them, *provided feedback* to students about their performance, and then *re-taught* the procedures if necessary. Such thoroughness is particularly important at lower grade levels, when children have had little experience with the routines of school.

As Viviana explained in her previous comments, she teaches her first graders how to behave when the need arises. On the first day of school, for example, she taught them to turn their chairs around to face her when she gives instruction to the whole group. Even though the whole process lasted less than a minute, Viviana managed to demonstrate the behavior, had students practice, provided feedback, and explained the rationale for the routine.

VIVIANA: All right, children, I want you to turn your chairs around to face me. Let me show you how to do that. [She selects a child, stands her up and turns her chair around to demonstrate.] Did you all see that? José, can you do that? [The child turns his chair around properly.] Good for you. Now let me see everyone's chair like that. [She makes a big thing of looking up and down each row checking the chairs.] Very, very good. You did that very well. By turning your chairs around like this, you won't have to strain your necks trying to see what I'm doing [she twists her neck around to illustrate], and I'll be able to see everybody's beautiful face.

Throughout the day, Viviana reinforces this procedure repeatedly: "Turn your chairs around and face me. Very good, you remember how."

Different Approaches to Teaching Rules and Routines

Barbara, Garnetta, Viviana, and Ken all have clear expectations for students' behavior and make these expectations absolutely clear to students. Nonetheless, the four teachers introduce rules and routines in very different ways. These differences reflect their beliefs about what works best for their particular students in their particular contexts.

Ken and Garnetta provide an interesting contrast. In the following transcriptions, you can see how they introduce rules to their students on the first day of school.

Ken: The Bill of Rights

In this situation, Ken was working with a group of students he had taught the year before in fifth grade. Since they were familiar with him and with each other, they began with suggestions that emphasized what many teachers would consider privileges, rather than rights (or rules) needed to ensure a productive learning environment. Note how Ken allows these suggestions (since they were seriously contributed), but works to shape the list to include more fundamental rights pertaining to opportunities to work. Figure 4-1 presents the list of rights that emerged from continuing discussion.

FIGURE 4-1
The Final Bill of Rights

Students' Bill of Rights

Students in this class have the following rights:

- To whisper when the teacher isn't talking or asking for silence.
- To celebrate authorship or other work at least once a month.
- To exercise outside on days there is no physical education class.
- To have two-minute breaks.
- To have healthy snacks during snack time.
- To participate in choosing a table.
- To have privacy. No one may touch anyone else's possessions without permission.
- To be comfortable.
- To chew gum without blowing bubbles or making a mess.
- To make choices about the day's schedule.
- To have free work time.
- To work with partners.
- To talk to the class without anyone else talking.
- To work without being disturbed.

Teacher's Bill of Rights

The teacher has the following rights:

- To talk without anyone else talking, or moving about, or disturbing the class.
- To work without being disturbed.
- To have everyone's attention while giving directions.
- To yell or punish someone who is not cooperating.
- To send someone out of the group, or room, or to the office.

KEN: I want to spend some time thinking about what your rights in school are. I don't want to just take last year's Bill of Rights. You're older and have probably changed in a lot of ways. I want to do a brainstorming session and write down things that you consider a right in school. I'm going to do a little editing, something I don't usually do, but I don't want to waste time on silly things, like throwing water balloons in the classroom. Okay, what rights do you have? [Ken moves to chalkboard and calls on children. As children state rights, Ken writes down what they say; sometimes he rewords a bit if student gives him permission.]

STUDENT: The right to whisper when the teacher isn't talking.

STUDENT: The right to have a party twice a month.

STUDENT: The right to go outside everyday after 9:15 and before 12:15.

STUDENT: The right to a 2-minute break between every working period.

STUDENT: The right to a snack everyday.

STUDENT: The right to sit next to whoever you want. [Ken writes: "The right to choose a table."]

STUDENT: The right for the table to stay together unless it wants to break up.

KEN: That's really an elaboration of the previous right, so I won't write it down, okay?

STUDENT: The right to privacy—so no one else takes what you have. So no one touches your stuff without permission.

KEN: This is very different from last year's list. You've really changed. This is good.

STUDENT: The right to use chairs on the floor to lean.

KEN: Can I write down, "The right to be comfortable?" [Boy agrees.]

STUDENT: The right to chew gum, without blowing bubbles. (Everyone begins to murmur, "Yeah . . .")

KEN: We'll put it up, but we'll have to think about it. I like the way you qualified it about the bubbles.

STUDENT: The right to make choices about the day's schedule.

STUDENT: The right to free work time.

Suggestions appear to be at an end. A few kids mutter things like "There must be more things to put up that we haven't thought about." Ken stands silently and waits. Kids are unable to come up with much more.

KEN: I don't think this is complete yet. I remember some things from last year that aren't here. But I'm going to copy this down and post it. We're going to have to work on this, and define these. I think you've left out some very basic rights that you have. The right to privacy hits on it. [He asks two girls to bring another movable chalkboard to the front of the room. He labels the new board "Teacher's Bill of Rights."] What rights do I have?

STUDENT: The right to talk without anyone else talking.

STUDENT: The right to work without being disturbed.

KEN: I really thank you two. These are beautiful.

STUDENT: The right to have everyone's attention when giving directions.

STUDENT: The right to yell at a person if they're not cooperating.

STUDENT: What do you mean by yell?

KEN: David's a little uneasy about that one.

STUDENT: The right to punish.

There are a few negative reactions among the kids. Ken writes punish under yell.

STUDENT: To send someone out of the room if they're bad.

There's a discussion about what that means: out of the room to the office? just out of the group? how long?

KEN: These will have to be defined as we go along. [Indicates on the board that there is some question about the last one that needs to be resolved.] Lindsay, do *you* have the right to talk without anyone else talking? You gave this right to me. Do you have this right?

STUDENT: We should have this right too. [Two boys in the front are talking.]

KEN: Like right now, when kids are talking and you're talking. How do you feel? [She indicates that she doesn't like it.] I'm going to add that right to the kids' list. [He does so.] You gave me another wonderful right: To work without being disturbed. Should you have that right too?

STUDENT: Yeah. [He elaborates on what that means.]

KEN: How many agree?

There's consensus. Ken adds that right to kids' list.

STUDENT: But what about #1 [the right to whisper]? How does that go with the right to work without being disturbed?

KEN: Karen's worried that there's a conflict between #1, whispering, and #15, the right to work without being disturbed.

Student tries to clarify how there is not really a conflict.

KEN: Do you have the right to yell at other kids if they're not cooperating?

STUDENT: No, kids can't yell at other kids. That's the teacher's job.

KEN: You're assuming that I as the teacher will yell at kids who call you names, pick on you, things like that.

STUDENTS: Yeah . . . . [There's general agreement.]

KEN: You've given me very strong rights. You also have a very interesting list. I'm going to post it. But our bill of rights isn't completed. We'll have to think some more about the rights and define them more carefully, especially the chewing gum.

Later, Ken shared his thoughts with us about this interaction:

You know, I think every teacher should do this every year. It's really fascinating the way the list changes so much fro m year to year. Sometimes I get real traditional things. Sometimes the kids don't "reach" very far—unlike *this* class. The bill of rights teaches you so much about the kids in your class; the list always reflects their concerns and their views of what classrooms are all about. You can see where they're from, what's happened to them in the past, what their expectations are. Making a bill of rights forces them to open up . . . to think about what they'd really like the classroom to be. It almost becomes a wish list—we wish we had these things. And then, of course, it forces me to ask myself, why not? *Why* can't they have these things? After all, if they're willing to take on the responsibilities, well, then, why shouldn't they enjoy the rights?

Some of the things on the list seem a lot more "special" than they really are. Take the two-minute break between classes, for example. In reality, every time you switch classes, it takes about that long anyway. So you define it as the break. You're acknowledging that it takes that long and saying that it's all right to talk during that time. Instead of fighting them for two minutes, you're saying, "I know it's going to take that long and it's okay." I'm not sure why it's so important to them—maybe it's getting ready for seventh grade, when they know they'll have five minutes between classes. In any case, allowing students to have that two-minute break in the bill of rights legitimizes something that's going to happen anyway.

Another thing—you read the literature on gifted and talented education, and it talks about how we want kids to be fluent idea-producers, to be able to make choices, to engage in problem-solving, to critique ideas. Well, here's a real-life problem—what rights should you have in this classroom? Now brainstorm, come up with ideas, critique them, decide which ones you can live with and which ones you can't. It's so much more real than anything you find in a G&T [gifted and talented] catalog. The kids have to live with the list they come up with; it stares them in the face every day. And it makes the classroom more *real.*

Garnetta: Stranded on an Isolated Island

In the following scenario, we see how Garnetta helps to make the need for rules vivid for her third-grade students. Notice how her students readily suggest classroom rules, consequences, and rewards. In fact, Garnetta needs to do little prompting during the discussion. Her students' responses reflect their experiences at McKinley, where teachers have been taught "Assertive Discipline," a widely used program developed by Lee and Marlene Canter (1992). Assertive Discipline emphasizes the right of teachers to determine and insist upon appropriate behavior from students; it distinguishes teachers who interact with students in an assertive manner from those who are nonassertive ("wishy-washy") or hostile. In classrooms using Assertive Discipline, it is common to see a set of posted rules, rewards, and penalties.

GARNETTA: We're going to go on an imaginary trip, on a boat. [She describes what the boat is like.] But a storm comes up and the boat capsizes, and we all go overboard. Luckily, we find a lifeboat. We all get on the little lifeboat, and we get to an island. Things are real nice for a few days, but after a while they get kind of disorganized. [She elaborates on how kids begin to take other kids' clothes, other kids' food, how people do whatever they want to do.] So we have a problem. We're missing something we need to make life on the island better for us all. What are we missing?

STUDENT: Rules.

GARNETTA: Right. We need to make some rules. . . . What would be some good rules for our island?

STUDENT: Don't mug somebody.

STUDENT: Don't snatch somebody's food.

STUDENT: Don't take anybody's clothes.

STUDENT: Don't beat nobody up.

GARNETTA: These are really fine rules for our island. . . . But what if somebody didn't follow them, what if someone did something wrong?

STUDENT: Make them do 15 pushups.

GARNETTA: What do we call that?

STUDENT: Consequences.

GARNETTA: Right. What are consequences?

STUDENT: If you break the rules, you gotta pay the price.

GARNETTA: Let's say that everyone did everything just right. What could we do then?

STUDENT: We could get rewards. [Students begin to murmur: Yeah, we could get some treats, some candy, some popcorn parties.]

GARNETTA: Yes, we could have some wonderful treats. Life on the island would be a lot better then. But, you know, we have to leave the island and come home, because school is starting. We build a new boat and we come back to New Brunswick, and we come to school. Now let's think about what we need in our class. How can we make it good in *here*?

STUDENT: We gotta have rules and consequences and rewards here, too.

GARNETTA: Okay, you want to suggest a rule?

STUDENT: Stay in your seat. [Garnetta writes what students say on the board.]

STUDENT: Raise your hand to be recognized.

GARNETTA: Excellent rule.

STUDENT: Think before you do something.

GARNETTA: Oh, I like that one. Yes, I do.

STUDENT: Don't play around. No horseplay.

STUDENT: No fighting.

GARNETTA: Definitely. That's certainly a rule we want to have.

STUDENT: Don't run in the classroom.

STUDENT: Don't chew gum.

STUDENT: Don't talk when the teacher's talking.

GARNETTA: Well, what if *you're* talking or giving a report?

STUDENT: Listen to *whoever's* talking.

GARNETTA: Oh, I like that, because when you listen quietly to someone who's talking, you're showing what?

STUDENT: Respect. Show respect for other people.

GARNETTA: Okay, I'm going to add those rules: "Be respectful" and "Don't talk while others are talking or giving reports." Okay, now let's think of consequences. If you break the rules, what could we do?

STUDENT: If you be bad, the teacher can call your parents and talk to them and talk to the principal.

STUDENT: If we have a party that week, the person can't go, they gotta go to the office.

STUDENT: Stay after school.

GARNETTA: Yes, definitely.

STUDENT: Write your spelling words 300 times each.

STUDENT: No, a thousand times.

GARNETTA: I'm going to just write "do a written assignment" instead. You all come up with these really big punishment assignments, but if I ever did anything like that, you'd just hate it. You know, all of these are pretty severe. What about consequences for something more minor.

STUDENT: No treats.

STUDENT: No special games.

GARNETTA: Okay, that's more balanced. Now let's look at rewards. What kind of rewards can you suggest?

STUDENT: Give the kids something, like a piece of cake or stickers.

GARNETTA: I'm going to write "stickers or other treats." That can include lots of things.

STUDENT: You get to go outside.

GARNETTA: Okay, you could get to go outside to play.

STUDENT: Have a party.

GARNETTA: Oh, yes, we like parties, don't we?

STUDENT: See a movie.

STUDENT: A peanut hunt—we did that last year. [She explains.]

GARNETTA: Gee, that's out of sight. I'll have to find out more about how to do that. Any more suggestions? [Class is quiet.] Okay, well this is a good list, but I'm going to add one more thing to the rewards list: "Send a good note home to parents." I especially like that. That's going to be one of our most important ones. [She and the students discuss why that's a good thing to do.] Okay, on this list we have all the rewards we use in this school. Let's go over these lists real quick and review, and then I'll write them up on posters. We'll be talking some more about these in the days to come. [The class reads the lists out loud with her. A boy wants to add "Don't name call" to the list of rules. Garnetta agrees to add it.]

Later in the day, Garnetta talked with us about her approach to setting rules:

I talk with them a lot about why we need rules. I think they need a very clear structure to follow, especially since some of them come from homes where there's very little structure. The rules need to be clear and they need to understand what happens if you follow the rules and what happens if you don't follow them. You can see that they're very used to talking about rules, consequences, and rewards, because everyone in the school uses the same kind of system. They know what kind of behavior is expected here, and they know what happens if you misbehave. But I don't tie a particular reward or consequence to a particular rule. Because if all of a sudden something happens with a child who never breaks a rule, you don't want to be tied into a severe consequence like going to the principal. That would be devastating. You have to look at the particular situation and decide which consequence. What's on the board is not the order of severity. First would be "no treats," then "stay after school," then "do a written assignment" (that's often an essay about what happened or a letter of apology), then "send to office," and last "call parents."

CONCLUDING COMMENTS

A while back, we heard a professor of education recount the story of her daughter's first week of kindergarten (Delpit, 1995). After each of the first four days of school, the mother asked her daughter what she had learned. The child's answers were succinct: on the first day she learned "to sit still"; on the second day she learned "to walk in a straight line"; on the third day she learned "to raise her hand"; and on the fourth day she learned "to be quiet." On the fifth day, the mother decided not to ask any more questions!

Obviously, the teacher in this story did a thorough job of teaching her students how to behave, and it's likely that she had few behavior problems in succeeding weeks. Nonetheless, we find this story somewhat sad and disturbing. Although we have emphasized the importance of establishing behavioral expectations early in the year, rules and routines should not be the *most salient* aspect of schooling for children. As you plan the first few weeks, make sure you balance the teaching of rules and routines with a variety of learning activities that students will find meaningful, enjoyable, and memorable. We want our students to understand that they will learn more in our classes than simply how to behave.

SUMMARY

In this chapter, we discussed two important functions of rules and routines in the classroom: (1) to provide a structure and predictability that help children to feel more comfortable; and (2) to reduce the complexity of classroom life, allowing you and your students to concentrate on teaching and learning. We outlined two broad categories of behavioral expectations—*rules for general conduct* and *routines for specific situations*—and emphasized the need to teach these explicitly.

When Deciding on Rules for General Conduct, Make Sure They Are:

- necessary
- reasonable
- understandable
- consistent with instructional goals and with what we know about how people learn
- consistent with school rules

Plan Routines for Specific Situations:

- class-running routines
    administrative duties
    procedures for student movement
    housekeeping responsibilities
- lesson-running routines
    routines governing use and distribution of materials
    routines for paper headings, homework procedures, what to do
      if you finish early
- interaction routines
    routines specifying when talk is permitted and how it is to
      occur
    routines for students and teachers to use to get each other's
      attention

Teach Rules Explicitly:

- define terms
- discuss rationales
- provide examples

Teach Routines Carefully:

- explain
- demonstrate
- practice
- give feedback
- reteach

Remember, developing good rules and routines is only the first step. For rules and routines to be effective, you must actively teach them to your students. Time spent on rules and routines in the first weeks of school will pay off in increased instructional time throughout the year. Make sure, however, to balance the teaching of rules and routines with learning activities that are meaningful and memorable.

ACTIVITIES

1 *Preparing for the first day:* Throughout the summer, teachers get ready for that first day of school. So many tasks need to be accomplished, it can be overwhelming. We hope this activity will make the process a little more manageable.

a Develop a set of rules for your classroom. About five or six rules should be sufficient. For each rule, list examples you will discuss with students to make the rules more meaningful.

b Obtain a copy of the school handbook, or talk to the principal or another teacher, to determine the school rules. Check your rules against the school rules to ensure that there is no conflict.

c Below is a list of areas for which you will need specific behavioral routines. Use this list to help you think through the ways you expect your students to behave.

Class-Running Routines:

Entering the room at the beginning of the day
Going to the bathroom
Lining up to leave the room
Taking attendance
Fire drills
Moving through the hallway
Sharpening pencils
Leaving the room at the end of the day

Lesson-Running Routines:

Distributing materials
Paper heading
Homework distribution
Homework collection
What to do when seatwork has been completed

Interaction Routines:

Talking during seatwork
Hand-raising during whole-class discussion
Behavior during interruptions (e.g., a visitor comes to the door; an announcement comes over the loudspeaker)
Signalling the teacher for help during independent seatwork

d Not all of these routines can be taught that first day. You need to decide on priorities and teach routines when it is most appropriate (and most likely to be remembered). Decide which ones are necessary for the first day.

2 You may decide, as Ken has, that developing a Bill of Rights is the strategy that best suits you and your students. During the brainstorming session, you may be confronted with some unexpected suggestions from your students. This can be problematic: on one hand, you don't want to squelch student initiative by vetoing too many of their ideas; on the other hand, you are the adult in charge and know what you and the school can tolerate.

A little practice on what to say to "unusual" ideas might help. Listed below are some student suggestions. What would be your response? Is there a way to incorporate or modify a suggestion to make it workable for you? Is there a way to say no in a manner that makes sense to the student? Give it a try!

a We should be able to walk around the classroom without our shoes on.
b We deserve stickers for bringing in our homework every day.
c We should be able to bring in toys to school.
d We should have a joke-telling time everyday before lunch.
e We should be able to select one day a week when we don't have to do homework.
f We should be able to write notes to each other.
g We should be able to call you by your first name.
h We should be able to lie down on the floor to do our work.

We posed the first situation to our group of teachers and asked their opinions, first privately and then as a group. These are their thoughts:

VIVIANA: I would tell them that it would be all right to take off their shoes as long as they wouldn't play with them and they could pay attention to what is going on in class. I, too, take off my shoes!

GARNETTA: I would say, fine, but what would happen if you stepped on a staple. You know how the carpet seems to collect staples. I would see what their solutions would be. I know there are days when my feet have had enough and I take off my shoes.

KEN: That's fine. It sounds sort of comfortable. But I'd ask them, "Are there any problems with this idea?" Someone might say, "Yeah, it will smell," or "We might trip over our shoes," or "You could step on a tack," or "You could stub your toe." I would then say, "Okay, how can we try to make sure these things don't happen?" And it would go on from there.

BARBARA: I originally wrote down okay as long as we were careful, but then I changed my mind. I would tell them that I wish we could take off our shoes, but if a fire drill happened no shoes could be a safety hazard. It wouldn't be safe to leave the building with no shoes on.

When the teachers came together, Barbara's thought about the fire drill shed some new light on the situation. Ken quickly agreed with Barbara and brought up the point that parents would be irate if they knew their children went outside without shoes in the winter. He also added that there was broken glass on the blacktop and the children could get cut. He envisioned lawsuits brought against him and the school.

Viviana and Garnetta, however, both still felt that taking shoes off was okay in their settings. Viviana felt that perhaps a fire drill occurring during this time was more like real life: "Do you keep your shoes on all the time at home, just in case a fire breaks out? No, you exit the house the way you are dressed or undressed, whichever the case may be. I want my children to experience life and feel like the classroom is their home."

Garnetta was also unwilling to sacrifice the comfort of those special times when children can unwind and cuddle up to a good book or work in a group on the carpet. "My school yard is well kept and free of any glass," she told us. "It would be okay in an emergency to take my children outside without their shoes."

This exercise clearly demonstrates that responses vary according to personal preference, district practices, expected parent response, and school environment. Once your students arrive at a list of rights, it's a good idea to share the list with some of your colleagues and get their input. They may come up with a "red flag" that you hadn't thought of. The children will understand the legitimate reasons for editing their original list as long as you provide an explanation.

REFERENCES

Canter, L., and Canter, M. (1992). *Assertive discipline: Positive behavior management for today's classroom.* Santa Monica, CA: Lee Canter & Associates.

Delpit, L. (May 1995). Informal comments at a conference celebrating the retirement of Courtney Cazden from Harvard Graduate School of Education. Cambridge, MA.

Emmer, E. T., Evertson, C. M., and Anderson, L. M. (1980). Effective classroom management at the beginning of the school year. *The Elementary School Journal, 80*(5), 219–231.

Gumperz, J. J. (1981). Conversational inference and classroom learning. In J. Green and C. Wallat (Eds.), *Ethnography and language in educational settings.* Norwood, NJ: Ablex Publishing Co.

Kounin, J. S. (1970). *Discipline and group management in classrooms.* New York: Holt, Rinehart and Winston.

Leinhardt, G., Weidman, C., and Hammond, K. M. (1987). Introduction and integration of classroom routines by expert teachers. *Curriculum Inquiry, 17*(2), 135–175.

Rosenshine, B. (1980). How time is spent in elementary classrooms. In C. Denham and A. Lieberman (Eds.), *Time to learn.* Washington, D.C.: U.S. Department of Education.

Shuy, R. (1988). Identifying dimensions of classroom language. In J. L. Green and J. O. Harker (Eds.), *Multiple perspective analyses of classroom discourse.* Norwood, NJ: Ablex Publishing Co.

Skinner, E. A., and Belmont, M. J. (1993). Motivation in the classroom: Reciprocal effects of teacher behavior and student engagement across the school year. *Journal of Educational Psychology, 85*(4), 571–581.

Solomon, D., Watson, M. S., Delucchi, K. L., Schaps E., and Battistich, V. (1988). Enhancing children's prosocial behavior in the classroom. *American Educational Research Journal, 25*(4), 527–554.

Webb, N. M. (1985). Student interaction and learning in small groups: A research summary. In R. E. Slavin, S. Sharan, S. Kagan, R. Hertz-Lazarowitz, C. Webb, and R. Schmuck (Eds.), *Learning to cooperate, cooperating to learn.* New York: Plenum Press.

Wertsch, J. V. (1985). *Vygotsky & the Social Formation of Mind.* Cambridge: Harvard University Press.

FOR FURTHER READING

Canter, L., and Canter, M. (1992). *Assertive discipline: Positive behavior management for today's classroom.* Santa Monica, CA: Lee Canter and Associates.

Emmer, E. T. (1988). Classroom management and discipline. In V. Richardson-Koehler (Ed.), *Educator's handbook: A research perspective.* New York: Longman Inc., 233–258.

Emmer, E. T. and Evertson, C. M. (1981). Synthesis of research on classroom management. *Educational Leadership, 38,* 342–347.

Evertson, C. M., Emmer, E. T., Clements, B. S., Sanford, J. P., and Worsham, M. E. (1994). *Classroom management for elementary teachers* (3rd edition). Boston: Allyn & Bacon.

Chapter Five _____

Gaining Students' Cooperation

_____

Not too long ago, we spoke with Cheryl, a first-year teacher whose class was giving her a hard time. It was only October, but she was close to tears as she talked about the disrespectful and disruptive behavior of her fifth graders. "I'm more like a cop than a teacher," she told us, and she was both surprised and dismayed by the antagonism she felt toward her students. She had always "loved children so much." What had gone wrong?

As we talked, it became clear that Cheryl's problem was not due to an absence of clear rules and routines:

> It's not like they don't understand what I want. On the first day of school, we talked a lot about the rules. You know, whisper quietly, don't interrupt, raise your hand to speak. . . . I thought we were off to such a great start. They were so well-behaved! But now they just don't seem to care. I'll remind them about a rule, like listening when the teacher is giving a lesson, and for a few minutes they're okay, but then they start shouting out, getting up to sharpen pencils, throwing erasers back and forth. I get so frustrated, I just start yelling—something I said I'd never do. I don't know . . . I just don't understand how to get them to _follow_ all those great rules I set up.

This first-year teacher had learned a sad fact of classroom life: having clear, reasonable rules and routines doesn't automatically mean that everyone will follow them. To achieve order, you must find ways of _gaining students' cooperation_. As Walter Doyle (1986) has suggested, classroom order is like conversation: it can only be achieved if both parties agree to participate. If students are resistant, classroom events turn into a series of hostile showdowns, and teaching becomes "a contest of wills" (Clark, 1989, p. 22). (Figure 5-1 illustrates the difficulty Calvin's teacher faces.) Unfortunately, Cheryl was never able to gain her students' cooperation, and she left teaching at the end of the year disillusioned and discouraged.

What can you do to prevent this situation from occurring? How can you get students to comply willingly with classroom rules and to become productively in-

FIGURE 5-1
Calvin's teacher has difficulty gaining his cooperation. (Calvin and Hobbes © *Watterson. Dist. by Universal Press Syndicate. Reprinted with permission. All rights reserved.*)

volved in learning activities? As you reflect on these questions, keep in mind the unique characteristics of classroom groups that we discussed in Chapter 1. Recall that, unlike most other social groups, students do not come together voluntarily. They are a captive audience, often required to work on tasks they have not selected and in which they may have little interest. Remember, too, that classroom groups are formed somewhat arbitrarily; students do not usually choose their peers *or* their teachers, yet they are expected to cooperate with both. Recalling these special characteristics may make it easier to see why teachers must work to gain students' cooperation.

In this chapter, we examine four approaches to this task. The first approach focuses on *establishing a positive relationship with students.* It is based on the assumption that teachers who have their students' respect and affection are more likely to gain their cooperation (Good and Brophy, 1994). The second approach emphasizes the importance of *fostering students' motivation to learn* (Brophy, 1987). As Kounin's (1970) work has shown, students who are interested and involved in the academic work at hand are less likely to misbehave. The third approach involves *sharing responsibility with students.* Here we assume that students who are allowed to exercise some autonomy and to make decisions about their own behavior will be more committed to acting responsibly. Finally, we discuss the *use of rewards to encourage and reinforce appropriate behavior.* The rationale for this approach is the psychological principle that behavior followed by a reward tends to be repeated.

ESTABLISHING A POSITIVE RELATIONSHIP WITH STUDENTS

Like Cheryl, beginning teachers may assume that they will have a few behavior problems if they "love and respect" children. They envision a classroom characterized by harmony and good will and are disappointed and disillusioned when students "test the limits" and begin to misbehave. But what does it mean to "respect children"? In real life, what does "respecting children" look like?

One answer comes from the study we discussed earlier by Emmer, Evertson, and Anderson (1980). This research indicated that, in addition to having rules and procedures, effective classroom managers *expressed concern for students* in several ways. First, teachers established a classroom environment that was *safe and secure* (i.e., they prevented children from hurting each other, physically or verbally, and they themselves refrained from abuse). Second, they *treated children fairly* and provided opportunities for them to be successful and to receive recognition. Third, teachers were *sensitive to children's anxieties and needs;* for example, they planned beginning-of-the-year activities to ease children's entry into the world of school (instead of administering an intimidating diagnostic test on the first day). Fourth, they created a classroom atmosphere that was *relaxed and pleasant;* although it was work-centered, teachers allowed breaks for activities like playing tapes and CDs. Finally, teachers had good *communication skills;* they not only knew how to listen well, they were also able to express their feelings to students.

From this portrait of a concerned teacher, we can see that respect for children goes beyond warm, "fuzzy" feelings. Respect is demonstrated through the planning and the behavior of effective managers—the way they structure academic tasks so that children can experience success, they way they schedule class activities, the way they communicate with students. Furthermore, this portrait describes a teacher who is clearly *in charge,* a teacher who is able to keep the peace and who does not allow children to attack each other—in sum, a teacher who can create a *classroom environment that is relaxed and comfortable, but orderly and productive.*

It is obvious that the four teachers with whom we are working are able to create this kind of classroom environment. Listening to them speak about their classes and observing them in action, their efforts to build good relationships with their students are striking. They play games with children during free time, share snacks, and talk about their families, hobbies, and trips. They reveal their feelings and encourage children to reveal theirs.

> On the first day of school, Ken has his students create record album covers that tell something about themselves; each album cover is to contain a title, the names of twelve songs, and an illustration. As we watch, Ken circulates throughout the room, commenting on each person's "self-portrait." His comments are personal and specific: "I like that drawing. It really looks like you." "That's a neat title; it could be a rap song." "You're calling yourself Mad Man? Is that what you want to tell me about yourself?" By the end of the period, he has learned a good deal about the self-perceptions of his 23 students, and he has connected personally with each one of them.

> Viviana is teaching a lesson on feelings. She shows the class pictures of people with different kinds of feelings: happiness, excitement, anger, love. They talk about what each picture is portraying. She shows a picture of a little boy by a fence with a ball and bat. "What do you think he's feeling?" "Sad," says one girl. "Lonely," volunteers another. Viviana asks, "Why do you think he's sad and lonely?" "Because the other children won't let him play ball with them." "What could you do to fix things?" "Invite him to play." After the pictures, she has the children portray different feelings. They get to the feeling of love, and they all joke about the fact that her name is Mrs. Love. One by one the children hug her to express "their love for Mrs. Love." Afterwards she tells us: "I try to

teach them how to deal with their feelings. I tell them that sometimes I get angry at my husband and I count to ten so that I don't say something I may regret later. I tell them, if you get angry, count to ten or do something until you cool off. You can hop, jump, ride a bike. Then you can talk with the person about what made you angry and you're less likely to say words you'll regret later on."

A few weeks later, we watch Viviana teach a phonics lesson. A child at the chalkboard is having difficulty and writes a word incorrectly. Viviana reminds the class, "Remember, we don't laugh." She goes to help the boy and makes a mistake herself. "Oh my goodness, I made a mistake. Are you going to laugh at me? If you do, how will I feel?" The children tell her she'll feel sad. "Yes, I'll feel sad, like this boy over here. [She points to a picture of a boy with a very sad face.] "Instead of laughing, what do you need to do?" she asks the class. "Help you." "That's right, you need to help me."

Barbara stands by the door waiting to greet her children after recess. It's clear as they enter the classroom that they're angry and upset. The story quickly comes out: A new kid from a higher grade caused an unbelievable amount of conflict and fighting out on the playground. So many kids were sent to the principal that he had to meet with them in the auditorium! Unfortunately, Barbara doesn't have a chance to discuss the situation with her class because they have to change rooms for science and social studies. She tells them that they'll talk the next day. Later, she describes what happened: "The delay worked out well, actually, because it allowed them to calm down a little before we talked. Because of the schedule, it worked out that the only time we could talk was during language arts period—and would you believe it—I was being observed by the principal. I began by reading them 'All I Really Need to Know I Learned in Kindergarten.' I love that poem—especially the part about a snack and a nap every afternoon. We talked about what stood out for them as they heard it. Somebody picked up on the part about how wars happen because people butt in. I asked, "Is that what happened yesterday?" Then it all began to pour out. . . . I wasn't reprimanding or laying blame; I just tried to help them find alternative ways of dealing with the problems they were encountering. . . . Kids need a safe place to discuss heated, emotionally charged issues, and I try to create that kind of classroom."

Garnetta's class is working in small groups, comparing present-day life with life in the days of King Arthur. Two boys begin to argue. Garnetta quickly goes over and begins to talk quietly with them. She sees that one of them has written "electricity" as one of the differences, but has misspelled it. She congratulates him on thinking of electricity and helps him to spell the word correctly. They get back on task. Later she talks to us about the incident and the boys involved: "Tony's very volatile; he gets in trouble every day, but not in here, usually in the lunch room. In here, Tony and I have developed our own special rapport. He loves doing things for me, like feeding the animals and sharpening pencils. Even so, he tests the limits. Often I'll see him watching me out of the corner of his eye. He *wants* me to stop him. He wants limits. And because he and I have a relationship, the others follow. Tony's a leader in this class. You have to find the leaders of the class and talk to them and get a rapport established with them. . . . It takes some time. . . . It's not going to happen the first day, but as long as you have a hand on 'Johnny' who is not going to act out during your lesson because you and he have respect for one another, the other ones will follow."

These examples of relationship-building echo the results of a study by Chris Clark (1989). In an effort to define "good teaching," Clark spoke with about 60 elementary and secondary teachers and their students. His conversations revealed that, for teachers, the essence of good teaching is in the arena of human relation-ships: "Teaching is good when a class becomes a community of honest, nurturant, and mutually respectful people" (p. 16). Students' views of good teaching also stress relationships: teachers are good when they tell stories of life outside school, when they laugh with students, when they make sure that students don't feel lost or humiliated, when they take the time to learn who their students are and what they like, and when they are *both a friend and a responsible adult.*

In today's diverse classrooms, teachers and students often come from different cultural and linguistic backgrounds. This means that learning who your students are and what they like is considerably more challenging: How do you connect with chil-dren if you speak different languages and have different interaction styles? We already broached this subject in Chapter 3, when we talked about designing the physical envi-ronment. Here are some additional suggestions to keep in mind (Kottler, 1994):

Use photographs to communicate without words.   Take pictures of the children engaged in various activities to take home to parents; display photographs around the room; invite students to bring in pictures of themselves and their families; use photographs for get-acquainted activities.

Develop a portfolio for each child.   Make a list of everything the child can do without using language (build, sort, match, categorize, sequence, copy, draw, mimic, make faces, pantomime). Note interactions with other people. Determine which instructional activities the student enjoys the most and which he or she tries to avoid. Think about whether these preferences might reflect cultural values. Find out what activities the child pursues after school. Include photographs of the child and samples of work.

Explore students' family backgrounds.   Where did the student come from? Was it a rural or urban setting? Why did the family move? How long has the child been in this country? How many people are in the family? What are the lines of author-ity? What responsibilities does the child have at home? Does the child care for younger brothers and sisters or elderly grandparents? Ask children to draw pictures of themselves with their families. Determine the family's attitude toward learning English. Is the child encouraged to speak English at home or not? (We will speak more about this in Chapter 11.)

Explore students' school backgrounds.   Have the children had *any* schooling? What kinds of instructional strategies are they used to? In their previous schooling, was there an emphasis on large group instruction, memorization, and recitation? What kinds of expectations were there for appropriate behavior? Were students ex-pected to be active or passive? independent or dependent? peer-oriented or teacher-oriented? cooperative or competitive?

Be sensitive to cultural differences and how they may lead to miscommunication. Do students nod their heads to be polite or to indicate understanding? How do they think about time? Is punctuality expected or is time considered to be flexible? (See Chapter 12 for further discussion of cultural differences.)

Learn to pronounce students' names correctly.   In the classes of our four teach-ers, there are children whose names can be a challenge: Isatu ("eye-sa-too"); Nanatsu; Iaesi ("ee-si"); Wei Hou ("wee-how"); Hiji ("Hai-jai"); Yevgenyi;

Zureyma; Daniel ("Donny-el"); Aminatu; Ayesha and Aisha (pronounced identically). In order to convey your respect for your students, it's important to spend time learning how they wish to pronounce and spell their names.

Learn a few phrases in the students' native languages.   It can mean a lot to students if you can welcome them to school each day with a few phrases in their native languages: *Ka hue?* ("What's happening?" in Fijian); *Apa khabar?* ("How are you?" in Malaysian); *"¿Que tal?"* ("How goes it?" in Spanish) (Kottler, 1994, p. 11). Ken tells about a girl in his class who had recently come from Mexico and was feeling unhappy and uneasy in her new setting: "One day she came in, and I said, 'Buenas dias' and she got this huge grin on her face. When I saw her reaction, I tried to learn some common Spanish phrases. Whenever I'd use them—in my awful accent—she'd smile and correct me. It was really something; it changed the whole nature of our relationship."

One final note about establishing positive relationships: In recent years, the fear of being accused of sexual harassment and physical abuse has made teachers wary of showing students any physical affection. Although our four teachers share this wariness, they do not want to forego all physical contact. Ken still pats students on the back when he's praising them for particularly fine work. When children reach out to hug Barbara and Viviana, they still hug back. And Garnetta tells us:

> There was a time when I actually stopped hugging or touching in any way because of the bad publicity, but I just couldn't continue doing that. I felt like I just didn't bond as well with that class. My children are young, and they need love. But you do have to be careful.

It's important to remember that these teachers have been in their districts for many years and have solid reputations. As a new teacher, you are in a very different situation. Speak with your colleagues about the policy in effect in your school; some schools actually direct teachers to "teach but don't touch." Even if there is no explicit prohibition against touching children, you need to be cautious so that your actions are not misconstrued. For example, when children stay after school, it's a good idea to keep the door open and to notify other teachers that you are in your classroom with one or more of your students.

FOSTERING STUDENT MOTIVATION TO LEARN

We sometimes speak about students' motivation as if it were a stable, unchangeable characteristic, like gender or eye color. From this perspective, some children are motivated, and some aren't. Some youngsters come to school wanting to learn, and some don't. This can be a comforting point of view: If motivation is an innate characteristic, then we don't have to spend time and energy figuring out ways to motivate students, particularly those who show little interest in school.

In contrast, some educators argue that motivation is an acquired disposition that is developed through experience and is amenable to change. It can also be situation-specific, varying with the nature of the particular activity. Thus, students can be enthusiastic about reading Judy Blume's novel, *Tales of a Fourth-Grade Nothing,* but can appear bored and uninterested when it is time to do spelling sentences.

If motivation is amenable to change (and we think it is!), then it follows that teachers are responsible for trying to stimulate the interest and involvement of students who appear unmotivated. A recent study on classroom motivation, however, suggests that this does not always happen. In fact, Skinner and Belmont (1993) found that teachers' actions actually "magnify" students' initial levels of motivation (p. 580). When children enter the classroom already motivated, teachers tend to respond positively and to provide additional support, affection, and encouragement. When children enter the classroom exhibiting a *lack* of motivation, however, teachers may respond negatively and become coercive and neglectful—thus exacerbating students' initial lack of interest.

To assist teachers in stimulating children's motivation, Jere Brophy (1987) reviewed relevant theory and research and derived a set of principles that teachers can apply in their classrooms. (See Table 5-1.) These principles are based on the idea that motivation to perform a task depends on *students' expectation of success* and *the value they place on the task* (Feather, 1982). These two factors work together like a multiplication equation: if either one is missing (i.e., zero), there will be no motivation.

Some of the principles that Brophy has developed focus on ways of increasing students' expectation of success:

Provide opportunities for success. If tasks appear too difficult, students may be afraid to tackle them. You need to make sure that instruction is on an appropriate level for each student. You may have to modify assignments for different students or provide additional help. For example, when Garnetta reviews cursive writing, she gives some of her students an alphabet page that requires them to trace over dashed letters. Other students have to complete an alphabet in which every fourth or fifth letter is missing. Still others write most of the alphabet on their own, with just a few letters already present as cues. These differentiated assignments increase all children's chances of success.

Teach students to set reasonable goals and to assess their performance. Some children think anything less than 100 on a test is a failure, while others are content with a barely passing grade. You may have to help students set goals that are rea-

TABLE 5-1
FOSTERING STUDENTS' MOTIVATION TO LEARN

1. Provide opportunities for success.
2. Teach students to set reasonable goals and to assess their performance.
3. Help students to recognize the relationship between effort and outcome.
4. Relate lessons to students' own lives.
5. Model interest and enthusiasm.
6. Include novelty and variety in your lessons.
7. Provide opportunities for students to respond actively.
8. Allow students to create finished products.
9. Provide opportunities to interact with peers.

sonable and obtainable. On the first day of school, Garnetta has her students write about their goals for third grade. These are discussed and posted on the front bulletin board, where they can serve as daily reminders: "I want to learn how to write in cursive." "I want to know timetables and divided by." "I will try to get straight A's." "I want to learn multiplication." And from a new child, "I want to make new friends." Similarly, on the first day of school, Ken gives his students their report cards from the previous year and copies of their standardized achievement test scores. He asks them "to sit and reflect and begin to set some goals." He encourages them to write these down. Then he distributes a blank report card to each student, telling them to "think about what you'd like to get in each subject." He stresses that this is "just the beginning" of the process and that they will continue to develop real objectives for the academic year.

Help students to recognize the relationship between effort and outcome.   Do you recall the story of the "little train that could"? Despite all the odds against her, she chugged up the mountain muttering "I think I can, I think I can, I think I can." And she did. . . .

In contrast to the little train, some youngsters proclaim defeat before they've even attempted a task. When they don't do well on an assignment, they attribute their failure to lack of ability, not realizing that achievement is often a function of effort. You may have to make this relationship explicit. Whenever possible, point out students' improvement and help them to see the role of effort: "See, you did all your math homework this week, and it really paid off. Look at how well you did on the quiz!"

Other motivational strategies address the *value* portion of the expectancy × value equation (Feather, 1982):

Relate lessons to students' own lives so that the content is more meaningful and relevant.   A recent study of motivational strategies (Newby, 1991) has demonstrated that on-task behavior is higher in classrooms where teachers provide students with reasons for doing tasks and relate lessons to students' personal experiences. Unfortunately, Newby found that first-year teachers use these "relevance strategies" only occasionally. (See Figure 5-2.)

FIGURE 5-2
It's important to point out the relevance of learning activities.

Observations of our four teachers provide numerous examples of attempts to link academic tasks to children's lives. In math class, for example, Barbara often creates word problems that incorporate her students' names and interests: "Mark collects baseball cards. His collection is worth $57.85. He purchases five new cards valued at $6.35. . . ." When Ken's class does writing, the topics come from the students' own lives. He asks them to write about what they're good at, what they can teach others, how they feel about school. Viviana and Garnetta teach map skills by having students make maps of the classroom and the neighborhood. Garnetta's students also play a game in which they write the directions to their houses. These are then read aloud and students try to guess whose house is involved.

Model an interest in learning and express enthusiasm for the material.   Before Barbara introduces students to the novel, *Mr. Popper's Penguins,* she first discloses that "penguins are one of my favorite animals." Her enthusiasm for penguins is apparent—on the first day of school, students' name tags prominently feature a picture of a penguin; a five-foot high, plastic penguin stands in the library corner; stuffed animal penguins perch on Barbara's desk; as days go by, dates on the class calendar are covered by paper penguins.

Include novelty/variety elements.   Garnetta's students play "Wheel of Fortune" to practice vocabulary. Barbara distributes the advertising flyers from supermar-

Ken's students manipulate tacks to learn about probability.

kets, assigns each child a designated amount of money, and has her students "go shopping." Viviana's students jump, hop, clap, and march when she's teaching them about verbs that depict action. When Ken's students learn about sampling procedures, they work with M&M's™, extrapolating from a small bag in order to predict how many of each color would be contained in a half-pound bag.

Provide opportunities for students to respond actively.   So often the teacher talks and moves, while students sit passively and listen. In contrast, when Ken's class studies probability, students work in small groups, gently tossing tacks and graphing how many land with the points up and how many land with the points down (and it's *not* 50-50!). Barbara's students make bubble solution, go outside to blow bubbles, and discuss what they saw, how the bubbles felt, and what they looked like. Then they come back in and write poems, essays, or stories about the experience.

Allow students to create finished products.   Creating a finished product gives meaning and purpose to assignments. After Garnetta's students finish their research on the solar system, each child constructs an eight-foot mural of the planets that they can take home. When Viviana's students learn about seeds, they construct displays for the district's "Academic Fair." Barbara's students participate in the "Invention Convention": they define a problem (e.g., scratching your back in an out-of-the-way place) and then construct an invention to solve the problem. In addition, students write ads for their inventions, which are compiled in a book that resembles a Sears catalog. When Ken's students have a writing assignment, the due date is called the "publication date." At that time, they "celebrate authorship" by reading and discussing their work (and, of course, by sharing some treats).

Provide opportunities to interact with peers.   All four of the teachers allow children to work in small groups to accomplish tasks. For example, Viviana's students work in pairs during math, manipulating Unifix™ cubes to demonstrate two-digit numbers. In Ken's class, students form simulation teams to experience first hand the hardships of pioneer life.

SHARING RESPONSIBILITY WITH STUDENTS

A third approach to gaining students' cooperation is to provide opportunities for them to exercise some autonomy and to make decisions. None of us like to feel controlled or manipulated, and it seems clear that students who feel empowered will be more likely to share the responsibility for seeing that classroom norms are enforced.

We already touched on this topic in the last chapter, when we discussed the idea of allowing students to participate in rule-setting. But shared decision-making doesn't end on the first day of school; it is an ongoing process. For example, Barbara allows students a key role in determining the seating arrangement:

> Whenever we choose the seating, I allow students to have some input. I ask them to write down a list of three students they'd like to sit next to. I tell them that I'll do my best to see that they sit next to one of their choices, but I explain that I'm counting on them to make wise choices—to choose someone who can act as a partner, someone they can sit next to without causing a commotion or interfering with others. I tell

them that I realize the importance of sitting with friends, but that learning has to be the primary concern. When I decide on the seating, I try to honor their requests, but I can also separate overly social kids or kids who just don't get along. In this way, I can prevent problems from occurring. The kids really like this system. They realize I'm trying to be considerate of their feelings, but I'm also protecting their opportunity to learn.

Whenever possible, Barbara also tries to build choice into the curriculum. During one visit late in the school year, we watched Barbara introduce a new project—writing a newspaper based on *Tuck Everlasting*, the novel they had just finished reading. In the following vignette, Barbara not only allows individuals to select the topic on which to write, but also to decide whether they will work alone or in groups.

BARBARA: Should we work in groups or not? [Students raise their hands in response to her question.] Edward?

EDWARD: I personally don't want to work in groups. I have an idea about what I want to do and how I want to do it, and it would be better if I could work alone.

BARBARA: Are there people who feel differently? How do you feel, James?

JAMES: I'd like to work in pairs.

BARBARA: Why?

JAMES: Because it's easier. You get more work done quickly.

BARBARA: Do you think writing this article is heavy duty work that will require a lot people?

CLASS: No-o-o-o.

BARBARA: Edward?

EDWARD: I don't mind pairs either, just not a large group.

ISATU: I go to enrichment, and it would help if I had a partner so I'd know what to do when I come back.

BARBARA: That's a good point. Jill?

JILL: Sometimes I prefer to work alone because I have serious thinking to do.

BARBARA: Can you think alone if you work in a pair? [She asks them to think about times when they worked in groups but they also had to think on their own.] It's always necessary to think alone, even if you're working in groups. [Talk turns to the actual writing assignments they will be doing. After discussing possible topics, Barbara returns to the question of how to organize students for the activity.] Okay, here's what we're going to do. You changed how I was thinking. I was thinking of having you work in threes, but you convinced me that pairs and singles would be good. It's 10:50. By 10:55, you should know if you want to work in pairs or singles and what you want to write about. I'll get my pencil and pad; you get yourselves organized. Come over to the round table and tell me what you want to write about and if you're single or pairs.

Like Barbara, Ken also structures opportunities for his students to exercise some choice. For example, he often allows his class to have input into the daily schedule. He'll tell them, "It's 1:45 and we have three things to do. What order should we do them in?" Sometimes, students are allowed to select the two assignments they will do in class and the one they will bring home for homework. Ken also believes that students should be able to make some decisions about the assignments themselves.

When students read a chapter in their novels, for example, they construct their own questions about the material and then answer them. Ken teaches his students to use Bloom's taxonomy of cognitive objectives (knowledge, comprehension, application, analysis, synthesis, and evaluation) and has them select the level at which they will construct their questions.

Occasionally, Ken even allows students to select the novels they will read in small groups:

> I brought in about a dozen sets of novels and had the kids examine them when they had some free time. They know there have to be three or four reading groups. They talked with one another about the books. I'd hear them say, "This looks good. Would you want to read this with me?" You know, it's funny. Teachers say, "You can't do this. Kids will just pick the books their friends read." I say, "That's right. And that's okay. In fact, that's exactly what *adults* do." When a friend says a book is good, that's when you want to read it. Kids are no different.

> Anyway, after everyone had had a chance to peruse the books, we took about 30 or 40 minutes one day to set up the groups. I told the kids, "Some people have picked this book, and this one. No one picked that one." Of course, we ended up with one group of only four and one group of nine, but generally, the kids were really cooperative. For example, one boy said, "I really wanted to read *Treasure Island,* but no one else picked it, so I'll take *Dies Drear* instead." I also tried to steer the not-so-good readers to fairly straightforward books, but in some cases, I decided to let them try a more challenging book. . . .

Although it is easier to share decision-making with students in higher grades, even Viviana and Garnetta are able to create opportunities for students to exercise independent judgment. For example, Garnetta sometimes allows children to select their own partners for groupwork. Instead of assigning classroom jobs, she puts the list on the board and allows children to choose the two they would like to do. She makes an effort to give students their first choice.

When Viviana's first graders work on spelling words, they have the option of using the spelling word in a sentence, drawing and labeling a picture showing the word, or incorporating the word in a sentence that describes a magazine picture. Viviana also tries to provide opportunities for students to monitor and regulate their own behavior. A good example is the way she handles the rubbery "spider rings" that appear at Halloween time. Instead of insisting that children take them off and put them in their desks, Viviana tells her students: "If you can pay attention and wear the ring, fine. If you think you'll have trouble, then take it off and put it in the desk."

Sharing decision-making can be difficult for teachers (Schmuck and Schmuck, 1988). When you're feeling pressured to "cover the curriculum" and to maximize learning time, it's easier to make the decisions by yourself. For example, assigning seats is faster than allowing students to participate in the process; informing students of classroom rules is simpler than developing a bill of rights. Involving students can be "messy" and time-consuming. Nonetheless, the opportunity to exercise judgment and to make decisions not only increases students' willingness to cooperate, but also enhances their independence, self-control, and socially responsible behavior (Solomon, Watson, Delucchi, Schaps, and Battistich, 1988). As Ken comments:

> Making decisions by yourself is a quick-fix solution that requires too much disciplining and reprimanding to maintain. In the long run, student decisions save time. There is less misbehavior when students help to decide.

REWARDING APPROPRIATE BEHAVIOR

Many effective managers find it useful to provide students with rewards for appropriate behavior and for involvement in academic work. The use of rewards in classrooms is based on the psychological principle of *positive reinforcement:* behavior that is rewarded is strengthened and is therefore likely to be repeated. One advantage of this approach is that it forces us to focus on the positive. Instead of vigilantly watching students for instances of misbehavior, we must be alert to instances of appropriate behavior. We must "catch 'em being good."

In this section, we discuss the kinds of rewards that are available to teachers, examine some problems that may diminish their effectiveness, and present some guidelines for their use.

Kinds of Rewards

Rewards can be divided into three categories: social rewards, activity rewards, and tangible rewards. *Social rewards* are verbal and nonverbal indications that you recognize and appreciate the way students are behaving. A pat on the back, a smile, a thumbs-up signal—these are commonly used social rewards that are low in cost and readily available.

Praise can also function as a social reward. Interestingly, however, research has shown that teachers use very little praise in classrooms. Jere Brophy (1981) reports that praise of good conduct appears only once every two to ten hours in the early grades and essentially disappears after that! Furthermore, praise can be used in ways that diminish its positive impact. For example, if public praise is given to only a few students, they may become known as "teacher's pets"—hardly a rewarding label. Another problem may arise when teachers praise students they don't particularly like, and inadvertently contradict the praise with frowns or other nonverbal indicators of disapproval. When that happens, the verbal praise is likely to be perceived as insincere (Brophy, Evertson, Anderson, Baum, and Crawford, 1981).

Despite the problems, Brophy (1981) concludes that "effective praise can be informative as well as reinforcing, can provide encouragement and support, and can help teachers establish friendly relationships with students" (p. 274). In order to be effective, however, praise must be *specific and sincere.* Instead of "you were so good this morning," try "I really like the way you came into the room, put away your coats, sat down, and immediately got out your books." Being specific will make your praise more informative; it will also help you to avoid using the same tired, old phrases week after week, phrases that quickly lose any impact (e.g., "good job"). If praise is to serve as a reinforcer, it also needs to be *contingent on the behavior you are trying to strengthen.* In other words, it should be given only when that behavior occurs, so that students understand exactly what evoked the praise.

> Viviana's students sit quietly while she speaks with a visitor by the door. When she turns back to the class, she tells them: "Thank you for being so quiet just now. It was so helpful. I was able to talk to Mrs. Johnson without being interrupted. By being quiet you helped the teacher."

In addition to pats on the back and verbal praise, some teachers institute more formal ways of recognizing accomplishment or cooperation. For example, they may select a "student of the week." Ken has developed an interesting variation of this program. Instead of deciding on the student of the week by himself, he and his students work together to develop the criteria (see Figure 5-3), and students vote each week to select the recipient of the award. (Another way of sharing responsibility and decision-making with students!) We asked Ken how he made sure that the weekly vote didn't degenerate into a popularity contest. Here's his response:

> Every Friday afternoon we sit in a circle and nominate people. Nominations have to be supported with references to the criteria. For example, "I nominate Paul. He helped me in math this week," or "I nominate Leah. She shared her snack with me or she helped a new student." When the list of nominees is complete, each child gets a ballot and we vote. The winner receives a certificate to take home, and we all write a note to the student giving three reasons why they deserved it.
>
> The class created the rule that you can win twice, but you can't win a third time until everyone in the class has won. Now maybe a kid who hasn't been picked begins to feel uncomfortable. I think that's okay. Maybe he'll think about not getting picked and begin to modify his own behavior. Maybe he'll hold a door for the other kids or stack chairs. I'll talk privately to a kid who isn't selected: Why do you think you haven't been chosen? What do you think you could do in order to be chosen as student of the week? When I see him begin to change his behavior, I make sure to point that out: "I want to thank Robert for holding the door for all of us."

FIGURE 5-3
Criteria for Student of the Week

The student of the week is a person who

1. is neat in work.
2. does homework.
3. is friendly to all classmates.
4. can be trusted and can be reliable.
5. helps others.
6. listens to the teacher's instructions.
7. respects other people's property.
8. is kind to people.
9. is responsible.
10. shares with other people.
11. treats everyone equally.
12. cooperates with students and teachers.
13. has self-control.
14. doesn't curse or doesn't talk back.
15. doesn't give up and always tries his or her hardest.
16. doesn't hurt others' feelings.
17. helps people with work.
18. uses gifts and talents well.

It's funny, I thought maybe this year I wouldn't do student of the week, but the class really wanted it. . . . And they do choose well.

In addition to social rewards, teachers often use *special activities* as rewards for good behavior. In the elementary grades, being a messenger, erasing the chalkboards, and being the line leader can be very reinforcing. (See Table 5-2 for additional ideas.) In Barbara's classroom, children who have behaved well receive the opportunity to have a private lunch in the classroom with her, or they may get to stay after school! Another rewarding activity is extra time on the class computer; since there are 27 children and only three computers, extra time is a valued privilege.

Our other three teachers also use activities as rewards. Garnetta gives her class free time and movies; Ken's students get a few extra minutes outside on the playground; and Viviana allows children to play learning games.

One way of determining which activities should be used as rewards is to listen carefully to students' requests. If they ask you for the opportunity to play a game on the computer, clean out the guinea pig's cage, or run the film projector, you can be confident that those activities will be reinforcing (at least for those particular children). It's also helpful to observe what activities students engage in when they have free time (e.g., do they play board games? run to the *Sports Illustrated* magazines in the library corner? trade baseball cards?)

Finally, teachers can use *tangible, material rewards* for good behavior—cookies, stickers, award certificates, candy, baseball cards, pencils. For example, Barbara's math class has particular difficulty remembering to bring in homework. In order to encourage this behavior, Barbara gives out stickers that can then be traded for special privileges. Garnetta's students all have sticker folders they made out of cardboard, and Garnetta dispenses cats, pumpkins, stars, and hearts of every conceivable size, texture, and smell. In addition to the rewards she distributes in class, there is a

TABLE 5-2
POSSIBLE REINFORCERS

Being first in line	Using the computer alone or with a friend
Choosing a game to play with a friend	Listening to music through earphones
Choosing a game for the class to play	Working with special art materials
Choosing a story for the teacher to read to the class	Leading a game
Having ten minutes of free time	Removing lowest test grade
Taking care of the class pet	Being excused from a homework assignment
Taking home the class pet for the weekend	Chewing gum at a specified time
Keeping a favorite stuffed animal on your desk for a day	Keeping score during a class game
Having breakfast or lunch with the teacher	Creating a bulletin board display
Reading a story to a class in a lower grade	Checking out a classroom game to take home
Reading a story to the principal	Having a private, three-minute talk with the teacher

schoolwide recognition program called GISMOS: Grand Incentive System for McKinley's Outstanding Students. By following established school rules, students earn purchasing power in the form of GISMOS points that can be used at the school store to purchase novelty items.

Problems with Rewards

The practice of rewarding appropriate behavior has been the focus of considerable controversy. In particular, educators have debated the legitimacy and ultimate value of *material* rewards. Even among our four teachers, there is disagreement. While Ken, Garnetta, and Barbara all use material rewards to some extent, Viviana does not, preferring to rely on praise and recognition.

One objection is that giving students material rewards in exchange for good behavior is tantamount to bribery. Proponents of this position argue that students should engage in appropriate behavior and activities for their own sake: they should be quiet during seatwork time because that is the socially responsible thing to do; they should do their homework so that they can practice skills taught during class; they should learn multiplication tables because they need to know them. Other educators acknowledge the desirability of such intrinsic motivation, but believe that the use of rewards is inevitable in situations where people are not completely free to follow their own inclinations. They ask: How many of us would go to work each day if we weren't going to collect a pay check at the end of the week?

Another major concern is that rewarding students for behaving in certain ways actually undermines their intrinsic motivation to engage in those behaviors. This concern requires us to distinguish between the use of rewards for teaching and reinforcing *appropriate classroom behaviors* and rewarding students for successful *academic performance* (e.g., getting an A on a vocabulary test). A long history of research on behavior modification has demonstrated that when students have difficulty behaving appropriately, rewards can be used to increase acceptable behaviors (e.g., following directions) and to reduce unacceptable behaviors (e.g., making distracting comments during discussions). (We will return to this topic in Chapter 6.) But what happens when you reward students, not for the behaviors required for an orderly environment, but for engaging in academic activities that they already know how to do—and even enjoy? Is it possible that providing rewards in a case like this can actually decrease students' intrinsic motivation?

This question was explored in an influential study conducted by Lepper, Greene, and Nisbett (1973). First, the researchers identified preschoolers who showed interest in a particular drawing activity during free play. Then they met with the children individually. Some children were simply invited to draw with the materials (the "no-reward" subjects). Others were told they could receive a "good-player" award, which they received for drawing (the "expected-reward" subjects). Still others were invited to draw and were then given an unexpected reward at the end (the "unexpected-reward" subjects). Subsequent observations during free play revealed that the children who had been promised a reward ahead of time engaged in the art activity half as much as they had initially. Children in the other two groups showed no change.

The study by Lepper, Greene, and Nisbett stimulated a great deal of research on the potentially detrimental effects of external rewards. Although the results were not always consistent, this research led educators to conclude that *rewarding people for doing something they already like to do decreases their interest in continuing that behavior.* Recently, however, the debate over external rewards has heated up once again. Judy Cameron and W. David Pierce (1994) conducted an extensive analysis of 96 previous studies and concluded that teachers can use rewards without worrying that their students will lose their intrinsic motivation. In fact, Cameron and Pierce found that verbal praise significantly *increased* intrinsic motivation, while unexpected tangible rewards had no effect. Even expected, tangible rewards did no harm, unless they were given simply for doing a task, rather than meeting a specified level of performance or completing a task. According to Cameron and Pierce's findings, this means that it's all right to say, "If you complete the assignment accurately, you'll get some free time at the end of the period" (reward contingent on completion and level of performance), but it's not all right to say, "Work on the assignment, and you'll get some free time at the end of the period."

Despite the persuasiveness of Cameron and Pierce's arguments, the debate is far from over. Already other researchers have challenged both their methods and their findings (*Harvard Education Letter,* 1995). At the present time, caution in the use of external rewards is clearly in order. Nonetheless, it still appears that the judicious use of rewards can help in the task of gaining students' cooperation and increasing their involvement in learning activities (Cohen, 1985).

Using Rewards Effectively

As you contemplate a system of rewards for your classroom, keep in mind the following suggestions.

Distinguish between rewarding appropriate behaviors and rewarding performance on academic activities.   Rewards (verbal, social, and tangible) can be helpful to teach students the behaviors needed for order and learning, such as speaking quietly, sitting still, focusing on schoolwork, and remembering to bring their homework. But don't wait for perfect performance; instead, shape youngsters' behavior by rewarding improvement.

Use verbal rewards to increase intrinsic motivation for academic tasks.   It seems clear that praise can have a positive impact on students' intrinsic motivation. But remember that intermediate students may be embarrassed by public praise, and they are good at detecting phoniness. In order to be reinforcing, praise should be specific, sincere, and contingent on the behavior you are trying to strengthen.

Save tangible rewards for activities that students find unattractive.   When students already enjoy doing a task, there's no need to provide tangible rewards. Save tangible rewards for activities that students tend to find boring and aversive.

If you're using tangible rewards, try to provide them unexpectedly, after the task performance.   In this way, students are more likely to view the rewards as information about their performance and as an expression of the teacher's pleasure, rather than as an attempt to control their behavior.

Be cautious about using expected tangible rewards. Be sure to make them contingent upon completion of a task or achieving a specific level of performance.   If you reward students simply for engaging in a task, regardless of their performance, they are likely to spend less time on the task once the reward is removed.

Make sure you select rewards that students like.   You may think that animal stickers are really neat, but if your students do not find them rewarding, their behavior will not be reinforced.

Keep your program of rewards simple.   An elaborate system of rewards is impossible to maintain in the complex world of the classroom. The fancier your system, the more likely that you will abandon it. Moreover, if rewards become too salient, they overshadow more intrinsic reasons for behaving in certain ways. Students become so preoccupied with collecting, counting, and comparing that they lose sight of why the behavior is necessary or valuable.

WHAT DO THE STUDENTS SAY?

While working on this chapter, we became curious about the perceptions of students in the classrooms of our four teachers. In particular, we were interested in their reasons for cooperating with their teachers. In each class, we met with students in small groups, either in a corner of the room or out in the hallway. We asked them to explain "why the kids in this class behave." They answered with disarming honesty, and within each class, students demonstrated extraordinary consistency.

Viviana's first graders seemed to have difficulty even understanding the concept of misbehavior. For them, behaving well was the only possible course of action. "We gotta behave," they told us, "because she's grown up and she's a teacher." Over and over, they insisted that "kids hafta listen to the teacher," that "we have to behave because she tells us to be good." When we described situations in which students *didn't* behave well, they looked at us blankly, as if they could not conceive of that possibility. One boy even told us, "My mother has educated me to behave well, so I never misbehave. *I'm not allowed to misbehave.*" A few children talked about wanting Mrs. Love to be happy: "Mrs. Love is good, and she's happy when we're good. She feels good when we listen." And one boy said he behaved well so that he would learn: "If you don't listen to the teacher you might not learn, and when you grow up someone might ask you a question and you won't know the answer, and you won't be able to have a good job, and then you won't make money."

In contrast, Garnetta's third graders had no difficulty understanding our question. They talked enthusiastically about the stickers they receive for good behavior. They proudly showed us their sticker folders, making certain we saw their favorites. They also told us about the candy they sometimes get when they've been "especially good," and about the pizza parties that they've earned. In addition, they emphasized that "Ms. Chain is real nice." We heard several variations on this theme: "Ms. Chain doesn't yell. "Ms. Chain cares about us." "Ms. Chain treats us real good. If we ask her to go somewhere, like the bathroom, she let's us go. Other teachers say wait until the other kids go." "Ms. Chain bought the guinea pigs for us—only the eighth-grade kids got guinea pigs." Students also described some of

Garnetta creates opportunities for students to do science experiments.

the projects they do, claiming that "in this room, we get interesting stuff to do." One boy talked excitedly about their research on the solar system, while another claimed: "This teacher is better than any other teacher I had because she teaches us a lot of things and gives us lots of science and math." One girl reported that "in this class, we get to bake bread (the story in our reading book was about making bread, so she let us do that). And she's going to let us make cupcakes, and she let us go with her to get fish for the bazaar." Finally, students described some of the "consequences" that they received if they broke the rules.

In Barbara's class, the students also stressed how "nice" their teacher was, how "she doesn't yell," and how "she makes things fun, even things we don't like." They talked about their science experiments, the arts and crafts activities they had done, the books they read, and the journals they kept. They were appreciative of the fact that they were allowed to work with other students and that they were given choices: "When we come in in the morning, we can write in our journals or read our books." "When we do science, we can do a poster, or a model, or a report." "When we watch movies, we can sit anywhere we want—even on top of our desks!" "When we read, we can go over to the library corner and lay on the rug." Finally, they talked about the way Barbara gives them free time, and how she plays board games with them ("not like *mothers,* who never play games with kids"). And one child seemed to sum it all up when he said: "She gives us what *we* want, so we give her what *she* wants."

We heard the same themes in Ken's class. These sixth-grade students talked about how "he makes work fun" and how "nice" he is—how he jokes, how he cares about kids, and how he really listens. One girl liked the way "we can tell him about our problems. We have journals and if we have a problem, we can write it down and tell him and he'll write back (like if you don't want to sit next to somebody or if you want to be in another reading group)." Students also mentioned the occasional use of rewards ("we get to play an extra game outside if we do a lot of good stuff") and penalties ("we have to stay in for recess and discuss what we did wrong"). The main theme, however, was the fact that "in Mr. K's class kids get to make decisions." Repeatedly, students talked about the options they were given (e.g., "We get to decide what order to do the work in"). They proudly pointed out the Students' Bill of Rights, the Teacher's Bill of Rights, and the Student-of-the Week program. One boy earnestly described the difference between Mr. K and "other teachers": "In here, kids make up the class rules. Some teachers don't care what kids think about what the rules should be. They come in the first day, hand out a paper with rules on it and say, 'These are the rules.' But in here, we can say what we think the rules should be."

Examining the similarities and the differences among these responses is intriguing. To some extent, the differences across classes seem to reflect developmental changes that occur in children's understanding of authority and obedience. William Damon (1977), for example, has pointed out that very young children view authority figures as having an inherent right to be obeyed. Thus, most of Viviana's children insist, "we gotta behave because she's grown up and she's a teacher." Later, Damon observes, authority comes to be understood as a reciprocal relationship: one person obeys another in return for the other's assistance and favors. We hear this type of reasoning when Garnetta's students tell us "she gives us stickers and candy" and when Barbara's students cite the way "she plays games with us." At a still later age, children begin to see authority as an earned commodity; those who have acquired specific abilities and experiences are entitled to obedience. According to Damon, the authority figure's respect for the welfare and rights of the subordinate is seen as particularly important. Although this theme emerged in discussions with both Garnetta's and Barbara's students, it was most striking in our talks with Ken's sixth graders, who repeatedly emphasized that "in Mr. K's class, kids get to have a say in what we do."

Beyond these developmental differences, we can see that students' responses largely reflect the four approaches we've discussed in this chapter. The students we spoke to described the ways their teachers demonstrate concern and caring; the assignments they get that are interesting and fun to do; the times they are allowed to exercise choice and self-regulation; and the rewards they receive for being good.

In addition, students talked about their teachers' "limits" and described the penalties that are invoked "if kids act up." We will explore limits and penalties in our next chapter, "When Prevention Is Not Enough: Protecting and Restoring Order."

SUMMARY

In this chapter we discussed the fact that having clear, reasonable rules and routines doesn't automatically mean that everyone will follow them. We reiterated the fact that students are a "captive" audience, stressed the need to gain students' cooperation, and suggested four approaches to this task.

Establishing a Positive Relationship

- Express concern for students' needs, anxieties, and fears
- Take the time to learn who your students are and what they like

Fostering Students' Motivation to Learn

- Keep in mind Feather's theory of motivation: expectation of success $\times$ value $=$ motivation
  - Provide opportunities for success
  - Teach students to set reasonable goals and to evaluate their own performance
  - Emphasize the relationship between effort and outcome
  - Relate lessons to students' own lives
  - Model interest and enthusiasm
  - Include novelty/variety elements
  - Provide opportunities for students to respond actively
  - Allow students to create finished products
  - Provide opportunities to interact with peers

Sharing Responsibility

- Share decision-making
- Provide opportunities for students to monitor their own behavior

Using Rewards

- Keep in mind the different types of rewards:
    social rewards
    special activities
    material rewards
- Be aware that rewarding people for doing something they already like to do decreases their interest in continuing that behavior
  - Think carefully about when and how to use rewards:
      Use rewards for activities that children find unattractive
      Use rewards for teaching the behaviors needed for order and learning
      Provide rewards unexpectedly, after performance of the desired behavior
      Select rewards that your students like
      Keep your reward program simple

Strive to create an environment that is relaxed and comfortable, but orderly and productive. Remember, classroom order is like conversation: it can only be achieved if both parties agree to participate.

ACTIVITIES

1 *Preparing for the first day:* In the previous chapter you were asked to consider the rules and procedures you would present on the first day of school. In this part of the activity, the focus will be on planning activities.

Using the following list of activities, prepare an outline for the first day of school: (1) an introductory, get-acquainted activity; (2) two content area activities (math, language arts, science or social studies); and (3) an art or creative drama project. In addition, select a book to read aloud and two games or "fillers" to use during "down time."

You may select any grade level you like. Describe each of your activities in narrative form. As you plan your day, keep in mind the ways of gaining students' cooperation. Code your plans with the following letters, indicating your intentions to motivate your students and build positive relationships.

a Provide opportunities for success. Don't barrage children with tests the first day. Plan activities they can do and feel good about.

b The content should be meaningful and relevant. What do children at your grade level like to do? Connect the activity to their lives.

c Allow for peer interaction. Students will be eager to rekindle friendships and get to know each other.

d Ensure active participation by all.

e Be sensitive to children's needs. Remember what it was like to be a child. For example, they have gone all summer being able to eat when they wanted. A snack time recognizes one of their needs. They also need breaks to move around. What about their fear or anxiety about the new class?

f Create a relaxed and pleasant atmosphere. Plan activities that you and the children will enjoy.

Example:

Activity	Code
Math: Bring in a watermelon to school. Have the students estimate how many seeds there are in the watermelon. Cut open the melon and have the students count the seeds in one slice. Have them estimate again how many seeds there are in the whole melon. Give out slices to eat and have them count the seeds. Graph the results.	a, b, d, e, f

We have also included in the Appendix a checklist of tasks to be accomplished before the opening of school. With careful preparation, your chances for an excellent school opening will be enhanced.

2 In addition to rule setting, how might you involve students in decision-making to develop a feeling of shared responsibility? In the following three vignettes, the teachers have directed the activity. Think about ways they could have involved students in the planning, directing, creating, or evaluating. Rewrite each vignette to show this more child-centered approach.

a It is creative writing time. Mr. Allen decided that since Thanksgiving was next week, his second-grade students should write about what they were thankful for. He gave each child a sheet of paper with the outline of a turkey on it and said they were to think about Thanksgiving and to write, inside the turkey, what they were thankful for. When they were finished, they could illustrate their stories. The children hung up their stories on the bulletin board and brought them home before Thanksgiving.

b Mrs. Peters felt that the unit her fourth-grade class completed on folk tales would lend itself to a class play. She chose *Paul Bunyon* and *Pecos Bill* as the stories to dramatize. The children were excited and Mrs. Peters gave out parts and assigned children to paint scenery. Mrs. Peters wrote a script and sent it home for the children to memorize. She asked parents to make the costumes. After three weeks of practice, the play was performed for the third-grade classes and the parents.

c Ms. Wilkins wanted her sixth-grade students to develop an understanding about ancient civilizations. She assigned a five-part project. Students had to research four civilizations (Egyptian, Mesopotamian, Indus Valley, and Shang); write a biography about Howard Carter, a famous archaeologist; describe three pyramids (step, Great Pyramid, Pyramid of Sesostris II); outline the reigns of five kings (Hammurabi, Thutmose III, Ramses II, David, and Nebuchadnezzar); and make a model of a pyramid. She gave the class five weeks to complete the project. She collected them, graded them, and then displayed them in the school library. The children were able to take them home the following week.

REFERENCES

Brophy, J. (1981). On praising effectively. *The Elementary School Journal, 81*(5), 269–277.

Brophy, J. (1987). Synthesis of research on strategies for motivating students to learn. *Educational Leadership, 45*, 40–48.

Brophy, J., and Evertson, C., with Anderson, L, Baum, M., and Crawford, J. (1981). *Student characteristics and teaching.* New York: Longman, Inc.

Cameron, J., and Pierce, W. D. (1994). Reinforcement, reward, and intrinsic motivation: A meta-analysis. *Review of Educational Research, 64*, 363–423.

Clark, C. (October 1989). The good teacher. Plenary lecture presented to The Norwegian Research Council for Science and the Humanities Conference: "Education from Cradle to Doctorate." Trondheim, Norway.

Cohen, M. W. (1985). Extrinsic reinforcers and intrinsic motivation. In M. K. Alderman & M. W. Cohen (Eds.), *Motivation theory and practice for preservice teachers* (Teacher Education Monograph No. 4). Washington, D.C.: ERIC Clearinghouse on Teacher Education, 6–15.

Damon, W. (1977). *The social world of the child.* San Francisco: Jossey-Bass Publishers.

Doyle, W. (1986). Classroom organization and management. In M. C. Wittrock (Ed.), *Handbook of research on teaching.* New York: Macmillan.

Emmer, E. T., Evertson, C. M., and Anderson, L. M. (1980). Effective classroom management at the beginning of the school year. *The Elementary School Journal, 80,* 219–231.

Feather, N. (Ed.) (1982). *Expectations and actions.* Hillsdale, NJ: Erlbaum.

Good, T. L., and Brophy, J. E. (1994). *Looking in classrooms* (6th edition). New York: Harper-Collins.

The Harvard Education Letter (January/February 1995). The debate over incentives heats up. *The Harvard Education Letter, 11*(1), 6.

Kottler, E. (1994). *Children with limited English: Teaching strategies for the regular classroom.* Thousand Oaks, CA: Corwin Press, Inc.

Kounin, J. (1970). *Discipline and group management in classrooms.* New York: Holt, Rinehart and Winston.

Lepper, M., Greene, D., and Nisbett, R. E. (1973). Undermining children's intrinsic interest with extrinsic rewards: A test of the "overjustification" hypothesis. *Journal of Personality and Social Psychology, 28,* 129–137.

Newby, T. (1991). Classroom motivation: Strategies of first-year teachers. *Journal of Educational Psychology, 83,* 195–200.

Schmuck, R. A., and Schmuck, P. A. (1988). *Group processes in the classroom* (5th edition). Dubuque, Ia: Wm. C. Brown Publishers.

Skinner, E. A., and Belmont, M. J. (1993). Motivation in the classroom: Reciprocal effects of teacher behavior and student engagement across the school year. *Journal of Educational Psychology, 85*(4), 571–581.

Solomon, D., Watson, M. S., Delucchi, K. L., Schaps, E., and Battistich, V. (1988). Enhancing children's prosocial behavior in the classroom. *American Educational Research Journal, 25*(4), 527–554.

FOR FURTHER READING

Jones, V. F., and Jones, L. S. (1986). *Comprehensive classroom management: Creating positive learning environments.* (2nd edition). Boston: Allyn and Bacon. (Chapter 4 discusses positive teacher-student relationships.)

Kottler, E. (1994). *Children with limited English: Teaching strategies for the regular classroom.* Thousand Oaks, CA: Corwin Press, Inc.

Purkey, W. W., and Novak, J. M. (1984). *Inviting school success—A self-concept approach to teaching and learning* (2nd edition). Belmont, CA: Wadsworth Publishing Company.

Schaps, E., and Solomon, D. (1990). Schools and classrooms as caring communities. *Educational Leadership, 48*(3), 38–42.

Schmuck, R. A., and Schmuck, P. A. (1988). *Group processes in the classroom* (5th edition). Dubuque, Ia: Wm. C. Brown Publishers.

Chapter Six _____

When Prevention Is Not Enough: Protecting and Restoring Order

Perhaps you've seen *Juggling for the Complete Klutz* (Cassidy and Rimbeaux, 1988), a lighthearted how-to book that has sold more than a million copies since its publication in 1977. In the foreword, author John Cassidy explains that his book began life "as a humble lesson plan for a sophomore English class." Cassidy was a student teacher, losing the daily battle for his students' attention. Teaching them to juggle was his response to Friday afternoon "post-lunch brain-haze."

Cassidy's solution may be unique, but his problem certainly isn't. No matter how hard you've worked to establish positive relationships with students and to involve them in meaningful learning activities, sooner or later instances of brain-haze and inattentiveness are bound to occur. If you don't know how to juggle, what can you do? And how do you deal with the *other* behavior problems and conflicts that inevitably crop up in classrooms? Before going any further, let's consider what those problems are likely to be.

WHAT'S IN STORE

Newspaper headlines about crime, violence, and vandalism sometimes convey the image of classrooms as "blackboard jungles," but in reality, most of the misbehaviors that teachers encounter are far more mundane—talking to neighbors, not having homework done, calling out, daydreaming, forgetting to bring supplies and books, teasing, name-calling, poking (Doyle, 1986). A national survey of teachers (Center for Education Statistics, 1987) indicates that problems such as these are widespread; more than half of the elementary teachers reported that in just the previous week a student had talked back to them (52 percent), whispered or passed a note (84 percent), or come late to class (74 percent).

Even if behaviors like these are not seriously disruptive, they can be aggravating and wearing. Furthermore, inappropriate behavior *threatens classroom order by interrupting the flow of instructional activity.* Lessons cannot proceed smoothly and efficiently if students haven't done their homework; class discussions become chaotic if children continually blurt out comments; and giving instructions is a waste of time if no one is listening.

PRINCIPLES FOR DEALING WITH INAPPROPRIATE BEHAVIOR

There is little research on the relative effectiveness of disciplinary strategies (see Emmer and Aussiker, 1990), but four principles guide our discussion. First, we believe that when dealing with misbehavior, *the overriding goal should be to keep the instructional program going with a minimum of disruption.* Achieving this goal requires a delicate balancing act. On one hand, you cannot allow inappropriate behavior to interrupt the teaching-learning process. On the other hand, you must realize that disciplinary strategies themselves can be disruptive. As Doyle comments, interventions are "inherently risky" because they call attention to misbehavior and can actually pull students away from a lesson (1986, p. 421). In order to avoid this situation, you must try to anticipate potential problems and head them off; if you decide that a disciplinary intervention *is* necessary, you need to be as unobtrusive as possible.

Watching our four teachers in action, it is clear that they recognize the importance of protecting the instructional program. In the following incident, Viviana sizes up a potentially disruptive situation and is able to maintain the flow of her lesson:

> It is Halloween time, and Viviana's students have just returned from art class, where they made masks. They enter the room wearing the masks, obviously excited and proud of the way they look. Viviana stands at the chalkboard, about to begin a language arts lesson. She takes a long look at her students and waits for them to get settled. Then, she moves to her desk, takes out a mask, and puts it on. She moves back to the chalkboard and announces, "Since you have your masks on, I will wear one too. We will do language arts with our masks on." Later, she tells us: "I had only two choices. It was clear that if I made them take their masks off, I'd be fighting with them the whole period; my lesson would go down the drain. If I let them wear the masks, and even put one on myself, I could keep the lesson going and get them involved. I couldn't let my lesson fall apart."

Our second principle is that *whether or not a particular action constitutes misbehavior depends on the context in which it occurs* (Doyle, 1986). There are obvious exceptions to this notion—punching another child and stealing property are obvious violations that always require a teacher response. But other behaviors are not so clear cut. For example, in some classes, wearing a hat, sitting on your desk, chewing gum, and talking to neighbors are all misbehaviors, while in other classes these are perfectly acceptable. What constitutes misbehavior is often a function of a particular teacher's tolerance level or the standards set by a particular school (Cairns, 1987). When determining a course of action, you need to ask yourself, "Is this behavior disrupting the ongoing instructional activity? Is it hurtful to other children? Does it violate established rules?" If the answer to these questions is no, disciplinary interventions may not be necessary.

"I'm a fidgeter," Barbara tells us. "When I first went for an interview for a teaching position, my mother told me not to wear any jewelry, because she knew that I'd play with it while I talked. Because of this, I'm sympathetic to the fidgeters in my class. If a kid has trouble sitting still and crawls all over his or her chair, I don't do anything—unless it's bothering other people. Sometimes I hear a child singing softly while working. I'll check to see if other people seem to be disturbed before doing anything. For me, that's the most important question: Is the behavior affecting others and denying them the right to instruction? If not, it's usually okay with me."

Considering the context has become more important as the home lives of many children have become more unstable and unsupportive. Sometimes teachers excuse the inappropriate behavior of certain students because "these kids can't help it." We hear teachers say, "What can you expect, with a family situation like that?" or "These poor kids are going through so much at home, I hate to make their lives more difficult by enforcing rules." As well intentioned as these teachers may be, not holding students accountable for appropriate behavior rarely helps. Children may protest limits, but they crave consistency, predictability, and structure—particularly when they live inconsistent, unpredictable, and unstructured lives out of school. Garnetta tells this vignette:

I have one girl in my class with serious behavior problems. Her mother is in and out of jail, and the child is shunted around to different relatives and friends. She's thin and frail, prone to tantrums, and *very* sensitive. She can't stand to be yelled at and needs a lot of TLC [tender loving care]. I have to be more mellow with her than with the other kids. For example, when I tell her she has to do her work, she'll say, "Okay, I'll be good, Mrs. Chain. Just give me a hug. Do you still love me?" I tell her, "I love you, and I'll hug you, but you still have to do your work."

Despite the need to enforce expectations for appropriate behavior, teachers need to be sensitive to conditions at home that make some children's lives a constant struggle. We recently learned about a second grader who was frequently late to school because he had to get himself up, wake his younger brother (a kindergartner), prepare breakfast, and get them both to school. When he would appear at the door of his classroom fifteen minutes late, his teacher would harshly berate him and send him to the office. It's true that the child was violating the school rule about not being tardy, but we think a more humane response would have been to welcome him to school with a warm hello, while working with the school social worker to see what could be done to improve the situation. After all, the fact that he got to school at all was quite an accomplishment.

The third principle that underlies our discussion is that *disciplinary strategies must preserve students' dignity.* Richard Curwin and Allen Mendler (1988), authors of *Discipline with Dignity,* put it this way:

Students will protect their dignity at all costs, even with their lives if pushed hard enough. In the game of chicken, with two cars racing at top speed toward a cliff, the loser is the one who steps on the brake. Nothing explains this bizarre reasoning better then the need for peer approval and dignity. (p. 27)

In order to protect students' dignity, it is important to avoid power struggles that may cause students to lose face with their peers. Our four teachers speak with misbehaving students calmly and quietly. They don't bring up past sins. They take care to separate the child's *character* from the specific *misbehavior;* instead of attacking the child as a person ("You're lazy"), they talk about what the child has done ("You have not handed in the last two homework assignments"). When more than a brief intervention is necessary, they try to meet with students privately.

On the second day of school, we witnessed a good example of disciplining with dignity in Garnetta's classroom. Even though it was so early in the school year, Tanya was already displaying the behaviors that had contributed to her notorious reputation:

> During the first hour of the morning, Tanya breaks down in tears, refuses to participate in a class activity, punches two children passing by her desk, and creates a fuss about her place in the bathroom line. She gets little work done without individual supervision, constantly asks Garnetta for assistance, and pouts if immediate help is not forthcoming. At 10:00, when Tanya is again in tears, Garnetta tells her class they have five minutes of free time. She goes over to Tanya and speaks quietly with her. The two of them go into the hallway. After a few minutes, Garnetta comes back alone; Tanya follows shortly. She sits down at her desk and begins to work on the assignment that Garnetta has just given. After about ten minutes, Garnetta asks Tanya to go on an important errand to the office. We are astounded by the smile on Tanya's face as she leaves the room. She returns shortly, and there are no problems for the rest of the morning.

> Later, we ask Garnetta to reveal what happened in the hallway. She tells us that she began by asking Tanya what was bothering her. Tanya reported that the boy next to her had said her shoes were ugly. "Do *you* think they're ugly?" Garnetta asked. "No," Tanya replied. They spoke for a few minutes about her shoes and how it feels when somebody says something bad about the way you look. Although this clearly had not been the cause of Tanya's problems all morning, Garnetta let it go, assuring Tanya that she would talk to the boy about his comment. Garnetta then talked about how glad she was that Tanya was in her class, pointed out good things Tanya had done that morning as well as the things that had been problematic, and encouraged her to work hard for the rest of the morning. She told her to go to the bathroom, wash her face, get a drink, and then return to the room. "When I saw her working so well, I wanted to give her an immediate reward. Children like Tanya often don't get to go on errands, because teachers are sure they'll misbehave in the hallways. So I sent her on an errand to let her know that I trusted her and that I liked her and that I knew she had been working well."

In this vignette, we see how Garnetta tried to avoid embarrassing Tanya by speaking with her privately; how she demonstrated concern for Tanya's feelings about the boy's nasty comments; how she focused on the appropriate behavior Tanya had demonstrated that morning rather than her misbehavior; and how she attempted to reinforce Tanya's on-task behavior and increase her feelings of self-importance by sending her on an errand. This encounter was not a magical cure. Although Garnetta was able to bring about definite improvements in Tanya's behavior, the child's problems were deep-rooted and persistent. Nonetheless, this vignette demonstrates the way Garnetta worked to communicate her expectations for appropriate behavior while preserving Tanya's dignity.

Another way of disciplining with dignity is to structure opportunities for students to assume some responsibility for regulating their own behavior. In Chapter 5, we talked about gaining students' cooperation by sharing responsibility and decision-making authority. In this chapter, we continue that theme by discussing strategies that involve students in solving the problems that arise in classrooms.

Finally, the fourth principle emphasizes the importance of *making sure a disciplinary strategy matches the misbehavior you are trying to eliminate.* Punching another child warrants more than a mild rebuke, while whispering to a neighbor probably doesn't deserve lengthy detention. Understandably, research indicates that teachers are least tolerant of disruptive behaviors that have a negative impact on other students (Safran and Safran, 1984). For example, a case study (Pittman, 1985) of "Mrs. Fisher," a first-grade teacher, indicated that she thought about misbehavior in terms of three categories. In the first category were *minor* misbehaviors—noisiness, socializing, wandering, and daydreaming. The second category consisted of behaviors that Mrs. Fisher considered *more serious*—arguing, fussing, acting boisterously, tattling, failing to respond to a group directive. In the third category were behaviors that she *never tolerated*—stealing, intentionally hurting someone, destroying property. When deciding how to respond to a misbehavior, Mrs. Fisher considered how serious it was, whether it was an isolated event or part of a recurring pattern, and who was involved. She then selected a course of action from a repertoire of disciplinary strategies that were also ordered in terms of severity—from nonverbal cues (e.g., catching the student's eye) and mild reminders to more severe rebukes (e.g., a failing grade in conduct for the day).

When deciding how to respond to a problem, it is useful to think in terms of these categories and to select a response that is congruent with the seriousness of the misbehavior. This is easier said than done, of course. When misbehavior occurs, teachers have little time to assess its seriousness, decide if it's part of a pattern, and select an appropriate response. And too often, the situation is ambiguous: since misbehavior often occurs when the teacher is looking somewhere else, it may not be absolutely clear who is doing what to whom. Beginning teachers may have even more difficulty responding appropriately if they lack a repertoire of strategies for dealing with misbehavior. All of these factors help to explain why beginning teachers sometimes ignore or react mildly to misbehavior that warrants a more severe response, yet overreact to behavior that is relatively minor.

With these four principles in mind—protecting the instructional program, considering the context, disciplining with dignity, and selecting a disciplinary strategy that matches the misbehavior—we turn now to specific ways of responding to inappropriate behavior.

DEALING WITH MINOR MISBEHAVIOR

As we mentioned in Chapter 4, Jacob Kounin's (1970) classic study of orderly and disorderly classrooms gave research support to the belief that successful classroom managers have eyes in the back of their heads. Kounin found that effective managers knew what was going on all over the room; moreover, *their students knew they knew,* because the teachers were able to spot minor problems and "nip them in the bud." Kounin called this ability "withitness," a term that has since become widely used in discussions of classroom management.

How do "with it" teachers deal with minor misbehavior? How do they succeed in nipping problems in the bud? In this section, we discuss both nonverbal and verbal interventions and then consider the times when it may be better to do nothing at all. (Suggestions are summarized in Table 6-1.)

Nonverbal Interventions

A while back, an 11-year-old we know announced that she could be a successful teacher. When we asked why she was so confident, she replied: "I know how to make *the look.*" She proceeded to demonstrate: her eyebrows slanted downward, her forehead creased, and her lips flattened into a straight line. She definitely had "the look" down pat.

The "teacher look" is a good example of an unobtrusive, nonverbal intervention. Making eye contact, using hand signals (e.g., thumbs down; pointing to what the child should be doing), and moving closer to the misbehaving student are other nonverbal ways of communicating disapproval. All of these convey the message, "I see what you're doing, and I don't like it," but since they are less directive than verbal commands, they encourage students to assume responsibility for getting back on task.

TABLE 6-1
DEALING WITH MINOR MISBEHAVIOR

Strategy	Advantages

1. Nonverbal interventions:
    Facial expressions
    Eye contact
    Hand signals
    Proximity
	Allow you to prompt appropriate behavior without
	    disrupting lesson
	Encourage students to assume responsibility for
	    changing behavior

2. Verbal interventions:
    Direct command
    Stating student's name
    Rule reminder
    Calling on child to participate
    Incorporating child's name into lesson
    Use of gentle humor
    I-message
	
	Straightforward
	Brief, unobtrusive
	Reinforces desired behavior
	Gets student back on task without even citing
	    the misbehavior; maintains flow of lesson
	Prompts a smile along with appropriate behavior
	Minimizes negative evaluations and preserves
	    relationships
	Points out consequences of behavior
	Promotes students' autonomy and responsibility
	    for actions

3. Ignoring the misbehavior	Unobtrusive; protects the flow of the lesson

Nonverbal strategies are most appropriate for behaviors that are minor but persistent—frequent or sustained whispering, staring into space, calling out or walking around the room, playing with a toy, and passing notes. Nonverbal interventions not only allow you to deal with these misbehaviors, they enable you to protect and continue your lesson.

> It's a few days after Christmas vacation, and we are observing in Garnetta's classroom. During a creative writing activity, two boys seated across the room from each other begin a "shooting match," using their pencils as "guns." They make convincing gun noises. Garnetta is working with another child; she stops and looks *hard* and *long* at both boys. They look back, immediately stop what they're doing, and get back to work. Garnetta finishes her conversation and begins to circulate around the room. She stops at both boys' desks and checks their work.

In the following incident, Ken is able to get rid of distracting objects and return a student to work without any verbal reference to what is happening:

> Ken is working with a reading group at his small group table. While he is speaking, one boy waves his spiral notebook in front of his face like a fan. Without breaking his sentence, Ken leans over and takes the notebook. A few minutes later the boy begins to play with his pencil. Ken also removes the pencil, without seeming to look at the boy and without a break in the pace of the lesson. The boy begins to participate.

As these anecdotes illustrate, a nonverbal cue is sometimes all that's needed to stop a misbehavior and get a student back "on task." In fact, a study of six middle school teachers (Lasley, Lasley, and Ward, 1989) found that the *most successful responses to misbehavior were nonverbal.* These strategies stopped misbehavior 79 percent of the time; among the three "more effective managers," the success rate was even higher—an amazing 95 percent.

Obvious advantage of using a nonverbal cue is that you don't distract other students while dealing with the misbehavior. As Barbara comments:

> Whenever you're involved in a verbal confrontation with one child, the others are "free-timing it." They're listening to *you* instead of doing their work. If a child is playing with a car, it's much more effective to simply walk over and take it. That way it's gone, and you don't have to worry about it anymore.

Placing a hand on a student's shoulder or physically guiding a child to pick up a pencil and get to work are also unobtrusive, nonverbal interventions that teachers have found helpful. Remember the cautions expressed in Chapter 5, however, about physical contact with students. We know a student teacher who tried to get a student on-task by taking the child's head in her hands and directing it away from the window toward the chalkboard. Later, the child complained about a stiff neck and accused the student teacher of "jerking" her head around. The student teacher immediately notified her cooperating teacher and principal about what had happened, and a phone call to the parents fortunately headed off further trouble. Incidents like these, however, point to the importance of avoiding any physical interventions that could be interpreted as abusive.

Verbal Interventions

Sometimes you find yourself in situations where it's just not possible to use a non-verbal cue. Perhaps you can't catch the student's eye, or you're working with a small group, and it would be too disruptive to get up and walk across the room to the misbehaving child. Other times, you're able to use a nonverbal cue, but it's unsuccessful in stopping the misbehavior.

In cases like this, you can use a *nondirective verbal intervention*. These allow you to prompt the appropriate behavior, while leaving the responsibility for figuring out what to do with the misbehaving student. For example, *simply saying the student's name* might be enough to get the student back on task. Sometimes it's possible to *incorporate the child's name into the ongoing instruction*. We witnessed Ken use this unobtrusive strategy during a small group discussion:

> Brian is slouching down in his seat and appears inattentive. Ken is praising the comment of another student: "Did you see the way Joey made that into any analysis question? He didn't just say, 'Brian is slouching in his seat,' he said . . . " Brian immediately sits up, with a small smile on his face and begins to participate in the discussion.

If the misbehavior occurs while a group discussion or recitation is going on, you can *call on the child to answer a question.* Consider the following example:

> Viviana is conducting a whole-group reading lesson—"The Hen and the Bread." She asks the class, "What is make believe in this picture and what is real?" The children scrutinize the illustration, and one by one hands go up into the air. She calls on a non-volunteer who appears to by daydreaming. "Fernando, what is make believe in this picture?" He is brought back to the task, looks at the picture, and slowly responds.

Calling on a student allows you to communicate that you know what's going on and to capture the student's attention—without even citing the misbehavior. But keep in mind what we said earlier about preserving students' dignity. If you are obviously trying to "catch" students and to embarrass them, the strategy may well backfire by creating resentment (Good and Brophy, 1987).

The *use of humor* can provide another "gentle" way of reminding children to correct their behavior. Used well, humor can show students that you are able to understand the funny sides of classroom life. But you must be careful that the humor is not tinged with sarcasm that can hurt students' feelings.

> Garnetta instructs her students to clean off their desks in anticipation of the next activity. One boy takes a paper, crumples it up into a ball and sticks it in his desk. Garnetta makes big eyes and says, "I saw that paper go *squish* into your desk." The boy and the class laugh. He takes the paper ball and puts it in the waste basket.

> Viviana sees a few students playing with toys inside their desks when they're supposed to by paying attention to the lesson. Very dramatically, she warns them: "You're going to make me mad, and when I get mad I make an *ugly face.* You don't want to see my ugly face, do you?" The children "shiver" with the thought of seeing her ugly face, put the toys away, and return to work.

An *"I-message"* is another way of verbally prompting appropriate behavior without giving a direct command. This strategy was developed by Thomas

Gordon, a clinical psychologist and author of *T.E.T.—Teacher Effectiveness Training* (1974). Gordon recommends that I-messages contain three components. First, the teacher *describes the unacceptable behavior* in a nonblaming, nonjudgmental way. This phrase often begins with "when": "When people talk while I'm giving directions . . . " The second component describes the *tangible effect* on the teacher: "I have to repeat the directions and that wastes time . . . " Finally, the third part of the message states the *teacher's feelings* about the tangible effect: "and I get frustrated." Barbara used a three-part I-message like this when her class failed to clean up after a particularly messy art activity: "When you leave the room a mess, I have to clean it up, and I may not want to do an activity like this again."

Other examples of I-messages are:

"When you come to class without your supplies, I can't start the lesson on time, and I get really irritated."

"When you leave your skateboard in the middle of the aisle, I can trip over it, and I'm afraid I'll break a leg."

Although I-messages ideally contain all three components in the recommended sequence, I-messages in any order, or even with one part missing, can still be effective (Gordon, 1974). We've witnessed our teachers use "abbreviated" I-messages. For example, Viviana communicates the importance of not laughing at people's mistakes when she states: "If you laugh at me when I make a mistake, then I'll feel bad." And Barbara honestly tells her class: "When you guys do that, it drives me up the wall."

There are several benefits to using Gordon's approach. In contrast to typical "you-messages" (e.g., "You are being rude," "You ought to know better," "You're acting like a baby"), I-messages minimize negative evaluations of the student. For this reason, they foster and preserve a positive relationship between people. Since I-messages leave decisions about changing behavior up to students, this approach is also likely to promote a sense of responsibility and autonomy. In addition, I-messages show students that their behavior has consequences and that teachers are people with genuine feelings. Unlike you-messages, I-messages don't make students defensive and stubborn; thus, they may be more willing to change their behavior.

Most of us are not used to speaking this way, so I-messages can seem awkward and artificial. With practice, however, using I-messages can become natural. We recently heard a four-year-old girl (whose parents had consistently used I-messages at home) tell her nursery school peer: "When you poke me with that pencil, it really hurts, and I feel bad 'cause I think you don't want to be my friend."

In addition to these nondirective approaches, there are also *more directive strategies* you can try. The most straightforward approach is to *direct students to the task at hand* ("Get to work on that math problem." "Your group should be discussing the first three pages"). You can also *remind the student about the rule or behavioral expectation that is being violated* ("When someone is talking, everyone else is supposed to be listening"). Sometimes, if inappropriate behavior is fairly widespread, it's useful to review rules with the entire group. This is often true after a holiday, a weekend, or a vacation.

Another strategy is to give students a *choice between behaving appropriately or receiving a penalty* for continued inappropriate behavior (e.g., "If you can't handle working in your group, you'll have to return to your seats"; "You either choose to raise your hand instead of calling out, or you will be choosing not to participate in our discussion"). Statements like these not only warn students that a penalty will be invoked if the inappropriate behavior continues, they also emphasize that students have real choices about how to behave and that penalties are not imposed without reason. Ken often uses this strategy. For example, when a boy in his class repeatedly called out during a spelling test, despite nonverbal cues and nondirective reminders, Ken told him: "Brain, you either choose to be quiet, or you will lose the opportunity to play soccer with the rest of the class." Brian protested in a shocked tone: "What am I doing?" In response, Ken calmly described his behavior and its effects: "You're calling out and disturbing people in the room, including me."

Sometimes, Ken also gives students a choice about the particular penalty that will be imposed if they choose to continue their inappropriate behavior. When Evan disregarded Ken's warning not to disrupt a social studies game the class was playing, Ken told him: "Evan, you leave me no choice—to bench you [i.e., exclude him from the game] or to give your whole team a penalty. Which do you want the next time you call out improperly?"

Deliberately Ignoring the Misbehavior

If misbehavior is extremely brief and unobtrusive, the best course of action may be *in*action. For example, during a discussion a student may be so eager to comment that she forgets to raise her hand; or someone becomes momentarily distracted and inattentive; or two boys quietly exchange a comment while you're giving directions. In cases like these, an intervention can be more disruptive than the students' behavior.

One risk of ignoring minor misbehavior is that students may conclude you're unaware of what's going on. Suspecting that you're not "with-it," they may decide to see how much they can get away with, and then problems are sure to escalate. You need to monitor your class carefully to make sure this doesn't happen.

Another problem is that occasional ignoring can turn into full-fledged "blindness." This was vividly demonstrated in a study of a student teacher named Heleen (Créton, Wubbels, and Hooymayers, 1989). When Heleen was lecturing, her students frequently became noisy and inattentive. In response, Heleen talked more loudly and looked more at the chalkboard, turning her back on her students. She did not allow herself to see or hear the disorder—perhaps because it was too threatening and she didn't know how to handle it. Unfortunately, Heleen's students seemed to interpret her "blindness" as an indication that noise was allowed, and they became even more disorderly. Heleen eventually recognized the importance of "seeing" and responding to slight disturbances, in order to prevent them from escalating.

DEALING WITH MORE SERIOUS MISBEHAVIOR: USING PENALTIES

During our discussions on misbehavior, Garnetta, Ken, Barbara, and Viviana repeatedly stressed the importance of following through on the rules and routines that you've planned and taught to your students. As Barbara put it, "If you tell kids to do something, then you have to make sure they do it. Otherwise, you're communicating that you don't really mean it."

Sometimes, nonverbal cues or verbal reminders are not enough to convince students that you really do "mean it." And sometimes misbehavior is just too serious to use these kinds of low-level responses. In cases like these, it may be necessary to impose a penalty in order to enforce your expectations for appropriate behavior.

The importance of enforcing expectations was clearly demonstrated in Emmer, Evertson, and Anderson's (1980) study of effective classroom management. When rule violations occurred in the classrooms of ineffective classroom managers, they often issued reminders and warned students of penalties, but they didn't act on their warnings. Inevitably, behavior problems increased in frequency and severity. In contrast, effective classroom managers dealt both quickly and predictably with rule violations. When they warned students that a penalty would result if the misbehavior didn't stop, the teachers made sure to follow through on the warning.

Emmer, Evertson, and their colleagues also found the effective classroom managers planned their penalties ahead of time. In some cases, teachers discussed penalties when they taught rules and procedures, so students understood the consequences of violating a rule from the very beginning. We saw Garnetta do this with her students in Chapter 4. This practice prevents unpleasant "surprises," and hopefully minimizes protests of blissful ignorance—"But you didn't *tell* me that would happen!"

Selecting Penalties

It's often difficult for beginning teachers to decide on appropriate penalties. One frustrated student teacher told us:

> I can't keep kids after school because they have to catch the school bus. I don't like keeping them in from recess or lunch because that's the only time I have for myself, and I've got to use it for preparation. My cooperating teacher says I'm not allowed to keep kids from going to "specials," because art, music, and physical education are legitimate, valuable parts of the curriculum. I was told by other teachers not to send kids to the office, because then the principal and my cooperating teacher will think I can't handle problems by myself. And my professors have told me never to use extra work as a penalty because kids will come to see schoolwork as punishment. *So what's left?!*

We posed this question to our four teachers and learned about the types of penalties that they typically use. The penalties fall into seven categories:

Expressions of disappointment.   We normally don't think of this as a penalty, but since students in these classes really like their teachers, they feel bad when their teachers are upset. In serious, almost sorrowful tones, our teachers express their disappointment and surprise at the inappropriate behavior and direct students to think about the consequences of their actions.

Loss of privileges.   In Barbara's, Garnetta's and Ken's classes, students who consistently misbehave may lose the highly valued privilege of free time. If they have "forgotten" to do their homework, they need to do it during this time. Ken tells us that, for his students, being eligible for the "student of the week" is extremely important; thus, losing eligibility for the week is also viewed as a serious penalty.

Time out.   In all four classes, students who distract other students or fail to co-operate with their peers must move to another part of the room until they are ready to rejoin the group. Viviana tells her students: "You decide when you can come back." When Ken has a student who constantly talks too much, he and the student agree upon a pleasant, quiet, and isolated place for the child to go if needed. They work out a signal that Ken uses to send the child to the agreed-upon spot if a verbal warning is ineffective.

Sometimes in-class time-out isn't possible or effective, and it's necessary to send a child out of the room. Barbara has worked out a system with another teacher so that she can send a child to his classroom if necessary. She simply writes the amount of time (e.g., "10 minutes") on a slip of paper that the child takes to the other teacher. In the other room, the child must sit quietly and do schoolwork, ignored by both teacher and students.

Time-out can be particularly effective with children who suffer from Attention Deficit Disorder (ADD) or Attention Deficit Hyperactivity Disorder (ADHD) (Rief, 1993). (See Chapter 12 for a discussion of the characteristics of ADD/ADHD.) These children have trouble dealing with the distraction and stimulation of the typical classroom environment; time-out can provide a much needed opportunity to calm down and regain self-control. Try to direct the student to time-out in a calm, positive manner and to be specific about the behavior that is causing the problem [e.g., "Sean, I need you to keep your hands to yourself. Please go to the 'think-about-it' chair until you are ready to sit without poking others" (Rief, 1993)].

Written reflections on the problem.   In Garnetta's classroom, students who consistently misbehave may have to write an essay about what they did, their thoughts about why it happened, and why it was inappropriate. In Ken's class, students who hurt other children write letters of apology to the individuals. Barbara sometimes has her students take out their journals and write about the problem that has occurred.

Visits to the principal's office.   All four teachers believe that "kicking kids out" is a strategy that should be reserved for major disruption. Only rarely do any of them send a child to the principal. Nonetheless, they realize that in extreme cases (like physical aggression), exclusion from the classroom and a meeting with the principal or disciplinarian may be necessary. Even so, Garnetta tells us, "I send along a note telling the principal to send the child back right away. I want my kids in here. They're not going to learn any of my curriculum in the principal's office."

Detention.   Sometimes Garnetta, Ken, and Barbara require students to meet with them after school for a few minutes. This gives them an opportunity to speak privately with students about the inappropriate behavior and to explore possible causes. Usually it's even possible for a "bus student" to meet for a brief period of time. If it's necessary for students to stay longer, parents are notified ahead of time. Ken also keeps students in the room at lunch time (although, as the student teacher we quoted at the beginning of this section observed, this requires him to eat his lunch in the room also). During this time, students make up missing work, and Ken can talk with students in a more private, less rushed manner.

Contacting parents.   All the teachers contact parents promptly if a student shows a pattern of repeated misbehavior. For example, in Barbara's classroom, the first time children don't do homework, she reminds them about her expectations. If shortly afterwards they "forget" again, she tells them, "It's my responsibility to let your parents know that you're not getting your work done and to ask them for help in seeing that you do it." She tries to say this, not in anger, but with an expression of serious concern. She wants to convey the idea that "between the two of us, maybe we can help you get it together." (Working with parents is discussed in more detail in Chapter 11.)

These penalties illustrate the ways Viviana, Garnetta, Barbara, and Ken choose to deal with problems when they have a degree of flexibility. In addition, there are times when they are required to follow school policies mandating particular responses to specific misbehaviors. In Viviana's school, for example, the vice principal (who serves as the school disciplinarian) requires that teachers send students to his office in cases of continual defiance, use of profanity, threats, physical assaults, fighting, and possession of weapons. Be sure to find out what your school policies are with respect to serious problem behaviors.

Selecting penalties that are logical consequences   Whenever possible, penalties should be *logically related to the misbehavior* (e.g., Curwin and Mendler, 1988; Dreikurs, Grunwald, and Pepper, 1982). For example, if students make a mess at the science center, a logical penalty would be to make them clean it up. If a child forgets his book and can't do the assignment, he must borrow someone else's book and do the assignment during free time or recess. A student who cannot work cooperatively in a group must leave the group until she decides she can cooperate. A student who hands in a carelessly done paper has to rewrite it.

Dreikurs, Grunwald, and Pepper (1982) distinguish logical consequences like these from traditional punishments, which bear no relationship to the misbehavior involved. An example of punishment would be to have students write "I will not mess up the science center" 50 times. Here are some other examples of punishments that are unrelated to the offense:

A child continually whispers to her neighbor. Instead of isolating the child (a logical consequence), the teacher makes her do an additional homework assignment in math.

A child forgets to get his spelling test signed by his parents. Instead of having the child write a letter home to parents about the need to sign the spelling test (a logical consequence), the teacher makes him stay in at recess.

A child continually calls out during a whole-class discussion. Instead of having the child make a cue-card to post on his desk ("I won't call out") or not allowing the child to participate in the discussion, the teacher makes him stay after school and clean the hamster cage.

According to Dreikurs and his colleagues, punishment is likely to be seen as an arbitrary exercise of power by a dictatorial teacher. Sometimes, children do not even associate the punishment with the misbehavior, but rather with the punisher. Instead of teaching students about the unpleasant results of their inappropriate behavior, unrelated punishments teach students only to make certain they don't get caught the next time around!

Imposing Penalties

It's frustrating when students misbehave, and sometimes we let our frustration color the way we impose penalties. In our careers, we've seen teachers scream at students from across the room, lecture students on their history of misbehavior, insinuate that they come from terrible homes, and attack their personalities. Clearly, behavior like this destroys children's dignity and ruins the possibility of a good relationship with them. How can you avoid creating a situation like this?

First, if you're feeling really angry at a student, it's a good idea to *delay the discussion.* You can simply say to a child, "Sit there and think about what happened. I'll talk to you in a few minutes." Barbara sometimes tells her students, "I'm really angry about what just happened. Everybody take out journals; we're all going to write about this situation." After a few minutes of writing, she's better able to discuss the misbehavior with students in a calm, dispassionate manner. Similarly, Ken may tell an individual student, "I do not like what I just saw. See me for a few minutes during free time so we can discuss this." By delaying discussion, everyone has a chance to cool off, and you'll be better able to separate the child's character from the child's behavior. Your message must be: "*You're* okay, but your *behavior* is unacceptable."

Second, it's a good idea to *impose penalties privately.* As we discussed earlier, students are very concerned about saving face in front of their peers. Public sanction may have the advantage of "making an example" out of one student's misbehavior, but it has the disadvantage of creating resentment and embarrassment. In fact, a study by Turco and Elliott (1986) found that fifth, seventh, and ninth graders viewed public reprimand as *the least acceptable method* of dealing with problems.

Barbara tells us how she dealt with Robert:

Robert was used to being the focus of the teacher's attention because of his annoying habits. I think he really enjoyed being yelled at, being the center of attention. His records indicated that he often seemed angry and unwilling to do what the rest of the class was doing. I knew I had to get him early on or he'd mess up my class. I vowed not to allow him to pull me off task. I decided to work with him individually, privately. In the beginning of the year he was chronically late to school and late to get started on everything. He'd have to sharpen his pencil, or rearrange his desk, or get a dictionary—he always procrastinated. So the first thing I did was take him aside and tell him what my expectations were. If he didn't get work done because he was late to school or late starting, then he had to miss free time. For three days after that he missed free time and was really angry with me. I refused to talk with him about his anger; I ignored it. Then he tried tears, and I ignored the tears. After the third day I reminded him about getting his work done. He got it done that day and had free time. Robert needed to know that I meant what I said. In addition, of course, I made positive comments to him about other things, so he wouldn't think I was just picking on him.

Third, *penalties should be imposed calmly and quietly.* Richard Curwin and Allen Mendler (1988) contend that the more *closely* you stand to the child and the *softer* your voice, the more effective you tend to be. When Garnetta reprimands a child, she moves over to the individual and speaks so softly that no one else can hear what is going on. Even when speaking to the whole class about misbehavior, her voice is amazingly soft and low—a striking contrast to her "instructional voice," which is loud and strong.

Finally, after imposing a penalty, it's a good idea to get back to the student and *re-establish a positive relationship.* At the beginning of this chapter, we saw how Garnetta sent Tanya on an errand after meeting with her in the hall. Similarly, complimenting a student's work or patting a back communicates that there are no hard feelings.

The Issue of Consistency

As Evertson, Emmer, and their colleagues (1994) note, "The dictum 'be consistent' has been repeated more frequently than the pledge of allegiance" (p. 101). Beginning teachers are taught that if they do not consistently enforce the rules, students will become confused, will begin to test the limits, and misbehavior will escalate.

On the other hand, teachers often feel trapped by the need for consistency. When a normally conscientious student forgets a homework assignment, it seems unreasonable to send the same note home to parents that you would send if a child repeatedly missed assignments. Furthermore, what is an effective consequence for one child may not be effective for another (Dreikurs, Grunwald, and Pepper, 1982). Staying after school might be a negative experience for a child who is eager to go home to play; for a child who has nothing special waiting at home, staying after school could actually be a positive, rewarding experience.

In order to get out of this bind, it's desirable to develop a *range of alternative consequences* that can be invoked if rules are violated. We already saw this in Chapter 4. You may recall that during our discussion, Garnetta explained how she and her class decide on a set of "generic consequences" that she chooses from: "no treats," "stay after school," "write an essay" (about what you did and why it was unacceptable), "send to office," "call parents." As Garnetta emphasized, she doesn't link a particular consequence to a particular rule, "because if all of a sudden something happens with a child who never breaks a rule, you don't want to be tied into a severe consequence like going to the principal. You have to look at the particular situation and decide which consequence."

Like Garnetta, some teachers develop a graduated list of generic consequences that can be applied to all misbehaviors. Others prefer to develop a graduated list of consequences for each important classroom rule. Richard Curwin and Allen Mendler (1988) suggest the following consequences for not bringing in homework:

1 Reminder
2 Warning
3 Student must hand homework in before close of school that day.
4 Stay after school to finish homework.
5 A conference between teacher, student, and parent to develop an action plan for completing homework on time.

Similarly, consequences for fighting on the playground might be (1) sitting on the bench; (2) having to go inside early; or (3) not going out at all.

Curwin and Mendler (1988) even recommend explaining in advance to students that "fair is not always equal." They contend that students should be taught it is impossible to have a single solution appropriate for everyone. Just as teachers design instruction to meet students' varying academic needs, they select consequences to meet students' varying social needs. A range of alternative consequences allows you to be *consistent* with respect to the behavior you expect from students, but *flexible* with respect to the selection of a consequence.

Penalizing the Group for Individual Misbehavior

Sometimes teachers impose a consequence on the whole class even if only one or two children have been misbehaving. The hope is that other students will be angry at receiving a penalty when they weren't misbehaving and will exert pressure on their peers to behave.

We decided to ask our four teachers what they think about this practice. Their responses were extremely consistent. All of them felt the practice was basically unfair and would undermine their efforts to create a caring community. They also believed the practice could backfire by teaching students that "it doesn't pay to be good since you'll be punished anyway." And Garnetta expressed concern about the animosity and physical fighting that might result from penalizing the group. She described instances of children vowing to "get back" at misbehaving students—"We'll take care of you after school."

When we asked our teachers if there were any situations that would prompt them to impose group penalties for individual wrongdoing, there was also remarkable consistency. All of the teachers cited the problem of stealing and described times when they had kept children after school or denied them free time in order to address the problem. Listen to Viviana:

> There was a time when one of my children stole some money from another child. I kept the whole class after school to discuss the problem. I told them, "I'm going to turn my back and I want the money returned. I don't need to know who did it. Let me know when I can turn back to you." Within a few minutes the money was returned, and Viviana dismissed the class.

Garnetta described a similar way of dealing with stealing:

> I said the whole class had to stay after school and explained that the girl's money was "missing." I told them we were going to help find it by spending a few minutes looking around the room. I said that if someone found the money they should put it on my desk. I helped to look too, and a few minutes later I went back to my desk. The money was there.

DEALING WITH CHRONIC MISBEHAVIOR

Some students with persistent behavior problems fail to respond to the routine strategies we have described so far—nonverbal cues, verbal reminders, and penalties. What additional strategies are available? In this section, we consider two basic approaches. Both require the active participation of students and provide them with opportunities to assume some responsibility for controlling their own behavior.

The first approach was developed by Thomas Gordon (1974), the psychologist whose "I-messages" were discussed earlier in this chapter. Gordon's approach sees classroom problems as conflicts that can be solved through a "no-lose method" of problem-solving. Next, we examine four self-management approaches based on principles of behavior modification—namely, self-monitoring, self-evaluation, self-instruction, and contingency contracting.

Gordon's No-Lose Method of Resolving Conflicts

For Thomas Gordon, the relationship between the teacher and the student is paramount, and the way to maintain a positive relationship is to avoid the use of power when trying to solve problems. Most teachers, according to Gordon, think in terms of winning or losing when they think about classroom conflicts:

> This win-lose orientation seems to be at the core of the knotty issue of discipline in schools. Teachers feel that they have only two approaches to choose from: They can be strict or lenient, tough or soft, authoritarian or permissive. They see the teacher-student relationship as a power struggle, a contest, a fight. . . . When conflicts arise, as they always do, most teachers try to resolve them so that they win, or at least don't lose. This obviously means that students end up losing, or at least not winning. . . . (p. 183)

Gordon offers a third alternative: a no-lose problem-solving method of conflict resolution. Appropriate for use with an individual child or with a group, Gordon's method has six steps. In Step 1, the teacher and the student (or students) *define the problem.* In Step 2, everyone *brainstorms possible solutions.* As in all brainstorming activities, suggestions are not evaluated at this stage. In Step 3, the *solutions are evaluated:* "Now let's take a look at all the solutions that have been proposed and decide which we like and which we don't like. Do you have some preferences?" It is important that you state your own opinions and preferences. Do not permit a solution to stand if it is not really acceptable to you. In Step 4, you and the students involved *decide on the solution that you will try.* If more than one student is involved, it is tempting to vote on the solution, but Gordon warns against doing this. Voting always produces winners and losers unless the vote is unanimous, so some people leave the discussion feeling dissatisfied. Instead, Gordon urges you to work for consensus.

Once you have decided which solution to try, you move to Step 5 and *determine how to implement the decision:* Who will do what by when? Finally, in Step 6, *the solution is evaluated.* Sometimes the teacher may want to call everybody together again and ask, "Are you still satisfied with our solution?" It is important for everyone to realize that decisions are not chiseled in granite and that they can be discarded in search of a better solution to the problem.

In the following example, we see how Barbara used this approach to solve a problem her students were experiencing at the end of recess each day. Note how she makes certain that everyone agrees on what the problem is, that she doesn't allow students to evaluate suggestions during the brainstorming phase of the activity, that she herself speaks against suggestions she doesn't like, and that she doesn't allow students to vote on the solution.

BARBARA: A few weeks ago, you were very upset about what was happening when you came in from the playground at the end of recess. We let it go for a while to see if the problem would go away by itself, but lately people have been telling me that things are still pretty bad out there. [Students begin to murmur in agreement and to comment on what is happening.] Can you tell me exactly what happens? After all, I'm not out there, so I don't really understand what's going on.

STUDENT: When the aide blows the whistle to come in, everyone gets in a big clump in the little alleyway by the door and then everybody pushes and shoves, and people start to fight, and then the aides get mad, and people get sent to the office, and . . . [she talks so fast it's hard to understand]

BARBARA: Wait—you have to help me. [She draws a map of the playground and the school on the board.] Now let's see if I understand. Everyone clumps up right here? [She points to an area on the map.] Okay, so this is the problem. We're all agreed on what it is? [There are signs of agreement.] Now, let's brainstorm some solutions. Remember, when we brainstorm, we let everyone have their say without evaluating. We'll evaluate all the suggestions at the end.

STUDENT: We come in a double door, and the doors are always kept closed until after we're lined up, and everyone gets smushed in so then it's hard to open the doors. If they were left open all the time, we could get in easier. [Barbara writes on board: "#1. Leave doors open all the time."]

BARBARA: Another idea? [She continues to solicit ideas and to write down each suggestion in a numbered list on the board.]

STUDENT: Open the doors right before the whistle is blown.

STUDENT: Call students to line up by class.

STUDENT: Line up by class and the quietest two classes go in first, one through each door.

STUDENT: Two classes line up by the fence, and two classes line up by the brick wall.

STUDENT: Get more aides. Right now there are only two.

STUDENT: Line up in one long line by the fence.

STUDENT: The classes play until the teachers come and get them.

STUDENT: The teachers wouldn't agree to that.

BARBARA: We're not evaluating now; we're thinking of solutions.

STUDENT: Have a different whistle signal for each class, one whistle for one class, two for another, etc.

STUDENT: Line up the way we do in the morning, each class in a different place.

STUDENT: I agree with that idea. . . .

BARBARA: Let's not evaluate now; we're still thinking of solutions.

STUDENT: Assign an aide to bring each class to their classroom.

STUDENT: Have classes go in different doors, like two classes could go in doors at the back and two classes could go in the doors on the side.

BARBARA: Are there any more ideas? [Suggestions seem to be at an end.] Okay, our next job is to quietly read these suggestions and think about them. Take two or three minutes to discuss the suggestions with your table group. Then I'll call you all back together again and we'll begin to evaluate as a whole class. [Students discuss the suggestions in their small groups.] Okay, what we'll do now is discuss each one and decide what we think about each suggestion. What I'd like to do is come up with a few suggestions to present to Mr. Fehn [the principal]. We'll decide how we want to present these later—if we'll write, or invite him to come to our class, or if I'll represent you. Okay, anyone want to react? [As students state positive or negative reactions, Barbara puts a plus or a minus sign by each suggestion that is mentioned.]

STUDENT: I like the idea of using more doors because that way kids would be separated and there wouldn't be so much pushing and shoving. [Barbara acknowledges this comment and puts a plus sign by that suggestion.]

STUDENT: I like the one about more aides. If there were more aides, then they could stop kids from pushing.

STUDENT: I don't think that's a good idea because it would cost money and the school doesn't have the money.

BARBARA: I'm going to write a dollar sign next to this one so you can think about the issue of money.

STUDENT: I like the idea of the teachers picking up the classes, but I don't think the teachers would like it.

BARBARA: Let me give you my perspective on that. My lunch time is from 11:57 to 12:37. I will tell you frankly and honestly that even though I adore you, my lunch time is very precious to me and I would not appreciate giving up part of that time every day to come pick you up.

STUDENT: Our table likes the idea of having two classes by the wall and two by the fence.

STUDENT: Our table likes #2, open the doors just before the whistle.

BARBARA: Sometimes people line up to go in before the aides blow the whistle. If people are already smushed in there, would opening the doors before blowing the whistle help? [There's some general discussion of Barbara's comment and this suggestion.]

STUDENT: I like the idea of lining up by class in different places. It works in the morning, so it would probably work in the afternoon.

STUDENT: I don't really like the idea of two classes lining up by the wall and two by the fence. Kids would still be too close, and they would still push. It might be better if they were farther apart, like maybe two classes could line up here and two could line up on the other side of the playground.

BARBARA: So you're really saying you like the idea of having classes line up in designated places. [Student agrees.]

STUDENT: I don't like the ones that say line up because we're supposed to be doing that now and it doesn't work.

BARBARA: Do you think it would help if you lined up in designated areas and used more doors? [The student agrees.]

STUDENT: Why don't we vote?

BARBARA: I don't want to vote because then there are winners and losers. But let's see if there are some we can eliminate. Let's sift out the ones that we think won't work. For example, I'm telling you that the one about having the teachers pick up the classes won't work because the teachers won't want to give up lunch. Let's look at the suggestions that have no marks next to them and the ones that have minus signs next to them. [She points to each one and asks, "Do you think this would work?" For each, the class says "no," and she erases.] Okay, let's see what's left. [There are only three left: use more doors; have classes assigned to different doors; have an aide assigned to each door.] Does anyone have any objection to these three? [One girl has reservations about one of the three and explains why.] Do you think you could live with it? [Girl indicates that she is willing to go along with the class.] Well, I think these three make a good package that we can present to Mr. Fehn. Let's talk tomorrow about how we want to present these ideas.

Approaches Based on Principles of Behavior Modification

Behavior modification programs involve the systematic use of reinforcement to strengthen desired behavior. Probably more research has focused on the effectiveness of behavior modification than any other classroom management approach, and dozens of books on behavior modification techniques are available for teachers (e.g., Epanchim, Townsend, and Stoddard, 1994; Evans, Evans, and Schmid, 1989; Sparzo and Poteet, 1989).

In recent years, however, educators have come to view full-blown behavior modification approaches as ill-suited for most regular classroom teachers (Evertson, 1989). First of all, a single teacher working with a class of 30 students cannot possibly keep track of—let alone systematically reinforce—all the desirable behaviors each student exhibits (Brophy, 1983). Second, in order to extinguish inappropriate behavior that is maintained by teacher attention, behavior modification calls for teachers to ignore the behavior. Although this is effective in one-to-one situations, ignoring misbehavior in the crowded, public environment of the classroom can cause problems to escalate (an issue we discussed earlier). This is even more likely to occur if teachers forget that ignoring is not a behavior management strategy by itself, but must be paired with attention for positive and appropriate behaviors. Finally, traditional behavior modification techniques emphasize external control by the teacher, rather than trying to foster internal control by the student (Kneedler and Hallahan, 1981).

For all of these reasons, educators have recently begun to recommend behavioral approaches that involve the student in *self-management:* self-monitoring, self-evaluation, self-instruction, and contingency contracting. The goal of these self-management strategies is to help students learn to regulate their own behavior. The perception of control is crucial in this process. As Anderson and Prawat (1983) observe, "Individuals who feel in control are much more willing to accept responsibility for their own behavior" (p. 62).

Self-monitoring   The object of self-monitoring is to help individuals gain an accurate picture of their own behavior. Some students may not realize how often they're out of their seats or how frequently they sit daydreaming instead of focusing on their work. Others may be unaware of how often they call out during class discussions or how many times they make nasty comments to other members of their small group. Youngsters like this may benefit from a self-monitoring program, in which students learn to observe and record their own behavior during a designated period of time. Interestingly, self-monitoring can have positive effects even when youngsters are inaccurate (Graziano and Mooney, 1984).

Before beginning a self-monitoring program, you need to make sure that students can identify the behaviors targeted for change. For example, some children may not know what "working independently on seatwork" looks like. You may have to demonstrate, explicitly noting all the component parts: "When I work independently, I am sitting down (without tilting back in my chair). I am looking at the paper on my desk. I am holding my pencil in my hand."

Students then learn how to observe and record their own behavior. This can be done in two ways. The first approach has individuals tally each time they engage in the targeted behavior. For example, students can learn to chart the number of math problems they complete during an in-class assignment, the number of times they blurt out irrelevant comments during a discussion, or the number of times they raise their hand to speak. For young children, the tally sheet might contain pictures of the appropriate and inappropriate behaviors. (See the "countoon" suggested by Jones and Jones, 1990, in Figure 6-1.)

FIGURE 6-1
An example of a "countoon." (*Vernon F. Jones and Louise S. Jones,* Comprehensive Classroom Management: Motivating and Managing Students, *Third Edition. Copyright 1990 by Allyn and Bacon. Reprinted with permission.*

COUNTOON

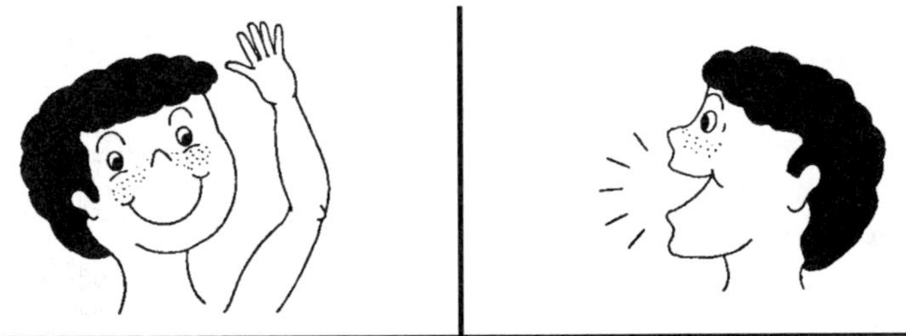

1	2	3	4	5	6	7	8	9	10	1	2	3	4	5	6	7	8	9	10
11	12	13	14	15	16	17	18	19	20	11	12	13	14	15	16	17	18	19	20
21	22	23	24	25	26	27	28	29	30	21	22	23	24	25	26	27	28	29	30
31	32	33	34	35	36	37	38	39	40	31	32	33	34	35	36	37	38	39	40
41	42	43	44	45	46	47	48	49	50	41	42	43	44	45	46	47	48	49	50

Count your hand raising   Count your hand raising

In the second approach, some sort of timer is used to cue individuals to observe and record the targeted behavior at regular intervals. At the designated time, students mark a recording sheet with a "+" or a "−," depending on whether they are engaged in the appropriate or inappropriate behavior.

These two approaches are well illustrated in an early study conducted by Broden, Hall, and Mitts (1971). In the first part of the study, Liza, an eighth-grade girl who had difficulty paying attention in history class, was directed to record her "study" or "on-task" behavior on the sheet shown in Figure 6-2. Before Liza began recording her behavior, she was on-task only about 30 percent of the time. During the self-recording phases, Liza averaged on-task rates of 76 percent to 89 percent.

The second part of the study involved Stu, an eighth-grade boy whose math teacher wanted to find a way "to shut Stu up" (p. 195). According to the teacher, Stu continually talked out in class, disturbing both the teacher and the other students. Having Stu record his talking-out behavior on the simple form shown in Figure 6-3 led to a decrease in his calling out, although the self-monitoring seemed to lose its effectiveness after a while (possibly because the teacher never acknowledged Stu's improved behavior).

Both Barbara and Ken have used self-monitoring approaches with students who did not respond to the simpler, routine strategies we have discussed. In Ken's class, we watched as this masterful teacher was driven to distraction by Jason, a boy who continually talked to his neighbors, to Ken, and to himself. Nonverbal signals, verbal directives, even penalties worked only momentarily. Eventually teacher and student agreed that Jason would sit at a separate desk in an isolated corner of the room, so he would not disrupt other students. But even there he constantly muttered while working on assignments, blurted out comments during class discussions, and

FIGURE 6-2
The recording sheet used by Liza

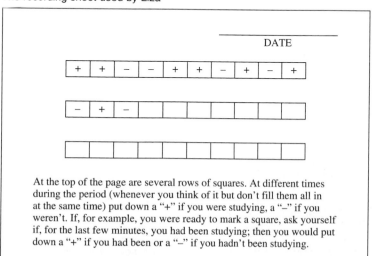

At the top of the page are several rows of squares. At different times during the period (whenever you think of it but don't fill them all in at the same time) put down a "+" if you were studying, a "−" if you weren't. If, for example, you were ready to mark a square, ask yourself if, for the last few minutes, you had been studying; then you would put down a "+" if you had been or a "−" if you hadn't been studying.

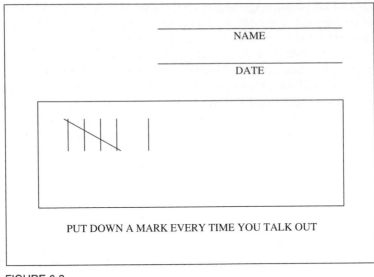

NAME

DATE

PUT DOWN A MARK EVERY TIME YOU TALK OUT

FIGURE 6-3
The recording sheet used by Stu

chattered with anyone passing by. When Ken spoke with him about this excessive talking, Jason denied that he was doing it. He seemed like an obvious candidate for a self-monitoring program.

One evening, Ken described the system that he and Jason developed:

> I decided to begin by focusing on only one of Jason's irritating behaviors—calling out during class discussions. I used the countoon form [see figure 6-1] so Jason could record the times he raised his hand and the times he blurted out. In some ways, it wasn't entirely successful: I'd see Jason raise his hand even when he had nothing to say, just to collect marks on the positive side of the countoon. On the other hand, I frequently saw him start to blurt out a comment and then catch himself, so he wouldn't have to record a "call-out." And when he did call out, I could give him a look and he'd reluctantly realize that he had to make a check on that side of the countoon. That did make him more aware of his own behavior, and I did see some improvement.

In Barbara's case, self-monitoring proved useful with a child who continually left the room to go to the bathroom. As in Ken's situation, when Barbara spoke with Louis about how frequently he left, he adamantly rejected her claim. Finally, they decided that Louis would keep count. Barbara placed a tin of bingo markers next to the bathroom pass, which was kept on a chalkboard ledge near the door. Whenever Louis took the bathroom pass, he had to take a bingo marker and put it on his desk. Each day, Barbara and Louis counted the number of bingo markers on his desk. The chips served as indisputable, concrete evidence of his trips. Within days, the number of markers began to decrease.

Self-evaluation   This self-management approach goes beyond simple self-monitoring by requiring children to make judgments about quality or acceptability of their behavior (Hughes, Ruhl, and Misra, 1989). Sometimes self-evaluation is linked with reinforcement, so that an improvement in behavior brings points or rewards.

There is evidence that even young children can learn to do this. In a study by Sainato, Strain, Lefebvre, and Rapp (1990), four preschool children who displayed high rates of inappropriate behaviors (hitting, tantrums, continual talking, lack of social responsiveness) were taught to assess whether they had exhibited appropriate independent seatwork behaviors (i.e., listening to the teacher's directions, sitting appropriately, working quietly). First, each child was photographed modeling the appropriate behaviors. These pictures were then mounted on construction paper, with a caption describing each behavior being modeled. Next to each picture were two faces: a happy face for "yes" and a frowning face for "no." The sheets of paper were covered with clear plastic and then placed in three-ring binders. Each of the four children received his or her own personalized binder. At the end of each independent seatwork period (20 minutes), the children assessed whether they had exhibited the behaviors, marking the yes or no with an erasable grease pencil. The results demonstrated that even these very young children could learn to accurately evaluate their behaviors. Furthermore, the self-evaluations produced immediate, substantial improvements in the children's behavior.

Self-instruction   The third self-management approach is self instruction, in which children learn to give themselves silent directions about how to behave. Most self-instruction strategies are based on Meichenbaum's (1977) five-step process of cognitive behavior modification: (1) an adult performs a task, while talking aloud about it, carefully describing each part; (2) the child performs the task while the adult talks aloud (overt, external guidance); (3) the child performs the task while talking aloud to self (overt self-guidance); (4) the child performs the task while whispering (faded, overt self-guidance); (5) the child performs the task while thinking the directions (covert, self-instruction). This approach has been used to teach impulsive students to approach tasks more deliberately, to help social isolates initiate peer activity, to teach aggressive students to control their anger, and to teach defeated students to try problem-solving instead of giving up (Brophy, 1983).

Self-instruction has usually been used in special education classes or in one-to-one settings (e.g., between therapist and client), but a study by Brenda Manning (1988) suggests that it can be successful in regular classrooms as well. Manning worked with first- and third-grade students who had been identified by their teachers as exhibiting inappropriate behavior in class—shouting out, constantly being out-of-seat, daydreaming, playing around with things in their desk, and disturbing others. Two times a week, for four consecutive weeks, Manning met with the children in a 50-minute session. First, she modeled appropriate behaviors (e.g., raising hands, staying seated, concentrating, keeping hands and feet to self). Then she had the students perform the behaviors while verbalizing aloud what to do: "If I scream out the answer, others will be disturbed. I will raise my hand and wait my turn. Good for me—see, I can wait!" Finally, students performed the behavior without speaking aloud, but they used "cue cards" as prompts ("I will raise my hand and wait my turn.") Observations of the students after the self-instruction training indicated significant increases in on-task behavior.

Although none of our four teachers have tried self-instruction with students, they have frequently used cue cards to prompt appropriate behavior. They tell us that sticky Post-it™ Notes are a useful "low-tech" tool for this purpose. Post-its™ can be stuck on desktops to remind children not to call out, not to tattle, or not to whine. They can be stuck on lockers to help students remember to wear their glasses or to bring their books to class. And one student teacher with a tendency to dominate class discussions applied Post-its™ to her lesson plans in order to remind herself to "KEEP QUIET AND LET THE KIDS TALK."

Contingency contracting   A contingency or behavior contract is an agreement between a teacher and an individual student that specifies what the student must do to earn a particular reward. Contingency contracts are negotiated with students; both parties must agree on the behaviors students must exhibit, the period of time involved, and the rewards that will result. To be most effective, contracts should be written and signed. And, of course, there should be an opportunity for review and renegotiation if the contract is not working (Evans, Evans, and Schmid, 1989).

Garnetta developed a contingency contract with Ronald, a child who was constantly out of his seat, did very little work, disrupted discussions, and frequently fought with other children. Garnetta told Ronald which behaviors she found most disruptive and irritating, and together they identified alternative, appropriate behaviors. Each day, they drew up a daily contract, listing the appropriate behaviors that Ronald agreed to work on (e.g., complete my work; raise my hand during discussion; don't get into fights). Then they discussed how many points each behavior was "worth" (e.g., don't get into fights = 4 points) and figured out point values so the total would be ten. At the end of each day, Garnetta and Ronald met to determine how many points he had earned and what his reward would be. In addition, Ronald was able to select a GISMOS item from the school store when he reached 25 points. (See Chapter 5 for a description of GISMOS—Grand Incentive System for McKinley's Outstanding Students.) The contract system proved to be effective in reducing Ronald's disruptive behaviors and promoting more appropriate social and academic behaviors.

An example of a contract appears in Figure 6-4.

DEALING WITH THORNY PROBLEMS

Although elementary classrooms vary a great deal, there are a few problems that always seem to crop up, regardless of the community or the school context. Every semester, student teachers from extremely different placements return to their seminars with similar tales of behavior that they find especially vexing or troublesome:

"I can't stand the constant tattling. Yet, I do want to know if somebody's doing something wrong."

"She took the eraser right out of his desk and then stood there and denied that she had done it."

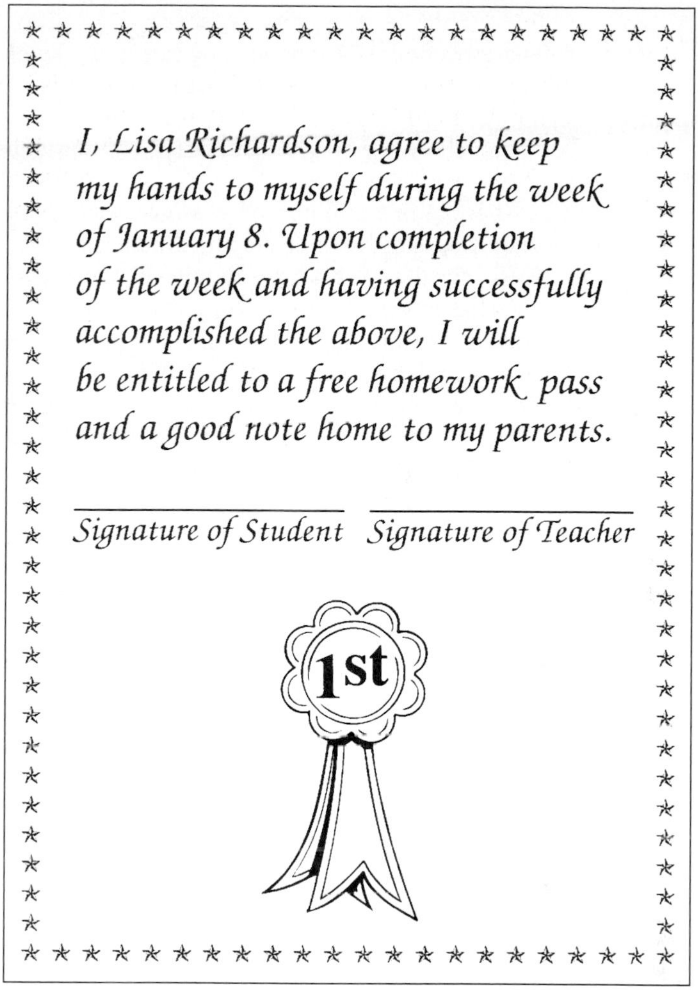

FIGURE 6-4
An example of a contract

"I can't believe it. I told him to go back to his desk, and he just glared at me and said, 'Make me.'"

It's impossible to generate recipes for dealing with these problems, since every instance is unique in terms of key players, circumstances, and history. Nonetheless, it is helpful to reflect on ways to deal with them *before* they occur and to hear some of the thinking that guides the actions of our four experienced teachers. In this section of the chapter, we will consider a variety of behaviors ranging from tattling to defiance. Some of these are merely irritating; some are far more serious. But all of them have the power to keep teachers awake at night wondering what to do.

Tattling

Fortunately, tattling is generally confined to the lower grades; *unfortunately,* it can become an epidemic if allowed to go unchecked, creating a negative atmosphere and wasting instructional time. Furthermore, if tattling is encouraged or condoned, children receive the message that only a "higher authority" can settle disputes and resolve problems.

All four teachers stress the fact that children need to understand the difference between alerting the teacher to a dangerous or hurtful situation and reporting minor infractions or perceived injustices. This may require explicit lessons, during which the class discusses what tattling is, how it affects the atmosphere in the classroom, and the importance of learning to settle one's own problems (Charles and Senter, 1995). Sometimes students need practice in distinguishing among situations that call for different responses: instances when a particular situation demands an immediate report to the teacher (e.g., you see a classmate about to jab someone with a pair of scissors); situations that they should try to resolve by themselves (e.g., your neighbor is mumbling to herself and it's annoying you); and situations that can be ignored (e.g., you see a classmate use the pencil sharpener when he shouldn't be). Of course, if you encourage students to try resolving their own problems, then you need to equip them with some strategies (e.g., using an I-message to the student who is being a bother).

Viviana, Garnetta, Barbara, and Ken try to convey the message that they are available for students when serious problems arise, but that they are uninterested in minor, petty complaints. When tattling does occur, they try to discourage it. Ken sometimes asks, "Why are you telling me this?" When the student explains ("Well, he took my paper . . . "), Ken follows up with questions such as

> "What else could you do, besides telling me?"
> "Is this serious?"
> "Can you talk to him?"
> "Do you want to write about it?"

Garnetta also suggests that children write about the problem and promises to read what they have written later, when she has the time. This usually discourages any further discussion, unless the situation is really upsetting to the child.

Very often, tattling occurs after lunch or recess, when students return to class with stories about problems that have occurred in the cafeteria or on the playground. Barbara deals with situations like these by telling students, "Unless you were hurt, I don't need to hear about it." If lunchtime or recess incidents begin to disrupt classroom life, however, it may be necessary to deal with the problem directly, either with the individual children involved or with the whole class. (See Barbara's problem-solving session described earlier.)

Cheating

As teachers increasingly emphasize collaboration, cooperative learning, and peer tutoring, both they and students are finding it harder to distinguish cheating and sharing. Furthermore, in classrooms where helping one another is the normal way of working, it can be difficult for students to shut off this mode of operation and move into individual, independent activities such as test-taking. Desks arranged in clusters can also contribute to the difficulty. As we discussed in Chapter 3, clusters foster discussion and sharing—even during a test, when students are supposed to work independently.

It's obviously better to deal with cheating before it occurs, rather than afterwards. Like tattling, cheating can be discussed in a class meeting, during which you can explain the difference between helping and cheating, demonstrate the expected behavior for various activities, and have students distinguish between situations when it's appropriate or inappropriate to share ideas. During independent activities, you can also minimize problems by separating desks, circulating throughout the room, and being vigilant. In the case of standardized testing, it's helpful to re-arrange the desks several days in advance, so students can adjust to the new layout.

When cheating does occur, a common response is to give the student a low grade or a zero on the assignment or test. This seems like a sensible solution at first glance, but it confounds the act of cheating with the student's mastery of the content (Cangelosi, 1993). In other words, a person looking at the teacher's grade book would be unable to tell if the low grade meant the student had violated the test-taking procedures or if it indicated a failure to learn the material. We prefer using a logical consequence; namely, having the student re-do the assignment or test under more carefully controlled conditions.

If a student cheats repeatedly, it's important to investigate the reasons for this behavior. Students may cheat on a test because they watched television instead of studying, but they may also cheat because their parents are putting excessive pressure on them to achieve, because they have unrealistic goals for themselves, or they do not have the skills or background necessary to succeed on the test (Grossman 1995). Clearly, these different causes of the cheating call for different responses.

Finally, you need to think about your response to the child who *gives* help on a task. Often, the desire to follow the teacher's directions and to stay out of trouble clashes with a child's desire to assist friends who are having difficulty (Bloome and Theodorou, 1988). This may be a particular dilemma for children who come from cultures that teach children to be generous; Hawaiian-American and Hispanic students, for example, may feel that helping friends is a necessity even though the teacher views it as cheating (Grossman, 1995).

Stealing

Like tattling, most stealing incidents occur in the early grades when students have less control over their impulses and when they are still learning the difference between sharing and taking what doesn't belong to them. Again, it's important to help young children distinguish between these two situations. Usually, a simple reminder about rules relating to personal property should help, but remember that a rule like "respect other people's property" has to be clearly operationalized for children.

In addition to age, cultural differences may also play a role in the confusion between sharing and taking. Some cultures emphasize sharing and generosity, while others stress private ownership (Grossman, 1995). For example, Grossman (1984) observes that when teachers try to explain that "what's mine is mine and what's yours is yours," Hispanic students may feel "bewildered, confused or even rejected and insulted." (p. 89)

If an incident of stealing does occur, and you know who the culprit is, you can have a quiet, private conversation about what has happened. If you are not sure that the child understands the difference between sharing and taking, it is best to avoid direct accusations: "I'm sure you forgot that his markers were in your backpack when you went home, but you need to bring them back tomorrow." When the child returns the markers, you can take a more instructional approach: "I'm glad you brought the markers back. You know, you shouldn't be putting other people's property in your backpack. Even though it was an accident, some people might call it stealing, and I know you wouldn't want to be accused of that."

Depending on the value of the property, the frequency of incidence, and the grade level you are teaching, it may be necessary to intervene more forcefully. As we mentioned earlier, all of our teachers have used whole-class pressure to have the stolen materials returned. Sometimes, you may even need to search backpacks and desks, contact families, or refer the problem to the principal; in the most severe cases, the principal may decide that the police have to be called in.

Profanity

The use of profanity in school has risen as children are increasingly exposed to inappropriate language at home and through the media. In deciding on a suitable response, it's useful to think about the reasons that students use profanity. Once again, age plays a role. Younger children may simply be echoing language they have heard used by friends, by family, or on television, with little or no understanding of the meaning. In this case, the appropriate response is instructional, not disciplinary. You need to explain that "we don't use words like that in school." You might ask the children if they know what the words mean and suggest they talk with their parents; it might also be helpful to contact parents and ask them to speak with their children.

Children may also use profanity because they hear it used frequently at home, and it has become a regular part of their speaking vocabulary. In this case, you can make it clear that language like that is inappropriate and unacceptable in school. Barbara reminds students that *she* doesn't use that language at school, and she doesn't expect *them* to use it either.

Finally, there are times when students angrily direct profanity toward another student or the teacher. When this happens, you need to stress that using language to hurt other people will not be tolerated and that there are more acceptable ways of expressing anger. Sometimes children are so angry that they blurt out profanities without thinking about the context. In this case, it's wise to allow them time to calm down before trying to discuss what happened. It's also helpful to address the reasons for their anger before addressing the inappropriateness of their language.

Defiance

When we asked Barbara, Garnetta, Ken, and Viviana to tell us about the ways they deal with defiance, our question was met with unusual silence. Finally, Ken ventured to explain that his students rarely acted in defiant ways, so it was hard for him to say what he'd do. The three other teachers murmured their agreement. We were initially skeptical, but as we talked, it became clear that the answer lay in the teachers' ability to prevent minor problems from escalating into major ones. Consider Garnetta's way of dealing with Ebony, a child who had "spent the entire second grade in the office":

> Ebony was constantly picking fights, calling names, and talking back to the teacher. I remember hearing one story about how she looked the student teacher straight in the eye and said, "Die . . . die . . . you drop dead in front of me." Obviously, I couldn't *wait* to have Ebony in my class. But when she came to me, one of the first things she said was "No one ever listens to me." I took that as my cue. I made sure to listen to her. And I'd always try to anticipate a problem. I'd see her beginning to act up—maybe going to poke someone—and I'd immediately go over and quietly tell her to come into the hall with me. I never got into an argument with her in front of everyone. I'd be real calm, and we'd go out, and I'd ask her what was happening. She'd tell me why she was mad, and I'd listen, and we'd talk about what she could do when she got that way. She hardly ever had to go to the office. But if I had let things go, the other child would have poked back. Then a fight would have erupted, and she'd have ended up in the principal's office again.

Now let's consider another example (adapted from Walker, Colvin, and Ramsey, 1995). This teacher-student interaction begins innocuously enough, but quickly escalates into an explosive situation:

> It's math time, and students are expected to complete problems assigned in the morning. Michael sits slouched in his seat staring at the floor, an angry expression on his face. The teacher sees that Michael is not doing his math and calls over to him from the back of the room where she is working with other students.

TEACHER: Michael, get started with your math.
MICHAEL: What math?
TEACHER: The math you didn't finish this morning.
MICHAEL: I did finish it.
TEACHER: Well, let me see it then. [She walks over to Michael's desk and sees that he has four problems completed.] Good. You have done four but you need to do ten.
MICHAEL: Nobody told me that!
TEACHER: Well, I announced it at the start of the morning that you had to do ten.
MICHAEL: I don't remember that.
TEACHER: Look at the board. See—math one through ten.
MICHAEL: I didn't see it. Anyway, why do I have to do this boring stuff?
TEACHER: Okay, that's enough. No more arguments. Math one through ten. Now.
MICHAEL: It's dumb. I'm not going to do it.
TEACHER: Yes you are, mister.
MICHAEL: Yeah? MAKE ME.
TEACHER: If you don't do it now you will have to do it at recess.
MICHAEL: F—- you.

TEACHER: That's enough!

MICHAEL: You want math. Here it is. [He throws the math book across the room.]

At first glance, it appears that the teacher is being remarkably patient and reasonable in the face of Michael's stubbornness, defiance, and abuse. On closer examination, however, we can detect a chain of *successive escalating interactions,* in which Michael's behavior moves from questioning and challenging the teacher to defiance and abuse, and for which *the teacher is also responsible* (Walker, Colvin, and Ramsey, 1995). Could the teacher have broken this chain earlier?

According to Walker, Colvin, and Ramsey (1995), the answer is yes. Defiant situations can usually be avoided if teachers do not corner a student, do not argue, do not engage in a power struggle ("I'm the boss in this classroom, and I'm telling you to . . . "), and do not embarrass the student in front of peers. Figure 6-5 summarizes their specific recommendations.

With this background, let's go back to Michael and see how another teacher might have dealt with the situation to prevent it from escalating.

It's math time, and students are expected to complete problems assigned in the morning. Michael sits slouched in his seat staring at the floor. The teacher notices Michael's posture and realizes that he is feeling upset about something. She goes over, crouches down so that she is on eye-level with Michael, and speaks very quietly.

TEACHER: Are you doing OK, Michael? You look a bit upset today.

MICHAEL: I'm okay.

FIGURE 6-5
Managing potentially explosive situations (adapted from Walker, Colvin, and Ramsey, 1995)

- Move slowly and deliberately toward the problem situation.
- Speak privately, quietly, and calmly. Do not threaten. Be as matter-of-fact as possible.
- Be as still as possible. Avoid pointing or gesturing.
- Keep a reasonable distance. Do not crowd the student. Do not get "in the student's face."
- Speak respectfully. Use the student's name.
- Establish eye-level position.
- Be brief. Avoid long-winded statements or nagging.
- Stay with the agenda. Stay focused on the problem at hand. Do not get sidetracked. Deal with less severe problems later.
- Avoid power struggles. Do not get drawn into "I won't, you will" arguments.
- Use crisis-prevention strategies. Inform the student of the expected behavior and the negative consequence as a choice or decision for the student to make. Then withdraw from the student and allow some time for the student to decide. ("Michael, you need to return to your desk, or I will have to send for the principal. You have a few seconds to decide." The teacher then moves away, perhaps attending to other students. If Michael does not choose the appropriate behavior, deliver the negative consequence. "You are choosing to have me call the principal.") Follow through with the consequence.

TEACHER: Well, good, but if you'd like to talk later, let me know. Meanwhile, you need to get going on your math.

MICHAEL: I already did the math.

TEACHER: Oh, I didn't realize that. Let me see how you did. [She checks the paper.] Okay, good for you, Michael. You've already done the first four. You're off to a great start. Do the fifth problem and then let me see how you've done. If you'd like to have more privacy, the round table is always there for you. [She walks away.]

Sexually Related Behavior

Our often repeated reminder to consider children's developmental levels is particularly relevant here. In an early childhood classroom, it's not unusual to see children occasionally rubbing their genitals. Usually they will stop as soon as you divert their attention or get them more actively involved in the lesson. Viviana simply tells her first graders that she wants to see everyone's hands on their desks. If the masturbation continues, however, she has a private conversation with the individual student:

> I don't want to embarrass the child, but if I don't stop it, the other children will see and start to make fun. Maybe the child doesn't even know this is not proper to do in school. I'll say something like, "I don't want you to put your hands inside your pants. It's not bad, but it's not something people do at school."

Depending on the situation, you might also contact parents, ask them to speak with their child, and suggest some simple ways of curbing the behavior—for example, having children wear pants that require a belt instead of pants with an elastic waist.

By the time students reach fourth grade, they generally know that masturbation is inappropriate in school. If you do see a youngster engaging in this behavior, however, you need to deal with the situation very discreetly—and before the other children notice and begin to taunt. Barbara uses this approach: "I've seen what you've been doing at your seat during quiet times, and it's not something you should be doing in school. Is everything okay?"

It's also necessary to consider developmental level when you see a child touching another child in a sexual way. Again, it's not unusual for kindergarten children to explore each other's bodies; a simple directive to stop and a reminder to "keep your hands to yourself" will usually take care of the matter. At intermediate grade levels (4-6), students need to be aware of what constitutes sexual harassment and to know that it will not be tolerated in the school environment. They also need to know that they can report incidents of sexual harassment and that the adults in the school will take action. (See "For Further Reading" for curriculum guides.)

At *any* elementary grade level, habitual masturbation and behaviors that are sexually precocious or explicit warrant investigation. Children who continue to masturbate even after you have spoken to them may have severe problems, and children who imitate adult sexual behavior may have witnessed such activity firsthand or experienced it themselves. In cases like these, you need to contact the appropriate child welfare agency. (See Chapter 13 for signs of abuse and reporting procedures.)

CONCLUDING COMMENTS

One afternoon after school, we talked with Garnetta about the problems her students bring with them to school. She displayed considerable empathy and insight into their home situations. Nonetheless, she emphasized that she had high expectations for their behavior and achievement:

> It's up to *us* to teach students to be responsible, to have standards, and to demand that work gets done. We can't simply say, "They can't help it," or "They didn't do it, so it's a zero." You've got to discuss expectations and keep plugging away. I see so many kids kicked out of class, and I think to myself, "Did you talk with them? What did you try before you gave up and sent them out?" Some days I feel like I've had it too. But then I remind myself that I'm in charge of this classroom. I'm responsible for what goes on here.

Garnetta's comments recall findings from a study on the ways teachers cope with problem students (Brophy and Rohrkemper, 1981). One basic factor that distinguished more effective teachers from less effective teachers was their *willingness to take responsibility.* They used a variety of strategies: some used behavioral approaches—negotiating contracts, providing rewards, praising desirable behavior—while others tried to build positive relationships, provide encouragement, and foster self-esteem. Regardless, effective teachers were willing to assume the responsibility for managing children's behavior. In sharp contrast, *less effective teachers tended to disclaim responsibility and to refer problems to other school personnel* (e.g., the principal, guidance counselor, etc.).

Clearly, our four teachers are willing to take responsibility for the behavior of their students. Like Garnetta, they recognize that they are "in charge" and that they are accountable for what happens in their classrooms. Furthermore, they are willing to admit when they themselves have contributed to misbehavior that occurs. Listen to Barbara:

> Sometimes, everyone will be getting into a heated discussion, and I sort of suspend the rule about raising hands. All of a sudden I realize it's getting chaotic. That's not the *kids'* fault. *I let it happen.* It would be unfair to lash out at them for calling out. I just say, "Whoa . . . this is getting out of hand. Let's calm down and remember to raise hands."

We agree with Barbara, Garnetta, Viviana, and Ken that teachers need to assume responsibility for children's behavior problems, and we hope that this chapter will help you to feel more competent in this area. Nonetheless, there are times when you have to recognize that a child's problem is so deeply rooted that you need special assistance. In this case, it's your responsibility to see that the child receives the help you're unable to provide. As Barbara observes:

> When you've gone the whole route, you've tried all the strategies you know, you've brainstormed solutions, and nothing works for more than one-and-a-half weeks, then you have to go for help. Sometimes you have to understand that the problem is bigger than what's going on in the classroom. The child has a greater need than you can fill. Sometimes I have someone from special services or a colleague come in and observe and then conference with me. The school psychologist has also been helpful.

For example, a few years ago I had a girl I just couldn't reach. She was a victim of sexual abuse. I liked her and she liked me, but I couldn't get her to change her behavior. She would sing in class. I'd say, "You can't do that. It disturbs other people." So she'd stop, but then she'd begin tapping her pencil. I'd take the pencil away, and then she'd take her beads off and rub the beads along the edge of the desk. I'd take her beads, and then she'd bang her head on the desk. She was finally classified as emotionally disturbed and is getting the kind of help she needs.

With experience, you learn to tell the difference between a student who's just being a pain in the neck and a student who's really in need. *And then it's your responsibility to get help for that child.*

We will return to this topic in Chapters 12 and 13, when we discuss helping children with special needs.

SUMMARY

Inappropriate behavior threatens order by interrupting the flow of classroom activity. In this chapter we discussed ways of responding to a variety of problems—from minor, nondisruptive infractions to chronic, more serious misbehaviors.

Guidelines for Dealing With Misbehavior

- Match your disciplinary strategy to the misbehavior.
- Try to keep the instructional program going with a minimum of disruption.
- Consider the *context* of students' actions. Behavior that is acceptable in one context may be unacceptable in another.
- Use disciplinary strategies that preserve the dignity of the student.
- Separate the student's *character* from the specific *misbehavior.*
- Encourage students to take responsibility for regulating their own behavior.

Strategies for Dealing with Minor Misbehavior

- Nonverbal interventions
- Verbal interventions:
    - Direct student to the task at hand
    - Call on student
    - Use gentle humor
    - Use an I-message
- Ignore misbehavior

Strategies for Dealing with More Serious Misbehavior

- Plan penalties ahead of time.
- Choose penalties that are logically related to misbehavior.
- Impose penalties calmly and quietly.
- Re-establish a positive relationship with the student as quickly as possible.
- Develop a range of alternative consequences.

Strategies for Dealing with Chronic Misbehavior

- Thomas Gordon's no-lose problem-solving method:
    Step 1: Define the problem.
    Step 2: Brainstorm possible solutions.
    Step 3: Evaluate solutions.
    Step 4: Decide on a solution to try.
    Step 5: Determine how to implement the decision.
    Step 6: Evaluate the solution.
- Behavior modification approaches
    Self-monitoring
    Self-evaluation
    Self-instruction
    Contingency contracting

Effective teachers are willing to take responsibility for managing students' behavior. Work on developing a system for dealing with misbehavior that suits your personality and your teaching style. You may have a student whose problems are too severe for you to deal with. If so, it is your responsibility to get this child outside help.

ACTIVITIES

1 Beginning teachers sometimes overreact to misbehavior or take no action at all because they simply don't know what to do or say. Read each of the following situations and devise a nonverbal intervention, a verbal cue, and an "I-message."

Example:	Nonverbal	Verbal	I message
You overhear a child call another child a name.	a "look"	"John."	"When you call another person a name, it hurts their feelings and that makes me sad."
A child is writing on her desk.	hand her an eraser	"We use paper to write on."	"When you write on your desk, the custodian complains to me, and I get embarrassed."

    a A child is copying from another child's paper.
    b A child is taking snacks from other children.
    c A little girl steps on everyone's coat in the coat closet.
    d A little boy scribbles all over another child's work.
    e A child spreads rumors about her friend.

2 When a misbehavior occurs, there usually isn't much time for careful consideration about logical consequences. We've listed a few typical misbehaviors for your practice. What are two logical consequences for each example?
    a Your class monitor keeps forgetting to clean the gerbil cage, and it is beginning to smell.

    b Tom always takes longer than the other children to get settled in after snack time, and most times he is still eating when it is time to get back to work.

    c Rachel spends her computer time playing with the contents of her purse.

    d As part of a laboratory group, Lou mishandles supplies, causing spills and complaints from his group members.

    e Meagan draws all over Shelissa's face with a purple marker.

    f Ross rubs glue all over his hands so that he can peel it off when it dries.

    g Ariana returns her novel with ripped pages and the cover missing.

3 Develop a behavior modification plan (e.g., self-monitoring, contingency contract) to deal with the following problems:

    a Arthur is larger than the other children in your second-grade class. A day has not gone by that a child hasn't come to you complaining of Arthur's hitting, pushing, or teasing them. You've talked to his parents, but they are at a loss about what to do.

    b Cynthia, a fifth grader, rarely completes her work. She daydreams, socializes with others, misunderstands directions, and gets upset when you speak to her about her incomplete work. The problem seems to be getting worse.

REFERENCES

Anderson, L. M., and Prawat, R. S. (1983). Responsibility in the classroom: A synthesis of research on teaching self-control. *Educational Leadership, 40,* 62–66.

Bloome, D., and Theodorou, E. (1988). Analyzing teacher-student and student-student discourse. In J. E. Green and J. O. Harker (Eds.), *Multiple perspective analyses of classroom discourse.* Norwood, NJ: Ablex, pp. 217–248.

Broden, M., Hall, R. V., and Mitts, B. (1971). The effect of self-recording on the classroom behavior of two eighth-grade students. *Journal of Applied Behavior Analysis, 4,* 191–199.

Brophy, J. E. (1983). Classroom organization and management. *The Elementary School Journal, 83*(4), 265–285.

Brophy, J., and Rohrkemper, M. (1981). The influence of problem ownership on teachers' perceptions of and strategies for coping with problem students. *Journal of Educational Psychology, 73,* 295–311.

Cairns, L. G. (1987). Behaviour problems. In M. J. Dunkin (Ed.), *The international encyclopedia of teaching and teacher education.* New York: Pergamon Press, pp. 446–452.

Cangelosi, J. S. (1993). *Classroom management strategies: Gaining and maintaining students' cooperation* (2nd edition). New York: Longman.

Cassidy, J., and Rimbeaux, B. C. (1988). *Juggling for the complete klutz* (3rd edition). Palo Alto, CA: Klutz Press.

Center for Education Statistics (1987). *Public school teacher perspectives on school discipline. OERI Bulletin.* Washington, D.C.: U.S. Department of Education.

Charles, C. M., and Senter, G. W. (1995). *Elementary classroom management* (2nd edition). New York: Longman.

Créton, H. A., Wubbels, T., and Hooymayers, H. P. (1989). Escalated disorderly situations in the classroom and the improvement of these situations. *Teaching & Teacher Education, 5*(3), 205–215.

Curwin, R. L., and Mendler, A. N. (1988). *Discipline with dignity.* Alexandria, VA: Association for Supervision and Curriculum Development.

Doyle, W. (1986). Classroom organization and management. In M. C. Wittrock (Ed.), *Handbook of research on teaching.* New York: Macmillan, pp. 392–431.

Dreikurs, R., Grunwald, B. B., and Pepper, F. C. (1982). *Maintaining sanity in the classroom: Classroom management techniques* (2nd edition). New York: Harper & Row.

Emmer, E. T., and Aussiker, A. (1990). School and classroom discipline programs: How well do they work? In O. C. Moles (Ed.), *Student discipline strategies.* New York: SUNY Press, pp. 129–165.

Emmer, E. T., Evertson, C. M., and Anderson, L. M. (1980). Effective classroom management at the beginning of the school year. *The Elementary School Journal, 80*(5), 219–231.

Epanchim, B. C., Townsend, B., and Stoddard, K. (1994). *Constructive classroom management: Strategies for creating positive learning environments.* Pacific Grove, CA: Brooks/Cole.

Evans W. H., Evans S. S., and Schmid, R. E. (1989). *Behavior and instructional management: An ecological approach.* Boston: Allyn and Bacon.

Evertson, C. M. (1989). Classroom organization and management. In M. C. Reynolds (Ed.), *Knowledge base for the beginning teacher.* New York: Pergamon Press, pp. 59–70.

Evertson, C. M., Emmer E. T., Clements, B. S., Sanford, J. P., and Worsham, M. E. (1994). *Classroom management for elementary teachers* (3rd edition). Boston: Allyn & Bacon.

Good, T. L., and Brophy, J. E. (1994). *Looking in classrooms* (6th edition). New York: Harper-Collins.

Graziano, A. M., and Mooney, K. C. (1984). *Children and behavior therapy.* New York: Aldine.

Gordon, T. (1974). *T.E.T.—Teacher effectiveness training.* New York: Peter H. Wyden.

Grossman, H. (1984). *Educating Hispanic students: Cultural implications for instruction, classroom management, counseling, and assessment.* Springfield, IL: Charles Thomas.

Grossman, H. (1995). *Classroom behavior management in a diverse society.* Mountain View, CA: Mayfield Publishing Company.

Hughes, C. A., Ruhl, K. L., and Misra, A. (1989). Disordered students in school settings: A promise unfulfilled? *Behavioral Disorders, 14,* 250–262.

Jones, V. F., and Jones, L. S. (1990). *Comprehensive classroom management: Motivating and managing students* (3rd edition). Boston: Allyn and Bacon.

Kneedler, R. D., and Hallahan, D. P. (1981). Self-monitoring of on-task behavior with learning disabled children: Current studies and directions. *Exceptional Education Quarterly, 2,* 73–81.

Kounin, J. S. (1970). *Discipline and group management in classrooms.* New York: Holt, Rinehart and Winston.

Lasley, T. J., Lasley, J. O., and Ward, S. H. (1989). Activities and desists used by more and less effective classroom managers. Paper presented at the annual meeting of the American Educational Research Association, San Francisco.

Manning, B. H. (1988). Application of cognitive behavior modification: First and third graders' self-management of classroom behaviors. *AERJ, 25*(2), 193–212.

Meichenbaum, D. (1977). *Cognitive behavior modification.* New York: Plenum Press.

Pittman, S. I. (1985). Cognitive ethnography and quantification of a first-grade teacher's selection routines for classroom management. *The Elementary School Journal, 85*(4), 541–558.

Rief, S. F. (1993). *How to reach and teach ADD/ADHD children.* West Nyack, NY: The Center for Applied Research in Education.

Safran, S. P., and Safran, J. S. (1984). Elementary teachers' tolerance of problem behaviors. *The Elementary School Journal, 85*(2), 237–243.

Sainato, D. M., Strain, P. S., Lefebvre, D., and Rapp, N. (1990). Effects of self-evaluation on the independent work skills of preschool children with disabilities. *Exceptional Children, 56*(6), 540–549.

Sparzo, F. J., and Poteet, J. A. (1989). *Classroom behavior: Detecting and correcting special problems.* Boston: Allyn and Bacon.

Turco, T. L., and Elliott, S. N. (1986). Assessment of students' acceptability ratings of teacher-initiated interventions for classroom misbehavior. *Journal of School Psychology,* 24, 227–283.

Walker, H. M., Colvin, G., and Ramsey, E. (1995). *Antisocial behavior in school. Strategies and best practices.* Pacific Grove, CA: Brooks/Cole Publishing Company.

FOR FURTHER READING

Canter, L., and Canter, M. (1992). *Assertive discipline: Positive behavior management for today's classroom.* Santa Monica, CA: Lee Canter and Associates.

Charles, C. M. (1989). *Building classroom discipline: From models to practice* (3rd edition). New York: Longman.

Curwin, R. L., and Mendler, A. N. (1988). *Discipline with dignity.* Alexandria VA: Association for Supervision and Curriculum Development.

Dreikurs, R., Grunwald, B. B., and Pepper, F. C. (1982). *Maintaining sanity in the classroom: Classroom management techniques* (2nd edition). New York: Harper & Row.

Girls and boys getting along: Teaching sexual harassment prevention in the elementary classroom (revised edition). (1995). St. Paul: Minnesota Department of Education.

Gordon, T. (1974). *T.E.T.—Teacher Effectiveness Training.* New York: Peter H. Wyden.

Grossman, H. (1995). *Classroom behavior management in a diverse society.* Mountain View, CA: Mayfield.

Stein, N., and Sjostrom, L. (1994). *Flirting or hurting? A teacher's guide on student-to-student sexual harassment in schools (Grades 6 through 12).* Washington D.C.: NEA Women and Girls Center for Change and the Wellesley College Center for Research on Women.

Walker, H. M., Colvin, G., and Ramsey, E. (1995). *Antisocial behavior in school: Strategies and best practices.* Pacific Grove, CA: Brooks/Cole Publishing Company.

Chapter Seven _____

Making the Most of Classroom Time

_____

On the first day of school, the academic year seems to stretch out endlessly. If you're a beginning teacher, you may wonder how you'll ever fill all the hours of school that lie ahead (especially if you're not even certain what you're going to do *tomorrow*). And yet, as the days go by, you may begin to feel that there's never enough time to accomplish everything you need to do. With assemblies, fire drills, announcements over the intercom, recess, clerical tasks, and holidays, the hours available for instruction seem far fewer than they did at first. Indeed, by the end of the year, you may view time as a "precious resource" (Goodlad, 1984)—not something that has to be filled (or killed), but something that must be conserved and used wisely. (Of course, your students may not share this view, as Figure 7-1 illustrates!)

This chapter focuses on the issues of time and time management. First, we look at the amount of school time that is actually available for teaching and learning. Much of our discussion draws on the Beginning Teacher Evaluation Study (BTES; Fisher, Filby, Marliave, Cahen, Dishaw, Moore, and Berliner, 1978), an influential project that examined how time is used in elementary schools and the relationship between time and achievement. Our purpose here is to provide you with a set of concepts that you can use to think about the way time is used in your school and classroom.

The second part of the chapter considers strategies for using classroom time efficiently. We discuss four complementary approaches—maintaining activity flow, minimizing transition time, holding students accountable, and limiting the disruption caused by students leaving the room for special instruction ("pull-outs)." As Linda Shalaway (1989) has commented, "Students only have so much time to learn in your classroom and you only have so much time to teach them" (p. 51). The wise use of time will maximize opportunities for learning and minimize opportunities for disruption.

CALVIN AND HOBBES   **By BILL WATTERSON**

FIGURE 7-1
Calvin doesn't agree that time passes quickly in classrooms. (Calvin and Hobbes © *Watterson.*
Dist. by Universal Press Syndicate. Reprinted with permission. All rights reserved.)

HOW MUCH TIME IS THERE, ANYWAY?

Although this seems like a straightforward question, the answer is not so simple. In fact, the answer depends on the kind of time you're talking about (Karweit, 1989). Most states mandate a school year of approximately 180 days, with a school day of six hours. This amounts to more than 1,000 hours of *mandated time* each year. But flu epidemics break out, and boilers break down; snowstorms cause delayed openings, and teacher workshops require early closings. Factors like these immediately reduce the time you have available for teaching.

Even when school is in session and students are present, only about five hours of the day are set aside for instruction, with the remaining time used for lunch, recess, and other breaks. Of these five hours, one is typically devoted to "specials"— art, music, and physical education, and four are allocated for instruction in academic areas—reading and language arts, mathematics, science and social studies (BTES; Fisher et al., 1978).

The way the four hours of *academic time* are distributed among the content areas varies considerably from school to school and even from teacher to teacher. For example, Nancy Karweit (1989) reports that in one school in Maryland, the time allocated to mathematics instruction ranged from 2 hours and 50 minutes per week in one classroom to 5 hours and 55 minutes per week in another. This translates into a difference of more than 100 hours over the course of the school year! Similarly, the BTES study (Fisher et al., 1978) found that in some fifth-grade classrooms 60 minutes per day were allocated to reading and language arts instruction, while in others 140 minutes per day were scheduled. Variations like these sometimes reflect differences in school policies and programs; however, they often reflect individual teachers' priorities and preferences (Schmidt and Buchmann, 1983), since teachers generally have a great deal of autonomy to determine what topics to emphasize.

Not only do elementary teachers vary in the time they allocate to various subjects, they also vary in the *amount of allocated time they actually use for instruction.* In some classes, taking attendance, collecting lunch money, distributing materials, and reprimanding misbehaving students consume an inordinate amount of time. Karweit (1989) describes a "one-hour" math class, for example, in which the first ten minutes were typically used to collect lunch money, and the last ten were used to line up the students for lunch—leaving only 40 minutes for actual instruction.

Situations like this are not unusual in the classrooms of teachers who lack efficient strategies for carrying out routine, noninstructional tasks. Leinhardt and Greeno (1986) provide us with a glimpse into the difficulties encountered by one beginning teacher, Ms. Twain, as she attempted to check homework at the beginning of math. Ms. Twain had two goals—to identify who had done the homework and to correct it orally. She began by asking, "Who doesn't have their homework?" In response, students did one of three things: they held up their completed work, called out that they didn't have it, or walked over to the teacher and told her whether they had done it or not. Ms. Twain then talked about the importance of homework and marked the results of this check on a posted sheet of paper.

Next, Ms. Twain chose students to give the correct answers to the homework problems:

> She called out a set of problem numbers (1-10) and assigned a child to call out the answers as she called the problem number. The student slowly called out the answers in order. (The first child chosen was the lowest in the class, did not have her work done, and was doing the problems in her head). Thus, for the first 10 problem answers, the teacher lost control of pace and correctness of answer; however, it was only when the child failed on the sixth problem that Twain realized the student had not done her homework . . . (p. 87)

Ms. Twain continued to call on students to give the answers, while the rest of the class checked their work. The last child chosen went through the sequence of problems quickly, but gave both the problem number and the answer, a situation that caused some confusion (e.g., "24, 27; 25, 64"). Ms. Twain's entire homework check took six minutes—and it was clear to the observers that she was never certain which children had done their homework.

In contrast, Leinhardt and Greeno describe a homework check conducted by Ms. Longbranch, a successful, experienced teacher. Ms. Longbranch first gave a cue, "Okay, set 43," and then began to call the children's names. Children who had done the homework simply responded, "yes." Those who hadn't done the work got up and wrote their names on the chalkboard. In 30 seconds—with a minimum of fuss—Ms. Longbranch was able to determine who had completed the assignment.

The next goal was to correct the work:

> The students took colored pencils out and responded chorally with the correct answer, a fraction in lowest terms. As the teacher called the problem, "1/12 + 1/12," they responded "2/12 or 1/6." Time to complete was 106 seconds. (p. 85)

We are not presenting Ms. Longbranch's homework check as a model to be copied in your classroom; indeed, her procedure may not be appropriate for your particular class. The important point is that Ms. Longbranch has established a routine that enables her to check homework efficiently, almost automatically, while Ms. Twain does not yet have a workable strategy. Although the difference in the time used by the two teachers is only about four minutes, it is probably sympto-matic of the ways they managed class time in general.

As you can see, the answer to our question, "How much time is there, anyway?" depends on whether we are taking about the number of hours mandated by the state, the number of hours school is actually in session and students are in attendance, the time scheduled for instruction, or the time actually used for instruction (Karweit, 1989). But even when teachers are actually teaching, students are not necessarily paying attention. We must consider still another kind of time—*engaged time or time-on-task.*

Let's suppose that while you are teaching, some of your students choose to pass notes about Halloween costumes, play with the latest action figures, or stare out the window. In this case, the amount of time you are devoting to instruction is greater than the amount of time students are directly engaged in learning. This is not an atypical situation. Research documents the fact that students tend to be "on-task" about 70 percent of the time (Rosenshine, 1980). Again, there are sizable variations from class to class. In the BTES, some classes had an engagement rate of only 50 percent (i.e., the average student was attentive about one-half of the time), while in other classes the engagement rate approached 90 percent (Fisher, Berliner, Filby, Marliave, Cahen, and Dishaw, 1980).

To some extent time-on-task reflects teachers' ability to motivate students and involve them in learning activities. (Recall our discussion of fostering students' motivation to learn in Chapter 5.) But other factors also come into play—for ex-ample, time of day (remember the case of post-lunch brain haze?) and day of the week (Friday afternoons are notorious). And some teachers insist that attention falls off (and misbehavior increases) when there is a full moon!

There are also substantial differences in engagement from activity to activity. During independent seatwork, for example, engagement is usually about 70 per-cent, while discussions led by the teacher yield engagement rates of 84 percent (Rosenshine, 1980). Why should this be so? Paul Gump (1982) suggests that some classroom activities prod students to be involved and "push" them along, while oth-ers do not. In a class discussion, external events (i.e., the teacher's questions, the other students' answers, and the teacher's responses) press students to pay attention. In seatwork and silent reading, materials (e.g., worksheets, textbooks) are simply made available; students must depend on their own internal pacing to accomplish the task. In other words, students must provide their *own* push—and sometimes the push just isn't there. (This is a topic we will pursue further in Chapter 8.)

Another type of time we need to consider is the *amount of time students spend on work that is meaningful and appropriate,* what Herbert Walberg (1988) calls *pro-ductive time.* We sometimes get so caught up in trying to increase students' time-on-task that we overlook the tasks themselves. We once saw first graders (not Viviana's!) spend 15 minutes of a 30-minute mathematics period coloring the bal-loons that appeared on their worksheet. The students seemed totally absorbed; in-deed, an observer coding time-on-task would have recorded a high engagement rate.

But what was the purpose of the activity? Coloring may be useful for developing children's fine motor skills, and teaching students to read color names is certainly a worthwhile objective. But coloring balloons is not mathematics, and in this case, fully half of the mathematics period was allocated to a non-mathematical activity.

One particular kind of productive time is the BTES concept of *academic learning time* (ALT)—the proportion of engaged time in which students are performing academic tasks with a high degree of success. Consider, for example, a situation in which students are completing a page of mathematics problems that involve two-digit multiplication. If they can accomplish the task with relatively few errors, it suggests that the task is appropriately matched to their level of achievement and that the teacher has provided sufficient preparation. If they get all the problems wrong, it doesn't matter how engaged they were; the time was wasted. The concept of ALT is an important contribution of the BTES; nonetheless, we often prefer to use the more general concept of productive time since we can imagine meaningful learning situations that are not characterized by a high degree of success. For example, in Chapter 9, you will read about how Barbara asked her students to build landfills that would not leach dangerous toxins into the ground. This was a complex problem-solving situation that did not result in much success; on the other hand, students learned an important lesson—namely, how difficult it is to build an environmentally sound landfill!

We began this section by asking, "How much time is there, anyway?" Figure 7-2 depicts our answer to this question. The bar at the far left shows the number of hours in the typical mandated school year—1,080. For the sake of argument, we will as-

FIGURE 7-2
How much time is there, anyway?

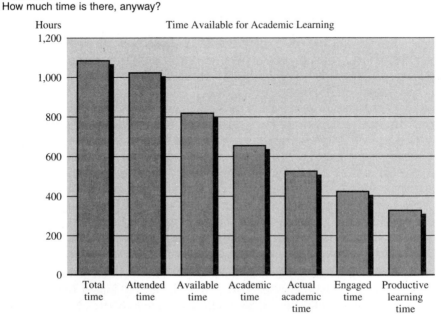

sume that student absences and school closings reduce this figure by ten days or 60 hours. Thus, the second bar indicates that "attended time" is 1,020. Since one hour of each day is generally spent in lunch and recess, only 816 hours are actually available for instruction (bar 3). Academic instruction is scheduled for 80 percent of this time, or 652 hours (bar 4). Given the need to carry out clerical and administrative tasks, we have only 522 hours for actual instruction (bar 5). If students pay attention 80 percent of that time, engaged time is 417 hours (bar 6). And assuming that students work on meaningful, appropriate tasks for 80 percent of the time they are engaged, we see that productive learning time is only 333 hours—less than one-third of "mandated" school time.

Obviously, our figures are estimates. As we have stressed, there are substantial variations from school to school and from classroom to classroom (Karweit, 1989). Nonetheless, the graph summarizes our fundamental point: *the hours available for learning are far more limited than they initially appear.*

INCREASING OPPORTUNITY TO LEARN

In addition to providing a conceptual framework that helps us to analyze the use of classroom time, the BTES also demonstrates the relationship between time and achievement. The findings are not surprising. *As allocated time, engaged time, and academic learning time increase, so does student learning;* of the three, academic learning time is the best predictor of achievement.

The BTES data made time a popular topic for reform-minded educators. In 1983, for example, the National Commission on Excellence in Education declared that we were "a nation at risk" because of "a rising tide of mediocrity" in our educational system. The report advocated a variety of reforms, including recommendations to extend the school day to seven hours and to lengthen the school year to 200 or 220 days.

Other educators argued that there was sufficient time for learning, but that it was used inappropriately (Karweit, 1989). These educators urged teachers to increase time-on-task and to eliminate wasted time. They criticized teachers for allowing students to work on homework during class and for using Fridays as "film day" (Lowe and Gervais, 1988). In some districts, supervisors armed with clipboards and stopwatches visited classrooms to monitor students' engagement rates—and the results were used in evaluations of teaching effectiveness. We know teachers who became wary of doing anything that was not directly related to the standardized achievement tests given at the end of the year. They eliminated "frivolous" activities like reading aloud to children, creative writing, hands-on science experiments, sharing time, and arts and crafts in order to provide more time for the practice of basic skills.

It's easy to go overboard in this search for more hours. First, expecting students to be on-task 100 percent of the time is foolish. Total engagement is not easy for *anyone;* it is especially difficult for students who must work on tasks they have not selected and sometimes find tedious and irrelevant. Second, eliminating activities like science experiments and reading aloud results in a curriculum devoid of interest, vitality, and variety; this might actually cause a loss of engaged time, since students are likely to become bored or disruptive. Third, some loss of instructional time to activities like taking attendance, collecting and distributing materials, and lining up is unavoidable in the crowded, group setting of the classroom.

With these qualifications in mind, it is still essential to consider reasonable ways of increasing students' productive learning time. We will discuss four strategies for achieving this goal: *maintaining activity flow, minimizing transition time, holding students accountable,* and *managing "pull-outs."* (see Table 7-1 for a summary.) Of course, these strategies not only maximize time for learning, they also help to create and maintain classroom order.

Maintaining Activity Flow

Good and Brophy (1994) observe, "four things can happen" when students must wait with nothing to do, and "three of them are bad: (1) students may remain interested and attentive; (2) they may become bored or fatigued, losing interest and ability to concentrate; (3) they may become distracted or start daydreaming; or (4) they may actively misbehave" (p. 138). Given the three-to-one odds that waiting will result in undesirable behavior and a loss of valuable learning opportunities, it's essential for teachers to learn how to maintain the flow of classroom activities.

Once again, we turn for guidance to the work of Jacob Kounin (1970). Kounin investigated differences in teachers' ability to initiate and maintain activity flow in classrooms. He then looked for relationships between activity flow and students' engagement and misbehavior.

TABLE 7-1
STRATEGIES FOR INCREASING STUDENTS' LEARNING TIME

1. Maintain activity flow	Avoid flip-flopping Avoid "stimulus-bounded events": being pulled away from the ongoing activity by an event or object that doesn't really need attention Avoid over-dwelling and fragmentation
2. Minimize transition time	Prepare students for upcoming transition Establish clear routines Have clear beginnings and endings (bring first activity to a halt, announce the transition, monitor the transition, make sure everyone is attentive, begin second activity)
3. Hold students accountable	Communicate assignments clearly Monitor students' progress Provide feedback
4. Manage "pull-outs" as efficiently as possible	Coordinate with special services to schedule pull-outs so they are not too disruptive Create a schedule showing when various students are present and when the whole class is together Establish a policy and procedures for having students who are pulled out complete work they miss

Kounin's research identified many differences in the ways teachers orchestrated classroom activities. In some classrooms, activities flowed smoothly and briskly, while in others activities were "jerky" and slow. Kounin even developed a special vocabulary to describe the problems he observed For instance, he found that some ineffective managers would terminate an activity, start another, and then return to the first activity. Kounin called this *flip-flopping*. It is illustrated by the following situation: A teacher finishes reviewing math problems with the class and tells students to take out their reading books. She then stops and says, "Let's see now. How many got all the [math] problems right? . . . That's very good. . . . All right, now let's get at our readers" (p. 94).

Kounin also observed *stimulus-bounded events,* situations in which teachers are "pulled away" from the ongoing activity by a stimulus (an event or an object) that really doesn't need attention. Kounin describes the case of a teacher who is explaining a math problem at the board when she notices that a student is leaning on his left elbow as he works the problem. She leaves the board, instructs him to sit up straight, comments on his improved posture, and then returns to the board.

Sometimes, teachers slow down the pace of activity by *over dwelling*—continuing to explain when students already understand or preaching at length about appropriate behavior. Another type of slow down is produced when a teacher breaks an activity into components even though the activity could be performed as a single unit—what Kounin called *fragmentation:*

> The teacher was making a transition from spelling to arithmetic as follows: "All right, everybody, I want you to close your spelling books. Put away your red pencils. Now close your spelling books. Put your spelling books in your desks. Keep them out of the way." [There's a pause.] "All right now. Take out your arithmetic books and put them on your desks in front of you. That's right, let's keep everything off your desks except your arithmetic books. And let's sit up straight. We don't want any lazy-bones, do we? That's fine. Now get your black pencils and open your books to page sixteen."

Flip-flops, stimulus-boundedness, over-dwelling, fragmentation—these are all threats to the flow of classroom activities. Not only do they result in lost learning time, they can also have a significant impact on children's behavior. When activities proceed smoothly and briskly, children are *more involved in work and less apt to misbehave.* Indeed, as Kounin concluded two decades ago, *activity flow plays a greater role in classroom order than the specific techniques teachers use to handle misbehavior.*

During one visit to Garnetta's classroom, we watched the skillful way she maintained the flow of activity in her math class. Students were using colorful cubes to solve division problems. For no apparent reason, there were innumerable interruptions that day. A messenger from the office wanted to know the number of children who had signed up for a special Saturday program; a child came to borrow an overhead projector for another teacher; and there was an announcement over the loudspeaker about after-school activities. All these interruptions occurred within a 15-minute period. Garnetta worked valiantly to keep the momentum going. She told the messenger from the office, "I'm in the middle of a lesson. I'll find out later and let the office know." When she turned to get the overhead projector, she first gave her class a task to do: "I'm going to give you a really tough problem while I take care of this business—two into . . . 88! Let's see if you can do that one!" The big number (88) bought Garnetta some additional time and created a special challenge for students. We heard murmurs like "That's not tough," and "Oh, that's easy," as they immediately began to manipulate the blocks to solve the problem.

We've seen Barbara maintain the flow of activity in the face of similar interruptions—and during equipment breakdowns, children's sudden illnesses, and the giddiness that springtime generates. During one March visit, we watched Barbara with her math class. In Bartle School, fourth graders are regrouped for math into four homogeneous classes. Barbara works with the group that is below grade-level. This spirited group of 24 is always a challenge (especially since math class is scheduled immediately after lunch and recess), but on this lovely spring day they came in unusually "wired" and rowdy. After settling them down, Barbara began a homework check. The assignment had asked children to solve word problems like the following: "If there are nine pieces of sports equipment and five of these are baseballs, what fraction are baseballs?" With Barbara's prodding, the homework check proceeded smoothly—until the last problem. Children had to determine how many letters were in the word MATHEMATICS and what fraction were vowels (4/11). There was substantial disagreement about the answer.

Children began arguing with one another, and for a moment it looked as if the lesson might fall apart. We wondered when Barbara was going to issue a firm reprimand and regain her students' attention. She didn't. Instead, she quickly settled the dispute by confirming the correct answer. Then she moved to the front-center of the room and said, "I'm thinking of a number that's between 66 and 92." Immediately, students quieted down and began to raise their hands with guesses:

STUDENT 1:   70?
  BARBARA: Greater than 70, less than 92.
STUDENT 2:   80?
  BARBARA: Greater than 80, less than 92.
STUDENT 3:   90?
  BARBARA: Greater than 90, less than 92.
STUDENT 4:   91?

While this game was going on, Barbara wrote some division problems on the board and motioned for a child to distribute paper. By the time students guessed 91, everyone had paper, and the problems were on the board. Barbara congratulated her students for their astute guesses. Then she directed the class to copy the problems and calculate the answers. As students bent over their papers, Barbara moved from desk to desk, distributing stickers for completed homework.

Later, we talked with Barbara about the class we had observed. We commented on the way she had managed to keep activities moving, shepherding her students along. With a good deal of fervor, she told us:

This is a difficult group. If there's any "down time" at all, things can get out of hand. If students have to sit and wait while paper is being passed out, that provides an opportunity for trouble. If they have to wait until I've written problems on the board, they start to talk and then it takes effort and time to get them back on task. *I've got to keep them involved every minute, or I lose them.* Besides, these kids are working below grade-level in math. They need every single minute of the period for math instruction.

Minimizing Transition Times

Kounin identified "flip-flopping" as one problem that can occur during transitions between activities. But transitions are vulnerable in other ways. An analysis by Paul Gump (1982, 1987) helps us to understand why transitions can be so problematic. First, Gump observes, there may be difficulty "closing out" the first activity—especially if students are deeply engaged. (Ironically, the very involvement that teachers strive to achieve makes it more difficult to get students to switch activities!) Second, transitions are more loosely structured than activities themselves (Ross, 1985). Since there's usually more leeway in terms of socializing and moving around the room, there is also more opportunity for disruption. In fact, in a study of 50 classes taught by student teachers, Marshall Arlin (1979) found that there was almost twice as much disruption during transitions (e.g., hitting, yelling, obscene gestures) as during nontransition time.

Third, students sometimes "save up" problems or tensions and deal with them during the transition time (Gump, 1982). They may seek out the teacher to complain about a neighbor, ask for permission to retrieve a book from a locker, or dump out the contents of their desks in search of a lost homework assignment. Although these behaviors are legitimate—and help to protect the adjacent activities from disturbance—they also make transitions more difficult to manage. Finally, there may be delays in getting students started on the second activity (Gump, 1982). Teachers may be held up because they are dealing with individual children's concerns or are busy assembling needed materials. Students may have difficulty settling down, especially if they are returning from physical education or recess.

Gump's analysis suggests that teachers can reduce the potential for chaos by *preparing students for upcoming transitions, by establishing efficient transition routines,* and *by clearly defining the boundaries of lessons* (Ross, 1985). These guidelines are especially important for children with Attention Deficit Disorder (ADD) or Attention Deficit Hyperactivity Disorder (ADHD), who have particular difficulty with transitions. (See Chapter 12 for the characteristics of children with these disorders.)

Advance Preparation Marshall Arlin's (1979) research revealed that transitions were far more chaotic when student teachers failed to warn students about the imminent change of activity. This often occurred because student teachers didn't even realize the period was about to end:

> The lesson was still continuing when the bell would ring. Not having reached any closure, the teacher, with some degree of desperation, would say something like "Okay, you can go," and pupils would charge out of the room, often knocking each other over. (Sometimes, pupils did not even wait for the signal from the teacher.) The teacher might

then remember an announcement and interject to the dispersing mob, "Don't forget to bring back money for the trip!" (p. 50)

In contrast, other student teachers in Arlin's study were able to prepare students for the upcoming transition. If they were about to dismiss the class to go to lunch, they made sure that desks were in order and that students were quiet and ready to leave. They made announcements while students were still seated and then lined children up in an orderly fashion.

Our four teachers are very skillful "clock watchers." They take care to monitor time and to inform students when an activity is drawing to a close. In the following scene, we see Garnetta warn her students that they will be changing activities in two minutes. We also see her spur them along by counting aloud, although she times her counting to match students' progress. Finally, she praises students for their cooperation:

10:15   Ladies and gents, you have approximately two minutes to finish up whatever sentence you're working on. Then put your papers in your creative writing book and put your heads down and show me you're ready.

10:17   Okay, I'm starting to count. One. We've got one person ready, now two people, four people. Table 2 looks excellent; Table 1 is excellent. I'm on two. [She circulates, walking closer to those who are not yet ready and watching as more and more students put their heads down.] I'm up to three. Table 1 is good; table 2, beautiful. [At table 3, Robert is still putting things in his desk.] Almost everyone is ready to go. Robert, are you ready? [He puts his head down.] Table 3, lovely.

10:18   [She speaks in a very quiet voice.] Okay, everyone knows our hallway rules. We'll stop at the bathroom and then go on to Basic Skills class. . . . Are we going to talk in the hallway? [Kids murmur, "No . . ."] Table 2 line up, Table 3, Table 1. [Children all push in their chairs and line up quietly.] Table 1, I really like the way you lined up.

10:19   [The class leaves the room in an orderly, quiet line.]

Not only do our teachers warn their students about upcoming transitions, they also prepare them for the activities that will occur after lunch, recess, or special classes. Here, we see Ken call his class together five minutes before they are to go to lunch. He reviews what the afternoon's activities will be and makes sure everyone has their materials out and ready:

KEN: Folks, I'd like everyone at their tables. [He pauses while students return to their seats from the various parts of the room where they have been working.] Now, before we go to lunch, I want to take five minutes so that you're all set for this afternoon. What are you going to need for this afternoon?

STUDENT: Page 39, page 40 [worksheets the students have been working on], and our newspapers.

KEN: Good. Take a minute to get those together and put them on your desks. What else?

STUDENT: We need our private journals with the answers to the questions.

KEN: Right. Get your private journals ready and on your desks.

STUDENT: We need our book reports.

KEN: Good. Is your book report on your desk?

STUDENT: We need our peer tutoring logs.
KEN: Yes. Get them out. I'm going to try to look at them this afternoon. We'll also watch the health video if we have time. Any problems? [Several students inform him about places they have to go that afternoon—to a second-grade class for peer tutoring, to band practice, to a yearbook meeting.] Okay, folks, see you later. [Students get up, get their coats, and leave for recess.]

The Use of Routines   In Chapter 4 we talked about the need to have clear, specific routines in order to keep the classroom running smoothly. At no time is the use of routines more important than during transitions (Ross, 1985). Well-established routines provide a structure to transitions that helps to prevent confusion and lost time. Routines are particularly crucial for children with ADD/ADHD who need predictability and consistency.

Barbara has instituted a routine for entering the room in the morning and settling in. This routine helps to ease the transition from home to school. When students come in, they immediately check the chalkboard to find out what they are to begin doing. Sometimes the board says "SQUIRT," and students know to begin Sustained, Quiet, UnInterrupted Reading Time. Sometimes the board says "JOURNALS":

It's 8:30. Students enter the room, glance at the board, go to their seats, and take out their journals. They quickly begin writing, as Barbara circulates. She gets the attendance form and silently notes attendance while students are working. Without a word, she hands the form to a boy who takes it to the office. He comes back in one minute. Barbara says, "Thank you, David." She continues to circulate, occasionally commenting to a child.

Viviana also has a well-established routine for beginning the school day:

Children begin arriving at 8:45. Viviana stands by the door. She greets each child with an enthusiastic "good morning" and a quick hug. The children go to the coat closet, hang up their coats, put their materials on the desks, and then leave the room for a bathroom stop. When they return, they go to their desks and sit quietly, comparing homework, putting things away, and chatting.

At 8:57, Viviana moves to her stool in the center front of the room.
"Good morning, children," she says.
The children respond chorally: "Good morning, Mrs. Love."
"How are you today, children?"
"Fine, thank you. How are you today?
"Fine, thank you."

Then Viviana sings a good morning song to the students. When she is done, they sing the song to her. At 9:00 she instructs them to stand and say the Pledge of Allegiance. They do so and immediately move into "My Country 'Tis of Thee." Then they turn to the calendar. Viviana asks a series of questions, all at a brisk pace: "What month is this?" "How many months are there?" "What are the months?" "What day is today?" "What day was yesterday?" "What day is tomorrow?" The children respond chorally to each question. At 9:10 they line up and leave for ESL class.

Viviana also has a routine that she uses whenever she erases boardwork in preparation for a new activity. The routine not only provides a structure to the transition that helps to keep children engaged, it also reinforces her first-graders' reading skills.

> Children are creating sentences by unscrambling words written on the chalkboard. They come to the last set of words:
>
> can   play   us   with   you
>
> One child volunteers: "Can you play with us?" Viviana acknowledges that the sentence is correct and asks if children can think of any other. No one can. Viviana praises the children for their good work and tells them that they will do more scrambled words another day. Then she says, "Now let's erase the board." As she goes to erase each word, she pauses, and the children read it aloud. When all the words have been erased, Viviana begins the next part of her lesson. "Okay children, now we're going to work a little bit with two vowel sounds."

Clear Beginnings and Endings   Arlin's (1979) study demonstrated that transitions proceed more smoothly if teachers bring the first activity to a halt, announce the transition, allow time to make sure that everyone is attentive, and then begin the second activity. In other words, smooth transitions are characterized by well-defined boundaries.

Sometimes, in an effort to maintain activity flow, teachers rush into the second activity without checking that students are "with them." Arlin (1979) writes: "Several times I noticed over 15 children continuing the previous activity while the teacher was giving directions for the new activity" (p. 50). Needless to say, those teachers then became exasperated when students asked questions about what to do.

In the following vignette, we see Viviana implement a transition with well-defined boundaries. Watch the way she gives explicit instructions for cleaning up, directs the orderly collection of materials, and pauses before beginning the second activity:

> Children are working on a place-value activity (tens and ones). They are using wooden blocks to show two-digit numbers. They are supposed to place the appropriate number of blocks on a card divided into a ones column and a tens column. As they work, Viviana walks around, commenting on their work. After about 15 minutes, she is ready to change activities. She gives instructions in a very quiet voice: "Okay, children. Put the cards together with a paper clip. Lesley, collect the cards." [Children begin to yell, "Can I collect the ones blocks?" "Can I collect the tens blocks?"] Viviana communicates her disapproval: "Too many people are talking to me at once. You need to be quiet and raise your hands." [The children quiet down.] "That's better. Okay, Alfredo, collect the tens blocks. Fernando, collect the ones blocks." [They do so.] "Okay, children, sit straight facing me. One, two, and . . ." [Children rush to get into their seats and face forward.] Viviana scans the room, checking that students are paying attention. Then she begins the next activity: "Yesterday I asked you to think about all the things you could buy in the supermarket that you divide into parts. . . ."

Our other three teachers also make certain that students are listening before they begin an activity. Often, they'll preface lessons with remarks designed to "grab" students' attention. Garnetta, for example, uses verbal cues like these:

"Let's get everything put away now. I want everybody with me 100 percent for this. It's important."

"Put everything else away. Now we're going to have some fun."

"We're doing this for the first time, so you all have to be quiet and listen very carefully."

"Please put your health books on your desks and look at me. Natasha, that's beautiful."

Although it's important to make sure that students are attentive before proceeding with a new lesson, Gump (1982) warns that waiting *too long* can cause a loss of momentum. He reminds us that a new activity will often "pull in" nonattending children. (Remember Barbara's use of the quiz game to capture her students' attention.) Gump writes: "Waiting for absolute and universal attention can sometimes lead to unnecessarily extended transition times" (p. 112). Clearly, teachers need to find the happy medium between rushing ahead when students are inattentive and waiting so long that momentum is lost. It's a delicate balancing act.

Holding Students Accountable

During a visit to Ken's class, we watched as Janice tried to get Monica to stop working on an assignment and do something with her. It wasn't clear exactly what Janice wanted to do, but Monica's reaction was unambiguous. "No," she responded firmly, "I want to do this *now*. I don't want to do it at recess, I don't want to do it at lunch time, and I don't want to do it for homework. I want to do it now."

Observing this interaction, we thought of Walter Doyle's (1983) comment that students tend to take assignments seriously only if they are held accountable for them. Your own school experiences probably testify to the truth of this statement. Even as adults, it takes a good deal of self-discipline, maturity, and intrinsic motivation to put your best effort into work that will never be seen by anyone else. And elementary students are *children*. Unless they know that they will have to account for their performance, it is unlikely that they'll make the best use of class time.

Furthermore, students are *unable* to make good use of their time if they are confused about what they're supposed to be doing. Teachers sometimes tell students to "get to work" and are immediately bombarded by questions: "Can I use pen?" "Do I have to write down the problems or can I just put the answers?" "Do we have to reduce to lowest terms?" "Can I work on the rug?" When this happens, precious class time has to be spent clarifying the original instructions.

In order to help children use their time wisely, teachers must *communicate assignments and requirements clearly, monitor students' progress,* and *provide feedback about performance* (Evertson, Emmer, Clements, Sanford, and Worsham, 1994). These practices minimize students' confusion and convey the message that school work is important. Let's see what our teachers and the research have to say about these practices.

Communicating Assignments and Requirements   One finding of the BTES (Fisher et al., 1980) was that students were more likely to have success on assignments when teachers provided clear, thorough directions. Interestingly, the number of explanations given *in response to students' questions was negatively associated with high student success.*What could account for this curious finding? One possibility is that when many students have to ask questions about an assignment, it means that their teachers failed to provide sufficient preparation. In other words, the original instructions were not clear or thorough enough.

Before students begin to work, you should explain what students will be doing and why, how to get help, what to do with completed work, what to do when they're finished, and how long they'll be spending on the task (Jones and Jones, 1986). You also need to make sure that students are familiar with your work standards—for example, what kind of paper to use, whether they should use pencil or pen, how to number the page, and whether or not erasures are allowed. After giving instructions, it's a good idea to have students explain what they will be doing in their own words. Simply asking "Does everyone understand?" seldom yields useful information.

During one visit to Garnetta's classroom, we watched her explain to her class that they were going to read about the life of Martin Luther King, Jr. and then write summaries. She emphasized that the summaries should be brief, containing only the most important ideas. Moreover, she stressed that they needed to be written in the students' own words:

> "I don't want you to just copy the information from the story. You've got to use your . . . [points to head; children call out "BRAINS"]. That's right, your brains. You and your partner will read the story, decide what the important facts are, and then *write them down in your own words.* Let's make sure that everyone understands this. I'm going to read the beginning of one of the stories in our reader. [Garnetta opens the reader and reads a few paragraphs. The children are clearly familiar with this story. Then she closes the book.] In your own words, what is happening in this story? What did I just read? [Children raise their hands. Garnetta calls on individuals to tell the story.] Good. You are *summarizing* the story. You're not telling the whole thing—only the *most important* things. And you're not just copying the words from the book. You're picking out the most important information, discussing it with your partner, and then you're writing it down in YOUR OWN WORDS."

It's often helpful to write the daily schedule and all work assignments on the chalkboard, so students can refer to them throughout the day. In Ken's class, the day's assignments are already on the chalkboard when students enter the classroom in the morning. A small chalkboard at the side of the room indicates how the morning will be structured. Each reading group is listed (by the title of the novel being read), along with its assignments and the time it will be meeting with Ken. After greeting students and taking attendance, Ken reviews the assignments with the class and checks that everyone knows what to do that morning. On another chalkboard is the schedule for the afternoon, along with due dates for the week's

CHAPTER 7: MAKING THE MOST OF CLASSROOM TIME 153

special assignments. For example, when Ken's students were studying the newspaper, the board read:

Newspaper Unit
Monday:	Analysis of a comic strip character
Tuesday:	Quotations from national/international news stories
Wednesday:	Worksheet on New Jersey news articles
Thursday:	Worksheet on local news articles
Friday:	Newspaper folders due

Communicating assignments clearly is especially important if you are working with low-achieving students or students who have a history of "forgetting" work. Barbara has devised a homework procedure that she uses with her low math class. At the beginning of the month, she provides each student with a folder in which all the assignments for the month are stapled. On the cover of the folder is a calendar, showing exactly what homework students are to do each night. In this way, students can't claim they "didn't know what to do," and if they're absent (a common occurrence among low-achieving children), they still know what the assignment is. One of Barbara's calendars appears in Figure 7-3.

Monitoring Student Progress   Once you've given directions for an assignment and your class gets to work, it's important to monitor how students are doing. The BTES found that teachers with high-achieving classes circulated around the room while students were working at their seats (Fisher et al, 1980). This practice enables you to keep track of students' progress, to identify and help with problems, and to verify that assignments are matched to students' ability. Circulating also helps to ensure that students are using their time well.

Observations of our four teachers revealed that they rarely sit down, unless they're working with a small group. In all four rooms, the teacher's desk is out of the way and used for storage, rather than as a place to sit.

Viviana's children are working with "Pattern Blocks," wooden blocks that come in several different shapes—squares, triangles, diamonds, hexagons, trapezoids. Each shape is a different color. The task is to use four blocks of the same color and shape to cover outlined figures drawn on a worksheet. Viviana introduces the activity: "Now this next page is *not baby stuff*. This one you really have to think about and read the directions. Let's read the first part out loud." [She calls on a child to read the first instruction: "Cover each figure with four blocks of the same shape."] The children begin to work. They are visibly excited, delighting in the ability to do the task: "This is easy, this is baby stuff." While they work, Viviana circulates, checking each child's paper: "You're supposed to use only one color. You're using two." "These are not the same shape, are they?" "Good for you. You are right!" When she see that all of the children are done, she returns to the front of the room and reviews what they did. "So you thought this first part was easy, right? Who wants to tell me what you did? Alfredo?" [Alfredo tells her that he used four blocks of the same color and shape to cover each figure.] "Okay, so what color did you use for the first one?" [She continues to review the page and then introduces the next part of the activity.]

SUN	MON	TUE	WED	THU	FRI	SAT
			1	2	3	4
5	6	7	8	9 Multiplication, Division Page 44	10 Word Problems Page 45	11
12	13 Fractions Pages 48–49	14 Symmetry Page 55	15 Subtraction Page 57	16 Multiplication, Division Page 59	17 Money Page 60	18
19	20 Word Problems Page 61	21 Check-up Page 64	22 Multiplication 2 Digit by 1 Digit Page 67	23 Multiplication Page 68	24	25
26	27 Subtraction Pages 69	28 Bar Graph Page 74	29 Addition, Subtraction Page 78	30 Multiplication Page 87	31 Check-up Page 84	

FIGURE 7-3
Barbara Broggi's Assignment Calendar

In classrooms where learning centers are prevalent, other forms of monitoring student performance and ensuring student accountability may be needed. A sign-in form by each learning center, for example, allows students to indicate that they have worked in a particular center; even kindergarten children can learn to check off or sign their names. The teacher can then pass by each center and readily determine which children have completed the centers. In addition, many teachers use response sheets that require students to perform some sort of written work associated with the center. These can be a simple fill-in-the-blank form, a small project, a review sheet, or a self-generated observation narrative. By requiring students to sign in and put something down in writing, the message is clear: The work done in centers is important and students are accountable.

Garnetta monitors students' progress on written work.

In addition to monitoring how students do on short, daily assignments, it's essential to *keep track of progress on long-term assignments.* By establishing intermediate check points, you can help children develop a "plan of attack." For example, if students are writing a research paper, you can set due dates on which they have to submit each stage of the assignment (e.g., the topic; preliminary notes; a list of references; the first draft; the final draft). Not only does this allow you to monitor children's progress, it also helps to lessen the anxiety that young children sometimes feel when faced with a large assignment.

Ken uses this approach when he has students write stories. Although the final draft is not due for a month, Ken breaks the assignment down into components that are due every few days. First, students discuss characters in books they've already read and select one character to analyze (e.g., appearance, personality traits, mannerisms). Then they create a character of their own, following the format they used for their character analysis. This sequence of activities is repeated for the setting, the problem or conflict, and the resolution of the problem. By the end of three weeks, students have the ingredients necessary for a story. Only then do they actually begin writing.

In order to monitor if students are regularly completing assignments, it's important to *establish routines for collecting and checking classwork and homework.*

Some teachers keep file folders for each child. These contain all of the worksheets and assignments for the day. Children complete their work and put it back in the file folders, which are then returned to the teacher's desk to await checking. Other teachers appoint student monitors to collect each assignment. If the monitors alphabetize the papers, it simplifies the task of noting whose work is missing. In some classes, students are assigned numbers that they put at the top of every assignment. This enables the monitors to put the work in numerical order, another way of making it easy to scan assignments. In Garnetta's classroom, there is a different paper monitor for each subject. These students collect assignments and tell Garnetta which students didn't turn in their work. She then writes those names on the chalkboard; when children complete their work, they turn it in to Garnetta and erase their names.

A very common system collecting work is to have shallow boxes or baskets labeled for each subject; when students are done with an assignment, they simply drop it in the appropriate basket. Interestingly, neither Ken, Barbara, nor Garnetta like this system. Ken tells us, "Whenever I've used boxes like this, my kids begin to think that the only important thing is getting the work done as quickly as possible so they can throw it in the box." Garnetta points out another potential problem:

> Boxes allow kids to slip by. I'd get home and find out that work wasn't there. I don't like to give zeroes; I'd rather have the work. So I try hard during the day to monitor who's turning in work and who's not, and I have kids finish their work during recess or some other free time. That way, when I get home at night, I have all the papers.

Barbara also finds that "kids slip by" when she uses boxes to collect work:

> I don't like boxes because it's not immediately clear who has done the work and who hasn't. I prefer to have my students put their work on a corner of their desks. Then I can go around the room, checking to see who's done the assignment. There's immediate, visible accountability.

Some schools have moved toward portfolio assessment to document student progress. This form of assessment relies on the gathering of student work samples, selected by either the teacher or the student. Although portfolios provide an "authentic" record of students' growth over time, the collection and storage of work samples can create organizational problems. Teachers use a variety of systems—plastic milk crates with hanging file folders, pocket folders, cubbies labeled with the children's names, and file cabinets with specific drawers designated for portfolios. In developing a system that's right for you, keep in mind that the students need access to their work, either to revisit works in progress or to update their portfolios.

Providing Feedback   Sometimes, turning in work to a teacher is like dropping it down a black hole. Assignments pile up in huge mounds on the teacher's desk, and students know that their papers will never be returned—graded or ungraded. From a student's perspective, it's infuriating to work hard on an assignment, turn it in, and then receive no feedback from the teacher. But a lack of academic feedback is not simply infuriating. It is also detrimental to students' involvement and achievement. The BTES (Fisher et al., 1980) documented the importance of providing feedback to children:

> One particularly important teaching activity is providing academic feedback to students (letting them know whether their answers are right or wrong, or giving them the right answer). Academic feedback should be provided as often as possible to students. When more frequent feedback is offered, *students pay attention more and learn more. Academic feedback was more strongly and consistently related to achievement than any of the other teaching behaviors.* (p. 27; italics added for emphasis)

If you circulate while students are working on assignments, you can provide them with immediate feedback about their performance. You can catch errors, assist with problems, and affirm correct, thoughtful work. As Viviana comments:

> I always correct papers as my children are doing them. That's the time to explain and correct mistakes. If children don't understand the first problem, they'll get all the rest wrong. This also allows students to take their work home every day, so parents can see how they're doing. Correcting work as students do it also means that I don't have to take home a huge stack of papers every night, and I can use that time for planning.

Sometimes you're just not able to monitor and correct work while it's being done. In this case, you need to check assignments once they've been submitted and return them to students as soon as possible. Checking or grading all the work done each day is an arduous task. Not surprisingly, first-year teachers often report that paperwork and grading are the most overwhelming aspect of teaching. To avoid being totally overwhelmed, you need to find ways to "make a molehill out of a mountain" (Shalaway, 1989). We asked our teachers how they handle the paperwork. Their ideas are listed in Figure 7-4.

You might also decide to allow your students to check their own work. Ken believes this has numerous educational benefits:

> If I correct assignments, *I'm* doing all the important work—the editing, the problem-solving, the analyzing of mistakes. That's what the *kids* should be doing, or at the very least, I should be doing it in front of them. They learn best by correcting their own mistakes, rather than reading somebody else's comments. And the most important stuff must be talked about. I prefer to have students discuss and correct work together, either in their small reading and math groups or as a whole class. I tell them, "Today at 2:00 you need to be ready to share your newspaper articles." We discuss what they've done, and the feedback session becomes an extension of the assignment.

Whether you correct work while it's being done, at home over a cup of coffee, or together with your students, the important point is that children *need to know how they are progressing.* If you don't provide them with frequent, specific, informative feedback, they may spend valuable time doing assignments incorrectly. Furthermore, a lack of feedback can be interpreted as a sign that you don't take their work seriously—and that provides a good excuse for fooling around.

- Model your record keeping after the report card you use. In this way, you'll be sure to have sufficient documentation for each category of the report card. For example, if the report card reads: "Is able to grasp main idea," make sure that you have attended to this skill, that you have examples of each child's achievement in this area, and that you have recorded their progress.
- Put some of the responsibility for keeping records on students. Teach them to keep track of their own progress. For example, they can construct a bar graph to record the number of spelling words they get right each week. Even kindergartners can date stamp their assignments.
- Whenever possible, correct in-class work while students are doing it, or as a group immediately afterwards.
- Collect in-class worksheets and then redistribute randomly for grading as a group. If students are assigned numbers, which they put at the top of their papers instead of their names, no one knows whose paper they're checking.
- Ask seventh- and eighth-grade students to help mark papers during lunch.
- Monitor that students complete in-class worksheets (e.g., a set of math problems) and homework, but don't grade these. Grade only quizzes and tests.
- Instead of correcting and grading every homework assignment, give periodic quizzes to check what students are learning.
- Give quizzes with 5 questions instead of 25.
- If you're drowning in paperwork, you're giving too much. Pare it down!

FIGURE 7-4
Ideas for Handling Paperwork

Managing Pull-Outs as Efficiently as Possible

Children with special needs are often "pulled out" of the regular classroom for special instruction. For example, students with learning disabilities may go to a resource room to work on reading and study skills; those who are "gifted and talented" may leave for an enrichment program; those with limited proficiency in English may receive instruction in English as a Second Language. (See Chapter 12 for a description of these special services and a discussion of the problems associated with pull-out instruction.) In addition, the whole class may go to "specials" like art, music, and physical education. With all these comings and goings, you may sometimes feel more like an air traffic controller than a teacher; furthermore, it may seem as though there is no time for whole-class instruction. One student teacher recently wrote about this problem in her journal:

> I am so frustrated as of this journal entry!! Where is there any time in the day?!! My kids get pulled out for so many different things I rarely have a solid hour with them all together! How can anyone teach the subjects that all students are supposed to get? Three kids go out on three days at different times for compensatory education. One girl goes out four days a week at different times for a one-hour block of resource room. Three more students go out three days at different times for a HOTS (higher order thinking skills) program. . . . Three-quarters of the class goes out once a week for chorus, band, and art club (and these are not even the specials, like music, gym, art, and library).

> Fourteen of my 24 kids go out of the room at scattered times throughout the entire week for music lessons. There is NO time in the day, and there is absolutely no consistency for the kids!!!

There is also no simple solution for this problem. All of our teachers face it to some extent (although special assistance is increasingly being provided in the regular classroom), and all of them find it frustrating. The best approach is to try to have input into scheduling. If you can work closely with special services personnel, you can develop a schedule that will minimize the fragmentation and ensure that there are some time periods when you will be able to instruct the whole class or a small group without excluding somebody. (See Figure 7-5.) For example it can be helpful to schedule "G & T" (gifted and talented), basic skills, and ESL (English as a Second Language) all at the same time. In this way, a large number of children can be out of the room simultaneously, rather than scattered throughout the whole day. (At Bartle School, these special services are now scheduled right before first period—8:00 to 8:40—so children do not have to be pulled out during the regular school day.) If you have students who require the maximum instruction possible in reading and math, make sure you don't schedule your own instruction in these content areas while they are out of the room. On the other hand, if children go to a resource room *in lieu* of receiving regular class instruction in these areas, then it's a good idea to schedule your own literacy and math instruction at that time.

Regardless of the scheduling, you need to find out the school's policy about requiring students who are pulled out to complete missed work. Consider another student teacher's journal entry:

> It seems to me that my special ed students are confused about what is expected of them, where they are supposed to be, whose class they belong to, etc. I certainly know that *I* feel very confused in regard to teaching them. Basically, they are out of class almost half of the school day. When they return to the classroom from being in the Resource Room, I often don't know what to do with them. . . . For example, is it fair to hold these children responsible for work that they weren't in class for? How fair is it to let them slide? Should I try to take them aside and explain what the class is doing? Amazingly, I have never been given a straight answer about whether or not these children are responsible for the work they missed. The "policy" seems to vary from week to week. This "laissez-faire" attitude is likely to doom students to always needing special services. It appears that there is little orchestration of objectives and material between the regular classroom teacher and special services personnel.
>
>   Usually, if children come into the class after being in the Resource Room, I have them simply join in with the class (or with their cooperative groups) wherever the class may be. But then it dawns on me that these are the children who are *least* likely to be able to pick up concepts in the middle of things and that a more effective routine needs to be established. Special needs children can get lost so easily!

If your school also has a laissez faire approach to this issue, you will have to establish your own policy. You will also need to think carefully about the procedures you want to implement to make children's leaving and re-entry as smooth as possible. You might appoint a special "buddy" for each student who is pulled out; bud-

Time	Monday	Tuesday	Wednesday
8:30- 9:00	out: Mark Tanya _____ journal writing	out: Mark Tanya _____ journal writing	out: Mark Tanya _____ journal writing
9:00- 9:30	out: Peter (Reading Group 2) _____ Reading Group 1	out: Terry (Reading Group 1) _____ Reading Group 2	out: Peter (Reading Group 2) _____ Reading Group 1
9:30- 10:30	out: Bonnie (Reading Group 1) _____ Reading Group 2	out: Jean (Reading Group 2) _____ Reading Group 1	out: Bonnie (Reading Group 1) _____ Reading Group 2
10:30- 11:15	Music	Phys Ed	Art
11:15- 12:00	out: no one Math	out: no one Math	out: no one Math

FIGURE 7-5
A Schedule Indicating When Children Are Available for Instruction

dies are responsible for orienting the students upon their return to the regular class-room. It can also help to have a special folder or box for each child who is pulled out so that you don't forget to put aside assignments or materials for children who are out of the room.

Even if you are able to have input into scheduling and to implement procedures to reduce the disruption, pull-outs can constitute a managerial nightmare and result in lost instructional time for the children who need it most. For this reason, more and more schools are trying to provide inclass support and assistance for children with special needs. We will return to this topic in Chapter 12.

CONCLUDING COMMENTS

Tracy Kidder's book, *Among Schoolchildren* (1989), describes one year in the life of Chris Zajac, an elementary teacher who's feisty, demanding, blunt, fair, funny, and hard-working. At the very end of the book, Kidder describes Chris's thoughts on the last day of school. Although she is convinced that she belongs "among schoolchildren," Chris laments the fact that she hadn't been able to help all her students—at least not enough:

> Again this year, some had needed more help than she could provide. There were many problems that she hadn't solved. But it wasn't for lack of trying. She hadn't given up. She had run out of time.

Like Chris, we all run out of time. The end of the year comes much too quickly, and some children's needs are much too great. Hopefully, the concepts and guidelines presented in this chapter will help you to make good use of the limited time you have.

SUMMARY

In this chapter we discussed time as a precious resource. First, we looked at the amount of school time that is actually available for teaching and learning. Then we discussed our strategies for increasing students' productive learning time. We reviewed research by Kounin demonstrating that activity flow plays a greater role in classroom order than specific techniques teachers use to handle misbehavior. We stressed the importance of minimizing transition times. We outlined ways of holding students accountable and helping them to use their time wisely. Finally, we talked about ways to cope with the managerial nightmare created by "pull-outs."

Types of Time

- *Mandated time:* the time the state requires school to be in session
- *Allocated time:* the time the state, district, school, and teacher allocate for instruction in various content areas

- *Instructional time:* the time that is actually used for instruction
- *Engaged time:* the time a student spends working attentively on academic tasks
- *Productive time:* The proportion of engaged time in which students are doing work that is meaningful and appropriate
- *Academic Learning Time (ALT):* the proportion of engaged time in which students are performing academic tasks with a high degree of success

The Relationship between Time and Learning

- As allocated, engaged, and academic learning time increase, so does student learning.
- Of the three, ALT is the best predictor of achievement.

How to Increase Hours for Learning

- Maintain activity flow by avoiding:
  - flip-flopping
  - stimulus-bounded events
  - over-dwelling
  - fragmentation
- Minimize transition time by:
  - defining boundaries to lessons
  - preparing students for transitions
  - establishing routines
- Hold students accountable by:
  - communicating assignments and requirements clearly
  - monitoring students' progress
  - providing feedback about performance
  - establishing routines for collecting and checking classwork and homework
  - maintaining good records
- Manage "pull-outs" as efficiently as possible
  - try to have input into scheduling
  - create a schedule showing periods of time when various students are present and when the whole class is together
  - establish (or find out) a policy about the responsibility of pulled-out students to complete work they missed
  - establish procedures for smooth transitions when students return to the classroom

By using time wisely, you can maximize opportunities for learning and minimize occasions for disruption in your classroom. Think about how much time is being spent on meaningful and appropriate work in your room, and how much is being eaten up by business and clerical tasks. Be aware that the hours available for instruction are much fewer than they first appear!

ACTIVITIES

1 Obtain a copy of the weekly schedule for the class you are observing. Analyze it to determine how much time is allocated each week to literacy (reading, language arts, creative writing, spelling, etc.), mathematics, science, social studies, art, music, and physical education. Next, select one subject that is taught while you are visiting the class. Observe for one complete period, carefully noting how much of the allocated time is actually used for instructional purposes. For example, let's suppose you elect to observe a 50-minute mathematics class. The allocated time is 50 minutes. But while you are observing, you note that the first five minutes of the period are spent checking to see who does or does not have the homework (a clerical job). In the middle of the period, the teacher asks students to get into groups of four, and moving into groups takes up another five minutes that is not actually spent in instruction. Then an announcement comes on over the loudspeaker, and the class discusses the announcement for another three minutes. Finally, the teacher wraps up class five minutes before the end of the period and gives everyone free time. Conclusion: Out of 50 minutes of allocated time, 18 minutes were spent on nonacademic or noninstructional activities, leaving 32 minutes of actual instructional time.

2 Read the following vignette and identify the factors that threaten the activity flow of the lesson. Once you have identified the problems, rewrite the vignette so that activity flow is maintained OR explain how you would avoid the problems if you were the teacher.

Mrs. P. waits while her second-grade students take out their fraction circles to begin the math lesson. When most of the children have placed the circles on their desks, she begins to remind the class of the work they did on fractions the previous day. As she explains the tasks they are about to do, she notices that Jack doesn't have his circles.

"Jack, where are your circles?"

"I don't know."

"This is the third time you don't have your circles. You didn't have them last week, and you had to stay in at recess one day and you also lost free time. What did I tell you would happen if you lost your circles one more time?"

"You were going to call my mother."

"That's right. Now go and write your name on the board while I see if I have an extra pack for you to use."

Mrs. P. goes to the supply closet and pulls out a pack of fraction circles for Jack. She then instructs the class to place the bag of shapes on the top left side of their desks.

"Take out the blue circle and place it directly in front of you." She checks to see that all students have complied.

"Now take out one of the four red pieces and place it on the blue circle. Be careful not to drop it, and do this without talking to your neighbor."

Mrs. P. circulates to see if the children are following directions.

"Now take out another red piece and place *it* on the blue circle."

The children do so. Mrs. P. then directs them to take out two remaining red pieces and place them on the blue circle, "one at a time."

"How many red pieces did you use to cover the blue circle?'

The class responds, "Four."

"And what is one piece called?"

"One fourth."

"I'd like everyone to say it together, please."

"One fourth!"

"Did I hear the back table? I want *everyone* to repeat it with strong voices!"

"ONE FOURTH!"

"Excellent. Now what are two pieces called?"

"Two fourths."

"I still didn't hear everyone. Let's hear Rhonda's table. (Rhonda's table responds.) Okay, how about Shakia's table? (They respond.) And now Reggie's table. Good."

As she passes Rob's desk, she notices a pink slip of paper. "Class, I almost forgot. Those children who have permission forms for the zoo trip need to give them to me now, so I can get them to the office."

Children proceed to hunt through their desks. Several ask permission to go get their book bags. Once all the slips are collected, Mrs. P. returns to the lesson and goes on to talk about thirds. She directs the children to put away the red pieces, to take out the three green pieces, and to cover the blue circle with the green pieces. Mrs. P. checks that students know each green piece is "one third." At the completion of this activity, Mrs. P. directs the students to put away the fraction circles and to take out their spelling books.

"Okay, children, turn to page 37 in your spellers and let's review the words for this week. Tanya, please read the first word and use it in a sentence."

As Tanya begins, Mrs. P. interrupts: "I'm sorry, Tanya, but I just realized that I forgot to tell you all what the math homework is. Everyone, take out your assignment pads and write down the assignment as I write it on the board." She takes a piece of chalk and writes, "Math—page 25, even problems only." The children copy the assignment. Mrs. P. scans the room to make sure everyone has written the assignment. When all the children are done, she directs them to return to their spellers.

"All right, now, where were we? Tanya, you were doing number one." When Tanya finishes, Mrs. P. has the class spell the word out loud and then moves on to next word. The class is on the fourth word when the bell rings for lunch.

"Oh my, I don't know where the time went. Okay, boys and girls, get ready for lunch. We'll continue with spelling when you get back."

3 Develop a routine or transition activity for each of the following situations. Remember, your goal is to use time wisely.

    a Beginning of the school day

    b Snack time

    c Returning from gym

    d Moving from small group time to independent seatwork

4 You want your fourth-grade students to do a research report on a famous inventor. They will also be creating their own inventions. As you plan this project, you will need to consider how to hold your students accountable. How will you:

    a convey requirements clearly and thoroughly?

    b monitor student progress?

    c maintain student interest?

    d provide feedback to students?

5 Interview two teachers about their policies and procedures with respect to pull-out instruction. Do they require students who are pulled out to complete the work they missed? If so, when do students do the work? How do they re-orient students when they return to class? Do they see any alternatives to pull out instruction?

REFERENCES

Arlin, M. (1979). Teacher transitions can disrupt time flow in classrooms. *American Educational Research Journal, 16,* 42–56.

Doyle, W. (1983). Academic work. *Review of Educational Research, 53*(2), 159–200.

Evertson, C. M., Emmer, E. T., Clements, B. S., Sanford, J. P., and Worsham, M. E. (1994). *Classroom management for elementary teachers.* (3rd edition) Englewood Cliffs, NJ: Prentice Hall.

Fisher, C. W., Filby, N. N., Marliave, R. S., Cahen, L. S., Dishaw, M. M., Moore, J. E., and Berliner, D. C. (1978). *Teaching behaviors, academic learning time and student achievement. Final report of Phase III-B, Beginning Teacher Evaluation Study.* San Francisco, CA: Far West Laboratory for Educational Research and Development.

Fisher, C. W., Berliner, D. C., Filby, N. N., Marliave, R., Cahen, L. S., and Dishaw, M. M. (1980). Teaching behaviors, academic learning time, and student achievement: An overview. In C. Denham and A. Lieberman (Eds.), *Time to learn.* Washington, D.C.: U.S. Department of Education, 7–32.

Good, T. L., and Brophy, J. E. (1994). *Looking in classrooms* (6th edition). New York: Harper-Collins.

Goodlad, J. I. *A Place called school.* New York: McGraw-Hill.

Gump, P. (1982). School settings and their keeping. In D. L. Duke (Ed.), *Helping teachers manage classrooms.* Alexandria, VA: Association for Supervision and Curriculum Development, pp. 98–114.

Gump, P. V. (1987). School and classroom environments. In D. Stokols and I. Altman (Eds.), *Handbook of environmental psychology.* New York: John Wiley & Sons, pp. 691–732.

Jones, V. F., and Jones, L. S. (1986). *Comprehensive Classroom Management: Creating Positive Learning Environments.* Boston: Allyn and Bacon.

Karweit, N. (1989). Time and learning: A review. In R. E. Slaving (Ed.), *School and classroom organization.* Hillsdale, NJ: Lawrence Erlbaum Associates.

Kidder, T. (1989). *Among schoolchildren.* Boston: Houghton Mifflin.

Kounin, J. (1970). *Discipline and group management in classrooms.* New York: Holt, Rinehart and Winston.

Leinhardt, G., and Greeno, J. G. (1986). The cognitive skill of teaching. *Journal of Educational Psychology, 78*(2), 75–95.

Lowe, R., and Gervais, R. (1988). Increasing instructional time in today's classroom. *NASSP Bulletin,* 19–22.

National Commission on Excellence in Education (1983). *A nation at risk: The imperative for educational reform.* Washington, D.C.: Government Printing Office.

Rosenshine, B. (1980). How time is spent in elementary classrooms. In C. Denham and A. Lieberman (Eds.), *Time to learn.* Washington, D.C.: U.S. Department of Education.

Ross, R. P. (1985). Elementary school activity segments and the transitions between them: Responsibilities of teachers and student teachers. Unpublished doctoral dissertation, University of Kansas.

Schmidt, W. H., and Buchmann, M. (1983). Six teachers' beliefs and attitudes and their curricular time allocations. *The Elementary School Journal, 84*(2), 162–171.

Shalaway, L. (1989). *Learning to teach . . . not just for beginners.* Cleveland, OH: Instructor Books, Edgell Communications.
Walberg, H. J. (1988). Synthesis of research on time and learning. *Educational Leadership, 45*(6), 76–85.

FOR FURTHER READING

Evertson, C. M., Emmer, E. T., Clements, B. S., Sanford, J. P., and Worsham, M. E. (1994). *Classroom management for elementary teachers.*(3rd edition) Engelwood Cliffs, NJ: Prentice Hall.
Kidder, T. (1989). *Among schoolchildren.* Boston: Houghton Mifflin.
Shalaway, L. (1989). *Learning to teach . . . not just for beginners.* Cleveland, OH: Instructor Books, Edgell Communications.

PART III

MANAGING SUBSETTINGS OF THE ENVIRONMENT

Chapter Eight

Managing Seatwork

In Chapter 1 we discussed our assumption that the tasks of classroom management vary across different classroom situations. We pointed out that the classroom is not a "homogenized glob" (Kounin and Sherman, 1979), but is composed of numerous "subsettings," such as opening exercises, sharing time, reading groups, transitions, and whole class discussions. What constitutes order in each of these subsettings is likely to vary. During transitions, for example, students may be allowed to sharpen pencils, talk with friends, and use the water fountain, but these same behaviors may be prohibited during a whole group discussion or a teacher presentation.

Variations in behavioral expectations are understandable, given the fact that subsettings have different goals and pose different challenges in terms of establishing and maintaining order. To be an effective manager, you must consider the unique characteristics of your classroom's subsettings and decide how you want your students to behave in each one.

This chapter focuses on *independent seatwork,* the situation in which the majority of children work independently on tasks while the teacher is involved with an individual or with a small group. We devote an entire chapter to this subsetting because independent seatwork can be particularly difficult for beginning teachers to manage; even for experienced teachers, seatwork poses a challenging set of "built-in hazards" (Carter, 1985) that must be well understood if they are to be overcome.

To be honest, this chapter almost didn't get written. When we sat down with our four teachers to discuss their views on independent seatwork, we found heated differences of opinion. On one hand, Ken told us he used seatwork every day: "I teach both mathematics and reading in small groups. I can't see any other way to do it, especially given all the ESL [English as a Second Language] kids in my class. That means the rest of the class *has* to work on their own. If you want to individualize instruction, seatwork is inevitable." Ken thought a chapter on the topic would be "invaluable, even fascinating, for new teachers."

On the other hand, Barbara—normally so soft-spoken and gentle—was vehemently negative: "I *hate* seatwork," she told us, "and I make a point to avoid it

Ken meets with a small reading group to discuss their novel.

whenever possible. I don't know why you'd ever want to have a chapter like this in the book." Similarly, Garnetta and Viviana claimed they never used seatwork, so they couldn't really contribute to the chapter. As Garnetta asserted, "If you write a chapter like this, it won't be about us." To these three teachers, seatwork clearly meant "filling in the blanks." The term itself conjured up images of bored, passive children, sitting alone at their desks, doing repetitive, tedious worksheets.

We debated, we moralized, and we shared anecdotes about the awfulness or the usefulness of seatwork. Eventually, we came to realize that there was no fundamental difference of opinion among us, that our dissension arose from the negative connotations of the term "seatwork." We all agreed that teachers sometimes need to assign independent seatwork so they can work with an individual or a small group (although the four teachers differ considerably in the amount of time they do this). We agreed that seatwork is too often busywork, that it frequently goes on for too long, and that too many teachers use seatwork as a substitute for active teaching. And we agreed that it shouldn't be this way.

This chapter will share the ways that Ken, Barbara, Garnetta, and Viviana work to make seatwork assignments meaningful and engaging. We will also discuss the unique challenges that seatwork poses—for both teachers and students—and provide suggestions for meeting these challenges. To set the stage for this discussion, we begin by considering three questions: (1) What does research say about the amount of time students spend doing seatwork? (2) What do they generally do during this time? and (3) What are the purposes of seatwork?

SEATWORK: HOW MUCH, WHAT, AND WHY?

The amount of time elementary students spend doing seatwork has long been a cause of concern among educators. One widely cited statistic comes from the BTES (Fisher et al., 1978), which found that seatwork sometimes constitutes as much as *70 percent of instructional time.* Research on mathematics instruction in the United States, Japan, and Taiwan provides an interesting cross-cultural perspective on independent seatwork. Stigler, Lee, and Stevenson (1987) found that first- and fifth-grade children in the United States typically spent *51 percent of their mathematics time working alone,* compared with 9 percent in Taiwan and 26 percent in Japan. Furthermore, American children spent only *46 percent of their class time in activities led by the teacher;* in Taiwan and Japan, the comparable figures were 90 percent and 74 percent. With some dismay, the investigators conclude that classes in the United States "were organized so that American children were frequently left to work alone at their seats on material in mathematics that they apparently did not understand well. . . ." (p. 70).

Figures like these prompted Linda Anderson (1985) to ask, "What are students doing when they do all that seatwork?" The answer is that in many classrooms, seatwork time is spent completing workbook pages and dittoed worksheets. Indeed, it has been estimated (Anderson, Hiebert, Scott, and Wilkinson, 1984) that in the course of a school year, an elementary child might complete a thousand workbook pages and skill sheets in reading alone! The vast majority of worksheets focus on discrete skills that students are to practice. A typical first-grade reading worksheet, for example, might ask a child to circle all the pictures that begin with a particular consonant. In mathematics, a first-grade worksheet might have students do basic addition problems printed inside balloons and then color the balloons according to a key (e.g., color the balloon red if the sum is 6; color the balloon blue if the sum is 8).

Why do American children engage in so much seatwork? What purpose does it serve? The answer to these questions depends on whether we look at seatwork from an instructional perspective or a managerial perspective (Anderson, 1985; Anderson, Brubaker, Alleman-Brooks, and Duffy, 1985). From an *instructional perspective,* the purpose of seatwork is to give students an opportunity to practice skills, synthesize and apply new knowledge, and develop independent work habits (such as learning to pace themselves and to check their work). Seatwork can also serve as a diagnostic tool for the teacher, providing a check on students' understanding (Chilcoat, 1990). From a *managerial perspective,* the purpose of seatwork is to keep students involved for a predictable period of time in quiet tasks that do not require close teacher supervision. As Ken pointed out, this way of organizing the class enables teachers to work with individuals and small groups and—theoretically at least— to tailor instruction to students' diverse needs. In other words, seatwork helps teachers deal with the heterogeneity of their classrooms.

THE CHALLENGES FOR TEACHERS

Seatwork poses unique managerial and instructional problems for the teacher. (These are summarized in Table 8-1.) First, it's difficult to keep track of what the rest of the class is doing when you are working with a small group. Careful monitoring requires the ability to "overlap" (Kounin, 1970)—to deal with simultaneous situations without becoming so immersed in one that you ignore the other. Overlapping can be a challenge for even the most experienced teachers. Ken honestly admits that he's been concerned about this for years:

> I've had people observe my classes to determine if students doing seatwork are really working. They generally say that the kids are on-task and that the talk I hear centers on work. But if you're working with a small group on the other side of the room, and kids are encouraged to help each other, how can you ever really be certain?

Second, although the managerial purpose of seatwork is to keep students engaged, it is easy for them to lose interest and become uninvolved, especially if the seatwork period is long. As we mentioned in the last chapter, seatwork requires students to pace themselves through assignments. Since there are no external signals (such as teachers' questions) to push students along (Gump, 1982), children may begin to doodle, pass notes, comb their hair, and sharpen pencils—until the teacher reminds students to get back to work. In fact, research has shown that engagement in seatwork often follows a predictable cycle (deVoss, 1979): Students begin their assignments; attention wanes; the noise level increases; the teacher intervenes; the children return to the assignment. This cycle can repeat several times, until a final spurt when students rush to complete their tasks before seatwork time is over.

A third problem that faces teachers is the fact that students work at different paces. They may *begin* seatwork at the same time, but they never *finish* at the same

TABLE 8-1
THE CHALLENGES OF SEATWORK

For the Teacher	For the Student
1. Keeping track of what the rest of the class is doing	1. Completing assigned work on their own
2. Keeping students on task	2. Understanding how and when to obtain the teacher's help
3. Dealing with the varying paces at which students work ("ragged" endings)	3. Understanding the norms for assisting peers
4. Selecting or creating seatwork that is clear and meaningful	4. Learning how to be effective in obtaining help from peers
5. Matching seatwork to students' varying levels of achievement	
6. Collecting, correcting, recording, and returning seatwork assignments	

time. Viviana observes that "it's common for some students to be on the second problem, while others are on number ten." Garnetta tells us that "Marie finishes everything in a minute—and if she doesn't have anything to do, she'll create havoc." Ken contrasts Dana and Jessica:

> Dana races to get everything done, and then she lords it over the others who are still working. Jessica is always ready to cry because she's the slowest; even if you gave her ten times as much time as everybody else, she still wouldn't finish.

You need to plan carefully in order to deal with ragged endings like these. On one hand, you need to plan activities for the Maries and Danas who complete their work earlier than you expected; if they must sit and wait with nothing to do, they'll inevitably distract students who are still working. On the other hand, you need to decide what to do about students like Jessica, who simply cannot complete assignments in the allotted time. Will you have them stay in at recess to complete their work? Will you provide an opportunity later in the day? May they do it for homework? And what will you do about students who are *capable* of finishing work in the allotted time, but do not?

A fourth challenge for teachers is to select or create seatwork that is clear and meaningful. Unfortunately, research indicates that too many of the worksheets assigned to students are confusing, meaningless, and unrelated to the rest of the reading and math program. For example, an analysis of reading workbooks, conducted by the National Academy of Education's Commission on Reading, concluded that many workbook exercises drill students on skills that have little value in learning to read. Consider the following task, cited in the Commission's report, *Becoming a Nation of Readers* (Anderson, Hiebert, Scott, and Wilkinson, 1985):

> Read each sentence. Decide which consonant letter is used the most. Underline it each time.
>
> 1 My most important toy is a toy train.
> 2 Nancy, who lives in the next house, has nine cats.
> 3 Will you bring your box of marbles to the party?

As the report's authors point out, if children can already read the sentences, it is unlikely that their reading ability will be improved by asking them to underline consonants. On the other hand, if they *cannot* read the sentences, it is difficult to see how underlining consonants will help.

A fifth challenge for teachers is to ensure that seatwork is matched to students' varying levels of achievement. The BTES has demonstrated that independent work should be performed at *a 95 percent success rate*. But the limited research on seatwork indicates that some children, particularly low achievers, may be unable to perform at this level. Linda Anderson and her colleagues (Anderson, Brubaker, Alleman-Brooks, and Duffy, 1985) observed in six first-grade classrooms of an urban school district. In each class they observed four target students (two high- and two low-achievers). They also talked with students about what they were doing and why. They found that children were often unable to complete successfully the tasks they were given:

Randy (Student 8) could not read all of the words used in the standard board assignment, which involved copying sentences with blanks and selecting a word from a list of options. Every time observers noted him doing this type of assignment, he became "stuck" (his word) because he could not decode the key words to make the choice and proceed.

Beth (Student 9) could only read about a third of the key words in a *Weekly Reader* article that students read in order to answer questions that they copied from the board. She could not read all of the questions either.

On a ditto with nine pictures of seasonal activities, Sean (Student 1) was to cut out and paste on the name of the season that matched the picture. After he quickly completed the assignment, the observer questioned him about it. He had matched only two out of eight correctly, he could not read any of the seasons' names, and he was not sure in what season one sledded, flew a kite, went camping in a tent, or went swimming outdoors.

Aaron (Student 13) was to compose sentences with new vocabulary words listed on the board. He could not read some of the words, he could not spell most of the words he wanted to write, and he soon bogged down and stopped attending to the task. (p. 130)

Finally, a sixth challenge is to collect, correct, record, and return all the paperwork assigned as seatwork—or to use activities that rely less on workbooks and skill sheets. We once observed second graders complete eight language arts worksheets during an hour-and-a-half of seatwork time. Since there were 27 students in this class, a quick calculation told us that this teacher would have *216* worksheets to grade that evening—in this one content area alone! This much paperwork can be unbearably tedious for both teachers and students, and we had to wonder about the educational value of all these worksheets. Ken also thinks about the issue of paperwork from an *environmental* point of view: "It's easy to use reams of paper, and if the work isn't really necessary—if it's really just busywork and you end up throwing a lot of it out—then you feel terribly guilty."

THE CHALLENGES FOR STUDENTS

We sometimes get so caught up in the problems that seatwork poses for *teachers* that we overlook the problems for *students*. In this section of the chapter, we consider four of the special challenges that students must confront when doing independent seatwork. (See Table 8-1.)

First, since the teacher is generally unavailable, students have to complete assigned work on their own. This statement may seem obvious, but it has several not-so-obvious implications. In order to complete assignments, students must maintain an internal push even when tasks are boring and personally irrelevant. They must remain free from distraction amid the crowded social environment of the classroom. They must decipher directions that are sometimes unclear. They must monitor their comprehension and recognize when they understand and when they do not.

The study by Anderson, Brubaker, Alleman-Brooks, and Duffy (1985) reveals that children often develop elaborate strategies that allow them to finish their work

CALVIN AND HOBBES   **By BILL WATTERSON**

FIGURE 8-1
Calvin's response to seatwork that is too difficult for him (Calvin and Hobbes © *Watterson. Dist. by Universal Press Syndicate. Reprinted with permission. All rights reserved.*)

even when they don't understand it. (Figure 8-1 depicts Calvin's rather special strategy.) For example, they may mark answers by matching the length of the word to the length of the blank, use pictures as cues for the correct answers, or simply ask others for answers.

> Randy (Student 8) could not read some of the words on the board assignment. Even when he did read some, he tried to decide on a word to go in the blank as soon as he came to the blank in the sentence, even if it was the second or third word. That is, he did not read the entire sentence to provide a context for the choice. When he did not figure out the answer immediately, he asked another child for the answer. In this manner, he often received most of the answers from others and completed this assignment without learning to read the new vocabulary words (ostensibly the purpose of the task).

> Beth (Student 9), unable to read enough of the *Weekly Reader* articles necessary to answer the questions, simply copied the questions and wrote answers that seemed logical to her, without consulting the articles. In the one instance when she did look, she searched for a number word to answer "How many legs does a grasshopper have?" She came to the phrase "five eyes" in the article and copied the number five. (pp. 131–132)

Students like Randy and Beth define success in terms of putting down an answer and finishing the assignment, even if the work makes no sense to them. As Richard, one of the target students gleefully commented, "I don't know what it means, but I did it" (p. 132).

A second challenge that seatwork poses for children is understanding how and when to obtain the teacher's help. Since the teacher is generally interacting with an individual or with a small group, gaining the teacher's attention is a lot like trying to get the attention of a store clerk who is busy with another customer (Cazden, 1988). Students must learn the appropriate ways to obtain assistance: Do they simply raise their hands and hope the teacher notices? May they call the teacher's name? Are they allowed to get out of their seats and walk over to the teacher? Must they wait until the teacher is finished with a particular group before asking their question? Unless procedures for obtaining the teacher's help are explicit, students who encounter problems with their work may become frustrated, unengaged, and disruptive.

In addition to learning the acceptable ways to obtain the teacher's help, students must meet a third challenge—understanding the norms for assisting peers. In some classes, teachers encourage students to work collaboratively, while in other classes giving or receiving help is tantamount to cheating (Rizzo, 1989). This latter situation can present a real dilemma for students. On one hand is their need to follow the teacher's directions—and to stay out of trouble. On the other hand is their need to complete the assignment successfully and to assist friends who are having difficulty (Bloome and Theodorou, 1988).

Finally, a fourth challenge for students is learning how to be effective in obtaining help from peers. It is important to recognize that even in situations where helping peers is permitted or encouraged, not all students are able to gain assistance. For example, students who are low in social status may be ignored or actually rejected when they seek help. A study conducted by Elizabeth Cohen (1984) illustrates this phenomenon. Cohen observed children in grades two through four working at learning centers. Students were told they had the right to ask for help and that they also had the duty to assist anyone who asked for help. Cohen found that children's social status was positively related to amount of peer interaction. Moreover, the more children talked and worked together, the more they learned from the curriculum. She concludes: "Those children with high social status have more access to peer interaction that, in turn, assists their learning. In other words, the rich get richer" (p. 184).

Children's ability to obtain peer assistance also depends on their ability to be "effective speakers." Research by Louise Wilkinson and her colleagues (Wilkinson and Calculator, 1982) indicates that students are more likely to get appropriate responses from their peers if their requests are *direct,* made to a specific *designated listener,* and perceived as *sincere* (i.e., the listener believes that the speaker really wants the information and does not already know the answer). Furthermore, effective speakers are flexible and persistent: if initially unsuccessful in obtaining help, they can *revise* and repeat their request.

These characteristics are illustrated in the following example (Wilkinson and Calculator, 1982, p. 97). Three first-grade students, Amy, Joe, and Dave, have been instructed to help each other on their reading work. In this excerpt, Amy first turns to Joe for assistance. When he refuses, she turns to Dave. Dave hesitates at first, but Amy persists, and he eventually provides the answer:

AMY: Ok, what, what's that word?
JOE: Don't ask me.
AMY: I'll ask him. What's that word [to Dave]?
JOE: Dave, do you know what we should write, like here?
AMY: Right here. [Several seconds elapse.]
        I want you to look at my paper. [Several seconds elapse.]
        Listen to this.
        I've got these words.
        I keep gettin mixed up, Dave.
        Dave, I keep gettin
DAVE: R the, the [The words requested by Amy are provided by Dave.]

In this very brief example, we can see why Amy is an "effective speaker." She directly frames her requests for help ("What's that word?" "I want you to look at my paper."); she requests help from a specific person (Dave); and she is obviously persistent. Unfortunately, not all children are so successful as Amy. In order to ensure that everyone benefits from working with peers, you will need to observe children's patterns of interaction and provide special assistance for those who are less effective speakers.

MINIMIZING THE HAZARDS

The research on seatwork sheds light on the special challenges or "hazards" associated with this particular subsetting of the classroom. How can you avoid—or at least minimize—these hazards? In this section of the chapter, we propose six guidelines derived from both the research on seatwork and the collected wisdom of our four teachers.

Check Worksheets for Clarity, Meaningfulness, and Appropriateness

As we have discussed, research suggests that students spend too much time doing seatwork that is neither clear, meaningful, nor appropriately matched to their achievement levels. Let's consider a few additional examples (adapted from Osborn, 1981). The worksheet in Figure 8-2 asks students to identify each picture and then circle the short vowel sound that is heard in the middle of each word. Possibilities for misidentifying a picture and therefore "making a mistake" are numerous: plane for jet; mice for rats; pan for pot; sheep for lamb; light for bulb; time for clock; bug for ant; jeep or truck for van. Obviously, successful completion of this task depends on a child's ability to identify the picture, and poor performance does not truly indicate if a child has difficulty hearing short vowel sounds.

Another example of a worksheet that may cause students problems appears in Figure 8-3. Here, the directions seem unnecessarily long and confusing. "Read the sentences. Fill in each blank with one of the words printed below" is shorter and probably easier for poor readers to understand. Moreover, children must realize that "box 1" refers to the space between the horizontal lines and understand that the "second sentence" refers to the second sentence in each space, not the sentence that appears after the numeral two. Although many students become sophisticated interpreters of workbook pages, those who are having difficulty with reading may find the page confusing. (For additional examples, see Osborn, 1984.)

In order to avoid assigning seatwork tasks like these, you must carefully evaluate commercially prepared workbook pages and dittoed worksheets. During one visit to Barbara's classroom, we saw her assign some dictionary skill sheets to her students. Later, we discussed the assignment, and Barbara told us what she thought about when she selected and screened the pages:

> I wanted to provide students with work they could do without me, so I could work with individuals who needed help on the ads for their inventions [a special language arts/science project they were working on]. First, I looked at whether the skills on these pages

FIGURE 8-2
Possibilities for making mistakes on this worksheet are numerous

meshed with the objectives of the fourth-grade curriculum. Then I made sure that the material had been previously presented by the librarian or by me, so that the pages would be practice and reinforcement—not instruction. We've worked on dictionary skills before—at the library, in spelling—so there was nothing new in these workbook pages. Then I checked the format to make sure it was familiar and understandable, and I checked that the directions were clear. If the pages had been confusing, that would have defeated the whole purpose.

Jean Osborn (1981) from the Center for the Study of Reading (University of Illinois at Urbana-Champaign) has developed a set of "Guidelines for Workbook

Read the first sentence in box 1. Use the sounds the letters stand for and the sense of the other words in the sentence to figure out what the word in bold print is. Then complete the second sentence by choosing one of the three words printed underneath. Print the word you choose in the blank. Finally, do what the third sentence tells you to do. Do the other boxes the same way.

1.   The boy **tripped** on the stairs.

      To **trip** means to _____.

            fall   step   hurt

      Put a T on the one who tripped.

2.   The girl **sipped** her soda.

      To **sip** means to _____.

            spill   drink   like

      Put an S on the one who is sipping.

3.   The boy **ripped** the page in the book.

      To **rip** means to _____.

            tear   read   fold

      Put an R on the page that is ripped.

4.   The dog **nipped** the postman.

      To **nip** means to _____.

            lick   chase   bite

      Put an N on the one who is nipped.

FIGURE 8-3
This worksheet may also cause students unnecessary problems

Tasks" that may be useful in determining whether a worksheet is suitable for your students. Some of these guidelines appear in Figure 8-4.

Present Seatwork Assignments Clearly

Once assignments have been selected or created, it is important to explain them clearly before sending children off to work. Unfortunately, research indicates that this does not always occur. The study by Emmer, Evertson, and Anderson (1980), for

---

1 Workbook tasks should be relevant to the instruction that is going on in the rest of the unit or lesson.

2 Some portion of workbook tasks should provide for a systematic and cumulative review of what has already been taught.

3 Instructions to students should be clear, unambiguous, and easy to follow; brevity is a virtue.

4 The layout of pages should combine attractiveness with utility.

5 Workbook tasks should contain enough content so that there is a chance a student doing the task will *learn* something and not simply be *exposed* to something.

6 At least some workbook tasks should be fun and have an obvious payoff to them.

7 Student response modes should be the closest possible to reading and writing.

8 Workbooks should contain a finite number of task types and forms.

9 The art that appears on workbook pages must be consistent with the prose of the task.

10 When appropriate, tasks should be accompanied by brief explanations of purpose for both teachers and students.

FIGURE 8-4
Guidelines for Workbook Tasks
(Adapted from J. Osborn, 1984)

example, indicated that less effective managers often gave unclear directions. They stated instructions vaguely and did not check to see whether the children understood the tasks. Not surprisingly, this resulted in off-task behavior, considerable talk as children tried to figure out what to do, and frequent interruptions of the teacher.

Furthermore, Linda Anderson's (1985) research on seatwork revealed that even when teachers provided introductory explanations, they rarely focused on the *purpose* of the seatwork or the *strategies* to be used. Instead, they emphasized procedural directions. Anderson recommends that teachers explain *why* students are doing what they're doing, describe the *strategies* to be used, and do a few *examples.* Indeed, studies of effective instruction (Rosenshine, 1980) demonstrate that students make fewer errors on seatwork when teachers provide "guided practice" before allowing students to work independently. As Viviana comments, "If I can catch students making a mistake on the first problem, I can prevent them from making that mistake all the way through the assignment!"

During one visit to Garnetta's classroom, we watched her introduce a letter-writing activity that was to be done as independent seatwork. She began by posing a hypothetical situation: James (a boy in the class) had a birthday party and invited the whole class. Everyone gave him presents. (The class enthusiastically discussed the various presents they could give him.) She then asked: "What could James do to thank us?" As various students suggested ways James could thank the class, Garnetta wrote the responses on the board: handshake; hug; send note; call and thank; give us something. Garnetta directed everyone to look at the list, while she continued:

Last week, we had a visitor, Miss Kinsey, who came and brought us all ice cream. I think we should thank her in some way. Think about the things we just came up with and let's decide what to do for Miss Kinsey. Can we hug her? ["No-o-o."] Can we shake her hand? ["No-o-o."] Can we write her a note? ["Yes."] Can we give her something? ["Yes."] Yes, we can send her notes, and we can send her pictures of us eating the ice cream.

After the students enthusiastically recalled the ice cream (vanilla with chocolate-covered almonds), Garnetta reviewed with the class the format for writing letters.

GARNETTA: Okay, what's the first thing that goes on our letter?
STUDENT: The heading.
GARNETTA: What goes in the heading? Edwin?
EDWIN: Dear. . . .
GARNETTA: No, that's in the greeting. [Pauses. No one volunteers.] I'll give you a hint. [She writes the number 35 on the board.]
STUDENT: The address!
GARNETTA: Good. [She writes the school's address on the board.] What's next? Something really important comes next.
STUDENT: The date!
GARNETTA: Yes. [She writes the date.] Okay, we've got the heading now. What comes next?
STUDENT: The greeting.

In this manner, Garnetta continued to review the format for letters. She left the model format on the chalkboard so that students could refer to it as they wrote their letters. She then instructed students that their letters had to contain at least five sentences (*not* five lines) and explained that the letter was to be written *independently*. She explained what to do if they were not sure how to spell a word. She answered questions the students had and told them that after they had finished their first draft, they should have another student check it. Then they were to write the final letter and draw the picture they would send. She showed them the paper to use for their final copies and put out paper and markers for their pictures.

There is an interesting postscript to this episode. About 15 minutes into the letter writing, a student went to Garnetta to show her his letter. She quickly scanned the page. Then she threw her hands up, gave a rueful laugh, and held a quiet but intense conference with him. He got a clean sheet of paper and returned to his desk to start again.

We were curious. The directions had been so clear. What could have possibly gone wrong? During a free moment, Garnetta came over and told us what had happened. Instead of a thank-you note to Ms. Kinsey, the boy had written a letter to a substitute who had been there the week before, apologizing for his poor behavior! We learned a good lesson: Even the most clear and thorough directions don't ensure that everyone will carry out the assignment as you intended!

Interestingly, a similar situation occurred a few days later, when we watched Ken explain a writing assignment that students were to do while he worked with small reading groups:

This assignment is going to be a challenge, so listen carefully. Instead of the usual book report, you're going to do something different. [He draws three intersecting circles on the chalkboard.] I want you to write about *three different books of your choice.* The first circle here represents a book I've read out loud to the class. What's one book I've read? [He calls on a student who responds.] Good. What's another? [He continues calling on students until about eight books have been named.] The next circle is a book you've read in your reading group. [He notices that Charles has his hand up.] Okay, Charles, you look like you can tell me *all* the books you've read in reading group. Go ahead. [Charles names six books.] Good for you. [He continues to call on students from various reading groups who recite the titles of five or six books.] Okay, so everyone's got about six books from reading group to choose from. Now this last circle is for any book you've read on your own. I'd suggest the most recent.

Now, take out the worksheet I gave you for evaluating pieces of literature. [This is a page that lists various "areas of criticism and analysis"—e.g., adventure, imagination, humor, emotion, illustrations, mystery and suspense, characters, pace, theme.] Your book report is going to be about one-and-one-half pages, so you obviously can't hit all these items. I want you to pick *one* of these categories and write a book report that compares the three books on this one category.

Let's practice this now and see how to think about it. Let's take one book I read to the class, say *Johnny/Bingo,* and for the reading group book, let's choose *The House of Dies Drear.* [He writes those names in two of the circles.] Okay, somebody suggest a topic for comparison. [Girl responds that both books have adventure.] Good. What would you say about the adventure in each book? [Boy describes some adventurous episode in each book.] Excellent. You guys are ready to become literary critics. Okay, let's change this circle to *The Trail of Anna Cottman.* What topic from this sheet would you use now? [Boy volunteers: Theme—good versus bad.] Good! How would you discuss the theme of good versus bad? Give me an example from each book. [Students volunteer examples.] All right. In your book report, you would need to write examples of this theme from each book. If you just say "there's the theme of good versus bad in each book," I won't really see it, but if you explain that in *Anna Cottman,* Anna was fighting the Yellow Lord, and in *Johnny/Bingo,* Johnny and Bingo were fighting the bank robbers, then I can understand what you mean. [The conversation continues with more examples of categories on which to compare the books they select.]

Okay, we've got seven minutes before gym. Jeff, give everyone a white sheet of paper. Start thinking of the three books you're going to choose. I want the list of the three books before we go to gym. Remember, I'm expecting your report to be about one-and-one-half pages. My goal here is not for you to tell me about *one* book, but to *compare three books.*

Just like Garnetta's instructions for the letter-writing activity, Ken's instructions were clear and thorough. He had explained what students were to do, suggested a strategy for beginning (i.e., select the three books, choose a category), and had modeled how to think about the comparisons. Yet a few minutes after Ken finished giving directions, a student raised her hand and said she was finished with her report. Incredulously, Ken went over to see what she had written. She had drawn the three circles and simply filled in the names of three books. She thought she was done. Once again we were reminded that although clear directions are necessary, they are not a surefire guarantee that students will know what to do!

Monitor Behavior and Comprehension

In Chapter 7 we discussed the fact that engagement rate during independent seat-work is often lower than engagement rate during teacher-directed activities. When children have to work on their own, without close teacher supervision and interaction, it's not uncommon for them to become distracted and lose the momentum needed to complete their assignments. For this reason, it is particularly important for you to monitor students' behavior.

In the following examples, we see the way Barbara and Ken are able to "over-lap" (Kounin, 1970)—to monitor the behavior of students doing seatwork, while continuing to work with an individual or a small group. As if they had "eyes in the back of their heads," both teachers manage to deal with simultaneous situations:

> Barbara is working at her desk with two children. She glances over at two girls who are whispering. "Sarah, are you helping Jessica?" [The girl says no.] "Then you're not to be talking." She asks the two children at her desk to check their papers for punctuation errors. While they are focused on their papers, she again scans the room and sees another person talking. "Louis, do you need help?" He shakes his head no and stops talking.

> Ken is working with a small reading group. He calls on a girl to read the question she has prepared. While the other students are answering her question, Ken scans the room. He silently signals a boy to come over and quietly tells him to leave his neighbor alone. The boy returns to his seat and begins to work. A few minutes later, Ken calls another boy's name and motions him over. He directs him to collect his materials and go work alone at a separate desk.

In addition to monitoring behavior, it's essential to monitor students' *understanding of their assignments.* In Chapter 7, we contrasted *engaged time* with *academic learning time*—the proportion of engaged time in which students are performing academic tasks with a high degree of success. As we pointed out, academic learning time is the best predictor of achievement. Clearly, it's not enough for students to remain busy and on-task. They must also understand what they are supposed to do and carry out their tasks successfully.

Monitoring comprehension can be particularly difficult when you're also involved with a small group of students. One hint is to spend the first five minutes of seatwork circulating throughout the room. Once you've checked that students understand what to do, you can convene your first small group. Evertson, Emmer, Clements, Sanford, and Worsham (1989) suggest that teachers circulate in the time between small group sessions, checking on students' progress and helping with problems.

> Garnetta has explained a reading/writing assignment that the class will carry out in pairs while she meets with individuals. Before she sits down, she circulates throughout the room. She notices Jason signaling another boy. "Jason, what's the problem?" She moves over to Jason and asks him if he has started the assignment. He reads orally to her and they quietly discuss what he is supposed to do. Garnetta moves to the small round table to work with a few children who need special help. When she is finished, she again moves around the room. As she approaches one cluster of children, a girl calls for her: "Ms. Chain, tell him what to do. He says he don't know what to do." Garnetta responds, "*You* tell him. He's your partner. And I'll listen." The girl explains the assignment. She asks: "Get

that?" The boy shakes his head no. The girl tells Garnetta, "He says he don't get what I'm saying!" "Okay, let's see if I can help." Garnetta explains again what the partners are supposed to do. She then continues to circulate before moving back to the small table.

Standing at the front of the room, Barbara gives instructions for a writing assignment and announces that she will be working with individuals at her desk. Slowly, she makes her way to her desk, stopping at various students' desks to see that they have begun to work. At Larry's desk, she crouches down: "You need to begin writing. Put these things away [the remnants from an earlier snack and a game he brought from home]. Now, what memory are you going to write about? [She discusses various ideas for the writing assignment.] Yes, those would be good memories to write about. Okay, you've got a bunch of ideas. Now get started." She circulates some more and then sits down at her desk and begins to confer with two students who need help on a project. When she finishes with them, she walks over to a student who had been whispering. Barbara instructs her to turn her desk around so she is not facing other students. She checks the girl's work and quietly discusses her progress on the assignment. She does another loop through the room, glancing at students' papers, answering questions, and providing assistance. Then she returns to her desk, where another child is waiting to discuss her work.

Watching Garnetta and Barbara monitor seatwork, we were struck by the very quiet, discreet way they interacted with each child. This kind of discretion appears to be important for students' achievement. Helmke and Schrader (1988) found that contact with individual students during seatwork was positively related to achievement only if it was private and discreet. They speculate on two reasons for this finding. First, audible comments may disturb everyone's concentration and progress; second, loud, public comments may be embarrassing and may have a negative effect on students' motivation or willingness to ask questions.

Teach Children What to Do If They Get Stuck

When children encounter problems with seatwork assignments, they need to know what to do. In particular, students need to understand how and when they can obtain your help. Effective managers often establish the rule that they cannot be interrupted during their time with small groups; however, they make it clear that they will be available for help in between group meetings. They tell students to skip tasks that are causing problems and to work on something else in the meantime.

Some teachers devise special systems that students can use to indicate their need for assistance. They may give children a "help" sign or a small red flag to keep on top of their desks. A child who needs help turns the help sign up or raises the red flag. In some classroom, students sign up for help on the chalkboard or on a clipboard (Evertson, Emmer, Clements, Sanford, and Worsham, 1989).

Systems like these allow you to scan the room periodically to determine who needs assistance and to provide help at an appropriate time. This practice is preferable to allowing children to come up to your desk or small group meeting area whenever they need help. We've seen classrooms where long lines of children were allowed to form by the teacher's desk. Not only is this distracting to other students, it's also a waste of time for the children waiting in line.

In addition to teaching children the procedures for obtaining the teacher's help, you need to make it clear whether or not students can ask peers for assistance. Most of the time, our four teachers not only allow peer assistance, they actively instruct students to help one another. Garnetta tells us:

> I believe that students learn from other students. Sometimes students understand the concept *better* when other students are teaching it. I try to have students work together as much as possible in order to avoid having students sitting there not knowing what to do.

In order to promote peer assistance, Barbara teaches her students, "Ask three, then me." Explicit encouragement like this may be necessary, since students are often reluctant to ask peers for help. A study of third-, fifth- and seventh-graders' attitudes toward help seeking (Newman and Schwager, 1993) sheds light on this reluctance: Across all grade levels, students saw the teacher as not only more likely to facilitate learning, but also less likely to think they were "dumb" for asking questions.

It's also important to note that all of the teachers work hard to explain what "helping" really means. They take pains to explain to students that simply providing the answer is not helping, and they stress the futility of copying (a practice that often irritates more diligent students, as Figure 8-5 illustrates). As Barbara tells us:

> In the beginning of the year we talk a lot about what is *helping* and what is *doing it for the other person.* We role play different situations. For example, we look at a page in the math book, and I pretend I don't know how to do a problem. I ask someone for help. Then I ask the class, "Was that good help? Was that *explaining* or was that doing the work *for* me?"

Although all our teachers firmly believe in the value of peer assistance, there are also times when they do *not* allow students to help one another. In these situations, they are careful to explain that the ground rules are different:

> It is almost the end of the school year. Barbara is explaining that students will be writing an essay that will go into their writing folders. These will then be given to the fifth-

FIGURE 8-5
Sometimes students don't like to help classmates who haven't tried to do the assignment on their own. (Calvin and Hobbes © *Watterson. Dist. by Universal Press Syndicate. Reprinted with permission. All rights reserved.*)

CALVIN AND HOBBES   **By BILL WATTERSON**

grade teachers so they can see the progress that students made in fourth grade. Barbara emphasizes the fact that students must work alone: "The only thing that is different about today's assignment is that it is to be done *independently*. What does independently mean?" [Boy responds, "Alone."] "Yes. You may not help one another. You may not have anyone edit or proofread your essay. I don't want to hear any peer conferencing today. This is to be a *silent* activity."

Teach What to Do If You're Done

Since students finish seatwork at varying times, they need to know what to do when they're done. Activities should be provided that are educational, but enjoyable. If students learn that they'll only be given more work to do, there's a danger that they'll learn to dawdle. Jones and Jones (1986) report the following anecdote:

> During a visit to a second-grade classroom, a student in one of our courses reported observing a child who was spending most of his time staring out the window or doodling on his paper. The observer finally approached the child and asked if she could be of any assistance. Much to her surprise, the child indicated that he understood the work. When asked why he was staring out the window rather than working on his assignment, the boy pointed to a girl several rows away and said, "See her? She does all her work real fast and when she's done she just gets more work." (p. 234)

In the classrooms of our four teachers, these are numerous activities for students who finish before others. They can work on a computer; they can do free reading, extra-credit assignments, or journal writing; they can tackle brainteasers and puzzles; they can work with manipulative materials, such as tangrams (seven plastic shapes that form a square when positioned properly) or pattern blocks. Finishing early also means that students can resume work on long-term, ongoing projects, such as social studies reports, science experiments, or book reviews.

Find Alternatives to Workbook Pages

Reliance on commercially prepared workbooks can lead to boredom and off-task behavior. In *Becoming a Nation of Readers,* Richard Anderson and his colleagues (Anderson, Hiebert, Scott, and Wilkinson, 1985) recommend that children spend less time completing workbooks and skill sheets:

> Workbook and skill sheet activities consume a large proportion of the time allocated to reading instruction in most American classrooms, despite the fact that there is little evidence that these activities are related to reading achievement. Workbook and skill sheet activities should be pared to the minimum that actually provide worthwhile practice in aspects of reading. (p.119)

Our four teachers provide students with innumerable alternatives to "filling in the blank." Viviana seems to speak for them all when she states:

> I rarely give my children worksheets to fill out. I really dislike them. Most of them don't make the children *think*. They're not challenging; they become tedious. Some of those skill sheets make children do so many problems—many more than they need. If they

can do the first five right, why give them ninety-five more? That's when children get bored and tired. I try to give my children work that will challenge them to think and to express themselves.

We asked Viviana, Ken, Barbara, and Garnetta to share some of their ideas for meaningful assignments that students can do while teachers are working with individuals or small groups. Here are some of their suggestions.

Reading   All four teachers encourage students to do silent reading, and Viviana and Garnetta also encourage children to read aloud to each other. This emphasis on reading is consistent with educational research. In fact, studies suggest that the amount of independent, silent reading children do in school is significantly related to gains in reading achievement (Anderson et al., 1984). Yet, the amount of time that children spend reading in the average classroom is small. An estimate of silent reading time in the typical primary school class is just *seven or eight minutes per day,* or less then 10 percent of the total time devoted to reading. By the middle grades, silent reading time may average 15 minutes per school day (Anderson et al., 1985).

Sometimes teachers are reluctant to use reading as a seatwork activity because they are convinced their students "won't just sit there and read!" (Cunningham, 1991). One fourth-grade teacher put it this way:

> I know reading is important and I know they need to do more of it but they just won't! Oh, some of them would, of course, and they'd love it but a lot of them wouldn't take it seriously. They'd read a page or two, then they'd get fidgety and start talking or cleaning out their desks. When a few started this, the others would stop reading too. They have to have something to complete and turn in and know that they are accountable for it or they just won't do it! (p. 188)

In order to avoid this problem, Cunningham suggests that teachers explain that since people learn to read better by reading, it's important to take time each day just to read. She also suggests that teachers stress that the alternative to reading is doing a worksheet (preferably a boring one). As Cunningham puts it, "Even children who do not like to read will sit and read for ten minutes when the alternative is another worksheet" (p. 290).

Writing   In addition to requiring and encouraging children to read, our four teachers create assignments that call for real writing (instead of simply filling in blanks). When Ken is teaching punctuation, for example, he has students pair up and have a conversation. They have to write it down and then punctuate it correctly. He also uses independent seatwork time to have students write reports for science, health, and social studies. And students always have writing to do in connection with the literature they are reading. Typically, students read a chapter or two in their novels, and then write questions (and answers) to ask other students during the small group meeting.

Since Ken teaches sixth grade, it's easy to see how his students can do independent writing, but these kinds of activities should go on at all grade levels. We've observed Viviana's first graders eagerly tackle writing assignments of all kinds. Sometimes Viviana gives them a set of pictures and they choose one on which to write. At other times, they "write" their favorite nursery rhymes by drawing pictures of the events in correct sequence. Viviana manages to incorporate writing in all subject areas—even mathematics. During one math lesson, for example, we watched students write "story problems." First, Viviana reviewed what a mathematics story problem was. Then she had a child create one for the class to solve. Finally, she had children work independently to create their own:

VIVIANA: I'm going to give you one second to think of a story problem. [She pauses.] Okay, Luis.

LUIS: Anita has four dolls. Her sister has three fewer dolls. How many dolls does her sister have?

VIVIANA: Good. What information is his problem giving us?

STUDENT: That Anita has four dolls.

VIVIANA: What else?

STUDENT: That her sister has three fewer.

VIVIANA: And what do we have to do?

STUDENT: Find out how many dolls her sister has.

VIVIANA: Who wants to illustrate this problem? Pedro? [He goes to the chalkboard and draws four little squares.]

VIVIANA: What do these represent?

CLASS: Ones.

VIVIANA: Now, how are you going to illustrate what the sister has? [He crosses out three of the squares.] Why did he cross them out?

STUDENT: Because fewer means less.

VIVIANA: Very good. Now, who wants to translate this illustration into numbers? Stephen? [He writes $4 - 3 = 1$ on the chalkboard.] And what does the one stand for?

STUDENT: The number of dolls that her sister has.

VIVIANA: Okay, so how will you answer the question? Andres? [Andres goes to the board and prints: "Her sister has one doll?"] It's a beautiful sentence, Andres, but is it an asking sentence or a telling sentence? [He changes the question mark to a period.] You were thinking about how story problems ask a question, right? Let's read this together, children. [They read the sentence aloud.] You know, you have become so proficient at this, I'm going to give you all a chance to make up some story problems now. I'm going to give you some paper, folded in half. On each side, write a story problem. Illustrate it with ones and tens and translate it into numbers. Then you can draw a picture to go with your problem. [The children cheer.] When you're finished, let me know and I'll check your problems while the rest are finishing. [She gives out paper. The class works quietly. Viviana meets with individuals at a small round table. As she checks children's papers, she not only looks at their mathematics, she also has them correct spelling and punctuation.]

While the students worked, we circulated through the room to see what children were writing. One boy turned to us and exclaimed, "I *love* story problems!" We asked why, and he responded, "Because I love to write!" (Figure 8-6 shows a story problem written by one of Viviana's first-grade students.)

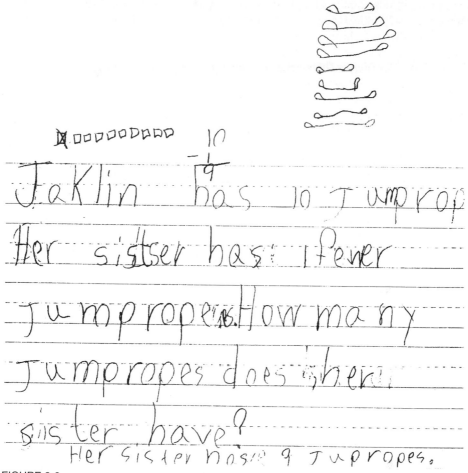

FIGURE 8-6
A story problem written by one of Viviana's first graders

In addition to content area assignments that require students to write, some teachers have students keep notebooks that they use "just for writing" on a daily basis. Teachers may specify a designated length of time for the writing (e.g., ten minutes) or a designated amount (e.g., "about a page"). In Ken's class, for example, students have private journals. To ward off students' complaints that they "don't know what to write about," Ken lists one or two suggested topics on the chalkboard every morning: "What are some things that glow?" "How would your life be different if you didn't need to sleep?" If these questions don't appeal to students, they may write on any topic they wish. Ken responds in writing in students' journals.

Some teachers we know have students brainstorm topics they know about—dogs, baseball cards, soccer—and topics they'd like to learn more about and list these ideas in their individual writing folders (e.g., "Topics I Can Write About"). This way they have ready topics at hand when it is writing time or when they have free time. Another option is to have each day designated for a different type of writing. Here is the writing schedule set up by one fifth-grade teacher (Cunningham, 1991):

Monday: Newspaper Day. *The teacher brought in his Sunday paper and read something that would be of interest to the students. After a two-minute brainstorming session, students wrote reactions to the article.*

Tuesday: Literature Connection. *The piece of literature that the teacher was reading to the class at the time was used as the springboard for writing.*

Wednesday: Social Studies/Science Connection. Students wrote about what they were learning in these content areas.

Thursday: The Real Thing. The teacher brought an object to school (a bar of soap, a rabbit, three dozen doughnuts, a boomerang) that was hidden under a blanket and unveiled with great fanfare.

Friday: "Surprise Me" Day. No topic was assigned on Friday, and students shared news with the teacher. During the week, whenever students wanted to tell him about something, he would say, "That would make a great Friday topic."

Listening   This is an often ignored aspect of language arts, but listening activities are a useful alternative to workbook pages. By providing students with books on tape, either commercial or teacher made, even less confident readers can follow along in the text and enjoy more complex books. Some teachers have more competent readers create listening tapes for other children in the class to use. Others encourage their less able readers to create book tapes for use in younger classes.

Ongoing Projects   Seatwork time can be viewed as an opportunity for students to continue work on long-term projects. In Garnetta's class, for example, students were studying a health unit on drugs. Students were responsible for mastering a particular part of the chapter in the textbook and teaching it to the rest of the class. Garnetta also encouraged them to do additional research, using encyclopedias and books from the library.

In Viviana's class, children studied "work." They drew pictures of people doing different kinds of physical work (lifting, pulling, carrying, pushing) and pasted them on cardboard so they could stand. Then they made a milk carton city, populated with their "workers." Although projects like these may begin as whole class lessons, seatwork time provides a chance for students to make progress on their own individual tasks.

Brainteasers and Puzzles   Ken often gives his students puzzles and brainteasers to solve during seatwork time. For example, when students study vocabulary words, he may give them five tasks to do for each word on the list (e.g., give an opposite; draw a picture; fit into a crossword puzzle; find out how many words you can make from the word; use in a sentence).

A particular favorite with Ken's students is a brainteaser called "Stinky Pinky" (Golick, 1987). Students must think of a rhyming pair of words that defines a nonrhyming phrase they are given. For example, an obese feline is a "fat cat," and a male who lies in the sun too long is a "tan man." Ken also challenges students to create their own "stinky pinkies" and other puzzles.

Learning Centers   Orignally found only in early childhood classes, learning centers are increasingly used in elementary classrooms as alternatives to paper-and-pencil seatwork. Centers can be simple, containing commercially produced activities in a folder, or more complex, incorporating science experiments, math problem solving, or story writing. Many teachers use centers to integrate a theme across content areas. Children are able to explore different aspects of the theme as they circulate, individually or in groups, among the learning centers. (See Table 8-2 for suggestions.)

When using centers, you need to think about how your students will move from center to center, how many children will be allowed in each center, how students will be held accountable, and what the acceptable noise level will be. It's also important to design activities that can be done by students with varying ability or to differentiate instruction in some way. At curriculum-based learning centers, for example, you can color-code activities according to different achievement levels. Students can self-select the level of difficulty or the teacher can

TABLE 8-2
SUGGESTIONS FOR LEARNING CENTERS

Science
   Simple experiments with lab sheets
   Observations over time with recording forms
   Exploring properties of objects and classifying them
Social Studies
   Recreating items used by different civilizations
   Creating charts or graphs of population trends
   Map making
Mathematics
   Math "challenges" and puzzles
   Manipulative activities
Art
   Holiday or thematic projects
   Crafts related to curriculum studies (quilting, quilling, origami, etc.)
Writing
   Class story writing (e.g., add-on stories)
   Rewrites of literature
   Writing plays or puppet shows
Computer
   Content-related programs
   Simulations
   Story writing

direct students to different colored activities (e.g., *blue:* single-digit addition; *yellow:* double-digit addition without regrouping; *red:* double-digit addition with regrouping).

A computer station can make an ideal learning center. In Ken's class, for example, computers are an integral part of the science curriculum. Students identify acid rain patterns around the world using a National Geographic Society computer network; practice navigation and rescue whales with *Voyage of the Mimi* (Bank Street College, 1985); and learn about marine environments with *A Field Trip into the Sea* (InView, 1990). According to Ken, software packages like these not only help his students learn about important science topics, they also teach students to use the computer as a research tool. There's also a social benefit: Since two to three students can work at each computer (one to work the mouse or keyboard, one to keep notes and record information, and one to help with decisions and to serve as time-keeper), they have to learn to collaborate. Ken contrasts this kind of computer use with computer-assisted-instruction (CAI):

> A lot of CAI is repetitive, fill-in-the-blank junk. It looks real nice, but there's not much academic benefit, and it doesn't promote active involvement. If a student gets stuck, there's no instruction; it just keeps repeating the question. Teachers have to be really careful about choosing software. It's possible to end up with something that's just a fancy workbook page.

Barbara also makes extensive use of the computer. In fact, the computers stay on all day so that students can work on stories and other writing assignments and make banners and cards using a printing program. In Garnetta's classroom, a favorite computer activity is "add-on stories"—two students begin a story on the computer, and then two students at a time go to the computer and add on a paragraph.

Cross-age Tutoring   This year, Ken began a program of cross-age tutoring with the primary classes in his school. Students went to a kindergarten, first-, or second-grade classroom where they tutored students in reading, writing, and social studies. They also helped the younger children do research on topics like seashells, spiders, and sharks. Each tutor kept a tutoring log in which he or she entered mini-lesson plans and the results of each day's lesson.

These are only some of the activities that can be used as alternatives to workbook pages. (Additional ideas can be found in sourcebooks listed at the end of this chapter; see "For Further Reading.") As you plan seatwork tasks, remember that even young children are capable of doing activities that are challenging and thought-provoking. We recently observed a kindergarten class, for example, where students circulated through various learning centers during seatwork time. They visited a literacy center where they listened to taped stories; they carried out scientific observations at a "cocoon center"; they discovered how many cups were in a pint by pouring water at a "liquid measurement center"; they used teddy bear counters and Pepperidge Farm™ goldfish to solve addition problems at a math center. As you can see, these "seatwork activities" don't even require students to be at their seats!

CONCLUDING THOUGHTS

In this chapter, we have tried to provide you with an understanding of the pitfalls and problems associated with independent seatwork, as well as suggestions for avoiding, or at least minimizing, these problems. We hope you will keep these in mind as you decide on the kinds of activities students will do during seatwork time, the way you will introduce seatwork assignments, and the rules and procedures you will establish to guide behavior.

The extent to which you will use independent seatwork in your classroom will depend on a number of factors—the heterogeneity of your class, the grade level you teach, district policy, the ability of your students to work without close teacher supervision, and your beliefs about the appropriateness of whole- or small-group instruction. Indeed, Viviana, Garnetta, Barbara, and Ken vary greatly in their use of independent seatwork. For example, Ken always teaches reading in small groups, since he has concluded that this practice best allows him to match students' interests with pieces of literature. The inevitable consequence is daily seatwork for those not meeting in the small group. In contrast, Barbara prefers to teach reading as a total class, selecting a piece of literature that children at varying levels of achievement can read together. Thus, she has less need to plan independent seatwork assignments for her students.

Similarly, both Garnetta and Viviana use whole group instruction for reading, a practice that is mandated by their district. Both teachers form small groups only as needed (e.g., to work on a skill with which a small number of students are having difficulty). Viviana tells us:

> I always introduce lessons to the whole group, but when I see a need I work with individuals. There are always some children who can move ahead quickly—children who swim. Others have trouble—they'll sink—and we have to rescue them. Then the teacher has to sit and work with them in a group. During those times, I'll have my children work independently on seatwork. But it's not a regular part of the day.

As you decide on the extent to which you'll use seatwork, keep in mind the trade-off that is involved. The primary advantage of seatwork is that it allows you to work with children in a small group and to tailor instruction to individual needs. The primary disadvantage is that children not in the small group must work on their own, without close teacher supervision and interaction. Fortunately, this disadvantage can be alleviated by using *groupwork*—the topic of our next chapter.

SUMMARY

If you plan to work with students individually or in small groups, you will need to use some form of independent seatwork. In this chapter we discussed some of the challenges seatwork presents to teachers and students. We also offered some suggestions for creating meaningful, appropriate assignments that students can do instead of traditional dittoes and workbook pages.

Challenges of Seatwork (for the teacher):

- Monitoring students
- Maintaining interest
- Coping with students' varying work paces
- Providing clear and meaningful assignments
- Matching seatwork to varying levels of achievement
- Handling the paperwork

Challenges of Seatwork (for the student):

- Completing work on their own
- Understanding how and when to get the teacher's help
- Understanding norms for assisting peers
- Learning how to be effective in obtaining help from peers

Strategies for Minimizing the Hazards of Seatwork

- Check workbook pages for clarity, meaningfulness, and appropriateness
- Present seatwork assignments clearly
- Monitor behavior and comprehension
- Teach children what to do if they get stuck
- Teach students what to do when they're done
- Use alternatives to traditional seatwork assignments

Alternatives to Filling-in-the Blanks

- Reading
- Writing
- Listening
- Ongoing projects
- Brainteasers and puzzles
- Learning centers
- Computer activities
- Cross-age tutoring

Think about how much time your students spend working independently, with peers, and with you. As you decide on time allocations for various kinds of groupings, remember the trade-off that is involved: seatwork allows you to work with children in small groups and to tailor instruction to individual needs, but it also means that children not in the small group must work on their own. Also keep in mind the limitations of commercially prepared seatwork, and choose seatwork assignments carefully. Find alternatives to workbook pages whenever possible. Many sources of quality seatwork are available—you don't have to create it all yourself. Seatwork does not have to mean busywork!

ACTIVITIES

1 Since we all need to use independent seatwork at some time, it's useful to explore alternatives to a ditto or workbook page. All of the following skills or concepts could be reviewed with a ditto. Select four, and for each one, think of a more active, engaging independent activity that would also provide an opportunity for review and reinforcement.

Example: 1st grade—letter formation—tracing letters in sand or salt; using finger-paints; making letters from clay

Grade Level	Skill/Concept	Seatwork Alternative
Kindergarten	The number "4"	
1st grade	Recognizing sight words	
2nd grade	Double-digit addition	
3rd grade	The sequence of events in a story	
4th grade	Using quotation marks	
5th grade	The parts of a flower	
6th grade	Geography terminology	
7th grade	French vocabulary	
8th grade	Character analysis in a short story	

2 Select a workbook page or a ditto sheet from your class or a class you are observing. Examine it, using the following questions as a guide. Suggest ways to improve the page or suggest alternative ways of reviewing the same skill or concept.

Question	Response	Suggested Improvement
Are the directions clear?		
Does the page organization facilitate students' understanding of the task?		
Does the activity reinforce the intended skill?		
Is the task meaningful?		
Are the pictures a help or a distraction?		

3 Analyze the weekly schedule of the class you are teaching or observing. Determine how much time is allocated to independent seatwork. During that seatwork period, observe three "target" students. (Try to select a high-, average-, and low-achieving student.) Note what activities each child is required to do during seatwork time. (Are the activities the same across achievement levels?) Every five minutes, record if the children are on-task or off-task. If possible, ask the children to explain what they are doing and why.

REFERENCES

Anderson, L. (1985). What are students doing when they do all that seatwork? In C. W. Fisher and D. C. Berliner (Eds.), *Perspectives on instructional time.* New York: Longman, pp. 189–202.

Anderson, L., Brubaker, N., Alleman-Brooks, J., and Duffy, G. (1985). A qualitative study of seatwork in first-grade classrooms. *Elementary School Journal, 86,* 123–140.

Anderson, R., Hiebert, E., Scott, J., and Wilkinson, I. (1985). *Becoming a nation of readers: The report of the Commission on Reading.* Washington, D.C.: National Institute of Education.

Bank Street College Project in Science and Math (1985). *Voyage of the Mimi.* New York: Holt, Rinehart & Winston.

Bloome, D., and Theodorou, E. (1988). Analyzing teacher-student and student-student discourse. In J. E. Green and J. O. Harker (Eds.), *Multiple perspective analyses of classroom discourse.* Norwood, NJ: Ablex, pp. 217–248.

Carter, K. (March-April 1985). Teacher comprehension of classroom processes: An emerging direction in classroom management research. Paper presented at the annual meeting of the American Educational Research Association, Chicago, Illinois.

Cazden, C. B. (1988). *Classroom discourse: The language of teaching and learning.* Portsmouth, NH: Heinemann.

Chilcoat, G. W. (1990). How to make seatwork more meaningful. *Middle School Journal, 21*(4), 26–28.

Cohen, E. G. (1984). Talking and working together: Status, interaction, and learning. In P. L. Peterson, L. C. Wilkinson, and M. Hallinan (Eds.), *The social context of instruction.* New York: Academic Press, pp. 171–188.

Cunningham, P. M. (1991). Making seatwork work. *Reading Horizons, 31*(4), 286–298.

deVoss, G. G. (1979). The structure of major lessons and collective student activity. *Elementary School Journal, 80,* 8–18.

Emmer, E. T., Evertson, C. M., and Anderson, L. M. (1980). Effective classroom management at the beginning of the school year. *Elementary School Journal, 80*(5), 219–231.

Evertson, C. M., Emmer, E. T., Clements, B. S., Sanford, J. P., and Worsham, M. E. (1994). *Classroom management for elementary teachers.* 3rd Edition Englewood Cliffs, NJ: Prentice Hall.

Fisher, C. W., Filby, N. N., Marliave, R. S., Cahen, L. S., Dishaw, M. M., Moore, J. E., and Berliner, D. C. (1978). *Teaching behaviors, academic learning time and student achievement. Final report of Phase III-B, Beginning Teacher Evaluation Study.* San Francisco, CA: Far West Laboratory for Educational Research and Development.

Golick, M. (1987). *Playing with words.* Markham, Ontario: Pembroke Publishers Limited.

Gump, P. V. (1982). School settings and their keeping. In D. L. Duke (Ed.), *Helping teachers manage classrooms.* Alexandria, VA: Association for Supervision and Curriculum Development.

Helmke, A., and Schrader, F. W. (1988). Successful students practice during seatwork: Efficient management and active supervision not enough. *Journal of Educational Research, 82*(2), 70–75.

InView (1990). *A field trip into the sea* (software). Pleasantville, NY: Sunburst Communications.

Jones, V. F., and Jones, L. S. (1986). *Comprehensive classroom management. Creating positive learning environments.* Boston: Allyn and Bacon.

Kounin, J. S. (1970). *Discipline and group management in classrooms.* New York: Holt, Rinehart & Winston.

Kounin, J. S., and Sherman, L. (1979). School environments as behavior settings. *Theory into Practice, 14,* 145–151.

Newman, R. S., and Schwager, M. T. (1993). Students' perceptions of the teacher and classmates in relation to reported help seeking in math class. *Elementary School Journal, 94*(1), 3–17.

Osborn, J. (1981). *The purposes, uses, and contents of workbooks and some guidelines for publishers.* Reading Education Report No. 27. Center for the Study of Reading, University of Illinois at Urbana-Campaign.

Osborn, J. (1984). The purposes, uses, and contents of workbooks and some guidelines for publishers. In R. Anderson, J. Osborn, and R. Tierney (Eds.), *Learning to read in American schools.* Hillsdale, NJ: Erlbaum, pp. 45–111.

Rizzo, T. A. (1989). *Friendship development among children in school.* Norwood, NJ: Ablex.

Rosenshine, B. (1980). How time is spent in elementary classrooms. In C. Denham and A. Lieberman (Eds.), *Time to learn.* Washington, D.C.: U.S. Department of Education.

Stigler, J. W., Lee, S., and Stevenson, H. W. (1987). Mathematics classrooms in Japan, Taiwan, and the United States. *Child Development, 58,* 1272–1285.

Wilkinson, L. C., and Calculator, S. (1982). Effective speakers: Students' use of language to request and obtain information and action in the classroom. In L. C. Wilkinson (Ed.), *Communicating in the classroom.* New York: Academic Press, pp. 85–100.

FOR FURTHER READING

Charles, L. H., and Brummett, M. R. (1988). *Connections: Linking manipulatives to mathematics.* Sunnyvale, CA: Creative Publications.

Friederwitzer, F., and Berman, B. (1986). *Math—Getting in touch: Activities with manipulatives.* New Rochelle, NY: Cuisenaire Co. of America.

Golick, M. (1987). *Playing with words.* Markham, Ontario: Pembroke Publishers Limited.

Johnson, T. D., and Louis, D. R. (1987). *Literacy through literature.* Portsmouth, NH: Heinemann.

Morrow, L. M. (1990). *Literacy development in the early years.* Englewood Cliffs, NJ: Prentice-Hall.

Routman, R. (1988). *Transitions form literature to literacy.* Portsmouth, NH: Heinemann.

Technology & Learning. Dayton, OH: Peter Li, Inc.

T.H.E. Journal (Technological Horizons in Education). Tustin, CA: T.H.E. Journal.

Wahl, M. (1988). *A mathematical mystery tour: Higher-thinking math tasks.* Tucson, AZ: Zephyr Press.

Chapter Nine _____

Managing Groupwork

Keep your eyes on your own paper.
Don't talk to your neighbor.
Pay attention to the teacher.
If you need help, raise your hand.
Do your *own* work.

For most of us, these are familiar instructions. We have heard them time and time again, spoken by teachers trying to instill the norms of the traditional classroom. (See Figure 9-1). Phrases like this are so much a part of the way we view classrooms that four-year-olds who have never even attended kindergarten use them when playing school.

As these instructions suggest, children in most classrooms work either alone or in competition. There are few opportunities for students to interact, to assist one another, or to collaborate on tasks (Gerleman, 1987; Goodlad, 1984; Graybeal & Stodolsky, 1985). We think this lack of interaction is unfortunate. Letting children work together in pairs or small groups has many advantages. We alluded to one advantage at the end of Chapter 8: If children can help one another during independent seatwork, they are less likely to "get stuck," to have to sit and wait for the teacher's assistance, and to become uninvolved and disruptive.

There are other benefits to groupwork. Working with peers on tasks can enhance students' motivation (Good and Brophy, 1991; Sharan, 1990). Groupwork also allows students to take an active role in their own learning—to ask questions, to allocate turns for speaking, to evaluate the work of others, to provide encouragement and support, to debate, and to explain—and some of these behaviors have clear academic payoffs. For example, research has consistently demonstrated that providing explanations to peers is beneficial to achievement (Swing and Peterson, 1982; Webb, 1985); in other words, the more children explain, the more they learn.

Opportunities for interaction also have social payoffs. When children work in heterogeneous groups, they can develop relationships across gender, racial, and

198

WARREN

"This class will stimulate your ideas and thoughts. And remember — no talking."

FIGURE 9-1
Students are rarely allowed to work together. (reprinted with permission)

ethnic boundaries (Manning and Lucking, 1993; Slavin, 1988). Groupwork can also help to integrate children with disabilities into the regular, mainstream classroom (Johnson & Johnson, 1980; Madden & Slavin, 1983). As our school-age population becomes increasingly diverse, fostering positive intergroup relationships grows more and more important.

Given all these benefits, why is there so little groupwork in elementary classrooms? Part of the answer has to do with the teacher's responsibility for keeping order and covering curriculum. In the crowded, complex world of the classroom, it's easier to keep order and cover curriculum when teachers do the talking, and students do the listening. Furthermore, if the school culture equates orderly classrooms with quiet classrooms, teachers may feel uncomfortable when groupwork raises the noise level. Consider this student teacher's journal entry:

> Every time I read about groupwork it sounds so great I'm ready to use it everyday. Then I attempt it in the classroom and I start having second thoughts. I love the learning that comes out of it, but I never feel in control when it is happening. The part that really upsets me is that I really do not mind if the class gets loud. It's the other teachers and the principal I worry about. There have been a few times when I was using cooperative learning and someone has come in to ask if I need any help or they will take it upon themselves to tell my class to be quiet. This really makes me angry. I feel like the only acceptable noise level is no noise at all.

Finally, groupwork has its own set of "built-in hazards" (Carter, 1985) that can make it particularly difficult for teachers to manage. In this chapter, we examine those special pitfalls. Then we discuss ways they can be minimized, drawing on the experiences of our four teachers, as well as the research and scholarly literature on groupwork. Finally, we describe four specific approaches to groupwork—STAD, Jigsaw and Jigsaw II, Group Investigation, and the structural approach to cooperative learning.

THE PITFALLS OF GROUPWORK

Let's begin by considering the recent experience of a student teacher named Tom. During an evening seminar for student teachers, Tom told us about his first attempt to use groupwork with his fourth-grade class:

> I couldn't wait to get my students into small groups. I didn't want to be like my cooperating teacher—she does all the talking and students are never allowed to work together. They seem so passive and so isolated from one another. Although she wasn't particularly enthusiastic about small group work, she gave me her blessing. I was really excited. I was sure that the kids would respond well if they were given the chance to be active and to interact.
>
> I decided to use small groups in science, since my cooperating teacher has given me the most freedom in this area. (I think she doesn't like science and doesn't think it's all that important, so she lets me do whatever I want.) I told the kids that they could choose their own groups. I figured that being allowed to work with friends would be really motivating.
>
> Well, just getting into groups was chaotic. First we had to move the desks from rows into clusters. Then there was lots of shouting and arguing about who was going to be in which group. The whole process took about ten minutes and was really noisy. My cooperating teacher was NOT pleased, and I was really upset when I saw what happened. My class is real heterogeneous—I've got blacks, whites, Hispanics, Asian-Americans. Well, the groups turned out really segregated. They also tended to be just about all boy or all girl. Even worse—I have one mainstreamed girl in my class (she's learning disabled and really hyperactive) and nobody wanted to work with her at all. I ended up *making* a group take her, and they were pretty nasty about it. And there's another kid who's real shy and quiet; I had to get him into a group too. It was really embarrassing for both of them.
>
> Finally, I got everyone settled down and they started to work on the assignment. We've been talking about seeds and plants, and each group was supposed to plan an experiment that they would actually carry out to demonstrate what plants needed in order to grow. I emphasized that they were supposed to work together and make sure everyone contributed to the plan.
>
> Well, it was a real mess. A couple of the groups worked out okay, but one group argued the whole time and never got anything written. In another group—all boys—they decided to just let the kid who was smartest in science plan the experiment. He kept coming up and complaining that no one else would do any work. And it was true. The rest just sat and fooled around the whole time. Another group had three girls and one boy. The boy immediately took charge. He dominated the whole thing; the girls just sat there and let him tell them what to do.

I had pictured everyone cooperating, helping one another, contributing ideas. But it didn't work out that way at all. And the noise—it just kept getting louder and louder. I kept turning off the lights and reminding them to use their "indoor voices." For a few minutes, they'd get quieter, but then it would get loud again. Finally, my cooperating teacher stepped in and yelled at everybody. I was really humiliated. I just couldn't control them. Right now I'm pretty turned off to using cooperative groups. I think maybe she's right. Maybe these kids just can't handle working together. Maybe I should just go back to having everyone sit and listen to me explain the lesson.

Unfortunately, Tom's story is not unusual. It illustrates all too vividly what can happen when teachers don't understand the problems associated with groupwork and don't work to prevent them from occurring. Let's take a closer look at four of these problems.

First, as Tom discovered, allowing children to form their own groups often leads to *segregation* among students in terms of gender and ethnicity. Have you ever had lunch in the cafeteria of a desegregated school? One glance is enough to see that members of each ethnic and racial group tend to sit together (Slavin, 1985). Similarly, at the elementary level, it is typical for boys to prefer sitting with boys, and girls with girls. It is important to recognize that strong forces operate against the formation of cross-ethnic, cross-gender friendships; left to their own devices, most children will choose to be with those they perceive as similar. An even greater barrier to friendship exists between children with disabilities and their nondisabled peers (Slavin, 1988). Public Law 94-142, passed in 1975 (and renamed in 1990 the Individuals with Disabilities Education Act), encourages the inclusion of children with disabilities in regular mainstream classrooms, but mere physical presence is not enough to ensure that these children will be liked, or even accepted.

A second problem of groupwork is the *unequal participation of group members.* Sometimes, this is due to what Garnetta calls the "freeloader" phenomenon, where one or two children in the group end up doing all the work, while the others sit back and relax. We saw this occur in Tom's class, when one group decided to have the best science student design the group's experiment. Although this might be an efficient approach to the task, it's not exactly a fair distribution of responsibility. And those who are freeloading are unlikely to learn anything about designing science experiments.

Unequal participation can occur for other reasons as well. Catherine Mulryan (1992) studied students' involvement in cooperative small groups in mathematics and identified six types of passive students (outlined in Table 9-1). It is worth keeping these in mind; although a desire to freeload may be at the root of some students' passivity, it is also possible that uninvolved students are feeling discouraged, despondent, unrecognized, bored, or superior.

Just as some individuals may be passive and uninvolved in the group activity, others may take over and dominate the interaction (Cohen, 1986). Frequently, the dominant students are those with high "academic status" in the classroom—those who are recognized by their peers as successful, competent students. At other times the dominant students are those who are popular because they are good athletes or are especially attractive. And sometimes dominance simply reflects the higher status our society accords to those who are white and male. Indeed, research has

TABLE 9-1
SIX CATEGORIES OF PASSIVE STUDENTS (FROM C. MULRYAN, 1992)

Category	Description	Typical Achievement Level
Discouraged student	The student perceives the group task to be too difficult and thinks it better to leave it to others who understand.	Mostly low achievers
Unrecognized student	The student's initial efforts to participate are ignored or unrecognized by others, and he/she feels that it's best to retire.	Mostly low achievers
Despondent student	The student dislikes or feels uncomfortable with one or more students in the group and does not want to work with them.	High or low achievers
Unmotivated student	The student perceives the task as unimportant or "only a game," with no grade being assigned to reward effort expended.	High or low achievers
Bored student	The student thinks the task is uninteresting or boring, often because it is seen as too easy or unchallenging.	Mostly high achievers
Intellectual snob	The student feels that peers are less competent and doesn't want to have to do a lot of explaining. Often ends up working on the task individually.	High achievers

shown that in heterogeneous groups, males often dominate over females (Webb, 1984), while whites dominate over African-Americans and Hispanics (Cohen, 1972; Rosenholtz and Cohen, 1985).

A third pitfall of groupwork is *lack of accomplishment.* In Tom's class, a significant amount of instructional time was wasted while children formed groups, and some groups didn't get anything done even when they had finally formed. The unproductive groups seemed to view the opportunity to interact as an opportunity to socialize. Their behavior undoubtedly distracted students who were trying to work. Furthermore, the noise and disruption was of particular concern to Tom's cooperating teacher and upsetting to Tom, who repeatedly asked students to use their "inside" voices—without success.

Finally, a fourth problem associated with groupwork is children's *lack of cooperation.* Tom tells us that "one group spent the whole time arguing." Although this kind of behavior is disappointing, it should not be surprising. As we have pointed out, most children have little experience working in cooperative groups, and the norms of the traditional classroom are dramatically different from the norms for successful groupwork (Cohen, 1986):

Ask peers for assistance.
Help one another.
Explain material to other students.

Check that they understand.
Provide support.
Listen to your peers.
Give everyone a chance to talk.

Children who are used to keeping their eyes on their own papers may find it difficult to learn the behaviors required by these new norms. Some may have difficulty giving clear, thorough explanations to their peers (Webb and Kenderski, 1984). Those who are not "effective speakers" may lack the skills needed to obtain assistance (Wilkinson and Calculator, 1982; refer back to Chapter 8 for the characteristics of "effective speakers"). Students whose cultural backgrounds have fostered a competitive orientation may have difficulties functioning in cooperative situations (Kagan, Zahn, Widaman, Schwarzwald, and Tyrrell, 1985). And students who are used to being passive may be unwilling to assume a more active role (Lazarowitz, Baird, Hertz-Lazarowitz, and Jenkins, 1985). As Elizabeth Cohen (1986) reminds us, "It is a great mistake to assume that children (or adults) know how to work with each other in a constructive collegial fashion" (p. 34).

In the next section of this chapter, we discuss some general strategies for managing groupwork. Remember, *successful groupwork will not just happen*. If you want your students to work together productively, you must plan the groups and the tasks carefully, teach students the new norms, and provide opportunities for them to practice the behaviors that are required. This takes time, and you may want to heed Ken's words of caution:

> If you want to do it right, you have to allot sufficient time to teach students how to work together. And in some schools, this could be viewed as taking time away from "covering the curriculum." It's a good idea to get administrative support before launching cooperative groupwork. That way, when your principal comes in to observe, he or she will understand what you're doing and why. You won't get asked, "Where is this in the curriculum guide?"

DESIGNING SUCCESSFUL GROUPWORK

Decide on the Type of Group to Use

Students can work together in a variety of ways. Susan Stodolsky (1984) has identified five different types of groupwork: helping permitted, helping obligatory, peer tutoring, cooperative, and completely cooperative. The first three groups all involve children assisting one another on individual assignments. In a *helping permitted group*, children work on their own tasks, and they are evaluated as individuals; however, they are allowed—but not required—to help one another. *Helping obligatory* situations differ only in that children are now *expected* to offer mutual assistance. In *peer tutoring*, the relationship between the students is not equal: an "expert" is paired with a student who needs help, so assistance flows in only one direction.

Cooperative groups differ from these helping situations in that children now share a common goal or end, instead of working on completely individual tasks. In a simple *cooperative group*, some division of responsibilities may occur. For example, a group researching the Civil War might decide that one child will learn about the causes of the War, while another learns about famous battles, and a third learns about important leaders. Tasks are carried out independently, but everyone's assignment has to be coordinated at the end in order to produce the final joint product.

More complex is a *completely cooperative group.* Here, students not only share a common goal, there is also little or no division of labor. All members of the group work together to create the group product. This was the type of groupwork that Tom used when he directed his fourth-grade students to plan an experiment demonstrating what plants need in order to grow.

It is important to keep these distinctions in mind as you plan groupwork. *Different types of groups are suitable for different types of activities, and they require different kinds of skills.* (See Table 9-2.) In helping situations, for example, students are ultimately responsible for completing individual tasks. Although these students need to know how to ask for help, how to explain and demonstrate (rather than simply providing the right answer), and how to provide support and encouragement, they do not need the more complex skills required in truly cooperative situations where they share a common goal. For this reason, helping situations are particularly useful when working with young children or those who are new to groupwork. Educators of young children often recommend Think-Pair-Share (F. Lyman, 1993, cited in L. Lyman, Foyle, and Azwell, 1993), in which students work on a question or problem individually and then pair up with another student to share responses and report to the teacher. "Sidework" like this, followed by interaction, may be

TABLE 9-2
DIFFERENT TYPES OF GROUPS

Type of Group	Skills Required	Example of an Activity
Helping permitted Helping obligatory	How to ask for help How to explain How to provide support and en- couragement	Using newspapers to learn about geography and current events; students help one another, but complete an individual worksheet
Peer tutoring	How to ask for help How to explain How to provide support and en- couragement	Tutor helps tutee to complete a set of math problems
Cooperative group	Divide group task into individual tasks Coordinate individual efforts to produce final group product	M&M™ activity: students count the number of candies in individual bag and then pool figures
Complete cooperative group	Take turns Listen to one another Coordinate efforts Share materials Collaborate on a single task Solve conflicts Achieve consensus	Building a landfill that doesn't leach toxins into the ground

and report to the teacher. "Sidework" like this, followed by interaction, may be more appropriate for very young children than full collaboration (Dowrick, 1993).

As an example of a helping situation, let's consider the following activity that we observed in Ken's class:

> Ken's students have been using newspapers to learn about geography and current events. Today, each student is to look through the newspaper and find five articles from cities in the state (other than their hometown), five articles from other states, and five articles from countries other than the United States. Students are expected to help one another, but each student is to complete an individual worksheet on which the geographical location, page number, and title of each article are to be listed. Then each student is to select an article to read in more depth and to write about how he or she "relates" to it; for example, what ideas does it trigger? what else do I know about the topic? why is the article particularly interesting to me?
>
> Students have the newspapers spread out all over their tables and on the floor. As we watch, we see lots of discussion about the assignment. Much of the talk is simple commentary on the articles students are finding: "Look, there's a flower show coming soon." "Penn State played Rutgers." "James Brown is singing in Los Angeles." "Guys, look at the top of page 11. . . ." But there are also requests for assistance: "I can't find a fifth article on a New Jersey city." "Is Franklin in New Jersey?" "I don't know how to relate to this article. Relating is hard. How do you think I should relate to this?"

In contrast to helping situations, cooperative groups require skills beyond requesting and giving appropriate assistance. Students must be able to develop a plan of action; they must be able to coordinate efforts toward a common goal; they must be able to evaluate the contributions of their peers and give feedback in a constructive way; they must monitor individuals' progress toward the group goal; they must be able to summarize and synthesize individual efforts.

During one visit to Garnetta's classroom, we observed a good example of a cooperative activity. The class was divided into groups of four or five to do "experimental math." Although students were required to carry out individual tasks, they had to coordinate their individual efforts if the groups were to be successful:

> Garnetta introduces the math activity by explaining that each student is going to receive a bag of M&M's™. The first task is to predict how many of each color are in the bag. Predictions are to be recorded on a "Candy Facts" page; a bar graph is then to be constructed and colored with the appropriate M&M™ colors (green, orange, yellow, red, light brown, and dark brown; blue was not yet a candy color). Once predictions have been made, students are to open their bags and count the actual number of M&M's™ of each color. This information is also to be recorded and then graphed.
>
> Garnetta also explains that once each student in the group is finished with the actual count, their figures are to be pooled. In other words, students are to find out the total number of each color in the group. This information is to be entered on a large "group graph" taped to the chalkboard. Each group member is to color at least one of the bars with the appropriate color.
>
> As students set to work, Garnetta reminds them of the rules: "You are to stay in your seats and work with your group. You cannot get up and go to another group. Use in-

door voices. If you have a problem, ask someone in your group. And remember, if you eat the M&M's™ you'll ruin the experiment. You've got to wait until the very end."

There is subdued excitement as group members begin to make predictions and color their graphs. Predictions vary tremendously. Some children guess that there will be eight or ten of every color, while others guess that there will be 25 or 30. There are lots of comments on each other's predictions: "That's way too high. There couldn't be *that* many!" "You think that's all the reds? No way!"

When children begin to open their bags, the excitement mounts. Some students go about the counting task very methodically. They separate each color into little clusters and then count each cluster. Some students line up each color and compare the length of the lines. Others are far more haphazard and have difficulty keeping track of which M&M's™ they've counted. Again, there is lots of comparing and commenting: "You got hardly any oranges!" "I got more light browns than anyone at the table!" "You should line yours up like I did."

When it's time to pool the individual numbers of each color, students call out their totals. In some groups, one person does the addition for everyone. In other groups, every group member writes down the numbers and does the addition. There are quite a few discrepancies: "I got 65 light browns." "Uh-oh, I got 58." Garnetta offers each group a calculator so they can check their work.

In the final step of this activity, the results of different groups are compared and also pooled. Under Garnetta's direction, the class works together to find out which color was most common and which color was least common.

In this experimental math lesson, we see that students were required to carry out an individual task. We can consider this a division of labor, since each student counted the M&M's™ in only one bag. In order for the group to complete the entire assignment, however, each member needed to do the task correctly. This structure provided an incentive for group members to monitor everyone's progress and to help one another. Moreover, students had to coordinate their individual efforts in order to produce a joint product—the group tally of each M&M™ color.

Completely cooperative groups with no division of labor present even greater challenges. Not only must students be able to take turns, listen to one another carefully, and coordinate efforts, they must also be able to share materials, collaborate on a single task, reconcile differences, compromise, and reach a consensus. Consider the following activity observed in Barbara's class, part of a science unit on the environment:

Barbara's class has been studying the environmental problems associated with *garbage.* Today's lesson is about landfills. Barbara explains what each group of five is to do: "The objective to today's activity is to build a landfill that doesn't leach toxins into the ground. On your lab tray are most of the materials you will need. You have a plastic container [a two-liter bottle from soda, with the top and bottom cut off]. You also have clay, cheese cloth, raisins, leaves, and plastic. All these can be used in your landfill. You'll also have to get soil from the big bucket on the side of the room, and a beaker of water from the water bucket. The only thing you can't use are the three little pieces of sponge. When you have built your landfill and you're satisfied that it won't leak, I'll come around and put red food coloring—the "toxin"—on each sponge. Then you'll put the three sponges on the top of the landfill and make it rain by pouring water from your beaker. We'll watch to see if the toxin comes through. If it doesn't, then your group has made a state-of-the-art landfill. You'll have 15 minutes to work."

Before the groups begin to work, Barbara reviews the roles for each group member. The *materials person* gets the lab tray, the dirt, and the water for the group; the *timekeeper* keeps track of the time; the *recorder* writes down what the group decides to do and draws a diagram of the group's landfill; the *facilitator* makes sure that everyone has a chance to participate; at the end of the lesson, the *reporter* will tell the class what happened.

In this activity, students had different roles to play, but they still needed to work together on the building of the landfill. They had to develop one plan, explain the reasons for their ideas, listen respectfully to one another, reject ideas without being destructive, reach consensus on which ideas to try, and take turns building the landfill. These are not easy skills to learn—even for adults.

As these three examples illustrate, the more interdependent students are, the more skills they need to cooperate successfully. It's a good idea to use simpler types of groups when you are just starting out. In Tom's case, we can see that he began with the most complex kind of groupwork. He set up a situation in which students who were not even used to helping one another were expected to cooperate completely. Moreover, he assigned an intellectually demanding task that required creativity and problem-solving. His students not only had to contend with an unfamiliar social situation, they also had to grapple with an unusually challenging academic task.

Decide on the Size of the Group

To some extent, the size of the group you use depends on the task you assign. Pairs are appropriate when students are using flash cards to drill one another on math facts, or when they are reviewing spelling words in preparation for a test. Groups of two are also easier for beginning teachers to manage (Johnson, Johnson, Holubec, and Roy, 1984), and teachers of younger students often prefer pairs over larger groups that require more elaborate social skills (Edwards & Stout, 1989/90).

This is definitely true of Viviana, who frequently has "neighbors" work together on tasks. In the following example, notice how Viviana provides step-by-step directions for her students; she doesn't simply put them in pairs and tell them to get to work. Note also that the structure of this activity is very similar to Think-Pair-Share.

Viviana's students are working on place value. She gives each child a worksheet that is divided into a tens column and a ones column. She explains: "Now, children, we're going to play a game. I'm going to give each pair of students a set of number cards. Put the cards between you and your partner." [She distributes the cards and checks to see that everyone has a partner.] Now, one person take the two top cards and put them side by side so that you make a two-digit number. Now, form the number on your worksheet using the tens blocks and the ones blocks. I want you to work individually and then check with your partner to see how your partner has made the number."

As the children work, Viviana walks around and checks what they are doing. Each partner makes the number on the place value worksheet by placing blocks in the appropriate columns. Then the partners confer. Sometimes they have represented the numbers exactly the same way. Sometimes, they discover that they have represented the numbers differently; for example, one child makes 67 with six tens and 7 ones; her partner has made 67 with 5 tens and 17 ones. They discuss the difference. Viviana helps them to see that they have each created 67 but in different ways. When pairs have completed the first number and checked their work with their partner, Viviana instructs them to reverse the two digits. She tells them: "Now remember, you don't have the same number, even though you are using the same cards. With a six and a seven you can make 67 or you can make 76."

In situations where the academic task requires a division of labor (e.g., the unit on the Civil War), it makes sense to form groups larger than two. Groups of three are still relatively easy to manage, but you need to make sure that two students don't form a coalition, leaving the third isolated and excluded (Cohen, 1986).

In general, educators recommend cooperative groups of four or five (Cohen, 1986), and six may be the upper limit (Johnson, Johnson, Holubec, and Roy, 1984). Keep in mind that as group size increases, the "resource pool" also increases; in other words, there are more heads to think about the task and more hands to share the work. It is also true, however, that the larger the group, the more difficult it is to develop a plan of action, allocate turns for speaking, share materials, and reach consensus.

Assign Students to Groups

In addition to deciding on the type and size of your groups, you must think carefully about group composition. As we mentioned earlier in this chapter, groupwork allows children to develop relationships with those who differ in terms of gender and ethnicity. Groupwork also helps to integrate children with disabilities into the mainstream classroom. For these reasons, groups should be heterogeneous with respect to gender and ethnicity, and children with disabilities should be included in groups with their nondisabled peers.

You also need to consider whether groups will be homogeneous or heterogeneous with respect to ability level. At times, homogeneous groups can be useful; for example, you may want to form a group of several children who are all having difficulty with a particular mathematics concept, or you may want to structure opportunities for children who are gifted and talented to work together on more advanced material (Robinson, 1990). In general, however, educators recommend the use of heterogeneous groups (Cohen, 1986; Johnson, Johnson, Holubec, and Roy, 1984; Slavin, 1988). One reason is that they provide more opportunities for asking questions and receiving explanations (Johnson, Johnson, Holubec, and Roy, 1984; Webb, 1985).

Just how heterogeneous your groups should be is still not clear. Research by Noreen Webb and her colleagues (1985) has shown that in groups composed of high-, medium-, and low-achieving students, those of medium-ability tend to get left out of the interaction. In fact, Webb (1985) argues that two-level groups (high-medium or medium-low) are most beneficial for all students. In contrast, other proponents of cooperative learning (e.g., Slavin, 1988) recommend that four-person teams consist of a high-achiever, a low-achiever, and two average-achievers.

Another variable you need to consider when deciding on group composition is social skill. Some children have unusual leadership abilities; others are particularly adept at resolving conflicts; still others are especially alert to injustice and can help to ensure that everyone in the group has a chance to participate. When forming groups, it makes sense to disperse children like these, so that each group has the benefit of their talents.

On the other hand, some children have extreme difficulty working with others. It makes sense to disperse *these* students, too. As Garnetta points out:

> Some children are really volatile—they come to school angry and disrupt whatever group they're in. Some children freeload and don't do anything; they just want to play. Some kids dominate. Some kids prefer to work individually. You have to be really careful who you place these kinds of kids with—and you certainly don't want to put them all together in one group!

Since group composition is so important, it is risky to allow students to select their own groups. We saw what happened in Tom's class: students segregated themselves according to gender and ethnicity; friends elected to be together—and did more socializing than work; the mainstreamed student and the social isolate were excluded. Experiences like this lead Ken to believe that students should rarely be allowed to select their own groups. As he puts it,

> If you allow children to select their own groups without carefully structuring the situation, the pitfalls are really there. You're inviting problems—especially if you're a beginning teacher. Just about the only time I allow my students to choose their own groups is when they're selecting novels to read. [See Chapter 5.] In that case, the groups are built upon the selection of the novel; it's not just "I want to work with this person," although that certainly enters into it.

Interestingly, Garnetta and Barbara allow their students to choose their own groups more frequently than Ken does, but not until the students have had substantial experience working in various kinds of groups with almost everyone in the class.

Teachers develop different systems for assigning students to groups. When Barbara forms heterogeneous groups, for example, she first writes each student's name on a note card, along with information about achievement and interpersonal relationships (e.g., with whom the student doesn't get along). Then she ranks students in terms of achievement level and assigns a top-ranked student and a bottom-ranked student to each of the groups. Next, the average students are distributed, keeping in mind the need to balance the groups in terms of gender, ethnicity, and social skill. Having each student's name on a note card allows her to shuffle students around as she tries to form equivalent groups that will work well together. Barbara comments, "It's impossible to form perfect groups, but at least this system gives me a fighting chance!"

Structure the Task for Interdependence

If you want to ensure that students cooperate on a task, you have to create a situation in which they need one another in order to succeed. In other words, you need to structure the task so that students are *interdependent.* A simple way to do this is to require group members to *share materials* (Johnson, Johnson, Holubec, and Roy, 1984). If one member of a pair has a page of math problems, for example, and the other member has the answer sheet, they need to coordinate if they are both to complete the problems and check their answers.

Another way to create interdependence is to create a *group goal.* For example, you might have each group produce a single product, such as a report, a science demonstration, a puppet show, or a story. A *group grade or group reward* is another way to stress the importance of collaborating. For example, suppose you want to encourage students to help one another with spelling words. You can do this by rewarding groups on the basis of the total number of words spelled correctly by all the members of the group (Johnson, Johnson, Holubec, and Roy, 1984). Similarly, you can give bonus points to every math group in which all students reach a predetermined level of achievement.

You can also promote collaboration by structuring the task so that students are dependent on one another for *information* (Johnson, Johnson, Holubec, and Roy, 1984). In Garnetta's M&M's™ math lesson, for example, group members had to pool their individual data to get a group count of the M&M's™ of each color. They needed each other in order to produce the group graph.

Finally, you can assign *different roles* to group members, requiring each role to be fulfilled if the group is to complete the task. In the landfill lesson that Barbara conducted, each group contained a materials person, a timekeeper, a recorder, a facilitator, and a reporter. In *Heritage,* a social studies simulation that Ken uses (Wesley, 1976), students form three-person racing teams that plot a course of travel from San Diego, California, to Bangor, Maine, stopping along the way at 15 important historical sites. Each team member plays a specific role—the driver, the navigator, or the leader. In each round of play, students change roles. The leader rolls the dice at the beginning of each round of play and selects a "fate card," which adds or subtracts miles that the team "travels." The driver computes the number of points the team earns each day and the miles gained or lost; he or she also moves the team's car symbol along the plotted course of travel on a large class map and writes a "Diary Entry" for the day. The navigator keeps a "Daily Travel Log," recording the number of miles gained or lost during the round of play, the number of hours traveled, the road and weather conditions, and other important information.

Even very young children can learn to carry out roles like these. One way of reminding them about their individual responsibilities is to place a different symbol on each person's desk. For example, you can give each student a star of a different color (Edwards and Stout, 1989/90). The child with the red star reads the instructions, the blue star records what the group does, the yellow star gets the materials, and the green star monitors the noise level. Recently, one student teacher we know used this strategy in a cooperative learning activity on spiders. After dividing her class into four-person groups, she gave each member of the group a different aspect of spiders to research (e.g., the structure of spiders; what they eat; how they construct webs). She also gave each group member a marker of a different color to use in recording his or her findings on posterboard. This student teacher reports: "[Using the different colors] made it visually easy for me to see if they did their part of the research, and the different colors . . . reminded them of the specific tasks they were to be engaged in."

Ensure Individual Accountability

As we discussed earlier in the chapter, one of the major problems associated with groupwork is unequal participation. Sometimes children refuse to contribute to the group effort, preferring to "freeload." Sometimes more assertive children dominate, making it difficult for others to participate. In either case, lack of participation is a genuine problem. Those who do not actively participate will not learn anything about the academic task; furthermore, the group is not learning the skills of collaboration.

One way to encourage the participation of all children is to hold all group members responsible for a task or a level of performance. You can do this by giving individual quizzes, by grading each individual's part of the total group project, or by having each student complete an individual worksheet or project. When Garnetta did the M&M's™ lesson, for example, all students had to complete their own set of worksheets with their individual predictions and actual counts, as well as the group tally.

Ken's *Heritage* simulation (Wesley, 1976) provides another good example of a task that fosters individual accountability as well as group cooperation. The number of miles that each team travels during a round of play is determined by the number of points the team accumulates. Team members earn points by carrying out the specific responsibilities associated with their particular roles; for example, the Daily Travel Log is worth ten points, and Diary Entries are worth 20 points. The better these are, the more miles the team is allowed to travel. In addition, each team member also has to complete three research reports on a historical site. Each research report is worth 40 points, so there is substantial pressure to do a good job. *Heritage* is structured so that the team will suffer if individuals do not participate or if they fail to do acceptable work; in other words, the success of the team depends on each person's contribution. This structure allows teachers to assign individual grades and to provide a group goal—being the first team to reach Bangor, Maine.

In addition to planning tasks so that individuals are held accountable, you need to monitor students' effort and progress during groupwork time. Our four teachers continually circulate throughout the room, observing each group's activity. In this way they can note problems, provide assistance, and keep students on-task. They are also careful to build in "progress checkpoints." For example, Barbara occasionally stops the groups' activity and asks each group to report, either verbally or in writing, on what they've accomplished. Similarly, Ken divides large assignments into components that are due every few days (see the section on "monitoring student progress" in Chapter 7). This allows him to keep track of how well groups are functioning.

If your groups include children with disabilities or those who have limited proficiency in English, you may have to modify the group task so that everyone can participate and everyone can succeed. Ann Nevin (1993) describes several cooperative learning situations in which teachers have made adaptations for students with especially challenging educational needs. For example, one teacher developed a science lesson so that Bobby, who was visually impaired and nonverbal, could be included:

> In a lesson in which the objective was for all students to identify different fruits by their seeds (color, size, shape, and number), each group was to complete a poster and, as a group, present it to the rest of the class. Posters were expected to include four or five different fruits and their seeds. Bobby's objective was to tactually [sic] explore each fruit and to stay with the group. The objective was explained to the students, and they were asked what other things Bobby could do to be part of the group's activities. The students suggested that Bobby paste some materials on to the poster instead of drawing them. Once all the groups had completed and corrected their posters as necessary, each made and ate a fruit salad. (p. 52)

Similarly, a social studies activity on the countries of Africa was modified to address the needs of an eighth grader with memory deficits, as well as limited reading and spelling skills:

Barbara checks in with a cooperative learning group.

The teacher asked each of six groups of four students to develop a memory aid, or mnemonic, to represent each of three sets of African countries being studied. The student with memory deficits was held accountable for one of the sets (a reduced assignment). All of the groups were successful in creating mnemonics that enabled them to remember both the names of the nations and their locations. (p. 53)

Teach Students to Cooperate

David and Roger Johnson (1989/90), two experts on cooperative learning, warn teachers not to assume that students know how to work together. They write:

People do not know instinctively how to interact effectively with others. Nor do interpersonal and group skills magically appear when they are needed. Students must be taught these skills and must be motivated to use them. If group members lack the interpersonal and small-group skills to cooperate effectively, cooperative groups will not be productive. (p. 30)

As the classroom teacher, *it is your responsibility to teach students to work together.* This is not simple process; students do not learn to cooperate in one 45-minute lesson. Indeed, we can think about the process in terms of three stages: team building, group skills training, and evaluation. Let's consider each of these briefly.

Team Building   Before students can work together productively, they must get to know one another and develop a sense of responsibility for the group. This can be accomplished by having groups engage in various nonacademic activities designed to build a team identity and to help students see the value of cooperation.

Having group members create a joint art project is one way of fostering a team identity. For example, when Barbara forms cooperative groups that will work together for several weeks, she begins by instructing them to decide on a team name. They then create a banner displaying the team name and an appropriate logo. Sometimes, Barbara gives each member of a team a marker of a different color; individuals can only use the marker they have been given, but the banner must contain all the colors. In this way, everyone has to participate in its creation.

Another activity that is useful for team building (particularly at the primary level) is making a "Things the ___ Team Likes" book (Graves and Graves, 1990). Each group gets a stack of pictures, and each student gets a turn to select a picture for the book. No picture can be included, however, unless all teammates agree that they like the picture. Once there's agreement, pictures are pasted on tagboard or construction paper, and team members provide labels or captions. This activity can be extended by having teams create "Things the ___ Team Likes to Do" books— or even "Things the ___ Team Hates to Do" books.

Group Skills Training   Recently, a student teacher wrote in her journal:

After my first disaster with working in groups, I decided I needed to write out a lesson plan for teaching my class how to participate in cooperative learning. I taught it just as I would a math lesson. I realized I could not expect them to know how to do something successfully if I had never taught them how. I would never expect them to be able to add two-digit numbers without training and practice; groupwork is the same thing.

This student teacher has learned an important lesson: Group skills training requires systematic explanation, modeling, practice, and feedback. *It's simply not enough to state the rules and expect students to understand and remember.* And don't take anything for granted: even basic guidelines like "don't distract others" and "use indoor voices" may need to be taught.

A particularly important skill to teach and encourage is asking for help. In Chapter 8, we discussed the difficulty that some students have in obtaining assistance. (See the section on the "effective speaker.") But even if students are effective communicators, they may be reluctant to turn to their peers. For example, Newman and Schwager's (1993) study of students' attitudes toward help seeking found that third-, fifth-, and seventh-grade students generally preferred to seek help from the teacher rather than from classmates. Students saw the teacher as not only more likely to facilitate learning, but also less likely to think they were "dumb" for asking questions. To counteract attitudes like these, you may need to give explicit instructions about when, to whom, and how to ask questions (Farivar and Webb, 1991). You can also encourage this behavior by reminding students that asking other group members can help them learn, by stressing that they're not alone in needing help, or by not responding to requests unless they're unsuccessful in obtaining help from their peers. (Remember Barbara's phrase: "Ask three, then me.") Keep in mind that low achievers—those most in need of academic help—are likely to be the most passive in seeking it (Newman and Schwager, 1993).

Let's see what teaching a group skill might look like in action. During a visit to Garnetta's classroom early in the school year, we observed a science lesson on the solar system. Students were working in pairs, researching information on the planet they had selected. Before the lesson began, Garnetta told us that students had not worked well together during the last science class: "Some people were guarding their work, not letting anybody else see. I knew I'd have to stress the importance of cooperation before we could work again in groups."

GARNETTA: Ladies and gents, there are a few things we need to discuss before we begin. Last time we did science, you were supposed to be working with a partner. Sometimes in school we don't always work with partners. For example, on a spelling test. What if you worked together on a spelling test and looked at someone else's paper?

STUDENT: You might get the answer wrong if the other person had it wrong.

GARNETTA: True. But what do we call it if you look at someone else's paper during a spelling test?

STUDENT: Copying.

GARNETTA: Yes. And that is what?

STUDENT: Cheating.

GARNETTA: Right. During a spelling test, you're supposed to work alone. But if I *tell* you to work together, that's different! What's the big word we use to describe that? The "C" work.

STUDENTS: Cooperation! [choral response]

GARNETTA: Right! We're going to use this big word today in science. Let's say you're work-
            ing on . . . Johnny, what's your planet?
JOHNNY: Venus.
GARNETTA: Okay, *you're* working on Venus, and he's working on Venus. [She points to a
            boy sitting across from Johnny.] If Johnny finds some really good information
            about Venus's atmosphere, should he hide it and not tell Raymond? [She
            mimes a child hiding his work.]
STUDENT: No. He should help him.
GARNETTA: Why?
STUDENT: Because he might not know the answer and they're supposed to work together.
GARNETTA: Okay. Let's say they're trying to find the answers to questions one and two, but
            the books they're using are written differently. Johnny doesn't have the answer
            to number one, and Raymond doesn't have the answer to number two. If they
            share the information, they can *both* do better. They can *both* answer one and
            two. And they'll probably both get good grades because they . . . what?
STUDENTS: Cooperated!
GARNETTA: Yes! Okay, I want to talk about one other thing that's important for today's sci-
            ence lesson. When people are working, I sometimes see this [she pretends to
            be a child whispering to another child]: "Hey, did you see so-and-so, he was
            down at the office 'cause he got in trouble. . . ." Are you going to get your work
            done if you're doing this?
STUDENTS: No.
GARNETTA: Right. If you're whispering like this, you're not *sticking to the task,* and you're
            not going to get your work done, and you're not going to . . .
STUDENTS: Learn!
GARNETTA: You got it. Okay, so I want you to remember these two things today. To *coop-
            erate* by sharing your information and to *stick to the task,* not playing around
            with your neighbor or talking about other stuff. And that way you will . . .
STUDENTS: LEARN!

It's helpful to begin by analyzing the groupwork task you have selected in order
to determine the specific skills students need to know (Cohen, 1986). Will students
have to explain material? Will they have to listen carefully to one another? Will
they have to reach a consensus? Once you have analyzed the task, select one or two
key behaviors to teach your students. Resist the temptation to introduce all the required group skills at once; going too far too fast is sure to lead to frustration.

Next, explain to your students that they will be learning a skill necessary for
working in groups. Be sure to *define terms, discuss rationales,* and *provide examples.* Johnson and Johnson (1989/90) suggest that you construct a "T-chart" on
which you list the skill and then—with the class—record ideas about what the
skill would look like and what it would sound like. Table 9-3 shows a T-chart for
"sharing."

Finally, you need to provide opportunities for students to practice the skill and
to receive feedback. You might have students role play; you might pair the skill
with a familiar academic task so that students can focus their attention on using the
social skill (Carson and Hoyle, 1989/90); or you might have students engage in exercises designed to teach particular skills. (Elizabeth Cohen's book, *Designing
Groupwork,* contains several cooperative exercises, such as "Master Designer" and

TABLE 9-3
A T-CHART FOR SHARING

Sharing	
Looks Like	Sounds Like
Leave the markers in the middle of the table where all can reach	Here's the marker.
Offer the markers to somebody else when finished using	Thanks for handing me the marker.
Return markers to middle of the table	I'm done with the marker; does anybody want it?
Take turns with the markers	Anybody need the red marker?

"Guess My Rule," which focus on helping and explaining, and Epstein's "Four-Stage Rocket," designed to improve group discussion skills.)

Regardless of the type of practice you provide, you need to give students feedback about their performance. They need to know how often and how well they have engaged in the new behavior. As Ken observes:

> Social skills need to be constantly reinforced. I have to tell my kids every day that I appreciate the way they're cooperating, or that I saw some groups doing a terrific job of explaining problems. As far as I'm concerned, teaching these skills is as important as teaching the math or the language arts.

In addition to providing feedback himself, Ken has found it effective to designate a "process person" for each group. This individual is responsible for keeping track of how well the group is functioning; for example, he or she may monitor how many times each person speaks. At the end of the groupwork session, the process person is able to share specific data that the group can use to evaluate its ability to work together.

Evaluation   In order to learn from their experiences, students need the chance to discuss what happened and to evaluate how successful they were in working together. One approach is to ask students to name three things their group did well and one thing the group could do better next time (Johnson & Johnson, 1989/90). You can also have students consider more specific questions, such as

Did you use "indoor voices?"
Did you take turns?
Did everyone carry out his or her job?
Did everyone get a chance to talk?
Did you listen to one another?
What did you do if you didn't agree?

For very young children, a simple checklist, like the one in Figure 9-2, can be helpful.

Name _____ Date _____

How was I in group today?
Did I . . .

	YES	NO
1. Share ideas?		
2. Encourage others?		
3. Let others speak?		
4. Listen to others?		
5. Do my job?		

FIGURE 9-2
A Checklist for Evaluating Group Skills

After individual groups have talked about their experiences, it is often helpful to have groups report to the whole class. You can encourage groups to share and compare their experiences by asking, "Did your group have a similar problem?" "How many groups agree with the way they solved their problem?" "What do you recommend?"

Unfortunately, there are times when teaching group skills and providing for practice and evaluation are just not enough to get particular children to cooperate. Some youngsters are so troubled, volatile, or hostile that they cause conflict no matter where they're placed. When this occurs, you may have no recourse but to exclude them from the activity and devise an individual assignment for them. In cases like this, Barbara tells students, "If you absolutely can't work with the group, then you'll just have to carry the whole load by yourself." (Then she makes sure that the individual activity is *less* enjoyable and *more* onerous than the group activity!)

FOUR SPECIFIC APPROACHES TO GROUPWORK

Several structured programs of cooperative learning have been developed to avoid the problems characteristic of groupwork and to encourage norms of effort and mutual support. Designed for use at any grade level and in most school subjects, all of these cooperative learning strategies are characterized by heterogeneous groups working together to achieve a common goal (Slavin, 1985). In this section of the chapter, we briefly examine four of these programs: STAD, Jigsaw and Jigsaw II, Group Investigation, and the structural approach to cooperative learning. You can learn more about these programs by referring to the references listed in "For Further Reading" at the end of this chapter.

STAD

Student Teams-Achievement Divisions (STAD) is a cooperative learning method developed and studied at Johns Hopkins University by Robert Slavin and his colleagues (Slavin, 1988). STAD is particularly appropriate for content areas where there are "right answers," such as mathematics, spelling, and grammar.

In STAD, the teacher presents a lesson, and students then work within their teams on an academic task. In other words, students help one another with the assignment instead of doing it as individual seatwork. Suppose the task is to complete pages in a spelling workbook. Students may take turns quizzing one another on the spelling words, do the exercises individually and then compare answers, or work together on each exercise. Their objective is to ensure that all team members master the material. Team members are told that they are not finished studying until everyone on the team feels confident about knowing the material.

Following team practice, students take individual quizzes on which they receive individual scores. In addition, a *team score* is calculated, based on team members' *individual improvement over their own past performance.* This is an extremely important feature: using improvement scores prevents low-achieving students from being rejected because they cannot contribute to the team. In STAD, the student whose quiz scores go from 57 to 67 contributes as much as the student whose scores go from 85 to 95.

Finally, teams that earn a designated number of points receive certificates recognizing their performance as a "Superteam," a "Greatteam," or a "Goodteam."

Jigsaw and Jigsaw II

In Jigsaw, one of the earliest cooperative learning methods (Aronson, Blaney, Stephan, Sikes, and Snapp, 1978), heterogeneous teams work on academic material that has been divided into sections. Jigsaw is particularly appropriate for narrative material, such as a social studies chapter, a biography, or a short story. Each team member reads only one section of the material. The teams then disband, and students meet in "expert groups" with other people who have been assigned the same section. Working together, they learn the material in these expert groups and then return to their home teams to teach it to their teammates. Since everyone is responsible for learning all the material, successful task completion requires students to listen carefully to their peers. Jigsaw also includes team-building activities and training to improve communication and tutoring skills.

Jigsaw II (Slavin, 1985) is a modification developed by the researchers at Johns Hopkins. It differs from the original Jigsaw in that all students of a team read the entire assignment. Then they are assigned a particular topic on which to become an expert. Like STAD, Jigsaw II uses individual quizzes and team scores based on individual improvement.

Group Investigation

Group Investigation, developed by Shlomo Sharan and his colleagues at the University of Tel Aviv (Sharan and Sharan, 1976, 1989/90) places students in small groups to investigate topics from a unit being studied by the entire class. Each group further divides their topic into individual subtopics and then carries out the research. Students work together to find resource materials, to collect and analyze information, and to plan and present a report, demonstration, play, learning center, or exhibition for the class. Evaluation focuses on both learning and affective experiences; assessment procedures may include comments from peers, students' self-evaluations, and questions submitted by groups for a common test, as well as evaluation by the teacher.

The Structural Approach to Cooperative Learning

The structural approach was developed by Spencer Kagan, director of Resources for Teachers (1990). According to Kagan (1989/90), "structures" are content-free ways of organizing social interaction among students. Structures usually involve a series of steps, with prescribed behavior at each step. A traditional classroom structure, for example, is the "whole-class question-answer" situation. In this structure, the teacher asks a question, children raise their hands to respond, and the teacher calls on one student. If that student answers the question incorrectly, the other children get a chance to respond and to win the teacher's praise. Thus, children are often happy if a classmate makes a mistake, and they may even root for one another's failure.

Kagan has developed a number of simple cooperative structures that can be used at a variety of grade levels and in many content areas. He emphasizes the need for teachers to select the structures that are most appropriate for their specific objectives. Some structures are useful for teambuilding or for developing communication skills; others are most suitable for increasing mastery of factual material or for concept development; and some can serve multiple objectives. Here are a few of the structures that our teachers find particularly helpful (Kagan, 1990). (See Table 9-4 for additional examples.)

Roundtable.   Each group has a piece of paper and a pen. The teacher asks a question with many possible answers. One student writes a response and passes the paper and pen to the student on his or her left. Roundtable can be used as a teambuilding activity, to introduce a lesson, to check for mastery of content, or to enliven drill and practice.

Talking Chips.   This is a good example of an easy social skills structure that can be added to a regular groupwork task to minimize both the freeloader phenomenon and the problem of one student taking over and dominating the interaction. Each member of a group is given a chip or some other kind of small object. When people want to talk, they must first place their chip in the center of the table—and they cannot talk again until everyone has used his or her chip, at which time the chips are retrieved and the process repeats.

Paraphrase Passport.   Here, the "ticket" needed in order to talk is not giving up a chip, but correctly paraphrasing the person who has just spoken. This structure encourages members of the group to listen to one another, and it gives individuals feedback about how their ideas are being interpreted by others.

TABLE 9-4
SOME OF SPENCER KAGAN'S COOPERATIVE STRUCTURES

Name	Purpose	Description	Functions
Match Mine	Communication	Students try to match the arrangement of objects on a grid of another student using oral communication only.	Vocabulary building. Communication skills. Role-taking ability.
Three-Step Interview	Concept Development	Students interview each other in pairs, first one way, then the other. Students then share information they learned with the group.	Sharing personal information such as hypotheses, reactions to a poem, conclusions from a unit. Equal participation. Listening.
Inside-Outside Circle	Multifunctional	Students stand in pairs in two concentric circles. The inside circle faces out; the outside circle faces in. Students use flash cards or respond to teacher questions as they rotate to each new partner.	Checking for understanding. Review. Tutoring. Meeting classmates. Sharing.

Adapted from Kagan, S. (1989/90). The structural approach to cooperative learning. *Educational Leadership, 47*(4), p. 14.

Numbered Heads Together.   This is a very effective way of checking on students' understanding of content and provides a cooperative alternative to "whole-class question-answer." Students number off within teams (e.g., one through four). When the teacher asks a question, team members "put their heads together" to make sure that everyone on the team knows the answer. The teacher then calls a number, and students with that number may raise their hands to answer. This structure promotes interdependence among team members: if one student knows the answer, everyone's chance of answering correctly increases. At the same time, the structure encourages individual accountability: once the teacher calls a number, students are on their own.

CONCLUDING COMMENTS

Although this chapter is entitled "Managing Groupwork," we have seen that there are actually a number of different groupwork situations, each with its own set of uses, procedures, requirements, and pitfalls. As you plan and implement groupwork in your classroom, it's important to remember these distinctions. Too many teachers think that cooperative learning is putting students into groups and telling them to work together. They select tasks that are inappropriate for the size of the group; they use heterogeneous groups when homogeneous groups would be more suitable (or vice versa); they fail to build in positive interdependence and individual accountability; they fail to appreciate the differences between helping groups and cooperative learning. The following example, taken from O'Donnell and O'Kelly (1994), would be funny—if it weren't true:

> One of our colleagues recently described an example of "cooperative learning" in his son's school. The classroom teacher informed the students that [they] would be using cooperative learning. His son was paired with another student. The two students were required to complete two separate parts of a project but were expected to complete the work outside of class. A grade was assigned to each part of the project and a group grade was given. In this instance, one child received an "F" as he failed to complete the required part of the project. The other child received an "A." The group grade was a "C," thus rewarding the student who had failed to complete the work, and punishing the child who had completed his work. In this use of "cooperative learning," there was no opportunity for the students to interact, and the attempt to use a group reward (the group grade) backfired. Although this scenario is not recognizable as cooperative learning to most proponents of cooperation, the classroom teacher described it as such to the students' parents. (p. 322)

This example illustrates the need for thorough training in cooperative learning. No three-hour class, no one-shot inservice workshop, and no chapter can adequately meet this need. Groupwork is an extremely challenging subsetting of the classroom, and successful management requires unusually careful planning and implementation. It is especially challenging for beginning teachers who are not yet experienced classroom managers.

Despite the potential pitfalls, we believe that groupwork should be an integral part of elementary classrooms. As was the case with independent seatwork, Barbara, Ken, Viviana, and Garnetta use groupwork to varying degrees, but all of them believe that students must learn to work together and that students can learn from one another.

After a meeting with our four teachers, during which we discussed the topic of small groups, Ken wrote us a brief note. In it, he reflected on the impact of groupwork on learning:

> The real advantage with small groups, at least from my angle, is increased learning. When kids interact with each other, when they speak to and listen to others, there is a greater level of involvement and increased support for learning. It is, of course, difficult to verify or assess this increase, yet I often hear kids talking about how they answered their questions and how the group affected their final product. Sometimes a child will say, "See, you guys, I was right and you talked me out of it!" Sometimes no one is really sure who came up with the answer; they all sort of pieced it together. For *my* kids, having to work alone on an assignment is a punishment.

Ken's reflections focus on the academic benefits of groupwork. But as we mentioned at the beginning of the chapter, groupwork has social payoffs as well. It's important to remember that the classroom is not simply a place where students learn academic lessons. It's also a place where students learn *social lessons*—lessons about the benefits or the dangers of helping one another, about relationships with students from other ethnic groups, about accepting or rejecting children with disabilities, and about friendship. As a teacher, you will influence the content of these lessons. If planned and implemented well, groupwork can provide students with opportunities to learn lessons of caring, fairness, and self-worth.

SUMMARY

We began this chapter by talking about the potential benefits of groupwork and about some of the special challenges it presents. Then we suggested strategies for designing successful groupwork. Finally we described some structured programs of cooperative learning.

Benefits of Groupwork

- Less idle time while waiting for the teacher to help
- Enhanced motivation
- More involvement in learning
- Greater achievement
- Decreased competition among students
- Increased interaction across gender, ethnic, and racial lines
- Improved relationships between mainstreamed students and their peers

Some Common Pitfalls

- Segregation in terms of gender, ethnicity, and race
- Unequal participation
- Lack of accomplishment
- Lack of cooperation among group members

Challenges of Groupwork

- Maintaining order
- Achieving accountability for all students
- Teaching new (cooperative) behavioral norms
- Creating effective groups

Designing Successful Groupwork

- Decide on the type of group to use (helping permitted, helping obligatory, peer tutoring, cooperative, completely cooperative)
- Decide on the size of the group
- Assign students to groups
- Structure the task for interdependence (e.g., create a group goal or reward)
- Ensure individual accountability
- Teach students to cooperate

Structured Programs of Cooperative Learning

- STAD
- Jigsaw I and II
- Group Investigation
- The Structural Approach to Cooperative Learning

Group work offers unique social and academic rewards, but it is important to understand the challenges it presents and not to assume that, just because a task is fun or interesting, the lesson will run smoothly. Remember to plan groupwork carefully, prepare your students thoroughly, and allow yourself time to develop experience as a facilitator of cooperative groups.

ACTIVITIES

1 For each of the following cases, choose the type of groupwork you would use (helping permitted, helping obligatory, peer tutoring, cooperative group, competely cooperative group) and briefly describe your reasons.

a You are teaching your heterogeneous math class how to tell time. Eight of the 17 students pick up the concept quickly, but the remaining students are having some difficulty.

b Your third-grade class is divided into three literature groups. Each group is reading a different novel, but each group has to define ten vocabulary words you have drawn from its book. Your main goal is for each child in each group to have the definitions correctly written to use as a study guide for a future quiz.

c In your homogeneous fifth-grade math class, you are reviewing the decimal equivalents of fractions. You want children to use flash cards to assist them in memorizing the equivalents.

d In sixth grade, your science class is studying rocks and minerals. You would like the students to work in groups of three to study the three types of rocks (igneous, metamorphic, sedimentary). Each group is to create a large poster showing the characteristics and examples of each type of rock.

e Your fourth-grade class just read tall tales in their literature anthology. To capitalize on their enthusiasm, you have them form groups to write and perform (complete with scenery and costumes) a play or puppet show based on one of the tall tales. You would like each member of the group to enjoy the many aspects of this project, from writing to acting.

2 You want your class to work on editing and peer-conferencing skills with the Halloween stories they've been writing. It is important to you that students be able to give and receive constructive criticism and feedback. You divide students into groups of three. How will you structure this activity? What roles will you assign? What are the social skills you need to teach and how will you teach them? What forms of accountability will you build in? How will you monitor the groupwork?

3 Choose two of the topics listed below. For each one, select an approach discussed in this chapter (STAD, Jigsaw, Group Investigation, or Numbered Heads Together). Describe briefly how you would use the cooperative learning strategy you selected. Use a different strategy for each topic.

Inventors and their inventions
Uses of plants
Linear measurement
Pioneer life
Character analysis
Using a thesaurus
Dinosaurs
Systems of the body
Nutrition

REFERENCES

Aronson, E., Blaney, N., Stephan, C., Sikes, J., and Snapp, M. (1978). *The Jigsaw classroom.* Beverly Hills, CA: Sage.

Carson, L., and Hoyle, S. (1989/90). Teaching social skills: A view from the classroom. *Educational Leadership, 47*(4), p. 31.

Carter, K. (March-April, 1985). Teacher comprehension of classroom processes: An emerging direction in classroom management research. Paper presented at the annual meeting of the American Educational Research Association, Chicago, Illinois.

Cohen, E. G. (1972). Interracial interaction disability. *Human Relations, 25,* 9–24.

Cohen, E. G. (1986). *Designing groupwork: Strategies for the heterogeneous classroom.* New York: Teachers College Press.

Dowrick, N. (1993). Talking and learning in pairs: A comparison of two interactive modes for six and seven year old pupils. *International Journal of Early Years Education, 1*(3), 49–60.

Edwards, C., and Stout, J. (1989/90). Cooperative learning: The first year. *Educational Leadership, 47*(4), 38–41.

Farivar, S., and Webb, N. (1991). *Helping behavior activities handbook: Cooperative small group problem solving in middle school mathematics (Report to the National Science Foundation.)* University of California, Los Angeles.

Gerleman, S. L. (1987). An observational study of small-group instruction in fourth-grade mathematics classrooms. *The Elementary School Journal, 88,* 3–28.

Good, T. L., and Brophy, J. E. (1991). *Looking in classrooms* (5th edition). New York: Harper-Collins.

Goodlad, J. I. (1984). *A place called school.* New York: McGraw-Hill.

Graves, T., and Graves, N. (1990). Things we like: A team-building/language development lesson for preschool-grade 2. *Cooperative Learning, The Magazine for Cooperation in Education, 10*(3), 45.

Graybeal, S. S., and Stodolsky, S. S. (1985). Peer work groups in elementary schools. *American Journal of Education, 93,* 409–428.

Johnson, D. W., and Johnson R. T. (1989/90). Social skills for successful group work. *Educational Leadership, 47*(4), 29–33.

Johnson, D. W., and Johnson, R. T. (1980). Integrating handicapped students into the mainstream. *Exceptional Children, 47*(2), 90–98.

Johnson, D. W., Johnson, R. T., Holubec, E. J., and Roy, P. (1984). *Circles of learning: Cooperation in the classroom.* Alexandria, VA: Association for Supervision and Curriculum Development.

Kagan, S. (1989/90). The structural approach to cooperative learning. *Educational Leadership, 47*(4), 12–15.

Kagan, S. (1990). *Cooperative learning: Resources for teachers.* San Juan Capistrano, CA: Resources for Teachers.

Kagan, S., Zahn, G. L., Widaman, K. F., Schwarzwald, J., and Tyrrell, G. (1985). Classroom structural bias: Impact of cooperative and competitive classroom structures on cooperative and competitive individuals and groups. In R. Slavin, S. Sharan, S. Kagan, R. Hertz-Lazarowitz, C. Webb, and R. Schmuck (Eds.), *Learning to cooperate, cooperating to learn.* New York, Plenum Press, pp. 277–312.

Lazarowitz, R., Baird, J. H., Hertz-Lazarowitz, R., and Jenkins, J. (1985). The effects of modified Jigsaw on achievement, classroom social climate, and self-esteem in high-school science classes. In R. Slavin, S. Sharan, S. Kagan, R. Hertz-Lazarowitz, C. Webb, and R. Schmuck (Eds.), *Learning to cooperate, cooperating to learn.* New York: Plenum Press, pp. 231–253.

Lyman. F. (1993). *Think-pair-share.* (Videotape). Washington, D.C.: National Education Association.

Lyman, L., Foyle, H. C., and Azwell, T. S. (1993). *Cooperative learning in the elementary classroom.* Washington, D.C.: National Education Association.

Madden, N. A., and Slavin, R. E. (1983). Cooperative learning and social acceptance of mainstreamed academically handicapped students. *Journal of Special Education, 17,* 171–182.

Manning, M. L., and Lucking, R. (1993). Cooperative learning and multicultural classrooms. *The Clearing House, 67*(1), 12–16.

Mulryan, C. M. (1992). Student passivity during cooperative small groups in mathematics. *Journal of Educational Research, 85*(5), 261–273.

Nevin, A. (1993). Curricula and instructional adaptations for including students with disabilities in cooperative groups. In J. W. Putnam, *Cooperative learning and strategies for inclusion: Celebrating diversity in the classroom.* Baltimore, MD: Paul H. Brookes Publishing Co., 41–56.

Newman, R. S., and Schwager, M. T. (1993). Students' perceptions of the teacher and classmates in relation to reported help seeking in math class. *The Elementary School Journal, 94*(1), 3–17.

O'Donnell, A., and O'Kelly, J. (1994). Learning from peers: Beyond the rhetoric of positive results. *Educational Psychology Review, 6*(4), 321–349.

Robinson, A. (1990). Cooperation or exploitation? The argument against cooperative learning for talented students. *Journal for the Education of the Gifted, 14*(1), 9–27.

Rosenholtz, S. J., and Cohen, E. G. (1985). Status in the eye of the beholder. In J. Berger and M. Zelditch, Jr. (Eds.), *Status, rewards, and influence.* San Francisco, CA: Jossey Bass.

Sharan, S. (1990). The group investigation approach to cooperative learning: Theoretical foundations. In M. Brubacher, R. Payne, and K. Rickett (Eds.), *Perspectives on small group Learning.* Oakville, Ontario: Rubicon Publishing Inc.

Sharan, S., and Sharan, Y. (1976). *Small-group teaching.* Englewood Cliffs, NJ: Educational Technology Publications.

Sharan, Y., and Sharan, S. (1989/90). Group investigation expands cooperative learning. *Educational Leadership, 47*(4), 17–21.

Slavin, R. (1985). An introduction to cooperative learning research. In R. Slavin, S. Sharan, S. Kagan, R. Hertz-Lazarowitz, C. Webb, and R. Schmuck (Eds.), *Learning to cooperate, cooperating to learn.* New York: Plenum Press, pp. 5–15.

Slavin, R. (1988). *Student team learning: An overview and practical guide* (2nd edition). Washington, D.C.: National Education Association.

Slavin R. E. (1989/90). Guest editorial: Here today or gone tomorrow? *Educational Leadership, 47*(4), p. 3.

Stoldolsky, S. S. (1984). Frameworks for studying instructional processes in peer work groups. In P. L. Peterson, L. C. Wilkinson, and M. Hallinan (Eds.), *The social context of instruction.* New York: Academic Press, pp. 107–124.

Swing, S. R., and Peterson, P. L. (1982). The relationship of student ability and small-group interaction to student achievement. *American Educational Research Journal, 19,* 259–274.

Webb, N. M. (1984). Sex differences in interaction and achievement in cooperative small groups. *Journal of Educational Psychology, 76,* 33–44.

Webb, N. M. (1985). Student interaction and learning in small groups: A research summary. In R. Slavin, S. Sharan, S. Kagan, R. Hertz-Lazarowitz, C. Webb, and R. Schmuck (Eds.), *Learning to cooperate, cooperating to learn.* New York, Plenum Press, pp. 147–172.

Webb. N. M., and Kenderski, C. M. (1984). Student interaction and learning in small-group and whole-class settings. In P. L. Peterson, L. C. Wilkinson, and M. Hallinan (Eds.), *The Social context of instruction.* New York: Academic Press, pp. 153–170.

Wesley, D. (1976). *Heritage.* Lakeside, CA: Interact Company.

Wilkinson, L. C., and Calculator, S. (1982). Effective speakers: Students' use of language to request and obtain information and action in the classroom. In L. C. Wilkinson (Ed.), *Communicating in the classroom.* New York: Academic Press, pp. 85–100.

FOR FURTHER READING

Cohen, E. G. (1986). *Designing groupwork: Strategies for the heterogeneous classroom.* New York: Teachers College Press.

Johnson, D. W., Johnson, R. T., Holubec, E. J., and Roy, P. (1984). *Circles of Learning: Cooperation in the classroom.* Alexandria, VA: Association for Supervision and Curriculum Development.

Kagan, S. (1990). *Cooperative learning: Resources for teachers.* San Juan Capistrano, CA: Resources for Teachers.

Slavin, R. (1988). *Student team learning: An overview and practical guide* (2nd edition). Washington, D.C.: National Education Association.

Special issue of *Educational Leadership* (December 1989/January 1990). *Cooperative Learning, 47*(4), pp. 1–67.

Chapter Ten

Managing Recitations and Discussions

Much of the talk that occurs between teachers and students is unlike the talk you hear in the "real world." Let's consider just one example (Cazden, 1988). In the real world, if you ask someone for the time, we can assume you really need to know what time it is and will be grateful for a reply. The conversation would probably go like this:

> "What time is it?"
> "2:30."
> "Thank you."

In contrast, if a teacher asks for the time during a lesson, the dialogue generally sounds like this:

> "What time is it?"
> "2:30."
> "Very good."

Here, the question is not a request for needed information, but a way of finding out what students know. The interaction is more like a quiz show (Roby, 1988) than a true conversation: the teacher asks a question, a student replies, and the teacher evaluates the response (Mehan, 1979). This pattern of interaction is called *recitation,* and several studies (e.g., Stodolsky, 1988) have documented the substantial amount of time that students spend in this subsetting of the classroom.

The recitation has been frequently denounced as a method of instruction. Critics object to the active, dominant role of the teacher and the relatively passive role of the student. They decry the lack of interaction among students. They condemn the fact that recitations often emphasize the recall of factual information and demand little higher-level thinking. (See Figure 10-1 for an example of this kind of recitation.)

An additional criticism focuses on the public evaluation that occurs during recitation. When the teacher calls on a student, everyone can witness and pass judgment on the response. In fact, as Phil Jackson (1968) comments, classmates "frequently join in the act":

Mr. Lowe's fourth-grade students have been reading some of *Aesop's Fables*. Today, they are focusing on "Androcles and the Lion." In this well-known fable, an escaped slave named Androcles earns a lion's gratitude for removing a large thorn stuck in one of the lion's toes. Later, Androcles is recaptured and is to be thrown to the lion, who has also been captured. When the lion's cage is opened, he rushes with a great roar toward his victim. At the last moment, however, he recognizes his friend and treats Androcles with gentleness and gratitude.

MR. LOWE:	Okay, let's start at the very beginning. What is the name of the slave?
STUDENT:	Androcles?
MR. LOWE:	Right. Now how was Androcles treated by his master?
STUDENT:	Cruelly.
MR. LOWE:	Good. So what did Androcles do?
STUDENT:	He escaped.
MR. LOWE:	Ah, yes. He escapes and he heads for the forest. He's wandering around and he meets a . . . a what, Jane?
JANE:	A lion.
MR. LOWE:	Yes, a lion. And something's wrong with the lion. What's wrong, Ari?
ARI:	He has a cut on his paw.
MR. LOWE:	Not exactly a cut. Tasheika?
TASHEIKA:	A thorn is stuck in his paw.
MR. LOWE:	Absolutely. A thorn. And this moaning, whimpering, distressed lion holds out his paw for Androcles, and Androcles does what?
STUDENT:	Takes the thorn out.
MR. LOWE:	Good, he takes the thorn out. Now the lion is so grateful that he leads Androcles to his cave, and they live in the forest together. But one day, when Androcles and the lion went out together, what happened?
STUDENT:	They were captured.
MR. LOWE:	Yes, and then what?
STUDENT:	Androcles is going to be thrown to the lion.
MR. LOWE:	Very good. Yes. And the lion is purposely starved for several days so that he will be even more ferocious. The Emperor and his court all come to the arena to see Androcles face the lion. They expect that the lion will do what, Billy?
STUDENT:	Kill Androcles.
MR. LOWE:	Yes, they think the lion will tear him to shreds. But what happens, Sivan?
SIVAN:	He recognizes Androcles and doesn't kill him.
MR. LOWE:	Right—because the lion is . . . what, class?
STUDENTS:	[Silence.]
MR. LOWE:	How does the lion feel toward Androcles?
STUDENTS:	[Students murmur a variety of responses.] Grateful. Happy. He likes him. Loving.
MR. LOWE:	Good, he is grateful to him for pulling out the thorn so he does not kill him.

FIGURE 10-1
An example of a poor recitation: *Aesop's Fables* as quiz show

> Sometimes the class as a whole is invited to participate in the evaluation of a students' work, as when the teacher asks, "Who can correct Billy?" or "How many believe that Shirley read that poem with a lot of expression?" At other times the evaluation occurs without any urging from the teacher, as when an egregious error elicits laughter or an outstanding performance wins spontaneous applause. (p. 20)

Not surprisingly, this public evaluation enables children to form opinions about who is "smart" and who is "dumb," and these opinions can influence their selection of friends. In a study of third- and fourth-grade classrooms, for example, Bossert (1979) showed that when recitation was the primary instructional strategy, children segregated themselves into homogenous friendship groups based on academic status in the classroom.

Finally, critics observe that the format of the recitation is incompatible with the cultural background of some students. A vivid illustration comes from Susan Philips (1972), who wondered why children on the Warm Springs Indian Reservation in Oregon were so reluctant to participate in classroom recitations. Her analysis of life in this Native American community disclosed a set of behavioral norms that conflict with the way recitations are conducted. As we have noted, recitations permit little student-student interaction, but Warm Springs children are extremely peer-oriented. During recitations, the teacher decides who will participate, while Warm Springs traditions allow individuals to decide for themselves if and when to participate in public events. Recitations involve public performance and public evaluation—even if a student has not yet mastered the material—but Warm Springs children are used to testing their skills in private before they choose to demonstrate them in public. Understanding these disparities helps us to see why the children would find recitations unfamiliar and uncomfortable.

Despite the validity of these criticisms, the recitation remains an extremely common feature of elementary classrooms. What is there about this instructional strategy that makes it so enduring in the face of other, more highly touted methods (Hoetker and Ahlbrand, 1969)?

We thought hard about these questions during one visit to Barbara's classroom, and our observation of a recitation she conducted provided some clues. The students had just read the first few chapters in their new novel, *The Cay* (Taylor, 1969). Barbara asked them to take out their books and to get ready to talk about what they had read. She perched on her stool in the front of the room.

BARBARA: Let's review what you read last night. First of all, what is a cay? [One girl raises her hand.] Only one person? [She pauses and a few more hands go up. Barbara calls on a volunteer.] Maggie?

MAGGIE: An island.

BARBARA: Any particular kind of island?

STUDENT: A very small island.

BARBARA: Okay. What did you find out about where the island was? [A boy raises his hand, but then lowers it.] Ben, you put your hand down, but you wanted to say something?

BEN: It's near Aruba.

BARBARA: Good. What else? [Barbara calls on a nonvolunteer.]

STUDENT: In the Caribbean.

BARBARA: Okay. [Barbara directs students to look at their individual maps and locate the island. When she is satisfied that everyone has located the island, she continues.] This story takes place in what time in history?

STUDENT: 1942.

BARBARA: Good. What important thing was happening then?

STUDENT   It was the middle of World War II.

BARBARA: Right. Where did most of the fighting take place in World War II?

STUDENT: Europe.

BARBARA: Okay, but are they in Europe? [She calls on a nonvolunteer.]

STUDENT: No.

BARBARA: Then why are they affected? [Barbara sounds very puzzled.]

STUDENT: It's a world war, so it affects a lot of places.

BARBARA: True, but why *this* place?

STUDENT: Because there are three submarines there.

BARBARA: But *why?*

STUDENT: Because of a supply of oil that was there.

BARBARA: So what? Why is oil important?

STUDENT: It's worth a lot of money.

BARBARA: Why?

Barbara leads a recitation on *The Cay.*

STUDENT: Because it's rare and we need it.

BARBARA: Okay, it's an important natural resource that's not plentiful everywhere.

Barbara's recitation helped us to identify five very useful functions of classroom recitations. First, the recitation allowed Barbara to review some basic facts about the story and to check on students' comprehension. Second, by asking intellectually demanding questions (e.g., why the war affected people in the Caribbean), Barbara was able to prod her students beyond low-level factual recall to higher levels of thinking. Third, the recitation permitted Barbara to involve students in the presentation of material—what Roby (1988) calls "lecturing in the interrogatory mood." Instead of telling students where the island was located, for example, or why it was affected by the war, Barbara brought out the information by asking questions. Fourth, the recitation provided the chance to interact individually with students, even in the midst of a whole group lesson. In fact, our notes indicate that Barbara made contact with 12 different students in just the brief interaction reported here. Finally, through her questions, changes in voice tone, and gestures, Barbara was able to maintain a relatively high attention level; in other words, she was able to keep most of her students "with her."

Later, Barbara reflected aloud on her use of recitation in this lesson:

Obviously, this was a directed lesson: one of my major goals was to get specific information to everyone without standing there and telling them. Because of this, all the talk was filtered through me. This was real different from a true discussion, when I'd encourage students to talk directly with one another and I'd pretty much stay out of things. Yet one of the interesting things about this kind of lesson is that even though I'm directing it, my kids don't really think of this as *teaching*. They see it more like a personal conversation with me, and don't realize that it's a "lesson."

One of the things I like about recitations is that I can push my kids to give more complete responses than they would in writing. Fourth graders are more comfortable talking than writing, so their oral responses tend to be more complete than their written ones. During a recitation, I can force them to expand on what they're saying, to substantiate their positions. I can also use their verbal responses as a model for the kind of answers that I'd expect on a written test or in a paper.

The recitation also allows me to find out what they don't have straight and to clear up misconceptions that they have about the material. I can also find out what they *bring* to the lesson. For example, in this lesson, I was really impressed by how much they had learned about geography in their social studies class. Since they go to another teacher for social studies, I didn't realize they knew so much about maps and climate. And they also knew more about World War II than I had anticipated.

As we can see, Barbara's recitation session was hardly a "quiz show" in which passive students mindlessly recalled low-level, insignificant facts. On the other hand, both the pattern of talk (teacher initiation, student response, teacher evaluation [I-R-E]) and the primary intent (to assess students' understanding of the reading) set it apart from another type of verbal interaction—the *discussion*. (Table 10-1, adapted from Dillon, 1994, summarizes the differences between recitation and discussion.)

In contrast to recitations, discussion is a form of verbal interaction in which individuals work together to consider an issue or a question. The discussion is in-

TABLE 10-1
DIFFERENCES BETWEEN RECITATIONS AND DISCUSSIONS

Dimension	Recitation	Discussion
1. Predominant speaker	Teacher (⅔ or more)	Students (half or more)
2. Typical exchange	Teacher question; student answer; teacher evaluation (I-R-E)	Mix of statements and questions by mix of teachers and students
3. Pace	Many brief, fast exchanges	Fewer, longer, slower exchanges
4. Primary purpose	To check students' comprehension	To stimulate variety of responses; encourage students to consider different points of view; to foster problem-solving and critical thinking; to examine implications
5. The answer	Predetermined right or wrong; same right answer for all students	Not predetermined right or wrong; can have different answers for different students
6. Evaluation	Right/wrong, by teacher only	Agree/disagree, by student and teacher

tended to stimulate a variety of responses, to encourage students to consider different points of view, to foster problem-solving, to examine implications, and to relate material to students' own personal experiences (Good and Brophy, 1994). In a discussion, individuals may offer their understandings, relevant facts, suggestions, opinions, perspectives, and experiences. These are examined for their usefulness in answering the question or resolving the issue (Dillon, 1994).

In order to make the distinction between recitation and discussion clear, let's consider another example, this time from Ken's class.

Eight students are sitting at the reading table with Ken, about to discuss the book they have been reading, *George Washington's Socks* by Elvira Woodruff (1991). They roll a die to see who goes first. A "two" comes up; thus, the second person from the end, Eric, goes first. Eric asks the other students an analysis question that he had prepared on the reading assignment. [Analysis questions require students to go beyond simple recall or comprehension to a deeper examination of the meaning.]

ERIC: Should Adam Hibbs have returned the General's cape instead of Matt?
SUZANNE: In a way, yes . . . because he was the soldier and Matt wasn't the soldier.
CHARLENE: I don't think so. Adam Hibbs should not have returned it because he could get in a lot of trouble for leaving his post.
LAUREN: I think Adam should have returned it because he was older and then he wouldn't have fallen on the bayonet.

The interaction becomes heated; several students speak at the same time. Ken looks at Eric and quietly murmurs: "You might want to get some control of this discussion."

ERIC: Okay, hold on. Jamie, what do you think?
JAMIE: For me, it's kind of in the middle. . . .

NEIL: Yeah, for me too, it's right smack in the middle. In a way I think he should have left it there, because he returns the cape and then—

SUZANNE: [interrupting Neil] the captain says, "You're in the war."

NEIL: And it's just a cape. What's the big deal? Somebody else could've given him a cape.

The discussion continues for a few more minutes. Then Ken asks Eric to read the answer he has prepared to his own question.

KEN: Comments about Eric's answer?

CHARLENE: If Adam Hibbs hadn't let Matt go, then maybe he wouldn't have gotten hurt.

LAUREN: Some of your answer goes along with the question, but then in the end, I think you were talking about something else. . . .

A few more comments are made on Eric's answer.

KEN: What a great analysis question! You saw all the debate, discussion it generated. I don't even have to judge the question; you can judge for yourself from the reaction. Okay, let's hear another question. Suzanne?

SUZANNE: Why did Matt return George Washington's cape?

ELEANOR: He didn't want the general to be cold.

MARK: Yeah, he would have frozen.

There's silence.

JESSICA: I think this is a comprehension question, not an analysis question.

KEN: Yes, it can be. But you can also answer it like an analysis question. When we want to figure out really why somebody does something, it's rarely so simple. Let's examine this more deeply. Let's take a look at page 47. Read it to yourselves and then let's continue. [Discussion continues about the reasons for Matt's returning the cape.]

As we can see from this excerpt, the predominant pattern in this interchange was not I-R-E, but initiation (by a student) followed by multiple responses (I-R-R-R). Ken essentially stays out of the interaction, except for making sure that students have an opportunity to speak when the interaction gets excited and pushing students to probe more deeply. In contrast to the recitation, students speak directly to one another. They comment on one another's contributions; they question; they disagree; and they explain.

Recitation and discussion are often confused. Teachers often say that they use discussion a great deal, when in fact they are conducting recitations. For example, in a provocative article entitled "What Teachers Do When They Say They're Having Discussions of Content Area Reading Assignments," Alvermann, O'Brien, and Dillon (1990) found that although 24 middle school teachers reported using discussion, only seven could actually be observed doing so; the others were using recitation and lecture with question-answer. These findings are consistent with observations of 1,000 elementary and secondary classrooms across the country, in which discussion was seen only 4 to 7 percent of the time (Goodlad, 1984). It is clear that real discussion is very rarely used in classrooms.

James Dillon (1994) suggests three major reasons for the infrequency of class-room discussion. First, discussion does not come naturally; it has to be learned, and it is difficult—for both students and teachers. Second, teachers themselves have had few experiences with classroom discussions and may not have received training and guidance in leading them. Finally, school culture is generally not supportive of discussion. If teachers feel pressured to "cover the curriculum" and to have students do well on standardized tests, they may consider discussion a luxury they cannot afford. In addition, providing opportunities for discussions means that teachers have to give up their role as *leader* and assume the role of *facilitator.* This can be difficult for teachers who work in schools that emphasize control and who are used to dominating or at least directing the conversation.

Educational critics frequently decry the use of recitation and promote the use of discussion, but both types of interaction have a legitimate place in the elementary classroom—if done well. As Tom Good and Jere Brophy (1994) write: "The oper-ative question about recitation for most teachers is not whether to use it but when and how to use it effectively" (p. 386).

This chapter begins by examining the managerial problems associated with recitations. Like seatwork and groupwork, this subsetting has its own set of "built-in hazards" (Carter, 1985)—unequal participation; loss of pace, focus, and in-volvement; and the difficulty of monitoring comprehension. Next, we consider what our teachers and the research have to say about minimizing these problems. We then turn to a consideration of discussions and offer some guidelines for man-aging this pattern of interaction.

THE PITFALLS OF RECITATIONS

Unequal Participation

Imagine yourself in front of a class of 25 children. You've just asked a question. A few children are wildly waving their hands, murmuring, "ooh, ooh," and clearly conveying their desire to be called on. Others are sitting quietly, staring into space, their expressions blank. Still others are slumped down as far as possible in their seats; their posture clearly says, "Don't call on me."

In a situation like this, it's tempting to call on a child who is eager to be chosen. After all, you're likely to get the correct response—a very gratifying situation! You also avoid embarrassing children who feel uncomfortable speaking in front of the group or who don't know the answer, and you're able to keep up the pace of the lesson. But selecting only those who volunteer or those who call out may limit the interaction to a handful of students. This can be a problem. Students tend to learn more if they are actively participating (Morine-Dershimer and Beyerbach, 1987). Furthermore, since those who volunteer are often high achievers, calling only on volunteers is likely to give you a distorted picture of how well everyone under-stands. Finally, restricting your questions to a small number of students can com-municate negative expectations to the others (Good and Brophy, 1994): "I'm not calling on you because I'm sure you don't know the answer."

Losing It All: Pace, Focus, and Involvement

In the early 1960s, a popular television program capitalized on the fact that "Kids Say the Darndest Things." The title of the show aptly describes what can happen during a recitation. When you ask your question, you might receive the response you have in mind. You might also get answers that indicate confusion and misunderstanding, ill-timed remarks that have nothing to do with the lesson (e.g., "There's gum on my shoe" or "I forgot my lunch money"), or unexpected comments that momentarily throw you off balance. All of these threaten the smooth flow of a recitation or discussion and can cause it to become sluggish, jerky, or unfocused.

Threats like these require you to make instantaneous decisions about how to proceed. It's not easy. If a student's answer reveals confusion, for example, it's essential to provide feedback and assistance. On the other hand, staying with that student can cause the lesson to become so slow that everyone else begins to daydream and fidget. During recitations, you are frequently confronted with two incompatible needs: the need to stay with an individual to enhance that child's learning and the need to move on to avoid losing both the momentum and the group's attention.

At one point in Barbara's lesson on *The Cay,* we saw a good illustration of this tension. Students had been talking about the problems faced by the main character, when Jessica suddenly raised her hand and asked, "If I got stranded on an island in the Caribbean, would it be possible for me to live?" The question was clearly out of sequence, but Barbara allowed it to stand. In fact, she responded, "*I* don't know." Turning to the class, she asked, "What do *you* think? Could Jessica survive?" That initiated a long interchange on the relevant factors: presence of food, water, shelter, temperature, animals, etc. Eventually, Barbara returned students' attention to the book:

BARBARA: Okay, we've been talking about Jessica's being stranded on an island and whether she could survive. How does this relate to the book?

STUDENT: Philip gets stranded on an island.

When we discussed this incident with Barbara after her lesson, she explained why she decided to pursue Jessica's question:

Jessica's question really floored me, and I was tempted to go on. We had been moving at a nice clip, and I didn't want to lose the flow. I also didn't want to lose the focus of the discussion. But she seemed sincere—it didn't seem like a ploy to get us off the topic—and she hardly ever participates. This book is really a challenge for her. I decided to let the question stand because I wanted to bring her into the conversation, to "move her up" in the eyes of the other kids, and to give her some credibility. Also, I decided I could use the question to bring up some of the problems that Philip, the character in the book, has to face. But I was taking a risk. It's so easy for a lesson to get way off target. When you're standing up there, it can get really scary. Sometimes, you don't have a clue what they're going to bring up when you ask a question. It's hard to tell a child we can't talk about that now, but if you follow every tangent someone brings up, you'll never get anywhere. If I decide not to talk about a question or a comment a child brings up, I try to write it on the board and remember to talk about it later, maybe during free time or lunch.

When "kids say the darndest things" during a recitation, it's easy to lose the pace of the lesson. But questioning sessions can also become bogged down if the teacher has not developed a set of verbal or nonverbal signals that communicate to children when they are to raise their hands and when they are to respond chorally. Without clear signals, students are likely to call out when the teacher wants them to raise their hands, or to remain silent and raise their hands when the teacher wants them to call out in a choral response.

Sometimes, questioning sessions get sluggish because ambiguity in the teacher's question makes it difficult for students to respond. For example, Farrar (1988) analyzed a social studies lesson in which the teacher asked a yes-no question: "Did you read anywhere in the book that Washington's army was destroyed?" When students responded, "No," and "Uh-uh," he rejected their answers. The result was confusion and a momentary breakdown of the recitation. In retrospect, it appears that the teacher was not really expecting a yes or no answer, but wanted a restatement of information that had appeared in the reading. Students responded to his *explicit* question, while he was waiting for the answer to his *implicit* question: "What happened to Washington's army?"

Difficulties in Monitoring Students' Comprehension

Recitations provide an opportunity for teachers to check students' comprehension, but doing so is not always easy. Recently, a fifth-grade teacher told us about a lesson taught by her student teacher, Rebecca. The class had been studying the human body, and halfway through the unit, Rebecca planned to give her students a quiz. On the day of the quiz, she conducted a brief review of the material by firing off a series of questions on the respiratory and circulatory systems. Satisfied with the high percentage of correct answers, Rebecca then asked, "Before I give out the quiz, are there any questions?" When there were none, she added, "So everybody understands?" Again, there was silence. Rebecca told the students to close their books and distributed the quiz papers. That afternoon, she corrected the quiz. The results were an unpleasant shock; a large number of students received D's and F's. During a post-lesson conference with her cooperating teacher, she wailed, "How could this happen? They certainly knew the answers during our review session!"

This incident underscores the difficulty of gauging the extent to which all members of a class really understand what is going on. As we mentioned earlier, teachers sometimes get fooled because they call only on volunteers—the students most likely to give the correct answers. In this case, Rebecca's cooperating teacher had kept a "map" of the verbal interaction between teacher and students and was able to share some revealing data: during a 15-minute review, Rebecca had called on only *six* of the 19 children in the class, and all of these had been volunteers. Although this allowed Rebecca to maintain the smooth flow of the interaction, it led her to overestimate the extent of students' mastery. Moreover, as Rebecca's cooperating teacher pointed out to her, questions that try to assess comprehension by asking, "Does everyone understand?" are unlikely to be successful. There's no accountability built into questions like this; in other words, they don't require students to demonstrate an understanding of the material. In addition, students who do not understand are often too embarrassed to admit it. (They may not even realize they don't understand!) Clearly, you need to find other ways to assess if your class is "with" you.

STRATEGIES FOR MANAGING RECITATIONS

Recitations pose formidable challenges to teachers. You need to respond to each individual's learning needs, while maintaining the attention and interest of the group; to distribute participation widely, without dampening the enthusiasm of those who are eager to volunteer; to assess students' understanding without embarrassing those who don't know the answers; to allow students to contribute to the interaction, while remaining "on course."

In this section of the chapter, we suggest five strategies for meeting these challenges. As in previous chapters, research on teaching, discussions with our four teachers, and observations of their classes provide the basis for our suggestions. Although there are no foolproof guarantees of success, these strategies can reduce the hazards associated with recitations. (Table 10-2 provides a summary of our suggestions.)

TABLE 10-2
STRATEGIES FOR MANAGING RECITATIONS

Strategy	Example
Distribute chances to participate	Pick names from a cup.
	Check off names on a seating chart.
	Use patterned turn-taking.
Provide time to think	Extend wait time to three seconds.
	Tell students you don't expect an immediate answer.
	Allow students to write a response.
Stimulate and maintain interest	Inject mystery and suspense.
	Inject humor and novelty.
	Challenge students to think.
	Incorporate physical activity.
Provide feedback to students	When answer is correct and confident, affirm briefly.
	When answer is correct but hesitant, provide more deliberate affirmation.
	When answer is incorrect, but careless, make a simple correction.
	When answer is incorrect but student could get answer with help, prompt or backtrack to simpler question.
	If student is unable to respond, don't belabor the issue.
Require overt responses	Have students hold up response cards, physically display answers with manipulative materials, respond chorally.
Use a steering group	Observe the performance of a sample of students (including low-achievers) in order to know when to move on.

Distributing Chances to Participate

Early in the school year, we watched Ken conduct a recitation using his "coffee cup system" of calling on students. (This was described briefly in Chapter 4, when we discussed interaction routines.) The lesson involved "summer maps" the students had created a few days earlier. Each student had selected a "key word" to represent a highlight of the summer and had printed it in the middle of a large piece of paper. Around the key word, students had placed related words, drawing lines among the words to indicate relationships. Ken used the summer maps in a variety of lessons and activities. He introduced students to the thesaurus, for example, by having them find synonyms for a word that appeared on their maps. The recitation we watched him conduct was based on this synonym activity:

> Ken stands toward the front of the room, a coffee mug in his hand. In the mug are small slips of paper, each one containing a letter of the alphabet.
>
> KEN: When I call your letter, tell me what word you found a synonym for and then give the synonyms. *Remember, the cup knows.* . . . [He pulls a paper from the cup. On it is printed the letter B.] Banana, give me a word.
>
> BANANA: [He is caught off guard.] I didn't finish yet.
>
> KEN: Aha, see, *the cup knows.* . . . [He pulls another paper from the cup: "I."] All right, Iceberg, give me a word.
>
> ICEBERG: Fun.
>
> KEN: What are the synonyms?
>
> ICEBERG: Amusement, play, sport, good time, pleasure, entertainment, enjoyment.
>
> KEN: [He turns to the class.] Did you hear that? I heard *seven* words for fun. How many people had fun somewhere on their summer map? [Students raise their hands. He acknowledges their hands with a nod.] Great job, Iceberg. [He pulls a new letter from the cup.] Obedient.
>
> OBEDIENT: Pain. Hurt. I just started, so I only have one.
>
> KEN: You have your thesaurus? [The boy nods.] Okay, keep working. [He pulls a new letter.] Lucky.
>
> LUCKY: Mission.
>
> KEN: That's a real space word. What's his keyword, anyone remember?
>
> CLASS: Space Camp.
>
> KEN: Good memory. Okay, Lucky, what are your synonyms for mission?
>
> LUCKY: Errand, task, job, assignment, duty.
>
> KEN: He got *five* synonyms. What do we know about five?
>
> STUDENT: It's a Fibonacci number
>
> KEN: Right. Well done, Aaron.

When we discussed this lesson with Ken, we asked him about the use of the cup to select students and what he had meant when he said, "The cup knows. . . . " We also commented on his students' strange "names." Ken explained:

> Using the cup helps me to make sure that I get around to everyone. Once a person's letter is called, I keep that slip of paper out of the cup so everyone gets a chance. I find that unless I use a system like this, I have trouble keeping track of who's gotten a chance to talk and who hasn't. And some kids are so eager to volunteer that they'd probably monopolize the whole lesson.

I tell the kids that the cup is going to call on people who are not ready. It's amazing, but it often works out that the first few people the cup calls aren't ready. I've had kids convinced that the cup really knows. In one class, we used to chant, "Cup, cup, wake someone up." This system works well for me. The kids know that I'm not looking around the room, hoping to catch someone who doesn't know the answer or who's not ready. It's purely random, but it serves to keep them on their toes.

About the strange names, I used to list the kids' names in alphabetical order and give them each a number. This way, things like taking attendance can go real quickly. The kids simply count off. A while back, I got the idea of giving students a letter of the alphabet instead of a number, and letting them choose a word that begins with that letter. When I take attendance, they "count off" in alphabetical order by saying their word. It's more personal than numbers. And it makes whole class lessons more fun when you call on "Obedient," "Knowledgeable," and "Vacuum Cleaner," instead of Susan or Mark.

Ken doesn't use the coffee mug for every recitation, and we are certainly not suggesting that you should do so. There are times when you won't want to call on students randomly, preferring to select particular individuals for particular questions. Nonetheless, the cup system helps Ken to sustain students' attention and to distribute participation widely and fairly. It also enables him to keep the pace moving, since he doesn't have to deliberate each time he calls on someone. Watching him, we recalled a study by McDermott (1977) of first-grade reading groups. McDermott found that turn-taking in the high-achievement group proceeded efficiently in round robin fashion, with little time lost between readers. In the low-achievement group, however, the teacher allowed the students to bid for a turn, and so much time was devoted to deciding who would read next that students spent only one-third as much time reading as students in the top group.

Instead of a coffee mug, some teachers use a list of names or a seating chart to keep track of who has spoken, placing a tick mark by the name of each child who participates. Other teachers use "patterned turn taking," calling on students in some designated order. The research evidence on the usefulness of this practice is inconclusive. Many educators (e.g., Kounin, 1970) argue that patterned turn taking leads to inattention, since children know exactly when they will be called on. But research by Jere Brophy and Carolyn Evertson (1976) found that the use of patterned turn taking in small reading groups leads to higher achievement. One explanation for this finding is that patterned turn taking allows more reading to occur, as in the McDermott study we just cited. Another explanation is that the use of a pattern ensures that everyone has an opportunity to interact with the teacher.

Whichever system you choose, *the important point is to make sure that the interaction is not dominated by a few volunteers.* As Barbara comments:

Students have to know they're going to be held accountable for the material. You've got to be the responsible adult. It's your job to keep everyone involved and to bring in the kids who are not talking. I generally ask, "What do *you* think?" or "Do you agree with what Peter said?" If a kid isn't comfortable talking, I may not call on them as frequently, and when I do, I try to be especially gentle. I'll ask something I know they know, or I'll call on them as soon as I see any gesture that indicates they're thinking about raising their hand. I also try to validate what the kid said, something like, "Peter just told us. . . . " But however I do it, I eventually get to everyone, and my kids know that.

"Getting to everyone" can be a daunting task, especially in a large class. One useful strategy is to allow several students to answer a question. In the following interaction, we see Garnetta increase participation by not "grabbing" the first answer and moving on:

GARNETTA: What do you do when you experiment?
STUDENT: Invent things.
GARNETTA: Okay, what else? [There's silence.] I'm going to put two letters on the board as a hint. [Writes IN.]
STUDENT: Investigate!
GARNETTA: Good! That's a big word. We traded one big word—experiment—for another—investigate. What does investigate mean?
STUDENT: When you be trying to find something out.
STUDENT: When you be a detective and try to find something out.
STUDENT: Finding out the facts—looking and finding out.
GARNETTA: Out of sight! [Writes on board: look at something, find out the facts, be a detective.]

At times, distributing participation is difficult not because children are reluctant to speak and there are too *few* volunteers, but because there are too *many*. The more teachers stimulate interest in a particular lesson, the more students want to respond. This means greater competition for each turn (Doyle, 1986), and "bidding" for a chance to speak can become loud and unruly. During one visit to Garnetta's class, we watched her deal with this situation. She and the students were talking about a movie they had just seen, *A Connecticut Yankee in King Arthur's Court*. The children were incredibly excited about the movie and were eager to share their reactions:

GARNETTA: Let's think about the ways people lived at the time of King Arthur. What did you see in the movie that was the same as the way we live now? [There are lots of "oohs," and calls of "Ms. Chain" as children compete for a chance to respond.] So many people want to talk, let's just go around, and hear one from everybody. Aleesha, you start.
ALEESHA: They rode horses and we ride horses. [Garnetta continues to call on students in order.]

Garnetta was able to use a "round robin" pattern of turn-taking because her class is small (15 students). This approach might not work so well in a larger class, where children seated at the "end of the line" sometimes feel cheated because they have nothing new to add. An alternative strategy is to have each child write a response and share it with one or two neighbors. This allows everyone to participate actively. You might then ask some of the groups to report on what they discussed.

It's also important to make sure that males and females have equal opportunity to participate. A recent review of the literature (Grossman and Grossman, 1994) reports that "teachers demonstrate a clear bias in favor of male participation in their classes":

> Teachers are more likely to call on a male volunteer when students are asked to recite; this is also true when they call on nonvolunteers. When students recite, teachers are also more likely to listen to and talk to males. They also use more of their ideas in classroom discussions and respond to them in more helpful ways (p. 76)

Similarly, *How Schools Shortchange Girls* (1992), a study commissioned by the American Association of University Women (AAUW), reports that males often demand—and receive—more attention from teachers. In one study of elementary and middle school students, Sadker, Sadker, and Thomas (1981) found that boys called out answers eight times more often than girls did. Furthermore, when the boys called out, teachers typically listened to the comment. In contrast, when girls called out, they were usually told to "Please raise your hand if you want to speak." In another study, Sadker and Sadker (1985) found that, even when boys do not volunteer, the teacher is more likely to solicit their responses.

Why would teachers allow male students to dominate classroom interaction by calling out? Morse and Handley (1985) suggest three possible reasons: (1) the behavior is so frequent that teachers come to accept it; (2) teachers expect males to be aggressive; and (3) the call-outs may be perceived by teachers as indicators of interest. Whatever the reasons, teachers need to be sensitive to gender differences in participation and use strategies to ensure that both males and females have opportunities to participate.

One final thought: While you're thinking about ways to distribute participation widely, keep in mind the suggestions we made in Chapter 3 when we talked about the action zone phenomenon: (1) move around the room whenever possible; (2) establish eye contact with students seated farther away from you; (3) direct comments to students seated in the rear and on the sides; and (4) periodically change students' seats so that all students have an opportunity to be up front.

Providing Time to Think Without Losing the Pace

In Chapter 4, we talked about the "what ifs" that plague beginning teachers: What if the kids don't listen to me? What if a student asks a question and I don't know the answer? A particularly common "what if" is associated with recitations: What if I ask a question and there's complete silence? The possibility of this situation haunts many of us as we plan our lessons.

One reason silence is so uncomfortable is that it's hard to interpret: Are students thinking about the question? Are they asleep? Are they so muddled they're unable to respond? Silence is also troubling to teachers because it can threaten the pace and momentum of the lesson (Arends, 1991). Even a few seconds of silence can seem like eternity. This helps to explain why many teachers wait less than *one second* before calling on a student (Rowe, 1974). Yet research demonstrates that if you extend *"wait time"* to three or four seconds, you can increase the quality of students' answers and promote participation. In fact, Garnetta finds it helpful to count silently to ten.

Sometimes, it's helpful to indicate to students that you don't expect an immediate answer. This "legitimizes" the silence and gives students an opportunity to formulate their responses. During Barbara's recitation lesson on *The Cay*, we saw her indicate to children that she wanted everyone to think for a while before responding:

BARBARA: What's one survival technique that CT used? [Children raise their hands.] Jim? [He had not raised his hand.]

JIM: Using a carved twig for fire.

BARBARA: Show us on the board how the twig was carved. While he's drawing, the rest of you think of another. [He draws a twig that has been carved. Barbara turns to the class.] Why would that burn more easily? [A few students raise their hands.] Everyone put your hands down and think for a minute. [There's a long pause. Then a few hands go back up; then some more. Finally Barbara nods to a student.]

GIRL: Because there are more places to burn?

BARBARA: Right.

Allowing children to write an answer to your question is another way of providing them with time to think. Written responses also help to maintain students' engagement, since everyone has to construct a response. In addition, students who are uncomfortable speaking extemporaneously can read from their written papers. We observed an example of this strategy when Barbara's class began their study of *Sarah, Plain and Tall* (MacLachlan, 1985). Barbara gave them the following directions:

BARBARA: Read the first chapter silently. While you do that, I'm going to give each of you a piece of paper. Write down just a little bit about each of the characters you meet. [When students have finished reading and writing, Barbara regains their attention.] Okay, you met Sarah. What did you learn about her?

Once you have selected someone to respond, it's also important to provide that student with an opportunity to think. This is another kind of wait time, and research has documented that here, too, teachers often jump in too soon (Rowe, 1974). Sometimes they provide the answer themselves or call on another child. This is particularly tempting if other students are frantically waving their hands. Watch the way Ken deals with this situation during a lesson on number sequences:

KEN: What is Sequence C? Robin? [Robin is silent. Other children in the class are waving their hands to answer and murmuring "ooh, ooh, Mr. K. . . . "] Let her take her time. This is tricky. Give her a chance. . . .

ROBIN: It's adding on every odd number, 1, 3, 5. . . .

KEN: Hmmm, I wonder if that continues. . . .

Stimulating and Maintaining Interest

In previous chapters, we have discussed Kounin's classic study (1970) of the differences between orderly and disorderly classrooms. One finding of that study was that children are more involved in work and less disruptive when teachers attempt to involve nonreciting children in the recitation task, maintain their attention, and keep them "on their toes." Kounin called this behavior "group alerting." Our observations of our four teachers reveal that they frequently use group-alerting strategies to stimulate attention and to maintain the pace of the lesson. For example, watch how Garnetta creates interest in her upcoming lesson by beginning with mystery and suspense:

GARNETTA: I need everyone to look up here while I draw something on the board. You know I'm not an artist, so this won't be perfect. [Students all murmur, "Amen." Slowly and deliberately, Garnetta draws a pattern of triangles and squares on the board. As she draws, students call out, "It's curtains." "It's a baseball field." "It's congruent shapes."] Now that I have your attention, I'm going to tell you what we're going to do. These are like pieces of a . . .

STUDENTS: Puzzle!

GARNETTA: Right. We're going to do a puzzle. I'm going to give you seven pieces of plastic. They're called Tangrams. You need to make a square with the pieces. You need to use *all* the pieces. You may work with a partner. The person next to you would be best.

Ken also injects suspense into recitations that could be dry and boring. For example, in a lesson on number sequences, students were to compare the rate at which "Fibonacci" numbers increase (1, 1, 2, 3, 5, 8, 13, 21, . . .) in comparison with sequences that square (1, 4, 9, 16, 25, . . .) or add ten (10, 20, 30, 40, 50, . . .):

KEN: Look at this. It's round 12 and Fibonacci and Squares are neck and neck. Which is going to win?

STUDENTS: [Chorally] Fibonacci.

KEN: Are you *sure?* Fibonacci started off *so slow* and it's going to get *higher* than squares? [With real amazement in his voice.]

STUDENTS: Yeah!

KEN: So . . . all you people who told me Fibonacci was going to come in last were wrong! They came in what?

STUDENTS: Second.

KEN: What came in last?

STUDENTS: Tens.

KEN: Yeah, all you hot shots who told me yesterday that my team was going to come in last, just look at the chalkboard. Tens came in last!

Children's interest can also be maintained if you inject some humor or novelty into the recitation itself. During an observation of Viviana's math class, she was discussing "story problems":

VIVIANA: I'm going to give you a few seconds to think of a story problem. [Pause while children think.] Luis?

LUIS: Anita has four dolls. Her sister has three fewer dolls. How many dolls does her sister have?

VIVIANA: What information is the problem giving us?

STUDENT: That Anita has four dolls.

VIVIANA: What else?

STUDENT: Her sister has three fewer.

VIVIANA: Three fewer what? Cats? [The children laugh.]

CLASS: [Choral response] Dolls.

Challenges to students can also be a way of keeping them on their toes. During another math lesson, for example, Viviana told her students, "This next one is not baby stuff. This one you really have to think about and read the directions." The excitement in the room was almost palpable, and afterwards we heard students murmuring, "This is easy, this is baby stuff, I can do this." Viviana's challenge is reminiscent of the behavior of "Teacher X," one of the subjects in Hermine Marshall's (1987) study of three teachers' motivational strategies. Marshall found that Teacher X frequently used statements designed to challenge students to think: "I'm going to trick you," "Get your brain started. . . . You're going to think," "Get your mind started," "Look bright-eyed and bushy-tailed" (stated according to Marshall, "with enthusiasm and a touch of humor"). This frequent use of statements to stimulate and maintain student attention was in sharp contrast to the statements made by the other two teachers in the study. In fact, Teacher Y and Teacher Z *never* used the strategy of alerting students to pay attention, and they rarely challenged students to think. The vast majority of their directives were attempts to *return* students to the task *after* attention and interest had waned.

Another day, we observed Viviana teach her students about action verbs. Although this can be deadly dull, the room was alive with excitement because Viviana allowed her children to engage in the actions they were studying:

VIVIANA: Let's stand up. Run in place. Run, run, run, run. Don't stop until I tell you to. [All the children run in place by their desks.] You are doing something. What are you doing?

STUDENTS: We're running.

VIVIANA: So run is an action. Something you are doing. Okay, stop. Let's . . . hop. [Children begin to hop in place.] Are you doing something?

STUDENTS: Yes.

VIVIANA: What are you doing?

STUDENTS: We're hopping.

VIVIANA: So hop is an action, something you are doing. [The pattern repeats as children jump and then skip around the room back to their desks.]

All too often, incorporating physical activity in a lesson leads to chaos rather than involvement. Viviana can use this strategy because she has established herself as the classroom leader. She tells us:

You have to know your class first. I'd never do this the first week of school. You have to have the rules and routines well established and make sure the children know exactly what you expect. I tell them, "This will be fun, but you have to listen carefully to my directions so that we can all learn." It's really important to wait until you know your class and your class knows you.

Providing Feedback Without Losing the Pace

As we discussed in Chapter 7, the BTES (Fisher et al., 1980) study documented the importance of providing feedback to students:

When more frequent feedback is offered, students pay attention more and learn more. Academic feedback was more strongly and consistently related to achievement than any of the other teaching behaviors. (p. 27)

But how can you provide appropriate feedback while maintaining the pace and momentum of your lesson? Barak Rosenshine (1986) has reviewed the research on effective teaching and has developed a set of guidelines that may be helpful. According to Rosenshine, when students give correct, confident answers, you can simply ask another question or provide a brief verbal or nonverbal indication that they are correct. If students are correct but hesitant, however, a more deliberate affirmation is necessary. You might also explain *why* the answer is correct ("Yes, that's correct, because . . . ") in order to reinforce the material.

When students provide an incorrect answer, the feedback process is trickier. If you think the child has made a careless error, you can make a simple correction and move on. If you decide the student can arrive at the correct answer with a little help, you can provide hints or prompts. Sometimes it's useful to backtrack to a simpler question that you think the child can answer, and then work up to your original question step by step.

There are times when students are simply unable to respond to your question. When that happens, there's little point in belaboring the issue by providing prompts or cues (Good and Brophy, 1994). This will only make the recitation sluggish. Ken allows students in this situation to "pass," and both he and Garnetta permit children to call on a friend to help. These practices not only help to maintain the pace, they also allow students to "save face." Meanwhile, the teachers make a mental note that they need to reteach the material to the individuals having difficulty.

We saw a good example of this situation in Viviana's class when she was introducing the concept of thirds. Her students had been working on "halves" with Cuisenaire™ rods. After seeing that two yellow rods were equivalent to one orange rod, and that each yellow rod was one-half of the orange, Viviana asked the children to take the blue rod (the "nine" rod):

VIVIANA: Everyone have the blue rod? Okay, divide it into equal parts. [A boy yells out, "Three greens." Viviana tells him that by yelling out he is not being fair to other children, not giving them a chance to figure out the answer. She scans the room and sees that everyone has three greens lined up with one blue.] How many greens equal one blue?

STUDENTS: Three.

VIVIANA: If you give one green to your friend, how many are left?

STUDENTS: Two.

VIVIANA: Good. If you give one green to your friend, what *fraction* have you given away? [There is silence. Children look puzzled. A few children try a guess: $\frac{1}{2}$? One? Two? Noting the extreme confusion, Viviana provides the answer.] You have given away one-third. And you kept two-thirds. We'll talk about this more tomorrow. Now we have to clean up and go to lunch. We need to collect the blocks. I want to see neat tables.

Afterwards, we spoke with Viviana about what had happened during the lesson. She told us why she had decided to "give up" on her question about thirds:

There was just too much confusion, and I didn't want the children to get frustrated. It was also too close to lunch time to start reteaching about thirds; when they're hungry, it's hard to think. It was better to just tell them the answer. Tomorrow I can pick up from where we left off.

We also talked with Viviana about how to provide appropriate feedback when children's answers are clearly incorrect. She was very emphatic as she talked about the need to be honest and clear. We think her perspective is worth remembering:

I strongly believe that teachers should not sugar coat their responses to children's an-swers for fear of hurting children's feelings. If the answer is wrong, the child needs to know it's wrong. *You can reject an answer without rejecting a child.* But you have to explain *why* the answer is wrong. I often ask other children to help out. When I get the right answer from another child, I go back to the first child and check to see if they now understand. It's important not to leave kids hanging.

Monitoring Comprehension: Requiring Overt Responses

A simple way to determine how well your students understand the material is to have them respond overtly to your questions. For example, you might give children cards reading "yes" or "no," colored red or green, or depicting a happy face or a sad face, which they then hold up in response to your yes/no questions. Students can also use small chalkboards or white laminated boards to write one- or two-word responses (Narayan, Heward, Gardner III, Courson, and Omness, 1990). In mathe-matics, students can use number cards or operation sign cards to show you the cor-rect answer. "Number fans" (Rief, 1993) are also useful for whole group responses; they can be used to indicate "strongly agree" (1), "I kind of agree" (2), or "I dis-agree" (3). (See Figure 10-2.) Barbara often uses "thumbs up" or "thumbs down" signals to check on students' comprehension:

BARBARA: Who can show me what I showed you yesterday about fractions? Let's say I have the fraction ¼. Okay, Brenda, take the chalk and go for it. [Brenda takes the chalk and goes to the board. She writes ¼, referring to the top number as the numerator and the bottom number as the denominator and explaining what each number represents.] How many people agree with that? Put your thumbs up if you agree, thumbs down if you disagree. [Barbara scans the room.] Okay, Brenda, we have total agreement.

You can also have children manipulate some material at their seats and physi-cally display their work. During one visit to Garnetta's class, she was reviewing di-vision with her students. She had students work with colored blocks at their desks, while one student did the division problem at the chalkboard:

GARNETTA: Okay, now count out 48. I see most of you have taken four ten blocks and eight ones blocks. Put the other ones away. We're going to divide the 48 by four. [There's a gasp, as if the children think that's too hard.] You're going to divide the 48 blocks into four groups. [One child murmurs, "Oh, that's easy!"]

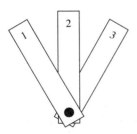

FIGURE 10-2
Number Fans (from Rief, 1993)
Number fans can be made by writing numerals on cardboard tag cards, hole punch one end and attach with a brad. Students hold up their answer to math problems or math facts.

> Rashad, you come to the board and do the problem while everyone else works with the blocks. Okay, let's see how many you put in each group. [She scans the room to see how the students did on the problem.] I want only hands.

STUDENT: 12.

GARNETTA: Everyone, look up here at the problem on the board. Rashad, what did you get?

RASHAD. 12.

GARNETTA: Okay, so everybody agrees. Now let's do this problem. [She writes $2/\overline{28}$ on the chalkboard.]

Another way of assessing students' comprehension is by having them respond chorally rather than individually. This allows you to scan the room and see who's having difficulty. Let's watch Viviana, who frequently uses this strategy:

> Viviana is seated behind a large abacus with 100 brightly colored beads. As she moves each bead across the rod, the children count out loud in unison.

VIVIANA: We have 100 beads here. It took us a long time to count by ones, didn't it? Now let's count by twos and see which way is faster. [The children count out loud by twos.] Which was faster?

STUDENTS: [Choral response.] By twos.

VIVIANA: What's another way to count? [She shoots her hand into the air, indicating that children should raise their hands.] Jose?

JOSE: By fives.

VIVIANA: Okay, let's go. [The class counts by fives.] Now which way should we . . . [Students start yelling out "by fives," "by tens."] Wait a minute, wait . . . wait . . . wait . . . You're not letting me ask the question. You're getting ahead of me."

Monitoring Comprehension: Using a Steering Group

Another way of checking on students' understanding is to observe a "steering group." This is a sample of students whose performance is used as an indicator that the class is "with you" and that it's all right to move on to a new topic (Lundren, 1972, cited in Good and Brophy, 1994). Be careful, however, about choosing students for the steering group. If you select only high achievers, their performance may lead you to overestimate the comprehension of the class as a whole.

During one discussion with Garnetta, she indicated that Joelle, a low-achieving student, was a key member of her mathematics steering group. She shared this example of how Joelle helps her to monitor the class's understanding:

> We were working on place value, and I wrote 382 on the board. I asked Joelle to tell us which number was in the ones column, which was in the tens column, and which was in the hundreds column and what that meant. He got it! And so I knew that everybody had gotten it!

MODERATING DISCUSSIONS

Thus far, the chapter has examined three major problems associated with recitations and has provided some suggestions for avoiding these problems. Now we turn to the second type of verbal interaction, the *discussion*. As we said earlier, although

the terms "recitation" and "discussion" are often used interchangeably, it is important to distinguish clearly between the two. (Refer again to Table 10-1.)

Let's consider this example of a discussion, witnessed in Garnetta's class early in
the school year. Here, students are working on a set of riddles designed to foster critical thinking—specifically, the ability to make inferences. Garnetta has chosen a
convergent task, rather than something more open-ended (e.g., a literature discussion). Although the answer in this situation is a predetermined right or wrong (more
characteristic of a recitation than a discussion), Garnetta has decided that this is more
appropriate for her students since they have had little experience with student-centered discussions. She also structures the interaction by instructing the children to
begin their comments with the words "I agree" or "I disagree." Before opening the
discussion, Garnetta first has the students put their desks in a circle so that they can
make eye contact. Then she reviews expectations for behavior:

GARNETTA: Now remember our rules for discussions. Talk in a normal tone of voice; don't
            scream at anyone. Use the words, "I agree with so-and-so," or "I don't agree
            with so-and-so." And one person speak at a time. All right? Okay, Aleesha,
            would you like to read the first riddle?

ALEESHA: [She reads.] "It eats insects. It has more than two legs. Is it a spider, dog, or bird?"

GARNETTA: [Nods.] Now the person who made up this riddle has provided some sentences
            with blanks to help you figure out the answer. The first one says, "It isn't a
            blank because it eats insects." The second one says, "It isn't a blank because
            it has more than two legs." We have to figure out what it is. Aleesha, what do
            you think goes in the first blank?

ALEESHA: Spider. [She reads, filling in the blank.] It isn't a spider because it eats insects.

VICTOR: I disagree because a spider eats insects.

TANAYA: I agree with Victor, because a *dog* won't eat insects.

VICTOR: Yeah. A bird don't eat insects, he eats worms.

JOSE: I disagree with Vincent. It says it has more than two legs, so it can't be a bird or a dog.

VICTOR: It *could* be a dog, because a dog has more than two legs, and a dog don't eat
          insects. And a bird has two legs.

LUCIA: It says it has more than two legs, so it isn't a dog, and it isn't a bird because it
         eats insects.

SHENEIKA: But it says it *isn't* a bird because it has more than two legs.

EDWARD: I agree with Sheneika. [He reads.] "It isn't a bird because it has more than two
          legs," and a bird only has two legs.

GRANDON: Yeah, and it isn't a dog because a dog doesn't eat insects, but a dog has more
           than two legs.

LUCIA: [Vehemently] It says, "It *isn't* a bird because it eats insects."

GARNETTA: I think some people are getting mixed up by the "its." You need to remember
            that "it" refers to the animal we're looking for, not the animal that is named in
            the sentence.

LUCIA: I think it should be "It isn't a bird because it eats insects. It isn't a dog because
         it has more than two legs." So it's a spider.

VICTOR: I agree it's a spider, but it should be like this: "It isn't a dog because it eats in-
          sects. It isn't a bird because it has more than two legs."

GARNETTA: Lucia, you still don't agree, do you?

LUCIA: No.

GARNETTA: Can someone help Lucia to understand?

As we can see, the predominant pattern here is not the I-R-E characteristic of a recitation. Once Garnetta reminded students of the rules for conducting discussions and focused them on the task at hand, she generally stayed out of the interaction, allowing the students to comment on the contributions of their peers. In fact, Garnetta intervened only to clarify Lucia's reasoning and to explain the referent for "it." Furthermore, the purpose of the interaction was to "go over material," but to engage in a problem-solving activity.

Several months later, we observed another discussion in Garnetta's classroom. This time, since her students had more experience with discussions, Garnetta chose an open-ended question about a story they had just read, *Buford, the Little Bighorn,* by Bill Peet (1993). Buford, "a scrawny little runt of a mountain sheep," has a huge pair of horns that cause him considerable difficulty throughout the story. At the very end, however, Buford discovers that his horns have some use after all. Using them as skis, he is able to escape from hunters and becomes a "star attraction" at a winter ski resort.

Garnetta's students are considering a question written on the chalkboard: "Suppose a vet offered to trim Buford's horns to a normal size. Do you think Buford would agree to that? Why or why not?" Once again, their desks are arranged in a circle, and Garnetta begins by reviewing the expectations for behavior:

GARNETTA:	My ladies and gents, let's review how to behave in a discussion. If someone's talking, we don't cut them off, right? Raise your hand, and I'll recognize you. Remember, you can't just say "I agree" or "I disagree"—you have to be able to *defend* your answer. What does that mean? Sheneika?
SHENEIKA:	You have to try to convince people you're right.
GARNETTA:	Okay, you have to give reasons why you think what you think. You have to explain. Luis, read the question for us. [He does so.] Thank you. Luis, you want to start us off, tell us what you think, and give us some supporting arguments?
LUIS:	Yes.
GARNETTA:	Yes, he should get his horns trimmed. [Luis nods.] Why do you say yes?
LUIS:	Cause they're too long, and if he fall down he can get hurt. [Victor's hand shoots up. Garnetta calls on him.]
VICTOR:	I disagree. In the story, when he fell, he ended up hanging on a tree. So the horns help him.
TANAYA:	I disagree 'cause the horns made him fall in the first place. He should take off his horns so the hunters won't get to him.
GRANDON:	I agree with Luis. If Buford don't get his horns cut, he'll trip and get hurt.
ALEESHA:	Yeah, I agree with Luis too. He'll fall if he don't get them cut.
SHENEIKA:	I disagree, because Buford, when he was walking, he fell, and his horns saved him.
VICTOR:	Yeah, and if he get his horns cut off, then the folks from all over the world won't come and he won't be a big star.
GARNETTA:	Do you want to say something, James?
JAMES:	I don't want him to get his horns cut off because then he won't be able to ski.
LUCIA:	What if there's that big pole sticking up out of the snow, and then there's the wires across, he could use his horns to hang on and go across the mountain. But he can't do that if he gets his horns cut.
GARNETTA:	Are you talking about the ski lift?
LUCIA:	Yeah. He can go on the ski lift if his horns are long.

EDWARD:	Yeah. How could he ski on his horns if they're cut? And he can't *roll* down.
GARNETTA:	Grandon, you look like you're trying to say something.
GRANDON:	If Buford get his horns off, they might just grow back. So why bother?
RASHAD:	But what if they get bigger and bigger?
GRANDON:	So he'll just go back to the vet.
RASHAD:	But the vet will just keep charging and charging!
VICTOR:	But it says the vet *offered* to trim his horns. That means he would be doing it for free.
GARNETTA:	Hmm, that's an interesting point. Julio, we haven't heard from you. You want to say something?
JULIO:	He was sad.
GARNETTA:	Yes, he was sad. What do you think he should do about his horns?
JULIO:	Cut them off.
LUCIA:	I disagree, cause if someone's chasing him, he can get away fast. [The discussion erupts in disagreement. Around the circle, there are lots of small debates going on.]
GARNETTA:	Ladies and gents. Ladies and gents. I think I have to remind you about the rules. We need to have one person talk at a time, and you need to listen to that person and not start talking with the people sitting next to you. Okay, now, Tanaya, what did you want to say? [Order restored, the class continues the discussion.]

Later that day, Garnetta talked with us about the discussion and the differences that she observed from the beginning of the year:

It used to be that two or three students dominated everything, and the others would not join the discussion. Victor used to jump on anybody who disagreed with him, and the other children actually seemed afraid to speak up. Now he's beginning to realize that other people are entitled to their opinions. Instead of just Victor and Lucia doing all the talking, just about everyone is willing to express an opinion. Sometimes I still have to intervene to make sure people get a chance to speak, but not as much. Like with Julio today. He's new, and he's real quiet; he needs an "invitation" to speak. But I'm pleased by the way people are willing to participate.

One of the problems we still have is that little subgroups develop around the circle, especially when the discussion heats up. We saw that today: Somebody would make a comment and then children turned to their neighbors and began debating among themselves. I had to keep pulling them back together. But that's okay. It takes time to learn how to participate in a discussion. They've made a lot of progress since the beginning of the year, but they still need the teacher to make sure they stick with the topic and listen to each other. If we want them to be problem solvers and to develop critical thinking skills, we've got to let them *practice.* And it takes practice on the part of the teacher too. We've got to learn to *guide* the discussion without taking over.

As Garnetta's comments suggest, it's not easy to conduct a good discussion, particularly for teachers who are used to dominating verbal interaction in the classroom. Dillon (1994) provides some extremely helpful guidelines for preparing and conducting discussions (see Figure 10-3). In addition, keep in mind three basic suggestions (Gall and Gillett, 1981):

1 *Limit the size of the group:* It's difficult to have a student-centered discussion with a large number of participants. In large classes, it's possible to use the "fishbowl" method, in which five or six students carry on the discussion in the middle of the room, while the rest of the class sits in a large circle around them and acts as observers and recorders. Another solution is to divide the class into small discussion groups of five, with one student in each group acting as a discussion leader.

2 *Arrange students so they can make eye contact.* It's very difficult to speak directly to someone if all you can see is the back of a head. If at all possible, students should move their desks into an arrangement that allows them to be face-to-face.

3 *Teach discussion skills.* Just as you need to teach students the skills for working in small groups, it is important to prepare students for participating in a student-centered discussion. Gall and his colleagues (1976; cited in Gall and Gillett, 1981) have developed a list of skills you may have to teach explicitly:

- Talk to each other, not just to the moderator.
- Don't monopolize.
- Ask others what they think.
- Don't engage in personal attack.
- Listen to others' ideas.
- Acknowledge others' ideas.
- Question irrelevant remarks.
- Ask for clarification.
- Ask for reasons for others' opinions.
- Give reasons for your opinions.

CONCLUDING COMMENTS

This chapter has focused on two different patterns of verbal interaction—recitations and discussions. It's important not to get them confused—to think that you're leading a discussion when you're actually conducting a recitation. Also keep in mind the criticisms that have been leveled against recitations, and reflect on how frequently you dominate the verbal interaction in your classroom. Ask yourself whether you also provide opportunities for student-centered discussion, during which you serve as a facilitator (rather than a questioner) and encourage direct student-student interaction. Reflect on the level of thinking you require from students. The classroom recitation can serve a number of useful functions, but *overuse* suggests that your curriculum consists largely of names, dates, facts, and algorithms (Cazden, 1988).

SUMMARY

We began this chapter by examining some of the major criticisms of recitation, as well as the useful functions it can serve. We then distinguished recitations from discussions. Next, we considered the hazards that recitations present to teachers and suggested a number of strategies for avoiding the problems. Finally, we looked at an example of a discussion, reflected on reasons for the infrequent use of discussion, and briefly considered a number of guidelines for managing this type of verbal interaction.

FIGURE 10-3
Guidelines for leading discussions (based on Dillon, 1994)

---

1 Carefully formulate the discussion question (making sure that it is not in a form that invites a yes/no or either/or answer), along with subsidiary questions, embedded questions, follow-up questions, and related questions.

2 Create a question outline, identifying at least three sub-questions and at least four alternative answers to the main question.

3 Present the discussion question to the class, writing it on the chalkboard or on an overhead transparency or on paper distributed to the class. After reading the question aloud, go on to give the sense of the question, identifying terms, explaining the relevance of the question, connecting it to a previous discussion or class activity, etc. End with an invitation to the class to begin addressing the question.

4 Initially, help the class focus on the question, rather than giving answers to it. For example, invite the class to tell what they know about the question, what it means to them.

5 DO NOT COMMENT AFTER THE FIRST STUDENT'S CONTRIBUTION. (If you do, the interaction will quickly become I-R-E.) In addition, do not ask, "What does someone else think about that?" (If you do, you invite statements of difference or opposition to the first position, and your discussion turns into a debate.)

6 In general, do not ask questions beyond the first question. Use instead non-question alternatives: *statements* (the thoughts that occurred to you in relation to what the speaker has just said; reflective statements that basically restate the speaker's contribution; statements indicating interest in hearing further about what the speaker has just said; statements indicating the relationship between what the speaker has just said and what a previous speaker has said); *signals* (sounds or words indicating interest in what the speaker has said); even *silence.* (Dillon acknowledges that deliberate silence is the hardest of all for teachers to do. To help teachers remain quiet, he recommends silently singing "Baa, baa, black sheep" after each student's contribution.)

7 Facilitate the discussion by
Locating: "Where are we now? What are we saying?"
Summarizing:"What have we accomplished? agreed on?"
Opening: "What shall we do next?"
Tracking: "We seem a little off track here. How can we all get back on the
    same line of thought?"
Pacing: "Just a minute, I wonder whether we're not moving a little too fast
    here. Let's take a closer look at this idea. . . . "

8 When it is time to end the discussion, help students to summarize the discussion and identify the remaining questions.

Characteristic Pattern of a Recitation

- I-R-E (teacher initiation, student response, teacher evaluation)
- Quick pace
- To review material, to elaborate on a text

Criticisms of Recitation

- The teacher plays a dominant role; the student, a passive one.
- There is a lack of interaction among students.
- Recall is emphasized over higher level thinking skills.
- Recitation promotes public evaluation which can lead to:
    Social segregation along academic ability lines
    Negative expectation effects
- Recitation format sometimes conflicts with students' cultural background.

Five Functions of Recitation

- Provides opportunity to check on students' comprehension
- Involves students in presentation of material
- Allows for contact with individuals in a group setting
- Helps to maintain attention level
- Offers an opportunity to push students to construct more complete responses

Characteristics of a Discussion

- I-R-R-R
- Student-initiated questions
- Student comments on contributions of peers
- Slower pace
- Intended to stimulate thinking, to foster problem-solving, to examine implications

Three Hazards of Recitations

- Unequal participation
- Losing the pace and focus
- Difficulty in monitoring comprehension

Strategies for Successful Use of Recitations

- Distribute chances for participation.
    Patterned turn-taking
    Names in a jar
    Using a checklist
    Ensure that males and females have equal opportunity to participate

- Provide time to think about answers before responding.
- Stimulate and maintain interest by:
    Injecting mystery/suspense elements into your questions
    Using humor, novelty
    Incorporating physical activity
- Provide feedback without losing the pace.
- Monitor comprehension by requiring overt responses.
- Monitor comprehension by observing a steering group.

Moderating Discussions

- Act as facilitator rather than questioner.
- Plan discussion question (and subsidiary questions) and outline.
- At the beginning of the discussion, focus on the question, not on answers.
- After the initial question, use non-question alternatives to keep discussion going.
- Manage the discussion by locating, summarizing, opening, tracking, pacing.
- Limit group size.
- Arrange students so they have eye contact.
- Teach discussion skills.

When planning your lessons, think about the extent to which you use recitations and discussions in your classroom. Think about the level of the questions you ask: Are all of your questions low-level, factual questions that can be answered with a word or two, or are your questions designed to stimulate thinking and problem-solving? Ask yourself if you consistently dominate the interaction, or if you also provide opportunities for real discussion among students.

ACTIVITIES

1 Visit a classroom and observe a recitation. On a seating chart, map the verbal interaction by placing a check in the "seat" of each child who participates. Analyze your results and draw conclusions about how widely and fairly participation is distributed in this class.

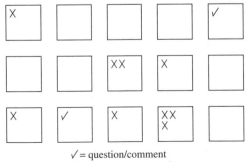

√ = question/comment
X = response to a question

2 Your colleague has asked you to help him figure out why his students are not paying attention in class. He would like you to observe him and offer feedback. What follows is a session you observed. Using what you know about distributing participation, stimulating and maintaining interest, and monitoring comprehension, identify the trouble spots of his lesson and provide three specific suggestions for improvement.

When you enter the class, Mr. B. is perched on a stool in front of the room with the science book in his hand.

MR. B.:   Who remembers what photosynthesis is? [No response.] Do you remember yesterday when we looked at green plants and we discussed how a plant makes its own food? [Mr. B. notices that Thea is nodding.] Thea, do you remember about photosynthesis?

THEA: Yeah.

MR. B.:   Well, can you tell the class about it?

THEA: It has something to do with light and chlorophyll.

MR. B.:   Good. Tom, can you add to this. [Tom was drawing in his notebook.]

TOM: No.

MR. B.:   Tom, Thea told us that photosynthesis had to do with light and chlorophyll. Do you recall our discussion from yesterday when we defined photosynthesis?

TOM: Sort of.

MR. B.:   What do you mean? Didn't you write down the definition with the rest of the class? Look in your notebook and tell me the definition. [Tom starts to page through his notebook. Many of the students have begun to whisper and snicker. Some are looking in their notebooks.] How many of you have found the page where we defined photosynthesis? [Seven students raise their hands.] Good. Would somebody read to me that definition? Thea.

THEA: Photosynthesis is the process of forming sugars and starches in plants from water and carbon dioxide when sunlight acts upon chlorophyll.

MR. B.:   Excellent. Does everyone understand? [A few students nod.] Good. Tomorrow we will be having a quiz about plants and photosynthesis. Tom, will you be ready for the quiz?

TOM: Sure, Mr. B.

MR. B.:   Okay, now let's all turn to page 135 in our science texts and read about the uses of plants.

3 Monitoring students' comprehension is sometimes problematic. Choose three of the following topics. For each one, suggest two different ways a teacher could elicit overt participation in order to determine student understanding.
   a Main characters and their traits
   b Fractional parts
   c "Greater than" and "less than" symbols
   d Syllabication
   e Spanish vocabulary words
   f State capitals
   g Types of clouds

4 We know that recitations and discussions are often confused. Observe and record ten minutes of a class "discussion." Then, using the following checklist, see if the verbal interaction actually meets the criteria for a discussion or if it is more like a recitation.

- Students are the predominant speakers.
- The verbal interaction pattern is not I-R-E, but a mix of statements and questions by a mix of teacher and students.
- The pace is longer and slower.
- The primary purpose is to stimulate a variety of responses, to encourage students to consider different points of view, to foster problem-solving, etc.
- Evaluation consists of agree/disagree, rather than right/wrong.

REFERENCES

The AAUW Report: How schools shortchange girls. (1992). Washington, D.C.: The AAUW Educational Foundation and National Education Association.

Alvermann, D., O'Brien, D., and Dillon, D. (1990). What teachers do when they say they're having discussions of content area reading assignments. *Reading Research Quarterly, 25,* 296–322.

Arends, R. I. (1991). *Learning to teach* (2nd edition). NY: McGraw-Hill, Inc.

Bossert, S. T. (1979). *Tasks and social relationships in classrooms. A study of instructional organization and its consequences.* Cambridge: Cambridge University Press.

Brophy, J. E., and Evertson, C. (1976). *Learning from teaching: A developmental perspective.* Boston: Allyn & Bacon.

Carter, K. (March-April 1985). Teacher comprehension of classroom processes: An emerging direction in classroom management research. Paper presented at the annual meeting of the American Educational Research Association, Chicago, Illinois.

Cazden, C. B. (1988). *Classroom discourse: The language of teaching and learning.* Portsmouth, NH: Heinemann.

Dillon, J. T. (1994). *Using discussion in classrooms.* Philadelphia: Open University Press.

Doyle, W. (1986). Classroom organization and management. In M. C. Wittrock (Ed.), *The handbook of research on teaching* (3rd edition). New York: Macmillan, pp. 392–431.

Farrar, M. T. (1988). A sociolinguistic analysis of discussion. In J. T. Dillon (Ed.), *Questioning and discussion—A multidisciplinary study.* Norwood, NJ: Ablex, pp. 29–73.

Fisher, C. W., Berliner, D. C., Filby, N. N., Marliave, R., Cahen, L. S., and Dishaw, M. M. (1980). Teaching behaviors, academic learning time, and student achievement: An overview. In C. Denham and A. Lieberman (eds.), *Time to learn.* Washington, D.C., U.S. Department of Education, pp. 7–32.

Gall, M. D., and Gillett, M. (1981). The discussion method in classroom teaching. *Theory Into Practice, 19*(2), 98–103.

Good, T., and Brophy, J. E. (1994). *Looking in classrooms* (6th edition). New York: Harper-Collins.

Goodlad, J. (1984). *A place called school.* New York: McGraw-Hill.

Grossman, H., and Grossman, S. H. (1994). *Gender issues in education.* Boston: Allyn and Bacon.

Hoetker, J., and Ahlbrand, W. P., Jr. (1969). The persistence of the recitation. *American Educational Research Journal, 6,* 145–167.

Jackson, P. W. (1968). *Life in classrooms.* New York: Holt, Rinehart and Winston.

Kounin, J. (1970). *Discipline and group management in classrooms.* New York: Holt, Rinehart & Winston.

Lundgren, U. (1972). *Frame factors and the teaching process.* Stockholm: Almqvist and Wiksell.

Marshall, H. H. (1987). Motivational strategies of three fifth-grade teachers. *The Elementary School Journal, 88*(2), 135–150.

MacLachlan, P. (1985). *Sarah, plain and tall.* New York: Harper & Row Junior Books.

McDermott, R. P. (1977). Social relations as contexts for learning in school. *Harvard Educational Review, 47,* 198–213.

Mehan, H. (1979). *Learning lessons: Social organization in a classroom.* Cambridge, MA: Harvard University Press.

Morine-Dershimer, G., and Beyerbach, B. (1987). Moving right along . . . In Virginia Richardson-Koehler (Ed.), *Educators' handbook, A research perspective.* New York: Longman, 207–232.

Morse, L. W., and Handley, H. M. (1985). Listening to adolescents: Gender differences in science classroom interaction. In L. C. Wilkinson and C. B. Marrett (Eds.), *Gender influences in classroom interaction.* Orlando, FL: Academic Press.

Narayan, J. S., Heward, W. L., Gardner III, R., Courson, F. H., and Omness, C. K. (1990). Using response cards to increase student participation in an elementary classroom. *Journal of Applied Behavior Analysis, 23*(4), 483–490.

Peet, B. (1993). *Buford, the Little Bighorn.* In Roger C. Farr and Dorothy S. Strickland (Senior Authors), *A most unusual sight. HBJ Treasury of Literature.* Orlando, FL: Harcourt Brace Jovanovich.

Philips, S. (1972). Participant structures and communicative competence: Warm Springs children in community and classroom. In C. Cazden, V. John, and D. Hymes (Eds.), *Functions of language in the classroom.* New York: Teachers College Press.

Rief, S. F. (1993). *How to reach and teach ADD/ADHD children.* West Nyack, NY: The Center for Applied Research in Education.

Roby, T. W. (1988). Models of discussion. In J. T. Dillon (Ed.), *Questioning and discussion—A multidisciplinary study.* Norwood, NJ: Ablex, pp. 163–191.

Rosenshine, B. V. (1986). Synthesis of research on explicit teaching. *Educational Leadership, 43*(7), 60–69.

Rowe, M. B. (1974). Wait-time and rewards as instructional variables, their influence on language, logic, and fate control: Part 1: Wait time. *Journal of Research in Science Teaching, 11,* 291–308.

Sadker, D., and Sadker, M., and Thomas, D. (1981). Sex equity and special education. *The Pointer, 26,* 33–38.

Sadker D., and Sadker, M. (1985). Is the OK Classroom OK? *Phi Delta Kappan, 55,* 358–367.

Stodolsky, S. S. (1988). *The subject matters: Classroom activity in math and social studies.* Chicago: University of Chicago Press.

Taylor, T. (1969). *The cay.* New York: Doubleday.

Woodruff, E. (1991). *George Washington's socks.* New York: Apple Paperback. Scholastic.

FOR FURTHER READING

Cazden, C. B. (1988). *Classroom discourse: The language of teaching and learning.* Portsmouth, NH: Heinemann.

Dillon, J. T. (1994). *Using discussion in classrooms.* Philadelphia: Open University Press.

Grossman, H., and Grossman, S. H. (1994). *Gender issues in education.* Boston: Allyn and Bacon.

Morine-Dershimer, G., and Beyerbach, B. (1987). Moving right along . . . In Virginia Richardson-Koehler (Ed.), *Educators' handbook, A research perspective.* NY: Longman, pp. 207–232.

Philips, S. U. (1983). *The invisible culture: Communication in classroom and community on the Warm Springs Indian Reservation.* New York: Longman.

PART IV

BEYOND THE CLASSROOM ENVIRONMENT

Chapter Eleven

Working with Families

"His parents actually admitted they can't control him at home, and yet they expect *me* to control him at school!"

"Do you believe they had the nerve to suggest that Sara be allowed to participate in free play even if she doesn't complete any work?"

"Joseph hasn't handed in homework for five days, and when I call to talk about it, they tell me it's *my* problem!"

Comments like these can be heard in almost any teachers' room you visit. It's not unusual for preparation periods, lunch time, and after-school meetings to become "gripe sessions" about parents' lack of cooperation, their unrealistic demands, and their irresponsibility.

Similarly, when parents get together, they often voice complaints about their children's teachers:

"How can she teach them anything if she can't even control the class? She shouldn't be a teacher if she can't make them behave."

"She just doesn't understand my child. Sara's so tense and anxious, she *needs* free play during school, even if she hasn't finished her work."

"He gives way too much homework—it's ridiculous that a fourth grader should have to work two hours a day on homework!"

As these comments indicate, parents and teachers are often at odds with one another. Indeed, Sara Lawrence Lightfoot (1978) has written: "One would expect that parents and teachers would be natural allies, but social scientists and our own experience recognize their adversarial relationship. . . . " (p. 20).

This "adversarial relationship" is unfortunate. Researchers have documented many advantages of close communication and collaboration between families and teachers. For example, parent involvement in their children's schooling is associated with higher academic achievement, better attendance, more positive student attitudes and behavior, and greater willingness to do homework (e.g., Becher, 1987; Epstein, 1984; Haynes, Comer and Hamilton-Lee, 1989; Henderson, 1987; Henderson, Marburger, and Ooms, 1986; Rich, 1988).

From a classroom management perspective, there are real benefits to working closely with families. First, *knowing about a child's home situation provides insight into the child's classroom behavior.* It's easier to understand why Johnny sits with his head down on his desk if you're aware that he spent the night in a homeless shelter; Carla's belligerence makes sense if you know that her mother just lost her job and her father is absent; and Jana's anxiety about getting all A's is understandable if you appreciate how much her parents pressure her to succeed. Furthermore, insights like these can help you decide what course of action to take when dealing with a child's problem. You're better able to judge if a suggestion that a parent read to a child is inappropriate because the parent can't read, or if a note home will lead to benefits or to beatings. (We discuss the issue of child abuse in Chapter 12.)

Second, *when families understand what you are trying to achieve, they can provide valuable support and assistance.* Most parents want their children to succeed in school and will do what they can to help. But they can't work in a vacuum. They need to know what you are trying to achieve and how you expect children to behave in your classroom. Familiarizing parents with your curriculum, routines, and policies minimizes confusion, misinterpretations, and conflict.

Third, *families can help to develop and implement behavior management plans.* Working together, parents and teachers can bring about improvements in children's behavior that would be impossible working alone. Garnetta shares this example:

> I had this boy in my class who was extremely disruptive. He wouldn't work, kept "forgetting" his homework, distracted other children, wandered around the room. You name it; he did it. The three of us—the mother, the boy, and I—talked about what we could do, and we decided to try a system of home rewards. We agreed that I would send a note home each day, reporting on the boy's behavior. For every week with at least three good notes, the mother added one Christmas present. In this way, what the child found under the tree on Christmas Day was directly dependent on his behavior. By Christmas, he had become so cooperative, I couldn't believe he was the same child. After Christmas, I observed some backsliding, so we all agreed to reverse the system: the mother took away one present each time a majority of the week's reports were negative. She didn't have to take many away!

As this example illustrates, parental cooperation in behavior management plans can be especially helpful because families have so many rewards at their disposal that are unavailable to teachers—a trip to the beach, a movie, pizza for dinner, or a new CD.

Finally, *parent volunteers can make classroom management easier by assisting in the classroom.* Parents can staff learning centers, read to children, help during writing conferences, and carry out some of the clerical and housekeeping duties that eat up a teacher's time. In the crowded, fast-paced, unpredictable world of the elementary classroom, an extra pair of hands (and eyes) can be a life-saver.

Given the obvious benefits of communication and collaboration between families and teachers, why is the relationship often so detached and distant? Why, at times, is it even strained and distrustful? In the next section of this chapter, we examine three barriers to close working relationships—teacher reluctance to involve parents, parent reluctance to become involved, and the changing nature of families. We then turn to our teachers and to the literature on parent involvement in order to suggest ways that families and schools can work together to educate children.

BARRIERS TO FAMILY-TEACHER COOPERATION

Teacher Reluctance to Involve Families in Schooling

A primary reason for teachers' reluctance to work with families is the *extra time and energy that are required.* Teaching is physically and emotionally exhausting, and reaching out to parents is sometimes viewed as one more burdensome task. Epstein and Becker (1982) remind us how much time it takes to make just one call home: "If a teacher telephones 30 parents and talks for 10 minutes to each, the teacher spends 5 hours voluntarily on the telephone with parents" (p. 103). Since this is obviously in addition to planning lessons and activities, grading papers, organizing cooperative learning groups, and creating bulletin board displays, it's understandable if teachers wonder whether the extra time required is worth the trouble. Furthermore, there are few external rewards to encourage teachers to spend time working with parents (Epstein and Becker, 1982), and teachers often lament the lack of support from their principals and other teachers.

In addition, *teachers' perceptions of families* undoubtedly contribute to the reluctance to seek greater parental involvement. Some teachers recognize that time is often a scarce commodity for parents, limited by responsibilities at work, household chores, and caring for other family members. These teachers question whether it is fair to ask already burdened parents to spend time working with children on academic activities or assisting in school (Epstein and Becker, 1982). As Ken told us one evening:

> Some parents are really stressed out. One family I'm thinking about owns their business. They work unbelievable hours. Meanwhile, I'm telling them to read to their kid. C'mon, are they going to do the accounts, or are they going to read to their kid? They're going to do the accounts. It's understandable.

Other teachers have been burned by encounters with angry, irresponsible, or apathetic parents. They would tend to agree with Anne Walde and Keith Baker (1990), who wrote that "far too many parents—and not just disadvantaged ones—simply don't give a damn. For them, school is a free babysitting service" (p. 322). Walde and Baker argue that many parents are not concerned with their child's education, do not want to be involved, or lack the skills needed to support their children. They describe numerous encounters with parents to support their assertion. Here is one example:

TEACHER: John isn't doing his homework.
PARENT: I know he isn't. He watches TV all the time and doesn't do his homework. I just don't know what to do.

TEACHER: Why don't you turn the TV off?
PARENT: Oh, he'd never let me do that!

Another reason for teachers' reluctance to involve parents in schooling has to do with *the level of authority and autonomy teachers enjoy within their classrooms.* As public servants, teachers are often exposed to criticism. Parents may blame them for children's problems (Vernberg and Medway, 1981) or question their professional competence (Power, 1985). It's not surprising that teachers sometimes become guarded and protective of their "turf." Lightfoot (1978) writes:

> The only sphere of influence in which the teacher feels that her authority is ultimate and uncompromising seems to be with what happens *inside* the classroom. Behind the classroom door, teachers experience some measure of autonomy and relief from parental scrutiny. . . . (p. 26).

Lightfoot concludes that teachers who are "more confident of their skills, expertise, and abilities" (p. 30) will be more likely to reach out to parents, and research supports her contention. In a study of factors that facilitate parent involvement, Hoover-Dempsey, Bassler, and Brissie (1987) found that *teacher efficacy* (teachers' beliefs that they can teach and that their students can learn) was the factor most strongly related to parent involvement.

Parent Reluctance to Become Involved in Schooling

Just as there are teachers who are reluctant to work closely with families, there are families who resist involvement. Some adults have unhappy memories of their own experiences as students. Listen to this father describe his reasons for not participating more fully in his son's schooling:

> They expect me to go to school so they can tell me my kid is stupid or crazy. They've been telling me that for three years, so why should I go and hear it again? They don't do anything. They just tell me my kid is bad.
>   See, I've been there. I know. And it scares me. They called me a boy in trouble but I was a troubled boy. Nobody helped me because they liked it when I didn't show up. If I was gone for the semester, fine with them. I dropped out nine times. They wanted me gone. (Finders and Lewis, 1994, p. 51)

Like this father, some adults remember school as an oppressive institution, not as a "place of hope" for their children (Menacker, Hurwitz, and Weldon, 1988). As sociologist Willard Waller (1932) wrote more than 60 years ago, "Each generation of teachers pays in turn for the sins of the generation that has gone before" (p. 59).

Other families believe that schooling should be "left to the experts" (Greenwood and Hickman, 1991). They may think they are showing their support for teachers by staying out of the way (Froyen, 1993); they may suspect that efforts to seek their involvement are merely attempts to shift responsibility (Froyen, 1993) and resent being asked to do the "teacher's job"; or they may feel they have little to offer teachers who have had years of training and experience.

Still other families feel guilty when their children have difficulties in school. They may become defensive and uncooperative when teachers try to discuss their child's problem and may be too embarrassed to disclose troubles they are having at home. Rather than deal with the child's problem, these families may try to deny what is occurring and to avoid communication with the teacher (Froyen, 1993).

Finally, some families are unnerved by the "threatening monolith" we call school (Lightfoot, 1978, p. 36). In the main office, high counters serve as barricades to the principal, and there are few spaces in which parents can sit and chat or speak privately with teachers. Overprotective administrators discourage "invading" parents from visiting classrooms or participating in educational activities. If parents are poor, uneducated, or have limited proficiency in English, these barriers to involvement are even more intimidating. Margaret Finders and Cynthia Lewis (1994) interviewed Latino parents and parents in two low-income Anglo neighborhoods about family involvement in schooling. They report that fear was a common theme among the parents they interviewed. One mother expressed her discomfort this way:

> Parents feel like the teachers are looking at you, and I know how they feel, because I feel like that here. There are certain things and places where I still feel uncomfortable, so I won't go, and I feel bad, and I think maybe it's just me. (p. 53)

Another mother conveyed the anxiety she feels because of the linguistic and cultural mismatch between home and school.

> [In] the Hispanic culture and the Anglo culture things are done different and you really don't know—am I doing the right thing? When they call me and say "You bring the plates" [for class parties] do they think I can't do the cookies, too? You really don't know. (p. 52)

The Changing Nature of the Family

In 1955, 60 percent of American households consisted of a working father, a homemaker mother, and two or more school-age children (Hodgkinson, 1985). Teachers sent letters home addressed to "Dear Parents," reasonably confident that two parents would read them, and schools scheduled "Parent Conferences" with the expectation that parents were the primary caregivers of their children.

Times have changed. Listen to Mary, a sixth-grade student teacher:

> One boy in my class is very bright, . . . but he never turned in assignments or participated in class discussions. He tended to annoy the students around him by doing strange things.

> Two weeks ago he missed two days of school. Last week he missed four. Some students saw him playing outside over the weekend, but he wasn't in school at all this week. There were no phone calls, and the social worker had to look into it.

> His uncle came to school today and told us that the father dropped him off with the grandparents Monday and hasn't been heard from since. He is officially a "missing person." The mother lives in another state and doesn't want the boy. His parents apparently went through a very messy divorce. Now this boy is tossed around with no

one who wants him. And we as teachers were concerned that he didn't do his *spelling homework!*

Stories like these have become all too common. The typical family of the 1950s now represents *less than 10 percent of our households* (Hodgkinson, 1985). The number of single-parent families has increased to a total of 9.7 million, almost all headed by women (Carlson, 1991), and more than half of the children born today will spend at least part of their childhood years in a one-parent home (O'Neil, 1991). The significant adults in many children's lives are not their parents at all, but grandparents, aunts, uncles, brothers, sisters, or neighbors (Davies, 1991). The "stay-at-home" mother is vanishing; indeed, in 1993, almost 60 percent of all children younger than six had mothers in the labor force (*The State of America's Children,* 1994). Many children come from non-English speaking homes, and their families are unfamiliar with schools in the United States (Epstein, 1988).

The changing nature of the American family has made communication and collaboration more difficult than ever. Nonetheless, research has found that it is *teachers' attitudes and practices—not the educational level, marital status, or work place of parents—that determine whether families become productively involved in their children's schooling* (Ames, 1993; Epstein, 1988). For this reason, you must not only understand the barriers to parent involvement, you must also be aware of the ways that families and schools can work together.

OVERCOMING THE BARRIERS: FOSTERING COLLABORATION BETWEEN FAMILIES AND SCHOOLS

Providing cookies for bake sales, attending school plays and athletic events, showing up for parent conferences, signing and returning report cards—these are the traditional ways parents have been involved in their children's schooling. But families and teachers can collaborate in other ways as well. Joyce Epstein and her colleagues at Johns Hopkins University (Epstein, 1984; Epstein and Becker, 1982; Epstein and Dauber, 1991) have studied comprehensive parent involvement programs and have identified different types of family-school collaboration. We have adapted Epstein's typology to provide a framework for our discussion.

Type 1: Helping Families to Fulfill their Basic Obligations

This category refers to the family's responsibility to provide for children's health and safety, to prepare children for school, to supervise and guide children at each age level, and to build positive home conditions that support school learning and behavior (Epstein and Dauber, 1991). Schools can assist families in carrying out these basic obligations by providing workshops on child development and parenting skills; establishing parent-support groups; creating parent resource centers and toy-lending libraries; communicating with families through newsletters, videotapes, and home visits; and referring families to community and state agencies when necessary.

Asking teachers to assume responsibilities for the education of *families,* in addition to the education of *children,* may seem onerous and unfair. Not surprisingly, some teachers hesitate to become "social workers," a role for which they are untrained (Olson, 1990). Others feel resentful and angry at parents who do not provide adequate home environments; in particular, teachers may "write off" parents who are poor and minority, believing that these families cannot or will not assist in their children's education (Olson, 1990).

Although these attitudes are understandable, you need to remember that your students' home environments shape their chances for school success. As the number of distressed, dysfunctional families grows, assisting families to carry out their basic obligations becomes increasingly critical. Indeed, James Coleman, professor of education and sociology at the University of Chicago, notes:

> Traditionally, the school has needed the support and sustenance provided by the family, in its task of educating children. Increasingly, the family itself needs support and sustenance from the schools . . . in its task of raising children. (Olson, 1990, p. 20)

Furthermore, research on parent involvement indicates that *most families want to become more effective partners with their children's schools.* Epstein comments: "Our data suggest that schools will be surprised by how much help parents can be if the parents are given useful, clear information about what they can do, especially at home (Brandt, 1989, p. 27). Although there are certainly a few families who cannot be reached, it appears that most parents are deeply concerned about their children's education; they simply do not know how to help.

What can you, as a teacher, realistically do to assist families in carrying out their basic obligations? Although you will probably not be directly involved in planning parent education workshops, writing newsletters on parenting, or creating videotapes, you can play an important, *indirect* role. You can let families know about available materials, motivate and encourage them to attend programs, bring transportation and child care problems to the attention of appropriate school personnel, and help families to arrange car pools (Greenwood and Hickman, 1991).

Ken, Viviana, Garnetta, and Barbara all work in schools that offer parent support groups through EPIC—Effective Parenting Information for Children (Hayes, Lipsky, McCully, Rickard, Sipson, and Wicker, 1985). EPIC provides teachers with training and manuals designed to prepare children to become responsible adults. It also offers opportunities for families to get together to share concerns and to discuss topics like communicating with children, discipline, resisting peer pressure, and home/school cooperation. Ken informs the families of his students about the EPIC support groups; if he sees a family with special needs, he makes sure that school personnel involved in EPIC know about the situation.

You can also educate families about relevant community and state agencies. Viviana, for example, routinely sends home the addresses and phone numbers of the Salvation Army, Catholic Charities, family planning organizations, dental clinics, and food distribution centers. Sometimes, she personally intervenes to connect her families with appropriate agencies. Listen to her story of Santiago, a child who had come from Nicaragua:

> Right away I noticed that Santiago had a lot of difficulty sitting still and paying attention. Sometimes he seemed liked he was in another world. One day, shortly after school

began, I talked with his grandmother when she came to pick him up. She told me that Santiago's father was still in Nicaragua and that Santiago lived with her, his mother, an older sister, and two little ones. She told me that Santiago had terrible problems sleeping, that he would wake up crying and fanning himself—as if he were trying to get flies away from him. She told me that Santiago had seen lots of people killed in Nicaragua, that he had seen bodies lying in the street, decomposing and covered with flies. I told the grandmother that we needed to get professional help for him and that I would see what I could do.

The next day, I found out that there was a Spanish-speaking person at a local mental health clinic, and I gave the grandmother the phone number. I told her to give the number to the mother, and I urged her to call. The clinic gave them an appointment right away and told the mother to bring all members of the family. It was such a good thing that they did! They found out that Santiago's older sister was contemplating suicide! As for Santiago, after working with him a number of times, they decided he needed medication to calm him down.

The change in Santiago was unbelievable. He was able to sit still, to pay attention, to do his work. He did fine after that. The mother came to see me and said, "Mrs. Love, you saved my family. My daughter was going to kill herself, and I didn't even know it." But she was worried about Santiago's medication; I assured her that they knew how much to give Santiago. We talked about her family and her jobs—she was working three jobs! Later, I found out the mother was laid off from two of the three jobs, and she didn't know what to do. I helped her go to welfare.

In addition to playing this indirect assistance role, there are times when it may be appropriate to work *directly* with families. You might be able to help them communicate more effectively with their children. If kindergartners are worried about separation, for example, you could share information with parents or caretakers about active or empathetic listening (see Chapter 13); if sixth graders are arguing about curfews, you might be able to encourage parents to provide necessary limits. Barbara remembers a child with many behavior problems, both at home and in school:

The mother really wanted him in my class, and I agreed to take him—with the stipulation that she listen to my suggestions about how to handle him at home. She was at her wit's end with the boy, so she agreed. I had to teach her how to say no to her son and how to reward his good behavior. The mother, the child's therapist, and I worked together as a team, and eventually we saw a lot of improvement in his attitude toward school and his relationship with his mother. It was a lot of work, and it was discouraging at times. But we were able to reach a very difficult child, and we got to the point where he was controllable in class. This not only made him feel good, it also caused less of a distraction for the rest of the class. It was worth the trouble.

Occasionally, a child's desperate plight prompts our teachers to take an even more direct role in helping families. Viviana, for example, tells us that every year her children seem to come from more impoverished families:

In New Brunswick, rents are very high, so two and three families rent an apartment together. Three families might rent a three-bedroom apartment, with a whole family sleeping in one bedroom. This means that some of the kids have to sleep on the floor.

This year I have a girl in my class who used to fall asleep every day. I asked her, "Why are you so sleepy?" She told me that she has to sleep on the floor; there are eight in her family and they all sleep in one room with two beds. I had a folding bed that I had bought for when my nephew came to visit. I went to her house and asked the mother if she would accept it. I said, "Do you mind if I give you the folding bed?" She was very pleased, and the girl doesn't fall asleep anymore.

Type 2: Fulfilling the Basic Obligations of Schools— Communicating with Families

It's the first day of school in New Brunswick. In Viviana's classroom, 19 parents are standing around the sides and the back of the room. The children are seated boy-girl and according to height. Viviana speaks in Spanish to the parents. She introduces herself and explains how she seated the children. She explains that they're the parents at home, but she's the mother in school. She says that they are all family, one big family, all Hispanic, and that they should come in if they need help; they are not alone.

She discusses the importance of homework and attendance. She explains that she is very firm about both. She will give a zero if children do not bring in their homework.

Viviana meets with parents on the first day of school.

She tells the parents that she gives homework every day but not on weekends, so the children can relax. She says that parents should not let their children fool them about being sick and not able to come to school. She says the school has a nurse and can check their children and send them home if they're really sick.

Viviana moves to a round table in the front of the room where workbooks are displayed. She picks up each workbook and explains that there is much work ("mucho trabajo") this year: spelling, social studies, English, math, science, health. Again, she emphasizes that the children must attend school in order to master the skills they need for first grade.

Viviana asks if the parents have any questions or comments. A woman in pink thanks her for her comments about being one big family. Then Viviana invites the parents to introduce themselves. They go around the room, saying who they are and pointing to their children. After the introductions are complete, the parents leave, kissing their children goodbye on the way out.

Epstein's second category of family-school involvement refers to the school's obligation *to communicate about school programs and children's progress.* Communications include the kind of face-to-face interaction with parents that Viviana has on the first day, as well as report cards and progress reports; memos, notes and newsletters; open houses and parent-teacher conferences; home visits; and phone calls. This is certainly the most commonly accepted way to work with parents, and there is no doubt that these communications are essential. The crucial question, however, is not only whether these communications occur, but *when they occur, whether they are being understood, and whether they lead to feelings of trust and respect or alienation and resentment.*

All of the teachers stress the importance of communicating with families *early in the school year—before* stressful situations occur. As Ken reminds us:

It takes effort for teachers to contact a parent, and so they often wait until some problem arises. Because of this, "communication" begins to have a negative connotation. We've got to communicate with parents even when there is no problem—when we've got good things to tell—and the more communication, the better. If you develop a personal connection with parents early, you have an easier time approaching them when you *do* have a concern.

We need to make sure that parents know our work schedules and the times we're free so they can call us. We have to put in the effort to send positive notes home. We have to find times for personal, casual communication. Take a few minutes to tell a parent about their child if you meet them in the school's hall or office. Treat parents respectfully. Appreciate that they take time to see you and communicate with you. Always remember that you and the parents are partners in the education of their child.

Recent research on family-school communication supports Ken's emphasis on partnership. A study by Lindle (1989), for example, indicates that maintaining a professional, businesslike manner is not the best way to gain the respect and support of parents. In fact, parents view "professionalism" as *undesirable;* they express dissatisfaction with school personnel who are "too businesslike," "patronizing," or who "talk down to us." Rather than a professional-client relationship, parents prefer an equal partnership, characterized by a "personal touch." (Sometimes, partnership is threatened by the use of educational jargon that parents may find difficult to understand; see Fig. 11-1.)

It is clear that the four teachers with whom we are working are able to create these kinds of partnerships with families. Let's consider the various ways they accomplish this.

Memos, Notes and Newsletters   So often, parents have no idea what is happening to their children for the six hours of each school day. Conversations like this one are not unusual:

PARENT: What did you do in school today?
  CHILD: Nothing.
PARENT: Well, did anything interesting happen?
  CHILD: No.
PARENT: *Something* must have happened.
  CHILD: We had pizza in the cafeteria.

Parents who are hungry for information appreciate a memo or note about current projects, future activities, and children's progress. On the first day of school, Barbara sends home a letter addressed to her students and their families (see Figure 11-2). In it she talks about schedules, snack, the curriculum, and homework policies. But the letter conveys more than this basic information: it communicates her desire for an open, ongoing relationship and sets the stage for the year ahead.

Weekly or monthly newsletters also help to keep parents informed about what is happening in school. In the lower grades, you can have a class meeting right before dismissal to review and record the day's events (see the form in Figure 11-3). On Fridays, you can fill in the newsletter just before lunch and then duplicate and send it home at the end of the day (Gruber, 1983). In the higher grades, students can fill out the form themselves at the end of each day or write a letter to parents on Fridays describing five events that occurred during the week.

FIGURE 11-1
The use of educational jargon sometimes impedes communication.

FRANK & ERNEST® by Bob Thaves

WELCOME!!!   LET'S HAVE A

WHALE OF

A YEAR

Sept. 6

Dear   and family,
    I hope you all had a fun-filled summer. I certainly did. But now I'm ready for a new school year. As I think about our time together there are some bits of information for me to share with you.

Specials: 10:20-11:08   Mon. P.E.
                           Tue. P.E.
                           Wed. Music
                           Thur. Art
                           Fri. Health

Lunch: 11:57-12:37 We will share the cafeteria with the fourth-grade class next door.

Snack: We will have a 15-minute break each morning for snacks and free time. I would encourage healthy snacks that we can eat while we play or talk.

Homework: You will be expected to do 20 minutes of reading outside of school each day. The books may be of your own choosing. You may also read with a parent, brother, or sister. Other homework assignments will be given as necessary to reinforce classroom skills, writing, or research. Everyone will develop a sense of responsibility for his/her own assignments, so an assignment pad will be helpful.

Ms. S. is our student teacher. She will be with us until the end of December.

Our language arts curriculum will be literature-based. That means that most of our reading will be done through novels and related activities. The other major component of our class is a program called "Creating an Original Opera." We will discuss this further as the year progresses, but I assure you it will be fun.

Well, if I tell you much more I won't have any surprises and any new information for Back to School Night on September 27th.

I am really looking forward to a great year.

Love,
Mrs Broggi

FIGURE 11-2
Letter from Barbara Broggi to her students and their families

    We asked Barbara, Ken, Garnetta, and Viviana to tell us the kinds of guidelines they keep in mind when they draft memos, notes and newsletters to families. Here are their responses:

    Memos, notes, and newsletters should be written in clear, concise language and should be edited for any misspellings or grammatical errors.

OUR WEEKLY NEWSLETTER WEEK OF _____	
MONDAY	
TUESDAY	
WEDNESDAY	
THURSDAY	
FRIDAY	
ADDITIONAL NOTES	

FIGURE 11-3
A sample newsletter format

Don't use educational jargon; it's a turn-off to parents. Remember that you won't be there to clarify what you meant.

When writing a note to a family, make sure you know the last name of the parent or guardian to whom you are writing. Often, the parent and the child do not have the same last name.

Tell children what is in the note. This will help to alleviate their fears and minimize the chance that the note will end up in the trash can.

If families don't read English, memos and notes must be written in their native language. (In Barbara's school, volunteer parents work as "parent advocates" to help teachers communicate with families who are Chinese, Filipino, Hispanic, Indian, Israeli, Japanese, Portuguese, and Russian.)

Send lots of positive notes home, such as "happygrams," award certificates, and success stories. Parents love to hear when their children are doing well.

If you want a parent to respond, create a tear-off sheet at the bottom of your note.

Don't write letters in anger. If you're communicating about a problem, wait until you've calmed down, and think carefully about what you want to say. Once your words are on paper, you've got a permanent document.

End letters with an invitation to call or meet with you if there is any question about the contents.

In order to facilitate the process of writing notes and memos, it's helpful to write each student's name on an envelope and place the envelopes in a convenient, obvious place. Once or twice a week, you can pull out an envelope and jot a brief, positive note to the family of that student. When all the envelopes are gone, you'll know that you've communicated once with each family (Gruber, 1985). It's also a good idea to make a "communication card" for each student on which to jot down any extra contact you have with a family member by phone, note, or in person (Gruber, 1985).

Phone Calls   In addition to written notes and memos, all four of our teachers use telephone conversations as a way of communicating with parents. In fact, Garnetta calls so frequently, her families know who's calling the minute she says hello.

Given the hectic lives that people lead, one of the main problems about telephone calls is making the connection! At the beginning of the school year, all four teachers find out when and how to contact the families of their students. (They're also careful about checking school records to see which parent should be contacted in cases of divorce.) Some businesses have strict policies about employees receiving phone messages, and a call during work hours may result in a reprimand. In cases like this, it's better to call in the evening or to send a note home. Garnetta says that she sometimes has to call at 10:30 in the evening to reach working parents.

All of the teachers also let parents know when they can receive telephone calls during the school day. (Barbara even gives parents her home phone number; she says that no parent has ever abused the information.) If parents call the school and leave a message, our teachers are prompt to return the call so that parents know they care.

Like memos and notes, phone calls should not be reserved for problems. Parents like to hear about their children's successes and improvement. If you've made contacts like these, it's easier to call when a problem *does* arise. Ken recalls a sensitive situation that occurred not too long ago:

> The class was having a discussion about drug abuse. I was talking about peer pressure to use drugs. I noticed this boy wasn't paying attention and doing a lot of talking, so I said something like, "Kids will try to convince you to use drugs, just like they try to convince you to talk when we're having a class discussion." The boy stopped talking, looked at me, and said, "Are you saying I'm going to use drugs?" We talked about what I had meant, and things were okay, but I realized I needed to call home in order to head off trouble. I didn't want the boy to go home and say, "Mr. K. said I'm gonna use drugs." I called home right after school. I was really glad that I had already spoken to these parents a lot, so that we had a good relationship going. I began by telling the parent that I was generally concerned about the boy's behavior in class lately (which I was), and that I felt something was going on. We talked about that for a while, and then I said, "By the way, this happened in school today. . . ." It was really important for me to talk about this with the parents, so that the situation didn't get misinterpreted.

We do have a few words of caution about using telephone calls to discuss sensitive issues or problems. First, talking on the telephone doesn't allow you to "soften" your messages with smiles, gestures, or body language; nor do you have access to parents' nonverbal language in order to judge reactions (Lemlech, 1988). For this reason, telephone calls are more likely to lead to misinterpretations than face-to-face interactions. Second, although it's important to contact parents about serious problems, frequent phone calls about minor misbehavior can be annoying. Furthermore, the practice can convey the message to both parents and children that the school can't deal with problems that arise; it's like saying, "Wait till your parents find out!"

Home Visits   Visiting students' homes is not very common, but it can be a valuable way of reaching parents who are reluctant to come to school. During the visit, you can discuss how the child benefits when the home and school work together, invite parents to visit your classroom, and encourage them to call you if they have questions or concerns.

In some school districts, teachers are encouraged to visit the homes of all students before school begins in order to listen and to learn about each family (Love, 1989). Other districts have created the position of home visitation coordinator or parent educator; this person is responsible for regularly visiting students' homes to discuss important events in the family's life, the child's progress in school, and ways parents can support and extend their child's learning (Olmsted, 1991).

Garnetta and Viviana stress the need to know about the community before you venture out. Both of them used to make regular home visits, but they are now far more cautious. Garnetta tells us:

A while back, I visited a child's home to talk about her progress in school and just to connect with the family. We had a nice visit. But two or three days later, I learned that her mom and dad and the older children were found guilty of possessing and selling drugs. I could have been in their home when a drug bust was made! Experiences like this have made me leery. I want to know the setting I'm walking into before I visit a parent's home these days.

Viviana has had similar experiences. As a result, she now asks another person (e.g., the school security guard) to go with her when she makes a home visit. She also asks for assistance from the district's Bilingual Community Liaison Coordinator, who is responsible for visiting children's homes.

Report Cards   Report cards have been the traditional way of communicating with families about a child's progress in school. Unfortunately, they are often not very informative. What exactly does it mean when children receive a C in reading? Are they on grade level or not? Are they having problems with vocabulary? with comprehension? with decoding?

Some report cards include grade-level designations, as well as grades, so that parents can see if their children are working "above," "on," or "below" grade level. This can also be confusing. To help families interpret these distinctions, Ken sends a note to parents (see Figure 11-4). In it, he explains that the report is a communication tool, not a score card, and invites parents to contact him if they are uncertain about what the report card is saying.

Another common problem with report cards is timeliness. During discussions with our four teachers, they repeatedly emphasized that parents need to know how their children are doing *throughout the marking period.* In other words, the report card should never come as a shock.

Some schools formalize the process of keeping parents informed. Garnetta and Viviana, for example, are required by their district to write progress reports for all of their children every four weeks. These summarize strengths the children possess, as well as areas that need improvement.

In addition to sending home letters and progress reports, you may want to develop a comment sheet to accompany the report card so that parents can easily write back to you. A comment sheet like this can tell you a lot about the clarity of the report card and the concerns that parents may have. Most parents will appreciate this opportunity to communicate and feel that you value their participation.

It's also important to include input from parents if your school is considering a change in the report card's format. Barbara, for example, served on a parent-teacher committee that evaluated the school's current report card and suggested modifications.

Back-to-School Nights   For many parents, open house or back-to-school night is the first opportunity to meet you and to see the classroom. It's also the first opportunity *you* have to show parents all the great things you've been doing and to tell them about the plans you have for the future. As Barbara says, "I put a lot of time, effort, and energy into my teaching, and I'm proud of it. I'm enthusiastic about what I do, and I want to share this with my parents. Plus, I like to show off!"

A Note to Parents Concerning Report Cards

Dear Parents,

This report card is designed to function as a communication tool more than as a score card, or even a record. So where there is question or confusion, please contact me so that we make sure we are communicating clearly.

Grade-level designations on the report card are not very easy to deal with. They are there so that I can say that one child might be doing very well On Grade Level, while the next child is doing very well Above Grade Level. It is very hard to draw those grade level differences.

It is also very hard to tell who deserves a Very Good and who deserves a Satisfactory. I think all the children in the class are expending great amounts of effort, some being more successful than others, so that is where I must draw the line. Those children who meet success more often than others on their tasks receive Very Goods. This may seem unfair to some; if it does, please contact me.

In Math, the only children Above Grade Level are the students in Mr. M   's class. The rest of the children are in various places in the sixth-grade book, some much further along and much more successful than others. I expect by the end of the year, some of these children will be in the seventh-grade book and will be considered Above Grade Level.

In Reading, the grade-level distinction is much more difficult to make. Many children are reading novels that, if the book's readability level were determined, I'm sure would be above sixth-grade level. That does not mean, however, that they are reading them as a seventh grader might. I am relying on the Wisconsin Design Reading tests to show me who has most successfully mastered the sixth-grade skills. Adding to that how well a child performs as a mature reader, I will decide who is above the normal sixth-grade level. Again, if you are uncertain about what your child's report card says to you, contact me.

There should be no surprises on the card for your child. We have discussed most of the grades already. I hope the other categories are clear to you, and I hope the comments are helpful. Lastly, I want to compliment you all on your success in raising such a fine batch of children. You've made my job that much more rewarding.

Mr. Kowalski

FIGURE 11-4
Letter from Ken Kowalski about report cards

Keep in mind that first impressions *do* matter, so you need to think carefully about how you will orchestrate this event. Here are some guidelines that emerged during our discussions with Viviana, Garnetta, Ken, and Barbara:

In order to increase attendance, don't just rely on the notices sent to parents by the school. Send a special invitation to families, indicating how much you are looking forward to meeting them. You can even have your students create invitations for their own families.

Make sure the classroom looks especially attractive and neat. Bulletin boards should display the work of *all* children, not just a few.

If you want parents to sit in their children's seats, make sure there are name tags on the desks. Have your students write notes to their parents and leave them on their desks.

Greet parents at the door, introduce yourself, find out who they are, and show them where their child sits.

Make sure your presentation is succinct and well-organized. Parents want to hear about your goals, plans, and philosophy, as well as the curriculum, schedules, and polices about homework and absences.

If parents raise issues that are unique to their child, let them know in a sensitive way that the purpose of open house is to describe the general program. Indicate that you're more than happy to discuss their concerns during a private conference. You may want to have a sign-up sheet available for this purpose.

Listen carefully to questions that parents have. Provide an opportunity for parents to talk about *their* goals and expectations for their children in the coming school year. This can begin the two-way communication that is so crucial for family-school collaboration.

Provide a sign-up sheet for parents who are able to participate in classroom activities (e.g., as a teacher's aide, guest speaker, or chaperone on field trips).

If refreshments are being served after the class meetings, join in conversations with parents. Clustering with the other teachers separates you from parents and conveys the idea that there is a professional barrier.

Prepare a packet of materials (e.g., a statement of curriculum goals, class schedule, homework policies, etc.) for parents who were unable to attend back-to-school night. Send it home, along with a note indicating how sorry you were that they had to miss the evening and how much you are looking forward to meeting them.

Given the hectic schedule of many parents, it may take some ingenuity to get a good turnout for back-to-school night. In Viviana's school, a sit-down dinner was held on back-to-school night this year, in order to entice parents to come and to make them feel welcome. You might also consider holding a supplemental "back-to-school Saturday morning" for parents who work nights and may not be able to attend school functions scheduled on weekday evenings. (Providing coffee and doughnuts could also increase attendance!) Another idea was devised by a student teacher we know: She made a videotape of her class in action, recording two or three minutes of each major activity and making sure that every child in the class was included. She and her cooperating teacher publicized the fact that the video would be shown at back-to-school night, and they were rewarded by a substantially larger group than in previous years. Another benefit was that parents who were unable to attend could borrow the videotape to watch at home or at school.

In addition to the regular back-to-school night, Ken has started having his own series of "parent evenings," each devoted to a different content area. On "science night," "social studies night," and "writing night," clusters of students make presentations about what they are doing in school in each subject. He reports that parents are extremely enthusiastic, but—take note—some of the other teachers in the building are unhappy with him!

CALVIN AND HOBBES   **By BILL WATTERSON**

FIGURE 11-5
Parent-teacher conferences provide a way of communicating with families. (Calvin and Hobbes ©
Watterson. Dist. by Universal Press Syndicate. Reprinted with permission. All rights reserved.)

Parent-Teacher Conferences   Schools generally schedule one or two formal
parent-teacher conferences during the school year. (See Figure 11-5 for Calvin's reaction to the prospect of such a conference.) Interestingly, these meetings are often
a source of frustration to both teachers and parents. Parents resent the formality of
the situation (Lindle, 1989) and find the limited conference period frustrating. As
one mother put it, "Ten minutes is ridiculous, especially when other parents are
waiting right outside the door. I need time to tell the teacher about how my child is
at home, too" (Lindle, 1989, p. 14).

Teachers, too, are sometimes unhappy with these formal conferences. Many find
the scheduling to be grueling. Ken observes, "It's hard to be pleasant, alert, sensitive, and productive when you're seeing families every 15 minutes for five or six
hours in a row!" Moreover, teachers agree with parents that the brief time allotted
often precludes meaningful exchange. Finally, teachers complain about the lack of
attendance: "The parents you *don't* need to see show up, while the ones you des-
perately *want* to talk with don't come."

Despite the problems, parent-teacher conferences are sometimes your only opportunity to have face-to-face interaction with members of a child's family, so it's
important to encourage families to participate. Amazingly, all four teachers report
that they generally have 100 percent attendance at parent-teacher conferences. This
is obviously not an accident. By conference time, Viviana, Garnetta, Barbara, and
Ken have already established a close relationship with families through notes, calls,
and home visits. They schedule conferences when parents can come, even if the requires appointments before school begins or in the evening. If necessary, they use
"incentives" to encourage attendance. Viviana, for example, enlists her children's
aid by promising a surprise to each child whose family attends! She also distributes
report cards at conferences, rather than sending them home with children.

All of our teachers stress the need to prepare carefully for conferences. Barbara
tells us:

> The first thing I do is collect samples of students' work and place them in individual
> folders. Using the report card as a model, I also prepare a profile of each student's aca-

demic progress and behavior. This helps to focus the conference and ensures that all important areas are discussed.

I try really hard to make the classroom particularly inviting. The students' work is displayed, and the room is neater than usual. I usually set up a table with adult-sized chairs so that we're both sitting on the same level. On the table I put a vase of flowers and a bowl of fruit or candies. Conference time is physically taxing. I need the refreshments, and I offer them to parents as a sign of hospitality.

Conferences can be tense—especially if you're meeting with family members for the first time—so all four teachers begin by trying to put parents at ease. They engage in small talk, offer candy or a cup of coffee, or share a funny incident that happened in school. They suggest leading with something positive: "Your son is a delight to have in class" or "Your daughter appears to be really interested in the topics we've been studying." They may share pictures of the student involved in various activities during the school day; this is especially helpful if family members have limited proficiency in English.

Next, they inform parents about the child's progress, pointing out both strengths and weaknesses. They document their reports by showing samples of students' work that they have collected for this purpose. They explain any strategies they are using to bring about improvements in academic work or behavior and try to enlist parents' support or assistance.

Although they try to provide parents with substantive information, our teachers emphasize the need *to listen.* They always allow time for parents to ask questions, and they solicit parents' suggestions. Remember, a conference should be a two-way conversation, not a monologue. *It's also critical not to assume that poor parents, uneducated parents, or parents with limited English proficiency have nothing of value to offer.* One mother in the study by Finders and Lewis (1994) expressed her frustration this way:

> Whenever I go to school, they want to tell me what to do at home. They want to tell me how to raise my kid. They never ask what I think. They never ask me anything.

Kottler (1994) stresses the importance of encouraging families from non-English-speaking backgrounds to help you understand their children's educational and cultural background. For example, you might ask them about past educational experiences, if the child is experiencing any cultural conflicts, what their educational goals for the child are, whether English is used at home, and if there are any special needs or customs you need to take into consideration.

Regardless of the family's cultural background, Ken stresses the need to be as responsive as possible.

> Sometimes parents have a particular request—for example, maybe they want to know immediately if a kid misses an assignment. Teachers sometimes resist requests like this and say, "That's not the way I do it. This is the policy in my class. The first time a child misses an assignment, I only give a warning, the second time . . ." I tell parents, "If you want it that way, we'll do it that way." I try to understand what the situation is at home and to be accommodating. And you know, it's the greatest feeling when a parent walks away from a conference and says *thank you*—thank you for understanding and for being responsive, thank you for not telling me I'm a bad parent.

If a parent is angry or upset with a particular approach or incident, our teachers also try hard not to respond with anger and defensiveness. As Viviana points out:

> It's important to let the parents get it out of their system. Don't fight it. Let it go. Most times the parent is reacting to what was told to them by their child and that is not always accurate. Once the emotions are spent, find out what prompted the tirade. Gather information. Then you can tell parents how *you* see the situation.

Our teachers emphasize the importance of not closing doors to further communication. When a problem needs to be resolved, they try to reach consensus on possible solutions, determine who will be responsible for doing what, and schedule a follow-up meeting. If a conference is not going well, they might suggest another meeting, perhaps with the principal on hand to mediate the discussion.

At the end of each conference, our teachers take a minute to summarize any decisions that have been made and to thank parents for coming. Sometimes, they follow up by sending a note home, expressing their appreciation for parents' attendance and reporting on children's subsequent progress.

Some schools have started to experiment with three-way conferences that include the teacher, the parent or caretaker, and the child (Davies, Cameron, Politano, and Gregory, 1992). Barbara, for example, provides parents with the option of having a regular two-way conference or a three-way conference, during which children can show pieces of work they feel represent their best efforts and share the goals they have for the rest of the year. Barbara restricts three-way conferences to the spring, since students are more experienced by this time at setting goals and assessing their own work. If families opt to have a three-way conference, students must prepare for the conference by completing the organizer shown in Figure 11-6.

In addition to formally scheduled parent-teacher conferences, our teachers look for chances to have more casual face-to-face meetings. As we saw earlier, Viviana capitalizes on the fact that many of her children's parents bring their children to school on the first day. Other opportunities occur in the morning, when her parents walk their children to school, or at the end of the day, when they come to pick them up.

Interestingly, all of our teachers agree that if parents show up unexpectedly during the teaching day, they will meet with them on the spot. Sometimes they assign the class independent work or ask an aide, another teacher, or the principal to supervise the class while they speak with the parent. As Garnetta tells us:

> If a parent felt it necessary and important to show up, you take care of it! They're not just coming in to chit chat. You cannot turn the parent away. If you do, there will be hurt feelings and anger. Parents need to feel you are accessible.

Ken agrees, but offers a word of caution:

> If a parent shows up angry or abusive, call the office and ask for assistance, or ask the teacher next door to cover your class so you can escort the parent to the office to discuss the matter with the principal or an appropriate third party.

Sending Home Student Work Many teachers send students' work home so that families can see how their children are doing in school, but the work doesn't always

Name _____ Grade _____ Date _____

1 Select 3 pieces of work to share and tell why those were selected.

a _____

_____

_____

b _____

_____

_____

c _____

_____

_____

2 This year I'm most proud of

3 I consider these to be my strengths:

4 A target area for improvement is:

5 Things I will do to try to improve are:

6 Overall, my fourth-grade experience has been:

7 Additional comments, if needed:

_____

Signature

FIGURE 11-6
Student Conference Organizer

arrive in very good condition. Sometimes it doesn't arrive at all! In order to avoid this problem, some teachers collect work over a week and then send it home in special envelopes that parents sign and return. If you're concerned that poor papers will be "lost" on the way, you can indicate on the envelope how many items should be inside. A parent response sheet might also accompany the work, to make it easier for parents to write back.

When you're sending home student work and tests, it's important to keep in mind that your written comments may be carefully scrutinized. Does children's work contain suggestions for improvement and specific praise for work well done, or is it so marked up with red slashes, zeros, and minus signs that it looks like an abstract painting? Remember, whatever you write on a paper is a communication to both child *and* parent.

You also need to think carefully about the kind of work you're sending home. Fill-in-the-blank worksheets are generally not products that children are proud to share, and they're unlikely to stimulate dinner conversation about what's happening in school. Social studies projects, science laboratory reports, and writing samples are not only more interesting, they're also more informative about what students have learned.

Ken believes strongly in the need to send home this kind of meaningful work. When students finish reading a novel, for example, he has them assemble a packet of the writing they've done about the story. He sits with each child, and together they evaluate the work as a whole. He might use items from the report card as a guide and ask students, "What grade would you give yourself for comprehension, for vocabulary, for making inferences?" Both the packet and the evaluation sheet are then sent home. Parents review the work and the evaluation, make their own comments on the sheet, and send it back so that Ken can see if everyone is in agreement.

Type 3: Family Involvement in School

Epstein's third type of family-school involvement refers to family members who come to school to attend student performances, athletic events, or other programs. It also refers to parents and other volunteers who assist in classrooms or in other areas of the school (Epstein and Dauber, 1991).

If you're teaching in a district where there has never been much parent involvement in school, special efforts may be needed to convince parents that you really want them to participate in the life of the school. When Bruce Davis (1995) became principal of an urban elementary school with no history of parent involvement, he immediately instituted a weekly awards assembly on Friday at 8:30 A.M. to which parents are invited. At the assembly, 44 students—two from each classroom—are honored as "students of the week" and "super readers of the week." Davis uses the assemblies as an opportunity to welcome parents to the school, to remind them about upcoming events, to make announcements of interest, and to encourage parents to become involved in the school. He reports that about 50 parents attend each week, many with cameras and video-recorders; some come *every* week, just to keep up with school news.

Classroom volunteer programs usually involve relatively few people, but even a few parents can provide considerable support. In Garnetta's classroom, for example, a mother comes in once a week to *assist with learning activities.* Depending on the day, she may work with small groups, tutor individual children, read aloud, type stories into a computer, staff a learning center, or supervise the production of a puppet show. She also helps to carry out *clerical and housekeeping chores,* such as preparing bulletin boards, organizing games and toys, filing work samples, and collecting book club money. When Garnetta directed a school play in honor of Martin Luther King, Jr., parents made costumes, applied makeup, and provided scenery and props.

Parents can also enrich the curriculum by sharing information about their jobs, hobbies, and cultural backgrounds. When Barbara's class reads *In the Year of the Boar and Jackie Robinson* (Lord, 1984), a novel about a little girl who comes to the United States from China, Barbara has parents who have come from other countries discuss their immigration experiences. As part of this study, her class has an ethnic food festival, during which families bring a typical food from their native country and eat with the children. Similarly, Viviana's school holds an Hispanic Cultural Festival; the highlight is a luncheon prepared and enjoyed by parents, teachers, and students.

If you decide to invite parents to participate in your classroom, you need to think carefully about how to recruit them. Sometimes parents don't volunteer simply because they're not sure what would be expected or how they could contribute. As we mentioned earlier, back-to-school night offers a good opportunity to make a direct, in-person appeal and to explain the various ways parents can assist. You might also send an invitation and a survey to families, soliciting their involvement. (See Figure 11-7, the survey sent by the principal in Barbara's school.) One

FIGURE 11-7
Bartle School's parent survey

BARTLE SCHOOL RESOURCE INFORMATION

NAME _____ ADDRESS _____

HOME PHONE _____ WORK PHONE _____

CHILD'S NAME _____

CHILD'S CURRENT HOMEROOM TEACHER _____

I am available to the Bartle Staff for the following activity:

_____ Tutor or mentor: subject(s) _____
_____ Speaker: subject(s) _____
_____ Activity chaperone: activity _____
_____ School assistant: activity _____
_____ Special projects help: examples _____
_____ Provide 2:30 PM workshop(s): topic _____
_____ Parent advocacy group _____
_____ Share hobbies: hobby _____
_____ After school homework _____

Please state any other way you could be a resource to the Bartle School Staff: _____
_____
_____

Please provide names of any other community members or resources you feel would be valuable to our staff: _____
_____
_____

Available hours/days during school week: _____
_____

kindergarten teacher we know periodically sends home "classified ads," listing specific jobs that need to be done and requesting parents' help. (Figure 11-8 shows the appeal she sent home before Halloween.)

When soliciting help, be sensitive to the fact that parents' time is also limited. Let them know that an hour once a week, once a month, or even once a year would be greatly appreciated by you and your students. Think of ways that families might assist at home (for example, typing stories that students have written). If a parent cannot come in without a younger sibling, you'll have to decide whether this is acceptable. In Highland Park's primary school, little ones can work in centers, listen to stories, or build with blocks right along with the other children—as long as

FIGURE 11-8
Another way of soliciting help from families.

CLASSIFIED NEWS

Help Wanted	Help Wanted	Help Wanted
Help needed on Thursday, October 31, for supervising cupcake decorating center in the morning.	Needed, parents to read "G" books during the week of October 28.	Wanted, parents to tape a Halloween book. Supplies included.
Parents wanted to read Halloween books to class on Thursday, October 31, morning or afternoon available.	Wanted! parents to read "G" books and record them on tape for our listening center. We will supply book, tape, and recorder. Please inquire.	Wanted! One parent to help make trick or treat bags on Monday, October 28.
One person needed for the Halloween Party to play pin the nose on the witch.	Help always wanted to help us in our math, art, and science centers every day!	Someone needed to help us paint our pumpkins on Thursday at 10:30 a.m.

THANK YOU!   THANK YOU!   THANK YOU!   THANK YOU!

I,_____, am replying to your ad in the classified news. I am very interested in helping our class with _____ on _____.

they do not create a disruption. The teachers have found that parents feel especially welcome when their toddlers are also welcome, and it's a good way to give little ones a preview of school.

Using family members as volunteers in the classroom requires you to become a "team leader of adults" in the classroom (Greenwood and Hickman, 1991). You have to assess parents' strengths, interests, and availability and determine appropriate roles for them to play. You need to plan and coordinate activities, assign meaningful tasks, provide direction and possibly even training. Despite these added responsibilities, the benefits can be substantial. Not only do you receive much-needed assistance in the classroom, but parents can obtain a better understanding of the classroom and become more comfortable in the school environment.

Type 4: Family Involvement in Learning Activities at Home

Epstein's fourth type of involvement refers to the ways families can assist their own children at home in learning activities that are coordinated with ongoing classwork (Epstein and Dauber, 1991). Interestingly, many parents say this is the kind of involvement they want most (Brandt, 1989). According to Epstein, surveys of parents have indicated that families want to know how to work with their own child at home in ways that help the student succeed and that keep the parents as partners in their children's education.

Despite parental interest in helping at home, this kind of involvement is often controversial. As we discussed earlier, some teachers believe that it's unfair to ask already overworked parents to assume teaching responsibilities; others question whether parents can really be helpful, given their "highly variable instructional skills" (Becker and Epstein, 1982, p. 86). Indeed, in a survey of teachers' attitudes toward parental involvement in learning activities at home (Becker and Epstein, 1982), about half of the 3,700 respondents had serious doubts about the success of such efforts.

It's also important to recognize that an emphasis on parental participation in learning activities at home may conflict with some families' beliefs and attitudes. For example, a mother in the study by Finders and Lewis (1994) explains why she stays out of her daughter's schooling:

> It's her education, not mine. I've had to teach her to take care of herself. I work nights, so she's had to get up and get herself ready for school. I'm not going to be there all the time. She's gotta do it. She's a tough cookie. . . . She's almost an adult, and I get the impression that they want me to walk her through her work. And it's not that I don't care either. I really do. I think it's important, but I don't think it's my place. (p. 52)

As Finders and Lewis (1994) comment, "This mother does not lack concern for her child. In her view, independence is essential for her daughter's success" (p. 52).

Similarly, when working with children from non-English-speaking backgrounds, you need to be sensitive to the families' attitudes toward learning English. Kottler (1994) tells of a case in which an Arab-American child's whole family attempted to learn English together by watching situation comedies on television and conversing in English about what they saw. The message this child received was clear: "If you want to succeed, you must learn to speak English." In contrast, the family of another Arab-American child emphasized the importance of maintaining their cultural heritage. Since Arabic was the only language allowed at home, the message this child received was very different: "Speak English only if you must, but Arabic is your real tongue" (p. 7). In a case like this, it is unrealistic to expect the family to assist the child in learning English at home.

Despite the potential problems surrounding Epstein's fourth type of involvement, it appears that communicating with parents about participation in learning activities at home has positive payoffs. A study by Ames (1993), for example, indicates that teachers' communications influenced "how parents talked to their children about school, whether they monitored their schoolwork, and how much time they spent helping their children learn; in other words, their involvement in their children's learning" (p. 47).

Since many children come from one-parent families or families in which both parents work outside the home, it is important to think carefully about realistic ways that families can participate in learning activities at home. (Figure 11-9 provides a list of suggestions.) If you are working with children from very poor families, you might consider setting up a "family resource library" so that families can check out educational games, activities, materials, and books to use with their children at home (Gruber, 1983).

During one meeting, we asked our four teachers to describe the ways they try to involve families in learning activities. Their responses can be grouped into three categories.

Activities Involving Reading and Books   Often teachers of young children encourage parents to read aloud on a regular basis. This is a wonderful way to create a supportive literacy environment at home, but it can be problem if parents aren't able to read. Viviana turns the tables: She gives her students books to read to their parents. She recalls how excited Eduardo's mother was the first time he read to her. She actually came to school the next day to tell Viviana how beautifully Eduardo had read, how he had translated each page, and how he had discussed the story with her in Spanish. Viviana tells us, "The parents are learning from the kids."

Activities Involving Joint Homework Assignments   Sometimes Ken tells his students to see whether their parents can solve math enrichment problems they've done in class. He believes it's exhilarating when children see that they've conquered really difficult problems that their parents can't do. And it gives them a chance to be the teacher: "All the tricks I play on them, they can now play on their parents." In conjunction with *In the Year of the Boar and Jackie Robinson*, Barbara has students interview family members about their ethnic background. Students make a family scrapbook with photographs, drawings, maps, and reports of interviews they've conducted. According to Barbara, "The really neat thing is that

Reading
Read stories to your child.
Read the comics section of the newspaper with your child.
Listen to your child read.
Help your child get a library card from the public library.
Find out about special activities at the public library for your child.
Set aside a special place for your child to keep books.
Subscribe to a children's magazine in your child's name.
Bring books for your child to read in the car while he or she waits for you to run errands.
Bring books for your child to read while waiting in a doctor's or dentist's office.
Read road and street signs while you're walking, driving, or riding somewhere.
Show your child how to use the telephone directory.

Writing
Make a mailbox for your child and leave notes in it.
Help your child write letters and notes to friends and relatives.
Help your child make a telephone/address directory of friends and relatives.
Help your child make birthday cards for friends and relatives.
Give your child a calendar to write down special events and mark off each day.
Help your child keep a scrapbook of his or her best school work.
Help your child make a journal or diary.

Mathematics
Help your child use a yardstick, ruler, tape measure for measuring objects around
    the house.
Show your child how to count change.
Help your child to tell time.
Help your child learn about measurement by following a simple recipe.

Television
Limit and screen your child's television watching.
Watch a television show together and discuss it.
Read a television guide and select a program to watch together.
Discuss and evaluate television commercials.

FIGURE 11-9
Suggestions for family involvement in learning activities at home (adapted from Gruber 1983, 1985)

parents find out things they didn't know either. They have to call their parents and aunts and uncles and cousins to find out information."

Supervising Homework   In interviews with 69 parents of first- through fifth-grade students, Hoover-Dempsey, Bassler, and Burow (1995) found that parents generally believed that involvement in homework was a "given" of parenthood. Many parents, however, expressed ambivalence about how much help they should provide and how independent their children should be. In addition, parents worried that they couldn't provide adequate help because they were unfamiliar with the topic being studied ("You would think I could do fourth-grade work, but sometimes I can't"); because they didn't understand the new ways subjects were taught ("My [math] language was different, because that was 30 years' ago language"); or because competing demands on their time made it difficult to help as much as they felt they should (pp. 444-445). Despite their worries, parents did not want less involvement in their children's learning at home; they simply wanted "to know better how to be involved" (p. 447).

Helping children with their homework can be especially problematic for parents who are not fluent in English and have had little formal schooling themselves. In a study of six Mexican-American families in California, Concho Delgado-Gaitan (1992) found that all of the parents believed it was their responsibility to assist with homework, but the parents of "novice" readers were unable to make sense out of the "reams of workbook pages and ditto sheets" that their children brought home (p. 510). Part of the problem was the "decontextualized drill and practice tasks [that] constituted most of the homework activities" (p. 511). Since these tasks depended on subject-matter knowledge covered in the classroom, they often caused a great deal of confusion and frustration.

You can support parents' desire to be involved by providing explicit information about your homework expectations and specific suggestions for working with children at home. Parents in the study by Hoover-Dempsey, Bassler, and Burow appreciated even simple suggestions as "Read for 15 minutes most nights"; "Say 'Let's go over this together' "; "Do about five math problems each night" (p. 446).

You can also reassure parents by emphasizing the importance of simply monitoring their children's school work, providing support and encouragement, and setting limits ("Doing math in front of the TV is not working" or "You have to do your homework before you can got out to play"). In fact, parents can help simply by asking to see their children's papers; this prevents papers from going directly into the trash can from the book bag. In Garnetta's class, for example, each student has a homework pad provided by the school. At the end of each school day, children copy the assignments listed on the chalkboard. Parents are required to review the homework pad each night and to sign it. When children come to school each morning, they put their homework and the pads on their desks for Garnetta to check. Garnetta remembers one boy who forged his father's signature. Since she had taught his brother, she knew what his father's signature looked like and she informed the boy that "the jig was up." As she puts it, "There was no use jumping all over the kid, but I wanted to make sure he took responsibility for getting the pad signed."

CONCLUDING COMMENTS

In 1976, Ira Gordon (1976), a well-known advocate of parent education and involvement, wrote these words:

We believe, with good evidence, that virtually all parents want a better life for their children than they have had. . . . We know that parents, when properly approached, want to be involved in the education of their children. . . . We have found that parents, regardless of region, race, or economic status, respond when the school reaches out to them in positive, nonthreatening, nonscolding, nonmanipulative ways. (p. 10)

This chapter has described different ways that teachers can reach out to families. Our suggestions vary considerably in terms of how common they are and how much time and energy they demand. As you get to know your students and their family situations, you will be able to decide which practices are most appropriate and most feasible.

As you consider the various alternatives, remember Gordon's message. This is an age of single parents; of mothers who work outside of the home; of grandparents, aunts, and neighbors who care for children; of increasing numbers of families whose cultural backgrounds differ from that of most teachers. Family-school collaboration has never been more difficult—but it has never been more essential.

SUMMARY

This chapter began by discussing the benefits to working closely with families. We then examined the barriers to family-teacher cooperation and stressed that teachers' attitudes and practices—not the education level, marital status, or work place of parents—determine whether families become productively involved in their children's schooling. Finally, we presented strategies for overcoming the barriers and for fostering collaboration between families and schools.

Benefits of Working Closely with Families

- Knowing about a student's home situation provides insight into the student's classroom behavior.
- When families understand what you are trying to achieve, they can provide valuable support and assistance.
- Families can help to develop and implement management strategies for changing behavior.
- Parent volunteers can make classroom management easier by assisting in the classroom.

Barriers to Family-Teacher Cooperation

- Teachers are sometimes reluctant to involve families in schooling because of
    The extra time and energy that are required
    Their perceptions that families are too overburdened, apathetic or irresponsible, or lack the skills needed
    The level of authority and autonomy teachers enjoy within their classrooms
- Parents are sometimes reluctant to become involved in schooling because
    They have unhappy memories of school
    They believe schooling should be left to the experts

They feel guilty if their children are having problems

They find schools intimidating and threatening places
- The changing nature of the family means that:

The number of single-parent families has increased

The "stay-at-home" mother is vanishing

The significant adults in children's lives may not be parents, but grandparents, neighbors, aunts, or uncles

Many children come from non-English-speaking homes

Fostering Collaboration between Families and Schools

- Schools can assist families in carrying out their basis obligations by providing parent education, establishing parent-support groups, referring families to community and state agencies.
- Teachers need to communicate about school programs and students' progress through memos and notes, phone calls, report cards, progress reports, and face-to-face interactions (e.g., Back-to-School night, parent conferences).
- Family members can serve as volunteers in classrooms.
- Families can assist their children at home on learning activities:

activities involving reading and books

activities involving joint homework assignments

supervising homework

providing encouragement and support

setting limits

Like Ira Gordon (1976), we believe that most parents will be supportive and helpful if schools reach out to them in welcoming ways. In this age of single parents, mothers who work outside the home, and children who come from diverse cultural backgrounds, meaningful family-school collaboration has never been more difficult, but it has never been more essential.

ACTIVITIES

1 In getting ready for the school year, you have decided to send a letter to the family of each student in your classes. The point of the letter is to introduce yourself, describe the curriculum, highlight a few upcoming projects, and provide information about what to expect the first day.

Select a grade level and write such a letter. As you write, think about the need to create a warm tone, to be clear and organized, to avoid educational jargon, and to stimulate interest and excitement about school.

2 Last week you conducted a parent conference with Mrs. Lewis, Joey's mother. During the conference you described his disruptive behaviors and what you've done to deal with them. You also explained that he is reading a half-grade below level. Mrs. Lewis seemed to accept and understand the information; however, the next day, an irate *Mr.* Lewis called. He told you that he had never seen his wife so upset and that he wants another conference as soon as possible to get to the bottom of the problem. He also intimated that the problem might be due to a personality conflict between you and his son. Although the phone call caught you off-guard, you scheduled the conference for two days later.

Consider the following questions:

a What will you do to prepare for the conference?

b How will you structure the meeting so that you can state your information in a productive way without being defensive?

c What sort of follow-up might you suggest?

3 Anita is extremely "forgetful" about doing homework assignments. She has received innumerable zeros and regularly has to stay for detention to make up the work. You have called her mother to report on this behavior and to ask for assistance, but her mother does not want to get involved. As she puts it, "I've got all I can do to handle her at home. What she does with school work is your responsibility."

Interview two experienced teachers about what they would do in a case like this, and then formulate your own course of action based on what you learn.

4 In an effort to involve parents in their children's education, you planned a project that required students and their families to work together. The activity involved collecting 15 different leaves, identifying them, and creating a booklet or chart to display the collection in an interesting way. As you survey students about their progress, you realize that two of your students are not receiving any help from home. Identify four ways that you can help these children, either by trying to get the families involved or by providing alternative assistance.

REFERENCES

Ames, C. (1993). How school-to-home communications influence parent beliefs and perceptions. *Equity and Choice, 9*(3), 44–49.

Becher, R. M. (1984). *Parent involvement: A review of research and principles of successful practice.* Washington, D.C.: National Institute of Education.

Becker, H. J., and Epstein, J. L. (1982). Parent involvement: A survey of teacher practices. *The Elementary School Journal, 83*(2), 85–102.

Brandt, R. (1989). On parents and schools: A conversation with Joyce Epstein. *Educational Leadership, 47*(2), 24–27.

Carlson, C. G. (1991). *The parent principle: Prerequisite for educational success. Focus 26.* Princeton, NJ: Educational Testing Service.

Davies, A., Cameron, C., Politano, C., and Gregory, K. (1992). *Together is better: Collaborative assessment, evaluation and reporting.* Winnipeg, MB, Canada: Peguis Publishers.

Davies, D. (1991). Schools reaching out: Family, school, and community partnerships for student success. *Phi Delta Kappan, 72*(5), 376–380, 382.

Davis, B. (1995). *How to involve parents in a multicultural school.* Alexandria, VA: Association for Supervision and Curriculum Development.

Delgado-Gaitan, C. (1992). School matters in the Mexican-American home: Socializing children to education. *AERJ, 29*(3), 495–513.

Epstein, J. (1984). *Effects on parents of teacher practices in parent involvement.* Baltimore: Johns Hopkins University, Center for Social Organization of Schools.

Epstein, J. L. (1988). How do we improve programs for parent involvement? *Educational Horizons, 66,* 58–59.

Epstein, J. L., and Becker, H. J. (1982). Teachers' reported practices of parent involvement: Problems and possibilities. *The Elementary School Journal, 83*(2), 103–113.

Epstein, J. L., and Dauber, S. L. (1991). School programs and teacher practices of parent involvement in inner-city elementary and middle schools. *The Elementary School Journal, 91*(3), 289–305.

Finders, M., and Lewis, C. (1994). Why some parents don't come to school. *Educational Leadership, 51*(8), 50–54.

Froyen, L. A. (1993). *Classroom management: The reflective teacher-leader* (2nd edition). New York: Macmillan.

Gordon, I. J. (1976). Toward a home-school partnership program. In I. J. Gordon and W. F. Breivogel (Eds.), *Building effective home-school relationships.* Boston: Allyn & Bacon, pp. 1–20.

Greenwood, G. E., and Hickman, C. W. (1991). Research and practice in parent involvement: Implications for teacher education. *The Elementary School Journal, 91*(3), 279–288.

Gruber, B. (1983). *Managing your classroom! An instant idea book.* Palos Verdes Estates, CA: Frank Schaffer Publications.

Gruber, B. (1985). *Classroom management for elementary teachers. An instant idea book.* Palos Verdes Estates, CA: Frank Schaffer Publications.

Hayes, T. F., Lipsky, C., McCully, T., Rickard, D., Sipson, P., and Wicker, K. (1985). *EPIC—Effective parenting information for children.* Buffalo, NY: EPIC.

Hayes, N. M., Comer, J. P., and Hamilton-Lee, M. (1989). School climate enhancement through parent involvement. *Journal of School Psychology, 27,* 87–90.

Henderson, A. T. (1987). *The evidence continues to grow: Parent involvement improves student achievement.* Columbia, MD: National Committee for Citizens in Education.

Henderson, A. T., Marburger, C. L., and Ooms, T. (1986). *Beyond the bake sale: An educator's guide to working with parents.* Columbia, MD: National Committee for Citizens in Education.

Hodgkinson, H. (1985). *All one system: Demographics of education, kindergarten through graduate school.* Washington, D.C.: Institute for Educational Leadership.

Hoover-Dempsey, K. V., Bassler, O. C., and Brissie, J. S. (1987). Parent involvement: Contributions of teacher efficacy, school socioeconomic status, and other school characteristics. *American Educational Research Journal, 24*(3), 417–435.

Hoover-Dempsey, K. V., Bassler, O. C., and Burow, R. (1995). Parents' reported involvement in students' homework: Strategies and practices. *The Elementary School Journal, 95*(5), 435–449.

Kottler, E. (1994). *Children with limited English: Teaching strategies for the regular classroom.* Thousand Oaks, CA: Corwin Press.

Lemlech, J. K. (1988). *Classroom management: Methods and techniques for elementary and secondary teachers.* New York: Longman, 1984.

Lightfoot, S. L. (1978). *Worlds apart: Relationships between families and schools.* New York: Basic Books.

Lindle, J. C. (1989). What do parents want from principals and teachers? *Educational Leadership, 47*(2), 12–14.

Lord, B. B. (1984). *In the year of the boar and Jackie Robinson.* New York: Harper & Row.

Love, M. J. (1989). The home visit: An irreplaceable tool. *Educational Leadership, 45*(2), 28.

Lueder, D. C. (1989). Tennessee parents were invited to participate—and they did. *Educational Leadership, 47*(2), 15–17.

Menacker, J., Hurwitz, E., and Weldon, W. (1988). Parent-teacher cooperation in schools serving the urban poor. *Clearing House, 62,* 108–112.

Nardine, F. E., and Morris, R. D. (1991). Parent involvement in the states: How firm is the commitment? *Phi Delta Kappan, 72*(4), 363–366.

Olmsted, P. P. (1991). Parent involvement in elementary education: Findings and suggestions from the Follow Through Program. *The Elementary School Journal, 91*(3), 221–231.

Olson, L. (April 4, 1990). Parents as partners: Redefining the social contract between families and schools. *Education Week,* April 4, 17–24.

O'Neil, J. (1991). A generation adrift? *Educational Leadership, 49*(1), 4–10.

Power, T. J. (1985). Perceptions of competence: How parents and teachers view each other. *Psychology in the Schools, 22,* 68–78.

Rich, D. (1988). Bridging the parent gap in education reform. *Educational Horizons, 66,* 90–92.

The State of America's Children Yearbook, 1994. Washington, D.C.: Children's Defense Fund.

Vernberg, E. M., and Medway, F. J. (1981). Teacher and parent causal perceptions of school problems. *American Educational Research Journal, 18,* 29–37.

Walde, A. C., and Baker, K. (1990). How teachers view the parents' role in education. *Phi Delta Kappan, 72*(4), 319–320, 322.

Waller, W. (1932). *Sociology of teaching.* New York: John Wiley and Sons.

FOR FURTHER READING

Davies, A., Cameron, C., Politano, C., and Gregory, K. (1992). *Together is better: Collaborative assessment, evaluation and reporting.* Winnipeg, MB, Canada: Peguis Publishers.

Davis, B. (1995). *How to involve parents in a multicultural school.* Alexandria, VA: Association of Supervision and Curriculum Development.

Gruber, B. (1983). *Managing your classroom! An instant idea book.* Palos Verdes Estates, CA: Frank Schaffer Publications, Inc.

Gruber, B. (1985). *Classroom management for elementary teachers. An instant idea book.* Palos Verdes Estates CA: Frank Schaffer Publications.

Henderson, A. T., Marburger, C. L., and Ooms, T. (1986). *Beyond the bake sale: An educator's guide to working with parents.* Columbia, MD: National Committee for Citizens in Education.

Phi Delta Kappan (January 1991). Special section on parent involvement, J. L. Epstein (Guest Editor), *72*(5), 344–388.

Strengthening partnerships with parents & community. (October 1989). *Educational Leadership, 47*(2).

Swap, S. A. (1987). *Enhancing parent involvement: A manual for parents and teachers.* New York: Teachers College Press.

Chapter Twelve

Helping Students with Special Needs

In many parts of the country, one visit to an elementary school is all that's needed to see that today's classrooms are far more diverse than ever before. Criticisms of tracking and ability grouping have resulted in more academically heterogeneous classrooms, with children who need instruction in basic skills next to those who qualify for "gifted and talented" programs. Recent increases in immigration, particularly from Latin America and Southeast Asia, have led to classes in which children come from a wide range of cultural and linguistic backgrounds. Efforts to achieve "inclusive classrooms" have meant that children with disabilities, who would have previously been taught in separate classrooms or even special schools, are now educated in the regular classroom.

In addition to being more diverse, classrooms also contain a greater number of children who are "at risk" because of conditions associated with poverty—maternal smoking, prenatal exposure to alcohol and drugs, low birth weight, lead poisoning, abuse and neglect, violence, and malnutrition (O'Neil, 1991). Poverty afflicts U.S. children more than any other age group, with 22 percent of all children living below the poverty line (Children's Defense Fund, 1994). African-American children are particularly affected; 44 percent live in poverty (Joint Center for Political and Economic Studies, 1990; cited in O'Neil, 1991). The message is clear: Large numbers of American children are likely to experience severe developmental delays, emotional disorders, and physical problems—and these problems put them at risk for school failure.

The increasing number of children who are at risk, along with the increasing diversity, make managing classrooms far more challenging than it used to be. Guiding and structuring classroom events is more difficult when numerous children are "pulled out" for supplemental instruction; when the language and culture of the classroom are in conflict with students' linguistic and cultural background; when some children are bored because work is too easy, while others are frustrated because work is too hard; and when children come to school troubled, malnourished or neglected.

How can you help the children with special needs who may be in your classroom? One answer is to be informed about the various special services that are available and to know how to obtain access to those services. Maynard Reynolds, a leading special educator, writes:

> It is too much to ask that a beginning teacher know about all of the problems he or she will encounter in teaching; but it is not too much to ask that the beginning teacher recognize the needs for support and assistance when challenging problems arise, and to understand that it is a sign of professionalism to seek help when needed rather than a sign of weakness. (Reynolds, 1989, p. 138)

You may recall Barbara's experience with a child in her class who had been sexually abused and demonstrated persistent behavior problems (see Chapter 6). Although Barbara tried every strategy she knew, she was unable to modify the child's behavior and eventually sought outside assistance. As Barbara stressed, when a child is really in need, "it's your responsibility to get help for that child."

Unfortunately, many beginning teachers do not know where to turn for help. They are unfamiliar with legislation mandating or encouraging programs for at-risk children. They don't understand their own responsibilities with respect to children with special needs. When children are "pulled out" for special instruction, teachers may not know where they're going, what they're doing there, or how they were selected. And they are unclear about helping children with special needs in the regular classroom.

Both this chapter and Chapter 13 are designed to address these issues. In this chapter, we focus on children with disabilities, those who are victims of poverty, those who come from different linguistic backgrounds, and those who are "gifted and talented." In Chapter 13, we turn to problems of substance abuse, violence, and child abuse and neglect.

We begin by providing an overview of services that exist to meet the challenges created by disability, poverty, limited-English-proficiency, and giftedness. For each topic, we briefly discuss the history, legislation, controversies, and services that are involved. Next we discuss the strategies for obtaining access to these services. Finally, we offer guidelines to keep in mind as you work with special needs children in your own classroom. Before going any further, however, it is important to make explicit two basic principles that underlie our discussion.

First, *teachers are responsible for all the children in their classes, including those with special needs.* As we have already emphasized, part of being responsible means seeking outside assistance when needed. It also means communicating and collaborating with special services personnel in order to provide children with a coherent educational experience. And it means *working with special children when they are in your room.* Unfortunately, some teachers seem to believe that they are "off the hook" once they refer a child for special services. A student teacher recently shared this story with us:

> There's a boy in my classroom who goes to a resource room every day for reading and math. When he's in the classroom, he sits in a back corner, basically doing nothing. My cooperating teacher gives him some worksheets to do, but doesn't even really monitor

to see if he does them. He never includes him in any of the class's activities. Sometimes the boy wanders around the room, looking at what the other kids are doing, and I get the feeling he'd like to do the lesson too, but my teacher doesn't make any attempt to involve him. When I asked about the boy, my teacher told me he can't do anything for the child, that his learning disabilities are just too great. He said he doesn't have the necessary expertise to help him—that he's not a special educator. So he just lets him sit. It makes me want to cry.

It is not unusual for regular classroom teachers to feel they lack the professional preparation necessary to help children with special needs (Semmel, Abernathy, Butera, and Lesar, 1991), and we can empathize with this feeling. Nonetheless, those who are hard to teach or to manage are just as much your responsibility as those who are "easy." The question is not *whether* to help, but *how.*

Second, *we believe that truly inclusive classrooms are those in which children learn to work and learn together, in which diversity is not just tolerated, but valued and respected.* It is not enough for children with special needs to be included physically; they must be included socially. This means that teachers must work hard to create a comfortable, caring environment; they must model sensitivity to differences; they must use a variety of instructional approaches geared to different learning and interaction styles; they must be willing to learn from other teachers, from support personnel such as special education teachers, speech/language pathologists, occupational therapists, and paraprofessionals, and from the children themselves. Listen to this teacher, initially resistant to the idea of having a child with severe disabilities in her class:

I started watching my own regular classroom students. They didn't treat him any differently. They went about their business like everything was normal. So I said, "If they can do it, I can do it. He's not getting in their way, they're treating him like everybody else. (Giangreco, Dennis, Cloninger, Edelman, and Schattman, 1993)

SPECIAL SERVICES FOR CHILDREN WITH SPECIAL NEEDS

Helping Children with Disabilities: Special Education

Helen is in Garnetta's third-grade classroom. She is repeating third grade this year, but her skills in reading and math are far below those of her classmates who have come directly from the second grade. In addition, Helen is extremely immature: she cries a lot, gets frustrated easily, and frequently falls out of her chair. Sometimes Garnetta finds Helen sitting under her desk. She's often defensive and denies her involvement in any misbehavior ("I didn't do it!"). Despite these behaviors, Garnetta says that Helen is "lovable" and reports that the child gets along well with her peers.

After observing Helen's behavior and academic performance during the first few weeks of school, Garnetta decided that Helen needed special help. She discussed the child with her principal and discovered that Helen had been referred for evaluation the previous year. Although she had been tested and the Child Study Team was ready to classify her as "perceptually impaired" (New Jersey equivalent of "learning disabled"), Helen's parents objected, and no action was taken.

Garnetta decided that Helen should once again be referred to the school's Child Study Team, and with the parents' consent, Helen was re-evaluated. Both the school psychologist and the Learning Disabilities Teacher Consultant (LDTC) administered a variety of tests and visited Garnetta's classroom to observe Helen's behavior. This time, Helen's parents agreed to Helen's classification. An individualized education plan (IEP) was developed for Helen. This specified that she would remain in Garnetta's classroom, but would go to a "resource room" every day, where a special education teacher would provide instruction for reading and math. The resource room teacher is responsible for grading her in these two subjects.

Helen's presence in Garnetta's class, the supplemental services she receives, and her individualized education program are a direct result of Public Law 94-142, enacted in 1975. (Table 12-1 provides a summary of significant federal legislation.) This landmark legislation mandated that "all handicapped children have available to them . . . a free appropriate public education which emphasizes special education and related services designed to meet their unique needs . . ." According to P.L. 94-142, handicapped students are:

TABLE 12-1
FEDERAL LEGISLATION RELATING TO SERVICES FOR CHILDREN WITH SPECIAL NEEDS

Special Need	Year	Legislation
Disability	1975	P.L. 94-142: mandated a free, appropriate public education for all handicapped children
	1990	Individuals with Disabilities Education Act: amended P.L. 94-142; substituted the term "disabilities" for "handicapped" but maintained the basic thrust of the law
Poverty	1965	Elementary and Secondary Education Act (ESEA): established compensatory education (Title I)
	1981	Education Consolidation and Improvement Act: transferred Title I programs to Chapter 1
Limited English Proficiency	1968	Bilingual Education Act (added as Title VII to ESEA of 1965): provided financial assistance to states and local educational agencies to design model programs to meet the needs of LEP children; the act stipulated that English-language proficiency was to be the goal of such programs, but implied that the child's language was to be used for content area instruction to prevent academic failure while the child was learning English
	1974	Equal Educational Opportunity Act (EEOA): specified that no state shall deny equal educational opportunity to an individual by failing to take appropriate action to overcome language barriers that impede equal participation by students in its instructional programs
Gifted and Talented	1970	P.L. 91-230, the Gifted and Talented Education Assistance Act: provided federal assistance for programs for students who are gifted and talented; mandated that the U.S. Commissioner of Education study the needs of gifted children and report to Congress.
	1978	P.L. 95-561, the Gifted and Talented Children's Act: provided funds to state educational agencies to assist in the planning and improving of programs for gifted students

those children evaluated as being mentally retarded, hard of hearing, deaf, speech impaired, visually handicapped, seriously emotionally disturbed, orthopedically impaired, other health impaired, deaf-blind, multi-handicapped, or as having specific learning disabilities. . . . (*Federal Register,* 1977, pp. 42478–43479)

Table 12-2 summarizes the primary provisions of the law: zero reject, nondiscriminatory evaluation, individualized educational programs, least restrictive environment, due process, and parent participation (Schulz, Carpenter, and Turnbull, 1991). These provisions help to explain why Helen's parents were able to stop her from being classified; why the school psychologist and the LDTC administered not one, but several tests; why a special committee developed an IEP specifying the services that were to be provided; and why she remained in Garnetta's classroom (the "least restrictive environment"), leaving for only one period a day to receive instruction in the resource room.

In 1990, amendments to P.L. 94-142 renamed it the Individuals with Disabilities Education Act (IDEA). The term "disabilities" was substituted for "handicapped," and a number of other modifications were made. But the essence of the law re-

TABLE 12-2
SIX PRINCIPLES OF P.L. 94-142

1. Zero reject	The right of *all* children with disabilities to receive an appropriate, publicly supported education, regardless of type or severity of disability.
2. Nondiscriminatory evaluation	The right to an accurate, fair evaluation, using a minimum of two tests, testing specific areas of educational need rather than focusing only on general intelligence, and considering racial and cultural factors.
3. Individualized education program (IEP)	The right to an individualized program established to meet the specific needs of the student; an IEP document is jointly developed by an interdisciplinary team; it must contain specific components—the child's current educational status; yearly goals; short-term objectives; documentation of the particular special education and related services that will be provided; the extent of time the student will participate in the regular education program; dates and duration of services; and criteria, procedures, and schedules for determining mastery of objectives.
4. Least restrictive environment	The right to be educated—whenever possible—in programs with nondisabled students; placement in special schools or special classes only when the disability is so severe that education cannot be accomplished in the regular education program with the use of supplementary aids and services.
5. Due process	The right of parents and school personnel to challenge the identification, evaluation, or placement of a disabled student and to initiate a due-process hearing, where both sides will be heard by an impartial hearing officer.
6. Parent participation	The right of parents to participate in the planning and implementation of the educational program and to have access to all educational records kept on their child; parents must give their consent before a child can be evaluated or placed in special education.

mained the same, including the principles that *all children should be educated in the regular classroom to the maximum extent possible, with the use of supplementary aids and services to help them achieve.* This principle is often known as "mainstreaming," and we can see it at work not only in Garnetta's classroom, but also in Barbara's:

> I have three children in my class who have been identified as perceptually or neurologically impaired. Each of the children works with a special services tutor who comes to the classroom several times a week. Her job is to help them with language arts and math, so they can make satisfactory academic progress in the regular classroom. But I'm still the "responsible" teacher: I grade the children in language arts and math, and I meet with the tutor every time she comes to tell her what I want done. She doesn't carry out a separate program; she reinforces the material that I'm teaching in the regular curriculum. Also, at the end of the day, she comes back to check that the students are organized to go home. She sees that they have their assignments written down and that their books are in their book bags. This is really a tremendous help, since I'm dealing with 27 students, trying to get everybody packed up and out the door on time.

It is important to point out that placement in the "least restrictive environment" does *not* necessarily mean that all students with disabilities are placed in the regular classroom for all or part of the school day. Indeed, the law allows placement in more "restrictive" environments: self-contained special education classrooms, special education day schools, hospitals, and residential schools. Recently, however, increasing numbers of educators have rejected the notion of a continuum of *placements*; they argue that it is far preferable to provide a continuum of *services* in the regular classroom, allowing children with disabilities to be educated with their nondisabled peers. Advocates of this position, often referred to as "full inclusion," contend that the regular classroom benefits children with disabilities academically because they are held to higher expectations and are exposed to more stimulating content. In addition, they benefit socially, since they can make friends with children from their own neighborhoods and can observe peers behaving in a socially appropriate manner. (Table 12-3 lists the assumptions that underlie arguments about inclusion.) Mara Sapon-Shevin, an education professor at Syracuse University, is a proponent of full inclusion:

> The idea is that these [inclusive] schools would be restructured so that they are supportive, nurturing communities that really meet the needs of all the children within them: rich in resources and support for both students and teachers. . . . As far as a rationale, we should not have to defend inclusion—we should make others defend exclusion. There's very little evidence that some children need segregated settings in which to be educated. . . . [W]e know that the world is an inclusive community. There are lots of people in it who vary not only in terms of disabilities, but in race, class, gender, and religious background. It's very important for children to have the opportunity to learn and grow within communities that represent the kind of world they'll live in when they finish school. (O'Neil, 1994/95, p. 7)

On the other side of the debate are educators who argue that it is essential to maintain a continuum of placements (e.g., Zigmond, Jenkins, Fuchs, Deno, and

TABLE 12-3
THE "INCLUSION" ARGUMENT

Proponents of Full Inclusion	Opponents of Full Inclusion
1. Labeling and segregation are inherently bad.	1. Labeling is not bad if the labels indicate real differences; it's the only way to ensure that funds go to the neediest children.
2. Students with disabilities aren't different from nondisabled students in any meaningful way; everyone is unique.	2. Students with disabilities are different from nondisabled children, precisely because of their disabilities.
3. Students with disabilities can best be served in regular classrooms because	3. Some children with disabilities may be best served in regular classrooms, but some may be better served in separate special educational programs because
teachers have lower expectations when all students in a class have disabilities	special education teachers have appropriate expectations for their students
they benefit academically because they are held to higher expectations and are exposed to more stimulating curriculum	they benefit academically because teachers are specially trained, can implement an appropriate curriculum, and can give more individualized attention
virtually all regular teachers can teach disabled students and are willing to do so	regular education teachers don't want children with disabilities in their classes and don't consider themselves prepared to serve them
students with disabilities can make friends with children in their neighborhoods and model appropriate behavior of nondisabled peers	students with disabilities are often isolated and rejected by their nondisabled peers; they need the social acceptance and comraderie of peers with similar disabilities
4. Special education is too costly, fragmented, and inefficient.	4. Opponents of special education just want to save money at the expense of needy students.
5. Many students in special education are not actually disabled, but are placed there because of faculty evaluations.	5. Most children in special education belong there; evaluations are generally reliable.
6. Nondisabled students benefit from having children with disabilities in their classes because they learn to accept and respect differences.	6. Nondisabled students suffer from having children with disabilities in their classes because the teacher has to spend too much time working with the disabled students.

Adapted from Webb, 1994, p. 4.

Fuchs, 1995; Zigmond, Jenkins, Fuchs, Deno, Fuchs, Baker, Jenkins, and Couthino, 1995). Jim Kauffman, a professor of education at the University of Virginia, reflects this point of view.

> I'm convinced that we *must* maintain the alternative of moving kids to other places when that appears necessary in the judgment of teachers and parents. . . . Sure, we ought to meet special needs in a regular class when that's possible. But there isn't anything wrong with meeting special needs outside the regular class if that is required. In fact, the law and best practice say we must consider both possibilities. (O'Neil, 1994/95, p. 7)

Critics of full inclusion worry that financially desperate school districts will use inclusion to reduce special education costs and "dump" children with disabilities in regular classrooms without support (Webb, 1994). Not surprisingly, many regular classroom teachers share this view. Indeed, they often resist full inclusion, afraid that they lack the expertise to meet children's special needs and worried about the time and effort that children with disabilities take away from other students (Semmel, Abernathy, Butera, and Lesar, 1991). Reactions can be extremely negative, especially if inclusion programs are imposed on teachers without consultation. One middle school teacher in a study conducted by Vaughn, Schumm, Jallad, Slusher, and Saumell (in press) reacted this way: "If you try to cram it down their throat, most of our faculty would just say 'No way, not on your life. I would rather pump gas' " (p. 14).

Advocates of full inclusion are careful to point out that including children with disabilities in the regular classroom does not mean placing unreasonable demands on teachers. A good program provides the supports necessary to make it work—aides, interpreters, planning time, administrative assistance, special materials and equipment. In Barbara's classroom, for example, a full-time teaching assistant works with Joey, a 12-year-old-boy with autism who has been included in regular classrooms since second grade. In addition, Joey and Barbara both wear a special device that allows him to screen out classroom background noise and to focus on the voice of the teacher. Barbara is extremely enthusiastic about Joey's presence in her class:

> Joey has been in the school for the last two years [since second grade], so his adjustment to my class wasn't a big issue. But he worries a lot, and once he's worrying about something, he really perseverates. In order to ease some of this worry, Joey and his third-grade class visited my class at the end of last year to see what life in fourth grade was like. The intent was to make Joey feel comfortable, but we decided that the whole class would come. The week before school started, we also had Joey come in so he could wander around the room, touch things, ask questions, talk with me. Even now, he comes in 15 minutes before the other students with Marge Trestka [the teaching assistant]. Partly it's so he doesn't get caught up in the hallway crowds, but partly it's so he can talk about what he's worrying about that day: a storm that's coming, a doctor's appointment, a friend who has a stomach ache. One of Marge's jobs is to refocus him when he starts worrying, so that worry doesn't overpower him.
>
> Since the other children know him, their adjustment wasn't a problem. On the first day of school, all I had to say was "Joey is here with Mrs. Trestka. You all know Joey and Mrs. Trestka, right?" What's been really fantastic is watching Joey and the other kids really beginning to work together and to be friends. They've always tolerated him, and treated him kindly, but they weren't *friends*. Making friends and developing a sense of humor are two big learning tasks for Joey. He's two years older than everybody else and he worries that makes the kids uncomfortable, but he doesn't. He's also real worried about "behaving appropriately." He asks Marge and me what he should or should not do.
>
> Watching Joey's progress this year has been fantastic. His *academic* progress was not so much the issue, because he's really bright, and Marge is there to help him. The biggest

thing for us has been watching his *social* development: his excitement when he's invited to someone's birthday party; when he decided to try out for the school talent show (and made it!); when he wanted to *give* Christmas presents, not just *receive* them. If he sat in a carrel all day (the way he used to), he'd never learn these behaviors. He's pleased with who he is now. He's beginning to want to be a part of the world around him; he doesn't find it such a scary place anymore.

Barbara is not alone in her very positive reaction to inclusion. Recent interviews with 19 general education teachers who had students with severe disabilities in their classes (Giangreco, Dennis, Cloninger, Edelman, and Schattman, 1993) reveal that despite their initial negative attitudes, 17 of the teachers described "transforming experiences" that led them to recognize the benefits of inclusion to themselves and to all the children. They began to realize that they *could* be successful and that including a student with disabilities was not so difficult as they had originally imagined. One teacher, for example, admitted: "At the beginning of the year, if I was making copies of something I might forget to count Jon: I just didn't deal with him" (p. 359). Later, however, her attitude changed:

> I just realized that he had been in my classroom for a month or so, and I had no contact with him really. I have a student in my classroom, and I don't think that I have even touched him. You know, I had so much physical contact with all the other first graders, patting them on the back, going up to them and talking to them. Other than saying "Hi, Jon" when he came into the room, I basically didn't have any contact with him. I started realizing at that point that I have got to have some impact on him. He's one of my students. I had always said, "I have 13 students plus Jon," and then I realized: Why am I saying "plus Jon?" He's one of my students. (p. 365)

Similarly, another teacher described this change:

> I started seeing him as a little boy. I started feeling that he's a person too. He's a student. Why should I not teach him? He is in my class. That's my responsibility, I'm a teacher!

And a third teacher commented:

> I made the full swing of fighting against having Bobbi Sue placed in my room to fighting for her to be in a mainstream classroom working with kids in the way that she had worked with them all year long. I'm a perfect example of how you have to have an open mind.

Paradoxically, the inclusion of children with more severe disabilities (who are *infrequently* included) may be more successful than the inclusion of children with ostensibly less severe and less obvious problems, such as learning disabilities (who are *frequently* included). One reason is that children with less severe disabilities may not get the level of support and the kind of instruction they need to succeed in the regular classroom. For example, teachers often find it particularly challenging to work with children who have Attention Deficit Disorder (ADD) or Attention Deficit Hyperactivity Disorder (ADHD), who may not even be eligible for special services. (See Table 12-4 for a list of the behavioral characteristics of ADD and ADHD. As you review the table, keep in mind that any one of the behaviors can be normal, especially in young children. It is when a child frequently displays a large

TABLE 12-4
CHARACTERISTICS OF CHILDREN WITH ADD/ADHD (ADAPTED FROM RIEF, 1993)

ADD	ADHD
Distractibility	The characteristics of ADD *plus*
Difficulty listening and following directions	High activity level (constantly fidgeting, falling out of chair, roaming around classroom)
Difficulty focusing and sustaining attention	Impulsivity and lack of self-control (blurts out; can't wait for turn; interrupts; talks excessively; can't stop and think before acting; engages in physically dangerous activities without considering consequences)
Difficulty concentrating	
Inconsistent performance in school work (can do task one day, but not the next)	
"Spaciness"	Difficulty with transitions
Disorganization	Aggressive behavior
Poor study skills	Social immaturity
Difficulty working independently	Low self-esteem
	High frustration

number of these behaviors at a developmentally inappropriate age that you may need to seek assistance.)

The argument over full inclusion is not the only controversy in special education. There is also heated debate over our current system of classifying or labeling disabilities. Educators who oppose classification point out that similar instructional processes appear to be effective with children who are given different labels (Oakes and Lipton, 1990; Stein, Leinhardt, and Bickel, 1989). They wonder, therefore, why classification is necessary—or even helpful—and they support the concept of "rights without labels" (Gartner and Lipsky, 1987).

Another criticism of our classification system is that labels make it seem as if disabilities are "real"—well-defined, easily identifiable, and permanent. Yet when children have mild or moderate learning difficulties, the inconsistencies from state to state—even district to district—make it clear that this is not always so. Indeed, we see large disparities in the percentages of children classified as emotionally disturbed, educable mentally retarded, and learning disabled (Reynolds, Wang and Walberg, 1987). To put it bluntly, a child may be classified as learning disabled in one state, emotionally disturbed in another, and not at all in a third. In 1984, for example, the percentage of special education students labeled as learning disabled varied from 30 percent to 67 percent among the 50 states, and from zero to 73 percent among 30 large cities (Binkard, 1986; cited in Gartner and Lipsky, 1987). These discrepancies suggest that the label assigned to a particular child is affected not only by characteristics of the child, but also by external factors—such as the criteria being used, the particular assessment instruments, evaluators' biases and competence, community and parental influences, and the availability of space and personnel in certain programs.

Problems with the category "mental retardation" provide a good example of the way external factors can influence classification. From 1976 to 1985, there was a substantial decline in the number of students labeled mentally retarded. A 1985 report by the United States Department of Education explains:

> These decreases . . . are the result of an increasing sensitivity to the negative features of the label itself and to the reaction on the part of local school systems to allegations of racial and ethnic bias as a result of the use of discriminatory or culturally biased testing procedures. (*Seventh Annual Report to Congress on the Implementation of the Education of the Handicapped Act,* 1985, p. 4)

During the same period, there was a *260 percent increase in the number of students classified as learning disabled* or the equivalent (e.g., perceptually impaired, neurologically impaired) (Slavin, 1989). It is likely that this increase in learning disabilities and the accompanying decrease in mental retardation is at least partly due to "classification plea bargaining" (Gartner and Lipsky, 1987, p. 373). Although understandable, these trends cast doubt on the validity and meaningfulness of the categories we use to label children.

Helping Children of Poverty: Compensatory Education

> It's 9:30, and Ken's class is working on vocabulary and dictionary skills. In a back corner, Danny is working on a writing activity with an aide provided by Chapter 1, a compensatory education program. Although Danny's family is not poor, he qualifies for Chapter 1 assistance because he scored in the 15th percentile on last year's California Achievement Test. The aide helps Danny with his story, following instructions provided in an activity folder that Ken has created.

At the beginning of each school year, our four teachers receive a list of students who will be receiving "compensatory education"—remedial programs intended to "compensate for" or overcome the problems associated with poverty. The current system of compensatory education began in 1965 as part of President Lyndon Johnson's War on Poverty. (See Table 12-1.) Since then, Chapter 1 (formerly known as Title I) has provided extra instruction in reading, writing, and mathematics to millions of children.

Chapter 1 funds go to schools on the basis of socioeconomic status (determined by the percentage of students who qualify for free lunches), but funds can be used to serve *any* student—like Danny—who scores substantially below grade level in math or reading tests. Although Chapter 1 programs have been shown to be effective in raising achievement, they have not been successful in closing the gap between Chapter 1 students and their peers (Slavin, 1989). Nonetheless, support and funding for Chapter 1 continue; during the 1991 and 1992 fiscal years, Chapter 1 received $6.1 billion, representing the largest component of the Elementary and Secondary Education Act of 1965 (Celis 3rd, 1993). About 5.5. million children in two-thirds of the nation's schools receive Chapter 1 services, and 70 percent of them are in elementary grades (Celis 3rd, 1993).

Compensatory education services are delivered in a variety of ways. As we just saw, a Chapter 1 aide comes to Ken's classroom to work with Danny. In contrast, Garnetta's entire class goes to a "basic skills classroom" each day.

> From 10:20 to 11:00, Garnetta's class works in the basic skills room. The compensatory education teacher provides remedial instruction to all students except one, who scored "too high" to be eligible. While the teacher works with a small group, Garnetta helps the others practice reading, language, and math skills on computers. Garnetta and the basic skills teacher meet together once a month to plan instruction. Garnetta selects three or four objectives which her students find particularly difficult, and the basic skills teacher reinforces these.

As these examples demonstrate, Chapter 1 services are delivered in a variety of ways. The most common method, however, is through "pull-out" programs, in which identified students leave their regular classmates in order to receive small group instruction from a Chapter 1 teacher. (See Chapter 7 for another discussion of pull-out programs.) Educators have become increasingly critical of this approach (Meyers, Gelzheiser, Yelich, and Gallagher, 1990; Stein, Leinhardt, and Bickel, 1989; Celis 3rd, 1993) and have identified a number of drawbacks associated with pull-out programs. One problem is a lack of consistency between what happens in the regular class and what happens in the Chapter 1 class (Allington and Johnston, 1989). Unless the two teachers communicate on a regular basis, they may use different (even contradictory) instructional approaches, emphasize different skills, and provide different kinds of materials. This can result in a disjointed, fragmented program—for the children most in need of a coherent educational experience.

Another drawback is the loss of instructional time that can occur when children are pulled out of the regular classrooms. Having to pack up, move to another room, and wait for everybody to arrive can substantially increase the time spent in transition. Once again, those most in need may actually be getting shortchanged.

Finally, when children are pulled out, they miss the regular classroom curriculum. It is not clear what should be done in this situation. Should the students be required to make up the work? If so, doesn't this put an additional burden on children who are already struggling to keep up with their peers? And when do you, the regular classroom teacher, find the time to provide the instruction they missed? The answers to these questions are not obvious. The following journal entry, written by a second-grade student teacher, captures the frustration that many teachers experience with respect to pull-out programs:

> Early in my placement, I was surprised to see so many children coming and going to special services. There are times during the week where half of my class is gone. . . . I sometimes feel frustrated by frequent scheduling dilemmas and guilty that I am often unable to find the time to teach the "pull-out" students the material they missed. The fragmentation and lack of instruction seem crazy. How can these kids be expected to "perform on grade level" when they aren't even in their classrooms?

Clearly, pull-out programs can create as many problems as they are intended to solve. On the other hand, results of a study on the effectiveness of a specially designed Chapter 1 program (Hiebert, Colt, Catto, and Gury, 1992) suggest that pull-out Chapter 1 programs "should not be summarily thrown out." These researchers implemented a program that was extremely effective in raising the literacy level of children with whom they worked; furthermore, students in the restructured Chapter 1 program not only had significantly higher performances than students in the district's regular Chapter 1 program, they also performed comparably to students in the middle of the class who were not eligible for Chapter 1. These results led the researchers to conclude: "It is doubtful that the Chapter 1 teachers would have been as effective within the classrooms. . . . The test of Chapter 1 programs should be whether children are learning to read, not where the instruction occurs" (p. 568).

Helping Children with Limited Proficiency in English

The students in Viviana's class are representative of a growing number of "language minority students"—students who come from homes in which a language other than English is spoken. Estimates of the number of language minority students vary considerably—from about 1.3 million to 3.6 million (Garcia, 1990). Although they live throughout the United States, about 62 percent of language minority students are clustered in Arizona, Colorado, California, New Mexico and Texas. The vast majority are of Spanish language background, but there are also sizable numbers of children with other European language backgrounds, Southeast Asian backgrounds (e.g., Vietnamese, Cambodian, Hmong), Asian backgrounds (Chinese, Korean), and Native American backgrounds. It is not uncommon in large school districts to have children representing as many as 25 different languages (Reynolds, 1989); in 1991, California's public schools served children speaking any one of about 100 languages (Lessow-Hurley, 1991).

Some language minority students may be fluent in English. Others, like Viviana's students, may enter school with limited English proficiency (LEP). Federal legislation provides funding and encouragement for programs to assist these children (see Table 12-1); however, there are no federally mandated programs like those provided for children who have disabilities or for those who come from impoverished homes. In fact, a landmark statement supporting the rights of LEP students comes not from the legislature, but from a Supreme Court case, *Lau v. Nichols* (1974), in which a group of Chinese students sued the San Francisco Unified School District for providing them with an education they could not understand. The Court found for the plaintiffs, stating:

> [T]here is no equality of treatment merely by providing students with the same facilities, textbooks, teachers and curriculum: for students who do not understand English are effectively foreclosed from any meaningful education. Basic English skills are at the very core of what these public schools teach. Imposition of a requirement that, before a child can effectively participate in the education program he must already have acquired those basic skills is to make a mockery of public education. We know that those who do not understand English are certain to find their classroom experiences wholly incomprehensible and in no way meaningful. (p. 27)

As a result of *Lau,* a number of states enacted legislation requiring services for LEP students, but laws change constantly and vary substantially from state to state. The state in which you teach may mandate such services or merely permit them; it may even prohibit them! Despite the variability, state laws generally call for the identification and assessment of LEP students and describe options for special services. Let's consider what these options are.

Bilingual education programs teach children in their native language as well as in English, thus allowing them to learn academic subjects while they're learning English. In some states, if there are a given number of LEP students in a district, speaking a common native language at approximately the same grade level, the district is required to provide bilingual programs. There are three types of bilingual programs (Romero, Mercado, and Vazquez-Faria, 1987): (1) *transitional* programs, where the goal is to have students move into English-only classrooms; (2) *maintenance programs,* where the goal is to maintain both languages, so that students achieve true bilingualism; and (3) *enrichment program,* where English-speaking students learn the language of the minority, and language-minority students learn English.

A major source of controversy involves the nature and pace of transitional programs—namely, when to move students into English-language instruction (Gersten and Woodward, 1995). Some bilingual educators believe that the transition to English should be extremely gradual; teachers in this kind of transitional bilingual program conduct academic instruction in the students' native language until students demonstrate a sufficient grasp of English to succeed in English-language academic instruction. Other bilingual educators favor the *immersion* approach, in which LEP students are taught English as they learn academic content, and the complete transition to English is made as early as first grade. The key to this approach is the use of "sheltered English," English that is sensitive to students' English proficiency and seeks to be comprehensible. (Judith Lessow-Hurley, 1991, points out the difference between immersion programs and "submersion programs," in which students are left to sink or swim.)

In Viviana's district, the bilingual education program is transitional and gradual. Three years of bilingual instruction are provided for children who come to school speaking Spanish; after that, children move into English-only classrooms. Viviana herself, however, is more an advocate of immersion. Although she wants her students to maintain their Spanish, she also wants them to learn English as soon as possible:

I used to teach every subject completely in Spanish and then translate everything in English. But after a while, I began to question whether this was a good approach. Translating everything was boring, exhausting, and time-consuming. Finally, I said, I'm going to try another way. In the beginning of the year I use Spanish a lot, but as time goes by I teach more and more in English, using Spanish explanations if I see the children don't understand. Of course, whenever I'm teaching new concepts, or demonstrating new skills, I'll use Spanish first. For example, when I teach compound words, I teach the concept in Spanish using Spanish vocabulary: "espanta" means "scare" and "pajaro" means "bird" or "crow." So "espantapajaro" means "scarecrow." The children understand this; they know what espantapajaro means, and they can give me other compound words in Spanish. Then I'll say, "You know, we have the same thing in English," and I'll show them compound words in English.

I also encourage the children to use English as much as they can. I tell them: "Spanish is a beautiful language, but you speak Spanish so much at home that I want you to have a chance to practice English when you're here. I want you to be bilingual, to know *two* languages. That's so much better than only knowing *one* language, like most kids around here. You're special." This year I'm trying something new. When I hold one finger up, that means they should use their first language; two fingers mean their second language. This seems to be working well. They feel proud that they can speak both. They *want* to learn English.

When LEP students come from many different language backgrounds, bilingual education programs are not practical. In this case, schools typically place children in regular English-only classrooms and pull them out for instruction from a specially trained teacher in *English as a Second Language.* Since the focus is on learning English, children with different native languages can be in the same room. Ken, for example, has six students—from Mexico, Korea, India, Sri Lanka, and Turkey—who leave his room for ESL instruction; there they join students who speak Russian, Hebrew, and Chinese.

Like special education and compensatory education, programs for LEP students have been the subject of emotional debate. The nature of this debate, however, is considerably different: The question is not only how special services are best provided, but also whether there should *be* special services. In other words, the controversy involves the very existence of such programs. Despite evidence that bilingual education improves academic performance of LEP students (Lessow-Hurley, 1991), opponents argue that such programs are unnecessary: "My grandparents learned English when they came to this country, and there were no special programs for them, so why can't *they?*" There are also unfounded fears that bilingual programs mean that students will never become proficient in English. These concerns reflect the strong feeling in our country that everyone should speak English.

Helping Children Who Are Gifted and Talented

It's easy to see that children who are disabled, poor, or unable to speak English may have problems in school, but we don't normally think of children who are gifted and talented as being at risk. Nonetheless, children who are bored by work that is too simple may begin to daydream or to become disruptive; students who are taunted by classmates for being "eggheads" or "nerds" may begin to fail on purpose; and children whose parents press them to be "the best" may develop unhealthy levels of perfectionism. Indeed, research has shown that gifted students are often in danger of underachievement, low self-esteem, and social and behavioral problems; within this population, young boys, adolescent girls, language minority students, and children with disabilities are particularly vulnerable (Whitmore, 1988).

Since we don't normally recognize this vulnerability, it is not surprising that federal legislation merely encourages, rather than mandates, special services and that minimal federal funding is provided. In 1980, for example, the amount spent by the federal government on programs for the gifted was less than 1 percent of the amount spent on children with disabilities (Kirk and Gallagher, 1983, cited in Schulz, Carpenter, and Turnbull, 1991). In the absence of federal mandates, state regulations determine whether there are special programs, which students are served, and the percentage of the state's resources that are committed.

Providing services for gifted students raises a knotty problem: how to define the concept of giftedness. Three of the most commonly accepted definitions appear in Table 12-5. As you can see, it takes more than unusual intellectual ability to be considered gifted; all the definitions include other attributes like creativity, commitment, and leadership.

Not only is it difficult to define giftedness, it is also difficult to identify those children who meet the definition. Sometimes, identification is based solely on standardized test scores, but standardized tests will not tap capacity for leadership or perseverance on tasks. Thus, it's generally recommended that school districts use multiple criteria, such as teacher, peer or parental nomination and examination of work samples. Even then, the process is problematic. States usually allocate fund-

TABLE 12-5
COMMON DEFINITIONS OF "GIFTED AND TALENTED"

Source	Definition
U.S. Commissioner Marland's report to U.S. Congress (1972)	Gifted and talented children . . . include those with demonstrated achievement and/or potential ability in any of the following areas, singly or in combination. 1. General intellectual ability 2. Specific academic aptitude 3. Creative or productive thinking 4. Leadership ability 5. Visual and performing arts 6. Psychomotor ability (p. 2)
P.L. 97-35, the Education Consolidation and Improvement Act (1981)	Children who give evidence of high performance capability in areas such as intellectual, creative, artistic, leadership capacity, or specific academic fields, and who require services or activities not ordinarily provided by the school in order to fully develop such capabilities. (Sec. 582; cited in Gearheart, Weishahn, and Gearheart, 1992)
J. S. Renzulli (1986)	Gifted behavior consists of behaviors that reflect an interaction among three basic clusters of human traits—these clusters being above average general and/or specific abilities, high levels of task commitment, and high levels of creativity. Gifted and talented children are those possessing or capable of developing this composite set of traits. . . . (p. 73)

ing based on a percentage of the total students enrolled in a district (Oakes and Lipton, 1990); for example, states might designate 2 percent or 5 percent of their students as gifted. Other states set the percentage based on the funding available. These variations mean that a child can be gifted in one state but not another, or one year when more funds are available—but not the next.

There is little agreement on the kinds of special services to provide for gifted students, and programs vary greatly from district to district. In Viviana and Garnetta's district, for example, special self-contained classes for gifted and talented children are housed at one particular elementary school. When children are identified as being gifted and talented, they transfer to this school. Garnetta tells us:

> I had a boy in my class last year who was new to the district. It didn't take long to see that the child was vastly superior to other children in terms of language ability. He had an incredible vocabulary, read way above grade level, and was extremely articulate. I spoke with my principal about him, and she got in touch with the head of the gifted and talented program in New Brunswick. He came to McKinley to observe the child and to test him. Within a week, the child was moved to a gifted and talented class. I really miss him, but it was good for him. The other kids were getting really annoyed with him. Whenever he'd give the correct answer to one of my questions, they'd ask, "Where did you learn that?" And they'd tease him a lot: they'd call him "smarty pants" and "know-it-all."

In contrast, Ken's district has no separate classes for gifted and talented children. This is partly due to the teachers' mixed feelings about such programs. Ken tells us:

> We believe all kids have gifts and talents. Our job is to build on each child's gifts and talents in the regular classroom. So we include enrichment activities and open-ended projects in our class work. We also offer special programs at lunchtime or after school, like working on the school newspaper or yearbook, but these are open to everyone. Every so often the district runs special districtwide projects for kids with special talents. We also have an enrichment math program that pulls sixth graders from around the district. These kids are identified by a battery of tests given by the math teacher.

In recent years, more and more districts have opted to teach gifted students in regular classes. One reason is the feeling that programs for gifted children are somehow "elitist" and that children need to learn to deal with different kinds of people. There is now a big push to meet gifted students' needs within the regular classroom, a movement that parallels the inclusion of children with disabilities (Willis, 1995). A second reason is financial; as school districts seek ways to save money, programs for gifted and talented children are being substantially curtailed or even eliminated.

OBTAINING ACCESS TO SPECIAL SERVICES

Where to Go for Help

Frequently, children who have special needs are identified and placed in special programs before they ever enter your classroom. When that happens, you are simply notified that Mariz, Zvi, and Ching-Chi will be receiving instruction in English as a Second Language; that Alison and James will be pulled out for "comp ed"; or that Sondra and José will be leaving for the "G & T" program once a week.

There are other times, however, when children with special needs are not identified until a regular classroom teacher is faced with a challenging problem and recognizes the need for assistance. Most often this occurs when a child exhibits extreme academic difficulties or behavior problems.

Not too long ago, a student teacher we know wrote the following journal entry:

> I'm really worried about one of my kids. She's unbelievably shy and withdrawn. It took me a long time to even notice her. She never participates in class discussions, never raises her hand, and never volunteers for anything. When I call on her, she looks down and doesn't answer, or her answer is so soft that I can't hear her. I've watched her during lunch time in the cafeteria, and she doesn't seem to have any friends. The other kids aren't mean to her—they act like she doesn't even exist—and that's sort of the way I feel too! I've tried to give her extra attention and affection, but she doesn't respond. Academically, though, she's doing fine. She turns in her work and it's always okay. I talked with my cooperating teacher about her, and she's concerned too. She says she's thinking of referring her. I don't even know what that really means. Who do you go to? Do you have to contact parents before you "refer" a child? Who decides whether to test her? I suppose I'll learn the whole process if my cooperating teacher *does* decide to go ahead and refer her, but I wish I knew more about this.

We shared this student teacher's concerns with our four teachers during a meeting to discuss special services. We asked them: "If this child were in your class, where would you go for help?" Their answers were revealing: although these four teachers work in neighboring districts, the procedures they follow are quite different. Garnetta would go directly to her principal. Ken would speak to the school's Student Assistance Counselor or members of a "core" team (composed of the principal, the nurse, the Student Assistance Counselor, and a specially trained teacher), since this child seems to be experiencing social or psychological problems. (He would go to the Student Assistance Team for academic problems.) Viviana would go to the guidance counselor in her school. Barbara would go first to the nurse to have the child's vision and hearing checked and then to her school's Student Resource Committee (SRC), similar to the core team in Ken's building.

This variation underscores the importance of becoming familiar with the procedures and resources in your own school. The best way to do this is to speak with people who can provide guidance and direction—experienced teachers, the principal, the school nurse, special educators, compensatory education teachers. Ken emphasizes that:

> what's important is that you talk with people. The more you talk with people, the less the problem is just yours, and that makes it easier to deal with. You also need to keep in mind that if you go to one special services person and you're in the wrong place, they'll bounce you to the right place. And be sure to build rapport with people involved in special services. If you build rapport, you're going to get help.

Exactly what kind of help will you receive when you make contact with your school's special services personnel? Generally, the first step is to provide you with additional suggestions for addressing the child's needs. These suggestions may include adjusting the curriculum, tutoring by a peer or an aide, implementing a behavior modification plan—even something as simple as changing the child's seat. If these interventions are not successful, and special services personnel believe the child should be considered for placement in special education, the classroom teacher initiates a formal request for evaluation.

Specific referral procedures vary from district to district, but the teacher usually completes a form describing the child's academic performance and classroom behavior and the interventions that have already been tried. The form used in New Brunswick, the district in which Garnetta and Viviana teach, asks for the following information:

- family information (parents' birthplace, education, occupation, residence, marital status; siblings)
  - contact with parents with regard to problem
  - steps that teacher has taken to deal with problem
  - description of the child's social and emotional adjustment (e.g., relationship with other children; attitude toward authority; effort; special interests and aptitudes)
  - previous schools attended
  - attendance record for last two years
  - standardized test data
  - achievement level in reading and mathematics
  - remedial services received
  - health record (to be completed by school nurse)

As we indicated earlier, P.L. 94-142 (now IDEA) requires that parental consent be obtained before a child can be evaluated. When parents give their permission, the referral process can proceed: the child is given a variety of tests, a conference is held with parents, and the results of the evaluation are discussed. If it is determined that the student's problems result from a disability, a classification is agreed upon, and an individualized education program is developed. A flow chart outlining this generic referral process appears in Figure 12-1.

What Information to Bring

It's important to approach special services armed with specific information about the child and about the interventions you've already tried. Complaints like "He's driving me crazy," "She constantly demands attention," or "He just can't hack it in the fourth grade" are not helpful. The more detailed your information can be, the more likely you are to receive assistance.

What kind of information should you bring? Here are some of our teachers' suggestions for children who are exhibiting inappropriate behavior or having academic difficulty.

- an overall description of the child (both strengths and weaknesses)
- a detailed description of the child's inappropriate behavior:
  when does the child exhibit the behavior?
  how frequently does the child exhibit the behavior?

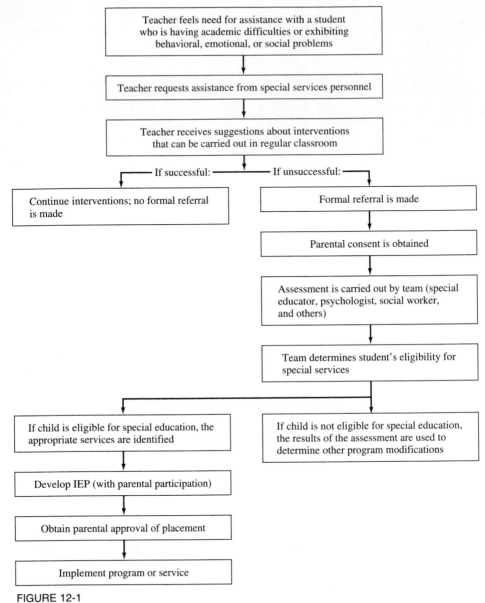

FIGURE 12-1
A typical referral process.

what antecedent events set off the behavior?
what is the duration of the behavior?
what is the reaction of other students in the class?
• a detailed description of the child's academic difficulties (with work samples to support your description)
    • information about the family (if possible)

- efforts on your part to correct or deal with the problem
- how you'd like to be helped or what type of help you believe the child needs

Once you've reported a problem, it's human nature to expect everybody to drop whatever they're doing and provide you with immediate help. But special services tend to be overworked and understaffed, and help is not always prompt. Barbara reminds us:

> You're dealing with the problem every day, and you're frustrated. You want an immediate resolution, but you have to be realistic. Special services is a slow process. I'm not the only person they deal with. They work with all the teachers in the building and with the kids who are already classified. It can take a long time for a child to be evaluated. But special services people will come in and consult with me. They'll give me ideas for working with a child, strategies I've forgotten to use. Or they'll fill me in on family histories. You've got to remember that they're not miracle workers. They're not wonders. But they *will* validate my problem, provide me with advice and support, and give time and understanding to a student.

HELPING CHILDREN WITH SPECIAL NEEDS IN A REGULAR CLASSROOM

In the introduction of this chapter, we stated our belief that classroom teachers must be responsible for teaching and managing all children in their classrooms, not just those who are "easy-to-teach." A learning disabled child who receives instruction in a resource room may leave your classroom every day for 45 minutes; a low-achieving student who qualifies for Chapter 1 tutoring may be pulled out three times a week for a half hour; and a youngster with limited proficiency in English may get ESL instruction an hour a day. But the rest of the time, these children are with *you*. What can you do to be responsive to their needs? In this section, we offer some guidelines to keep in mind as you try to meet the challenges of teaching at-risk children.

Examine Your Classroom Environment for Possible Mismatch

It's important to remember that problems do not always reside excusively within a child. Sometimes problems are the result of a discrepancy between a child's needs and the classroom environment. Barbara shares this example of an obvious mismatch:

> I have a boy in my class who's 5′6″ and weighs about 200 pounds. He's constantly picking up his desk with his knees and dropping it on the floor. It's disturbing and disruptive, but I can't blame him. I've had a request in for months for a bigger desk, but so far nothing has happened. Meanwhile, he's always fumbling and bumping into things and knocking things over. It's easy to get frustrated with him—he's got lots of other problems too—but it's clear that one contributing factor is that the physical setting is just too small for him!

As Barbara's story points out, we sometimes think of a child as disabled, when actually the problem is the result of a *disabling situation* (Gearheart, Weishahn and Gearheart, 1992). LEP children, for instance, may have problems in an English-only classroom if you tend to talk quickly, use idioms like "It's raining cats and dogs," and speak in complex sentences. They may be able to function admirably, however, if you implement specific environmental supports. (See Table 12-6, which lists suggestions provided by Romero, Mercado and Vazquez-Faria, 1987.)

A mismatch between the culture of the school and the culture of the home can also create a disabling situation. In Chapter 10, we discussed Susan Philips's (1972) work on the conflict between the teacher-oriented nature of classroom recitations and the peer-oriented upbringing of children on the Warm Springs Indian Reservation. More recently, numerous other instances of cultural mismatches have been identified (see Grossman, 1995). Wei (1980), for example, describes some of the problems Vietnamese-American students often experience in American schools:

> The American teachers' friendliness and informality are shocking to the Vietnamese students and hard for them to accept. The absence of honorific terms in the English language compounds the problem and makes the Vietnamese students feel uneasy and uncomfortable when talking with their teachers. They are reluctant to ask questions in class because such behavior seems aggressive and disrespectful to them. Their confusion is increased when, to their surprise, their teachers reward such behavior in class. . . . (pp. 13-14)

Similarly, Irvine (1991) points out that the classroom norm of raising your hand when you want to speak may conflict with the conversational norms in African-American culture:

> In a heated discussion, blacks frequently make their point whenever they can enter the discussion. Deference is given to the person who considers his or her point most urgent. Turn-taking is the style of whites, who usually raise their hands to be recognized. Teachers find black students impolite, aggressive, and boisterous when they cut off another student or fail to restrain themselves so that every student can have a turn to talk. (p. 29)

TABLE 12-6
STRATEGIES FOR HELPING LEP STUDENTS

Paraphrase questions and statements to allow for different levels of proficiency. Use synonyms to clarify the meaning of unknown words.

Make the language of the text comprehensible by interpreting it in simple, everyday language.

Enunciate clearly, with your mouth in direct view of the students.

Encourage classroom discussion of new information.

Establish a classroom environment in which children are not afraid to take risks and to use English.

Ask questions that require different degrees of English proficiency in responding. For example, allow students to respond nonverbally, to answer a yes-no question, or to provide a single-word answer.

When students respond to your questions, focus on the content, rather than on the form of the response.

Encourage children to tell about their culture. View ethnic and linguistic diversity within a classroom not as a problem, but as an asset from which both teachers and students can profit.

A final example is the conflict that may occur when European-Americans are in group situations with their Asian-American or Hispanic peers. Since members of these latter two cultures tend to place a high value on group harmony and consensus, they may think it rude when European-Americans are direct and forthright and push for the acceptance of their own ideas (Grossman, 1995).

In reflecting on your students' cultural backgrounds, it is helpful to ask yourself the following questions (Kottler, 1994, pp. 8-9):

1 Has the student been socialized to be an active participant or a passive recipient of information?

2 How is the concept of time viewed? Is punctuality important or is time flexible?

3 Are students expected to make eye contact with their teachers or look down out of respect?

4 Do students nod their heads to be polite or to show they understand?

5 Is the head considered sacred and therefore not to be touched?

6 Do parents regard teachers as experts and refrain from expressing differences of opinion?

7 Is cooperation or competition encouraged?

8 Is the family patriarchal, limiting educational aspirations for girls?

9 Is education or work valued more in the family?

10 Do students expect specific directions for carrying out tasks and therefore have difficulty choosing their own learning activities?

11 Do students not ask questions because they have been taught not to bother adults?

12 Is the student expected to tell the teacher what the teacher wants to hear (e.g., that an assignment is done when it hasn't even been started)?

13 Are expressions of emotion and feelings emphasized or hidden?

14 Are speaking or listening modes of communication preferred?

15 Do students exhibit low self-esteem and self-defeating behaviors because they feel they cannot succeed as a result of socioeconomic marginality and discrimination?

It is also important to examine the classroom environment when working with children with ADD/ADHD. Since these children are easily distracted, you need to arrange the classroom environment so that distractions are minimized. Furthermore, children with ADD/ADHD have a special need for classrooms that are predictable, secure, and structured, where behavioral expectations are clear, and where there are clear, fair consequences. Table 12-7 offers some suggestions.

In sum, before concluding that "the entire problem is the kid," it's necessary to examine your classroom situation and to reflect on ways the environment may be contributing to the child's difficulties. Here are some questions that our teachers ask themselves:

Where is the child sitting? Is the seat near a source of distraction? Is it too far from the teacher?

Is sitting in clusters too difficult for the child to handle? Should I move the child to a pair or to individual seating?

TABLE 12-7
HELPING CHILDREN WITH ADD/ADHD (ADAPTED FROM RIEF, 1993,
AND CH.A.D.D. FACTS, 1993)

- Provide structure, routine, predictability, and consistency.
- Make sure behavioral expectations are clear.
- Tape a copy of the schedule on their desks.
- Seat them close to you, among attentive, well-focused students (the second row is better than the first).
- Make frequent eye contact.
- Make sure their desks are free of distractions (provide cardboard dividers to block out distractions).
- Provide a quiet work area or a "private office" to which children can move for better concentration.
- Provide headphones to block out noise during seatwork or other times that require concentration.
- Provide opportunities to move around in legitimate ways (e.g., exercise breaks, doing errands).
- Use physical contact to focus attention (e.g., a hand on a shoulder).
- Develop private signals to help focus attention.
- Ease transitions by providing cues and warnings.
- Use positive reinforcement and behavior modification techniques.
- Modify assignments:
    cut the written workload

    break the assignment into manageable parts
- Limit the amount of homework.
- Allow more time on assignments or tests.
- Assist with organization (e.g., assignment pads; checklists; color-coded notebooks for different subjects; accordion folders for loose papers).
- Try to give students at least one task each day that they can do successfully.
- Try to call students when they are paying attention; use their first names before calling on them.
- Provide extra sets of books to keep at home so that children are not overwhelmed after an absence and to prevent problems caused by forgetting books.
- Provide access to a computer, along with keyboard and word processing instruction; do not remove access to the computer as a penalty.
- DO NOT PUNISH; DO NOT ASSUME CHILDREN ARE LAZY; DO NOT GIVE UP.

What type of academic work am I providing? Are assignments too mechanical? too dry? too long? Do they require too much independence? Do I ever allow choice?

How do I speak with the child? How do I praise the child? *Do* I praise the child?

What rules and routines have I set up and are they contrary to the student's ability to comply? Am I expecting quiet behavior too long? Am I setting the child up for failure?

Am I allowing an appropriate amount of time for completing assignments? for transitions?

Reflect on the Appropriateness of Your Expectations

Children with special needs are too often the victims of low expectations. Listen to Lori and Bill Granger, the parents of a child who was identified as being in need of special education:

> Children of Special Education are children of Small Expectations, not great ones. Little is expected and little is demanded. Gradually, these children—no matter their IQ level—learn to be cozy in the category of being "special." They learn to be less than they are. (1986, pp. 26-27, cited in Gartner and Lipsky 1987)

Sometimes, in our efforts to be understanding and sympathetic, we lower our expectations so much that we teach students to "be less than they are." We water down curriculum; we set "ceilings" rather than floors (Good and Brophy, 1994); we forgive inappropriate behavior since "they can't help it"; we place children in safe environments where they will never be asked to do things we "know they cannot do" (Gartner and Lipsky, 1987). And when, in fact, they cannot do them, when they behave inappropriately, and when they do not learn, our beliefs seem justified.

On the other hand, it's important not to set unreasonably high expectations that children cannot meet. Your expectations have to be achievable, appropriate, and flexible. Viviana shares this incident:

> Last year I had a child who had just moved here as a first grader. This boy would learn something one day and forget it the next. I couldn't understand what was going on. I began to get so frustrated; I'd say, "But you knew this yesterday!" The child was frustrated too, of course. Finally, I talked with the parents about the problem. The mother told me that she had been taking him to a clinic for lead poisoning. When he was a baby, he had eaten the paint chips in his apartment. I said, "Why didn't you tell me?" I wouldn't have gotten so frustrated with him!" Once I understood the problem, my entire attitude changed. That didn't mean I left him in the corner not doing anything, but I understood what was causing his memory problems.

Use Cooperative Learning to Foster Real Inclusion

In today's heterogeneous classrooms, it is essential to teach children to value and respect diversity and to work and learn together. As we stressed in Chapter 9, research has demonstrated that cooperative learning can promote positive social relationships between children with special needs and their peers. The use of cooperative learning can help to minimize the problem of children with special needs being isolated and rejected *socially,* even though they are included *physically* in the regular classroom. Furthermore, cooperative learning may be very useful when classrooms contain children from Hispanic backgrounds and from many Native American groups, since individuals in these cultures traditionally prefer collaboration rather than competition, dislike being singled out in front of an audience, and think it is bad manners to try to excel over others (Grossman, 1995; Losey, 1995; Putnam, 1993).

Ken tells us about a two-person team he created that has been beneficial to both students:

> I have one kid, Jeannie, who goes to a resource room, and another kid, Suzanne, who's considered "gifted and talented." When the class works on *Voyage of the Mimi* activities on the computer, they function as a team. Let's say their task is to find a whale that's caught in a trap. You're someplace in the ocean, you've got different nautical instruments and you're supposed to get to the whale. I know that Jeannie isn't going to be able to follow the complicated instructions on her own, and she doesn't have the patience to go through the necessary six or seven steps to come close to the whale. She's just not accurate enough. Also, you never get it on the first shot, so you have to deal with that frustration, and she's easily frustrated. But she can be a valuable part of the team. She can work the rulers to plot the points on the map, for example. And Suzanne can do the planning and the strategizing. She's not held back at all. Together, they do fine.

Enlist the Assistance of Other Students and Teachers

Teachers sometimes think that all support and assistance must come from them. But, as Ken's example illustrates, other children in the class can be extremely helpful. Students can serve as *tutors* on academic tasks, *buddies* who assist with difficult activities, or *advocates* who "watch out" for the welfare of children who have special needs (Gearheart, Weishahn, and Gearheart, 1992).

In addition, some schools are beginning to substitute "pull-in" programs for traditional "pull-out" programs. In this model, support personnel work with students who have special needs in the regular classroom. For example, a special education teacher and a regular classroom teacher may collaborate in planning a lesson, and then one teacher may lead it while the other attends to the children who may require special assistance.

This year, Barbara has teamed up for science with a special education teacher who teachers a self-contained class of "communication handicapped" children. The two teachers plan together and alternate teaching responsibilities (lead teacher and support teacher). Each day during science, the special education teacher and her class come to Barbara's room:

> All the children are integrated into cooperative learning teams. Each member of the group always has a special job, like materials to gather, timekeeper, reader, recorder. Since the special ed kids have a communication disability, they have problems with reading and writing, but they don't get out of the reading and writing responsibilities. Instead, they all have a "buddy" from my class who helps them do their jobs. There's been no embarrassment or nervousness about this at all. *They* know they have trouble with reading and writing, and *my* kids know they have trouble, and everyone approaches the matter very matter-of-factly. It's been really wonderful. The special ed teacher and I have a great time working together, and the kids really enjoy it.

Use a Variety of Instructional Strategies

Diverse classrooms demand diverse teaching approaches. It is unlikely that a steady diet of traditional instruction—whole-group teacher presentation, recitation, independent seatwork—will be successful when classrooms contain children who vary in terms of academic achievement, come from different linguistic and cultural backgrounds, and have a range of disabilities. The use of cooperative learning is one instructional alternative. There are others: group problem-solving, role-playing, debates, writing and reading workshop, computer-assisted instruction, peer tutoring, cross-age tutoring.

In recent years, teachers have become increasingly aware of the need to vary instructional approaches so that children who learn differently have equal access to instruction. Numerous schools have developed programs based on Howard Gardner's (1993, 1995) theory of "multiple intelligences" (MI). According to Gardner, people have at least seven types of intellectual capacities; *linguistic* (capacity to use language); *logical-mathematical* (capacity to reason and recognize patterns); *spatial* (capacity to perceive the visual world accurately); *musical* (sensitivity to pitch, melody, rhythm, and tone); *bodily-kinesthetic* (capacity to use the body and to handle objects skillfully); *interpersonal* (capacity to understand others); and *intrapersonal* (capacity to understand oneself). Clearly, schools have traditionally emphasized the development of linguistic and logical-mathematical intelligences (and have favored those who are relatively strong in these), while they have neglected and undervalued the other intelligences. Although Gardner does not advocate one "right way" to implement a multiple-intelligences education, he does recommend that teachers approach topics in a variety of ways, so that more children will be reached and more children can experience "what it is like to be an expert" (1995, p. 208). With this in mind, Barbara plans curriculum units that allow for a wide range of activities, from report writing, to puppet shows, to murals, to "hands-on" demonstrations and experiments. As Barbara puts it,

> I want all students to have the chance to work in ways that are comfortable for them, but I also want to "stretch" them and have them work in ways that are less comfortable. Children who are artistic should have the chance to do murals, but they also have to do writing!

Remember the Principles of Effective Management

Although you may feel you lack the skills needed to teach children who are especially low-achieving or those who have mild academic disabilities, research indicates that the teaching behaviors associated with outstanding achievement gains for these students are similar to the behaviors that are effective with *all* students (Slavin, 1989). In fact, effective teaching behaviors include many of the strategies we've discussed in earlier chapters:

- providing feedback to students
- providing specific, informative praise
- providing learning tasks that students can accomplish with a high rate of success
- using classroom time efficiently, minimizing transitional or noninstructional time
- limiting the use of punishment
- maintaining high engagement rates

• focusing on preventive management strategies, rather than disciplinary interventions

• creating a supportive, nonthreatening learning environment

This list reinforces Ken's viewpoint that working with children who have special needs often doesn't require different skills. As he puts it, "It's not such special stuff."

Team Up with Another Teacher for Support

All of our teachers stress the importance of turning to colleagues when you encounter difficulties with particular children. You might ask another teacher to visit your classroom to observe, offer advice, and validate your concerns.

Sometimes a student will get the best of you, and you find you simply have no more patience left. In order to prepare for times like this, you can work out an arrangement in which you can send the child to another teacher for a brief period of time. (Of course, this arrangement would work in both directions.) This gives you a break from frustration, provides time to think of another strategy, and frees the class of confrontation and disturbance.

CONCLUDING THOUGHTS

During a discussion on the growing numbers of children with special needs, Ken reminded us of the importance of focusing on the *strengths* that children bring to the classroom:

> It's really important to build a schedule and design activities that will lead to success, not just reaffirm that the kid fails a lot. Teachers have got to work with children's strengths and interests, not their weaknesses. A lot of the time, teachers say, "These are the areas where the child has problems, so I've got to spend all the time on remediating these." But skills are all interdependent; they can be taught in the context of activities that kids find interesting and appealing, activities that they can succeed on. *Children need to learn hope and success as much as they need to learn academic skills.*

Nancy Keller (1994), a middle school science teacher in Vermont, provides an excellent example of building on children's strengths. Keller had been teaching science for three years as part of a sixth- to eighth-grade team, when a new sixth-grade student arrived who had learning disabilities as well as behavioral and emotional problems. Andy was extremely loud and aggressive, and his verbal and physical threats frequently disrupted the class. An emergency meeting of Andy's regular teachers, a special educator, and the special services administrator was held to review the records from Andy's previous school and to consider ways of helping him develop more positive social behaviors.

Keller describes the meeting and its aftermath in these words:

> What stands out most for me about the initial IEP meeting was the positive manner and genuine concern that permeated the discussion. . . . The problem was defined not in terms of Andy's negative behavior, but in terms of how we could use his strengths to address his needs.

> I remember Andy being described as someone with a sense of humor, someone who regularly came to school, someone who liked being given special jobs or chores—someone who wanted to belong. Because Andy possessed these qualities, the problem was defined as finding ways we could build on them to help him become more successful in our classrooms. For example, because Andy liked being helpful, we gave him specific jobs to complete in each class. . . . Andy's jobs also provided occasions when we could work on his social skills. . . . I purposely planned tasks he could complete in which he had to use his "quiet voice." These tasks—such as distributing science supplies on lab days—were of genuine assistance . . . [and involved] appropriately asking a classmate what supplies were needed and then handing them out. (pp. 83-84)

Keller goes on to describe the kinds of classroom and peer supports that were put in place for Andy (e.g., having a regular teacher and a special educator team teach; using cooperative groups, peer buddies, and peer tutoring) and the progress he made over the next three years. Andy's time in middle school was "not a progression of one amazing success after another, but rather a series of stops and starts . . . successes and setbacks" (p. 89). Nonetheless, his story is a cogent example of the impact teachers can have when they work together as a team, when they have the support they need, when they are willing to try a variety of instructional formats, and when they focus on what children can *do*, rather than on what they *cannot* do.

SUMMARY

We began this chapter by stressing our belief that teachers are responsible for all the children in their classes, including those with special needs. Part of being responsible means seeking outside assistance when needed; it also means communicating closely with special services personnel; and it means working with special children when they are in your room. The purpose of this chapter was to describe services for children who are "at risk," to discuss strategies for obtaining access to these services, and to present guidelines for working with special needs children in your own classroom.

Special Services for Children with Special Needs

- special education for children with disabilities
- compensatory education for impoverished, low-achieving children
- language education for children with limited proficiency in English
   bilingual education
   ESL
   immersion
- programs for children who are gifted and talented

Obtaining Access to Special Services

- Become familiar with the resources in your own school—Student Assistance Counselors, Student Assistance Teams, CORE Teams, Student Resource Committees.

- Bring specific information about the child's problems: details about the behavior or academic difficulty, work samples, efforts on your part to correct the problem.

Helping Children with Special Needs in the Regular Classroom

- Examine your classroom environment for possible mismatch.
- Reflect on the appropriateness of your expectations.
- Use cooperative learning to foster integration and achievement.
- Enlist the assistance of other students and teachers.
- Use a variety of instructional strategies.
- Remember the principles of effective management.
- Team up with another teacher for support.

As the number of children with special need grows, the demands on teachers become even greater. Sometimes the problems can be overwhelming, especially for beginning teachers. When that happens, it's helpful to focus on children's strengths, rather than their deficits. In Ken's words, "Children need to learn hope and success as much as they need to learn academic skills."

ACTIVITIES

1 In the district where you are observing or teaching, interview a principal or the director of special services to determine procedures and policies for helping children who have special needs, in particular:

Children who are gifted and talented
Children with learning disabilities
Children with limited proficiency in English
Children who qualify for Chapter 1 assistance

2 Interview a principal or the director of special services to learn about the district's position with respect to full inclusion. Are any children with severe disabilities being educated in the regular classroom? If so, what kind of special supports are being provided for those children? Interview the teacher about his/her attitudes toward including a child with special needs who would normally have been educated in a special education classroom or sent to a special school.

3 At XYZ School, a meeting of the special services team was called to discuss two children having academic and emotional difficulties. The teacher of each child was invited to describe the situation. Mr. Ryan, a fifth-grade teacher, made the following presentation:

Mr. Ryan began by saying that he thought Olivia was having some difficulties at home that were affecting her ability to do her work in school. "Olivia's academic problems have been evident since the beginning of the school year. She's reading at a third-grade level, and she's doing fourth-grade math." He distributed reading and math worksheets for the committee to see. "However, recently her work and her work habits have gotten worse. I've talked to Olivia and her mom. Since her mother started working nights, Olivia has shown little interest in school. In a typical week, she'll have her homework done only one or two days, and she rarely finishes assignments in class. She has difficulty following oral directions and is slow at getting her ideas down on paper. Here are two typical writing papers; in each case, she only managed to get down two sentences in 25 minutes, and you can see that her handwriting is somewhat immature." He showed the committee two papers. "I have tried to limit the number of directions I give her and when oral directions are given, I also write them on the board. I've offered after-school help, but she needs to get home to watch her little sister. She's also having problems socially; in the last two weeks, she's gotten in five fights with the children in the class." He referred to a note pad he had brought. "On November fifth, for example, she accused another child of stealing a pencil and an eraser from her desk. It resulted in a lot of name-calling and loud insults. We finally found the pencil and eraser in the back of her desk, behind all her papers and books. I was worried about her before the problems at home surfaced, and now I'm really at a loss for how to help her. Do you have any ideas for me?" He took out a pen and opened the note pad to a clean sheet.

After Mr. Ryan's presentation, the team discussed ways of helping Olivia. Mr. Ryan left the meeting feeling that his concerns had been taken seriously and that he had received useful advice. Next, Mrs. Teller, a third-grade teacher, presented her concerns about Daniel:

Mrs. Teller began by stating that it was about time that someone did something for Daniel. "He has been disturbing my class since September. Look at his work." She handed out papers with many red circles and negative comments. "His work is sloppy, and he never finishes anything. I keep him after school and call his mother and still he doesn't try to get any better. He's one year below level in reading and still can't figure out long vowel sounds. I've had it with him. He doesn't seem to listen to me anymore. In all my years of teaching third grade, this boy is the worst one yet! He always interrupts the lesson by fooling around. I always end up yelling at him or sending him to the principal. What can you do to help me? I think he belongs in a special class."

The team members told Mrs. Teller that they needed more information before they could provide meaningful assistance and asked her to attend the next meeting when Daniel's case would again be discussed. Based on the guidelines presented in this chapter and the model provided by Mr. Ryan, rewrite Mrs. Teller's presentation to make it more effective.

REFERENCES

Allington, R. L., and Johnston, P. (1989). Coordination, collaboration, and consistency: The redesign of compensatory and special education interventions. In R. E. Slavin, N. L. Karweit and N. A. Madden (Eds.), *Effective programs for students at risk.* Boston: Allyn and Bacon, pp. 320–354.

Binkard, B. (1986). State classifications of handicapped students: A national comparative data report. *Counter-Point,* 12.

Celis 3rd, W. (February 22, 1993). U.S. school program criticized anew. *The New York Times,* A16.

CH.A.D.D. (1993). *Attention deficit disorders: An educator's guide (CH.A.D.D. Facts #5).* Plantation, FL: Children and Adults with Attention Deficit Disorders.

Children's Defense Fund (1994). *The state of America's children yearbook 1994.* Washington, D.C.: Children's Defense Fund.

Federal Register (1977). Washington, D.C.: U.S. Government Printing Office.

Garcia, E. E. (1990). Educating teachers for language minority students. In W. R. Houston, M. Haberman, and J. Sikula (Eds.), *Handbook of research on teacher education.* New York: Macmillan Publishing Company, pp. 717–729.

Gardner, H. (1993). *Multiple intelligences: The theory in practice.* New York: Basic Books.

Gardner, H. (1995). Reflections on multiple intelligences: Myths and messages. *Phi Delta Kappan, 77*(3), 200–209.

Gartner, A., and Lipsky, D. K. (1987). Beyond special education: Toward a quality system for all students. *Harvard Educational Review, 57*(4), 367–395.

Gearheart, B. R., Weishahn, M. W., and Gearheart, C. J. (1992). *The exceptional student in the regular classroom* (5th edition). New York: Macmillan.

Gersten, R., and Woodward, J. (1995). A longitudinal study of transitional and immersion bilingual education programs in one district. *The Elementary School Journal, 95*(3), 223–239.

Giangreco, M. F., Dennis, R., Cloninger, C., Edelman, S., and Schattman, R. (1993). "I've counted Jon": Transformational experiences of teachers educating students with disabilities. *Exceptional Children, 59*(4), 359–372.

Good, T. L., and Brophy, J. E. (1994). *Looking in classrooms* (6th edition). New York: Harper-Collins.

Granger, L., and Granger, L. (1986). *The magic feather.* New York: E. P. Dutton.

Grossman, H. (1995). *Classroom behavior management in a diverse society.* Mountain View, CA: Mayfield Publishing Co.

Hiebert, E. H., Colt, J. M., Catto, S. L., and Gury, E. C. (1992). Reading and writing of first-grade students in a restructured Chapter 1 program. *American Educational Research Journal, 29*(3), 545–572.

Irvine, J. J. (1991). *Black students and school failure: Policies, practices, and prescriptions.* New York: Praeger.

Joint Center for Political and Economic Studies (1990). *The declining status of black children: Examining the change, Summary of findings.* Washington, D. C.: Joint Center for Political and Economic Studies.

Keller, N. (1994). Integrating Andy. In *Toward inclusive classrooms* (NEA Teacher-to-Teacher Book). Washington, D. C.: National Education Association, 81–89.

Kirk, S. A., and Gallagher, J. J. (1983). *Educating exceptional children* (4th edition). Boston: Houghton Mifflin.

Kottler, E. (1994). *Children with limited English: Teaching strategies for the regular classroom.* Thousand Oaks, CA: Corwin Press.

Lau v. Nichols, 414, U.S. 563 (1974).

Lessow-Hurley, J. (1991). *A commonsense guide to bilingual education.* Alexandria, VA: Association for Supervision and Curriculum Development.

Losey, K. M. (1995). Mexican American students and classroom interaction: An overview and critique. *Review of Educational Research, 65*(3), 283–318.

Marland, S. (1972). *Education of the gifted and talented.* Washington, D. C.: U.S. Government Printing Office.

Meyers, J., Gelzheiser, L., Yelich, G., and Gallagher, M. (1990). Classroom, remedial, and resource teachers' views of pullout programs. *The Elementary School Journal, 90*(5), 533–545.

Oakes, J., and Lipton, M. (1990). *Making the best of schools: A handbook for parents, teachers, and policymakers.* New Haven, CT: Yale University Press.

O'Neil, J. (1991). A generation adrift? *Educational Leadership, 49*(1), 4–10.

O'Neil, J. (1994/95). Can inclusion work? A conversation with Jim Kauffman and Mara Sapon-Shevin. *Educational Leadership, 52*(4), 7–11.

Philips, S. (1972). Participant structures and communicative competence: Warm Springs children in community and classroom. In C. Cazden, V. John, and D. Hymes (Eds.), *Functions of language in the classroom.* New York: Teachers College Press.

Putnam, J. W. (1993). *Cooperative learning and strategies for inclusion: Celebrating diversity in the classroom.* Baltimore: Paul H. Brookes.

Renzulli, J. S. (1986). A definition of gifted behavior. In R. J. Sternberg and J. E. Davidson (Eds.), *Conceptions of giftedness.* New York: Cambridge University Press.

Reynolds, M. C. (1989). Students with special needs. In M. C. Reynolds (Ed.), *Knowledge base for the beginning teacher.* Oxford, England: Pergamon Press.

Reynolds, M. C., Wang, M. C., and Walberg, H. J. (1987). The necessary restructuring of special and regular education. *Exceptional Children, 53*(5), 391–398.

Rief, S. F. (1993). *How to reach and teach ADD/ADHD children.* West Nyack, NY: The Center for Applied Research in Education.

Romero, M., Mercado, C., and Vazquez-Faria, J. A. (1987). Students of limited English proficiency. In V. Richardson-Koehler (Ed.), *Educators' handbook: A research perspective.* New York: Longman, pp. 348–369.

Schulz, J. B., Carpenter, C. D., and Turnbull, A. P. (1991). *Mainstreaming exceptional students: A guide for classroom teachers* (3rd edition). Boston: Allyn and Bacon.

Semmel, M. I, Abernathy, T. V., Butera, G., and Lesar, S. (1991). Teacher perceptions of the regular education initiative. *Exceptional Children, 58*, 9–24.

Seventh Annual Report to Congress on the Implementation of the Education of the Handicapped Act (1985). Washington, D.C.: U.S. Department of Education.

Slavin, R. E. (1989). Students at risk of school failure: The problem and its dimensions. In R. E. Slavin, N. L. Karweit, and N. A. Madden (Eds.), *Effective programs for students at risk.* Boston: Allyn and Bacon, pp. 3–19.

Stein, M. K., Leinghardt, G., and Bickel, W. (1989). Instructional issues for teaching students at risk. In R. E. Slavin, N. L. Karweit, and N. A. Madden (Eds.), *Effective programs for students at risk.* Boston: Allyn and Bacon, pp. 154–194.

Vaughn, S., Schumm, J. S., Jallad, B., Slusher, J., and Saumell, L. (in press). Teachers' views of inclusion. *Learning Disabilities Research and Practice.*

Webb, N. (1994). With new court decisions backing them, advocates see inclusion as a question of values. *The Harvard Education Letter, 10*(4), 1–3.

Wei, T. T. D. (1980). *Vietnamese refugee students: A handbook for school personnel* (2nd edition). ERIC ED 208 109.

Whitmore, J. R. (1988). Gifted children at risk for learning difficulties. *Teaching Exceptional Children, 20*(4), 10–14.

Willis, S. (1995). Mainstreaming the gifted. *Education Update, 37*(2), 1, 4–5.

Zigmond, N., Jenkins, J., Fuchs, D., Deno, S., and Fuchs, L. S. (1995). When students fail to achieve satisfactorily: A reply to McLeskey and Waldron. *Phi Delta Kappan, 77*(4) 303–306.

Zigmond, N., Jenkins, J., Fuchs, L., Deno, S., Fuchs, D., Baker, J., Jenkins, L., and Couthino, M. (1995). Special education in restructured schools: Findings from three multi-year studies," *Phi Delta Kappan, 76*(7) 533-540.

FOR FURTHER READING

Educational Leadership. (December 1994/January 1995). Special issue on The Inclusive School, 52(4).

Gearheart, B. R., Weishahn, M. W., and Gearheart, C. J. (1992). *The exceptional student in the regular classroom* (5th Edition). New York: Macmillan.

Grossman, H. (1995). *Classroom behavior management in a diverse society* (2nd Edition). Mountain View, CA: Mayfield.

Kottler, E. (1994). *Children with limited English: Teaching strategies for the regular classroom.* Thousand Oaks, CA: Corwin Press.

Lessow-Hurley, J. (1991). *A commonsense guide to bilingual education.* Alexandria, VA: Association for Supervision and Curriculum Development.

Putnam, J. W. (1993). *Cooperative learning and strategies for inclusion: Celebrating diversity in the classroom.* Baltimore: Paul H. Brookes.

Rief, S. F. (1993). *How to reach and teach ADD/ADHD children.* West Nyack, NY: The Center for Applied Research in Education.

Schulz, J. B., Carpenter, C. D., and Turnbull, A. P. (1991). *Mainstreaming exceptional students: A guide for classroom teachers* (3rd Edition). Boston: Allyn and Bacon.

Slavin, R. E., Karweit, N. L., and Madden, N. A. (Eds.) (1989). *Effective programs for students at risk.* Boston: Allyn and Bacon.

Chapter Thirteen

Helping Students Who Are Troubled

In Chapter 12, we discussed the diversity that characterizes so many of today's classrooms and the growing numbers of children with special needs. We focused on children with disabilities, those who are victims of poverty, those who come from different linguistic and cultural backgrounds, and those who are gifted and talented. This chapter continues the discussion of children with special needs by examining the problems created by substance abuse, violence, and child abuse and neglect. Consider these statistics:

It is estimated that there are 28.6 million children of alcoholics in the United States; 6.6 million are less than 18 and most are enrolled in our schools (Newsam, 1992).

At least 10% of all births in the U.S. are to drug-addicted mothers, thus exposing their babies to serious lifelong problems (Walker, Colvin, and Ramsey, 1995).

The total number of teen pregnancies in 1991 was estimated at about 1.1 million; almost 70% of teen births were to unmarried girls (Children's Defense Fund, 1994).

The number of children reported to be abused or neglected almost tripled from 1980 to 1992, reaching nearly 2,700,000 in 1992 (Children's Defense Fund, 1994).

The number of children exposed to violence is increasing. In one survey of elementary school children on Chicago's south side, 26% reported having seen someone shot; 29% had witnessed a stabbing (O'Neil, 1991).

Approximately 6 to 8 million children in our country who are in need of mental health interventions receive no care whatever; other children, perhaps 50% of those in need of treatment, receive care that is inappropriate for their needs (Walker, Colvin, and Ramsey, 1995).

These alarming statistics mean that large numbers of America's youth are growing up in circumstances that delay their development; create physical, emotional, and psychological problems; and jeopardize their futures. (For a chilling picture of the plight of America's children, see Figure 13-1.) Furthermore, **when these youngsters come to school, their problems come with them.** Children who are frightened, hungry, or abused can't leave their problems at the door and participate wholeheartedly in classroom activities.

3	children die from child abuse.
9	children are murdered.
13	children die from guns.
27	children—a classroomful—die from poverty.
30	children are wounded by guns.
63	babies die before they are one month old.
101	babies die before their first birthday.
145	babies are born at very low birthweight (less than 3.25 pounds).
202	children are arrested for drug offenses.
307	children are arrested for crimes of violence.
340	children are arrested for drinking or drunken driving.
480	teenagers get syphilis or gonorrhea.
636	babies are born to women who had late or no prenatal care.
801	babies are born at low birthweight (less than 5.5 pounds).
1,115	teenagers have abortions.
1,234	children run away from home.
1,340	teenagers have babies.
2,255	teenagers drop out of school each school day.
2,350	children are in adult jails.
2,781	teenagers get pregnant.
2,860	children see their parents divorce.
2,868	babies are born into poverty.
3,325	babies are born to unmarried women.
5,314	children are arrested for all offenses.
5,703	teenagers are victims of violent crime.
7,945	children are reported abused or neglected.
8,400	teenagers become sexually active.
100,000	children are homeless.
1,200,000	latchkey children come home to houses in which there is a gun.

Reprinted with permission of Childrens Defense Fund, from The State of America's Children Yearbook, 1994.

FIGURE 13-1
One Day in the Life of American Children

During one meeting, our four teachers spoke sadly about the increasing problems their students face. They talked about six children sleeping in one bed; about absent fathers and drug-addicted mothers; about parents who are in and out of jail; about a youngster finding the body of his older brother who had committed suicide; about a child sleeping, eating, and doing homework in the car while his mother delivered newspapers; about a first grader who had to bring her mother home from a bar every afternoon after school. As they talked, their anger and compassion were obvious. Also obvious was their recognition that in today's society, teachers have to deal with issues that were unimaginable in an earlier era—issues that require knowledge and skills far beyond those needed to be an effective instructor.

How can you provide extra support for the troubled students who may be in your classroom? **First, you need to be alert to the indicators of potential problems.** As an adult immersed in the culture of youth, you will probably develop a good idea of what the behavior of a typical elementary student is like. This allows you to detect deviations or changes in a student's behavior that might signal the presence of a problem. In *Teacher as Counselor: Developing the Helping Skills You Need* (1993), Jeffrey and Ellen Kottler suggest that you learn to ask yourself a series of questions when you notice atypical behavior.

What is unusual about this student's behavior?
Is there a pattern to what I have observed?
What additional information do I need to make an informed judgment?
Who might I contact to collect this background information?
What are the risks of waiting longer to figure out what is going on?
Does this student seem to be in any imminent danger?
Who can I consult about this case?

Viviana tells us how she tries to be alert to problems her students might be experiencing:

Even when I'm giving a lesson, I'm always scanning the room from one end to the other. You have to have your eyes all over. When the children are supposed to be paying attention, it's easy to notice behavior that might mean there's a problem—sleeping, putting a head down on the desk, masturbating, fidgeting. I also watch for bruises. The other day, for example, Carlita came in with a bruise under her eye. I said, "How did you get that bruise?" She said that she had fallen. I decided to check it out with her grandmother who works in the cafeteria. I said, "You know, Carlita has a bruise under her eye." She said that she knew, that Carlita had fallen, and I left it at that. I was not too concerned because I have known the family for a long time—I had two of Carlita's siblings—and there's never been any indication of abuse. But I still watch. If a child seems to be "falling" too much, then I report it. DYFS [Division of Youth and Family Services] would have to be notified.

As Viviana's last comment suggests, **a second way you can help students with serious problems is to be informed about the various special services that are available and to know how to obtain access to those services**—a topic we have already discussed in Chapter 12. Since specific resources and reporting procedures vary from district to district, it is essential that you learn about the special services in your own school and find out if there are special referral forms. Depending on the situation, you may want to consult with the principal or vice principal, student assistance counselor, school social worker, substance awareness coordinator, nurse, guidance counselor, or member of a "core team" (a group of teachers, staff, student assistance personnel, and administrators who identify, refer, and support at-risk students experiencing problems). Some districts, like New Brunswick and South Brunswick, even have "School-Based Youth Services Programs" (SBYSP), centers located in schools where outside agencies provide a variety of support services to students and their families—health and dental screenings, recreation, psychological counseling, substance abuse programs, and teen parenting classes. New

Brunswick's elementary-level program, headquartered in Viviana's school, is directed by Dr. Marilyn Green. She describes "school-base":

> At the elementary level, the mental health component is the major thrust of our efforts because it has consistently been identified by both school personnel and families as the service that is most needed. We've found that families who need mental health services just won't go over to the mental health center, even if we set up the appointments for them. But they *will* come to us. We're part of the Community Mental Health Center of UMDNJ [University of Medicine and Dentistry, New Jersey], but we're located in the school, and we try to be user friendly. We see children and families every day from nine to five, and at least one day a week, we're open until 9:00 P.M.
>
> We work mainly through teacher referral, although children will often come on their own or direct their peers to us. When teachers spot a child who needs help, we provide them with a referral form that is mainly a behavior checklist, but also includes a section where the teacher can describe the child and the problem he or she is having. The teacher also contacts the family and tells them about the referral and asks if it's all right for a school-base counselor to contact them. It's very rare for parents to refuse our services. We emphasize to the family that we're not Board of Education employees, that school-base is part of the Mental Health Center. We also stress that we're bound by ethics and by law to ensure confidentiality. I feel that families trust us and that allows us to work more effectively with them.
>
> Once we get parental approval, we'll conduct an initial evaluation with the child and the family and determine a treatment plan that we discuss with them. We can do individual, family, and group counseling, but due to case load demands, we try to provide children with group counseling as their primary treatment. We run a variety of groups— for prevention as well as intervention. For example, I'm running two groups right now on anger management and conflict resolution. We also run grief groups for children coping with the loss of family members due to death, incarceration, separation, or divorce; groups about male/female relationships; and "Child Fit" groups that focus on nutrition and exercise and the link with mental health. That's where we can try to help the pre-anorexic or pre-bulimic adolescent.
>
> We can't provide all the services we'd like because of limited funding. Besides me, there are only three full-time clinicians and a half-time clinician—and we provide mental health services for all eight elementary schools [about 4,000 children]. However, since we're linked up with UMDNJ, we have access to all of the other services of UMDNJ. For example, we can refer a parent with a drug problem to UMDNJ's Addiction Recovery Service, or we can help set up an appointment at the Eric B. Chandler health clinic if there's a medical problem. That's what we're all about—helping families get the services they need.

A third way of helping is to develop communication skills that will allow you to work more effectively with troubled or disaffected youngsters. Although your job is not to be a counselor or a therapist, you *can* learn to listen and to talk to students in ways that have been shown to be effective in counseling situations. Thomas Gordon, a clinical psychologist and author of *Teacher Effectiveness Training* (*T.E.T.*, 1974; see Chapter 6), emphasizes the importance of knowing how to talk with students who are experiencing problems:

Talk can cure, and talk can foster constructive change. But it must be the right kind of talk. How teachers talk to their students will determine whether they will be helpful or destructive. The effective teacher, like the effective counselor, must learn how to communicate acceptance, must require some specific communication skills.

This chapter begins by examining some of the situations that teachers may encounter in today's elementary schools because of substance abuse, violence, and child abuse and neglect. We then move on to a discussion of the communication skills you can use to help students who are experiencing problems. These skills include attending and acknowledging, active listening, asking open-ended questions, and problem solving. As you will see, this chapter not only relies on the experiences of our four teachers and the research literature, it also draws upon the wisdom of counselors who work directly with troubled students in each of the three districts, New Brunswick, Highland Park, and South Brunswick.

WHAT ARE THE PROBLEMS? AND WHAT CAN YOU DO?

Substance Abuse

At one time, a section on substance abuse in an elementary classroom management book would have seemed ridiculous, but more and more teachers are seeing problems rooted in drugs and alcohol. In response, many schools have established Student Assistance Programs (SAPs) and have hired full-time Student Assistance Counselors (SACs). Note that the initials "SA" do *not* stand for Substance Abuse. The wording is deliberate. Although SAPs focus on identifying and helping students at risk for alcohol and other drug problems, they generally adopt a broad-based approach. There are two good reasons for this strategy. First, it's less stigmatizing to go to a *Student Assistance Counselor* than a *Substance Abuse Counselor.* Second, drug problems usually occur in conjunction with other problems—depression, abuse, academic difficulties, pregnancy (Gonet, 1994).

Substance abuse affects elementary classrooms in three ways: when children from chemically-dependent families enter school; when children have been prenatally exposed to drugs and alcohol; and when children themselves are substance abusers. Let's turn first to the problems of *children from chemically-dependent families.*

Amanda's father is an alcoholic who becomes aggressive and abusive when he drinks. At age 13, Amanda is her mother's primary source of support and works hard to make her family appear normal. She has assumed many adult responsibilities that would normally be carried out by the father of a household. At school, she is a very successful student; her teachers describe her as superdependable and motivated. They don't realize that she is filled with feelings of inadequacy and confusion, that her behavior is prompted by a compulsive need to be perfect. Nor do they notice that in between classes and at lunch time Amanda spends most of her time alone. Amanda avoids forming friendships because she is afraid of revealing the family secret. (Powell, Zehm, and Kottler, 1995)

Ricky, Amanda's 10-year-old brother, is a fourth grader whose teacher describes him as sullen, disrespectful, and obstructive. He frequently fights with other children and is often in the principal's office being reprimanded for some antisocial behavior. His mother claims not to understand his behavior; she reports that Ricky never acts this way at home and implies that the teacher is the cause of his perpetual negative attitude. Yet he often runs around the house, screaming and tearing things apart. At the core of Ricky's behavior is anger: he is enraged by the rejection he feels from his alcoholic father and resentful that his mother spends so much time wallowing in self pity. He soothes his pain by planning ways to run away. He is on the verge of jumping into his own life of addiction. (Powell, Zehm, and Kottler, 1995)

Substance abuse touches elementary classrooms every time children like Amanda and Ricky enter the room—and their presence is not a rare occurrence. It is estimated that *one in every four children* sitting in a classroom comes from a family in which one or both parents are addicted to drugs or alcohol (Powell, Zehm, and Kottler, 1995). When these children of alcoholics/addicts (COAs) are angry and disruptive like Ricky, it is relatively easy to recognize that a problem exists; it is far more difficult when children are compliant perfectionists like Amanda. Leslie Lillian, the Student Assistance Counselor at Ken's school, stresses that COAs can exhibit a wide variety of behaviors (see Table 13-1):

Some children become perfectionists and peacemakers. They want to prevent situations that might evoke their parents' anger because their parents' responses are so unpredictable. It's as if they think to themselves, "I'm not going to disturb anything; I'm not going to do anything wrong; I'll try and keep the peace, so that no one will be angry."

TABLE 13-1
CHARACTERISTICS OF CHILDREN OF ALCOHOLICS/ADDICTS
(ADAPTED FROM TOWERS, 1989)

Difficulty in creating and maintaining trusting relationships, often leading to isolation

Low self-esteem

Self-doubt

Difficulty in being spontaneous and open, caused by a need to be in control and to minimize the risk of being surprised

Denial and repression because of the need to collaborate with other family members in keeping "the secret"

General feelings of guilt about areas for which the child had no responsibility

Uncertainty about his/her own feelings and desires caused by shifting parental roles

Seeing things in an "all or nothing" context, which sometimes manifests itself in a perfectionist fear of failure

Poor impulse control, which may result in acting-out behavior, probably caused by lack of parental guidance, love, and discipline

Potential for depression, phobias, panic reactions, and hyperactivity

Preoccupation with the family

Abuse of alcohol and/or drugs

Some children become class clowns; maybe they've found that making people laugh breaks the tension, or maybe they're seeking attention. Others become very angry; they may begin to lie, or steal, or cheat. Some become sad and melancholy; everything about them says, "Nurture me." We see a whole spectrum of reactions—and it's the same spectrum of behaviors that we see in kids from violent homes.

It's important to understand that for COAs, family life revolves around the addiction. Rules are arbitrary and irrational; boundaries between parents and children are blurred; and life is marked by unpredictability and inconsistency. Leslie comments:

> These kids never know what they're going home to. One day, they may bring a paper home from school that's gotten a low grade, and the parent might say, "That's okay, just do it over." Another day, they might get beaten up for bringing home a paper like that.

Sadly, it's often difficult for COAs to reach out for help. In a chemically dependent family, everyone works to maintain the family secret. Tonia Moore, Highland Park's Student Assistance Counselor, finds that COAs move back and forth between "wanting to report the problem and wanting to deny there *is* a problem":

> A while back I worked with a sister and brother; the girl was in elementary school and the boy was in high school. Their mother was an alcoholic, and she would tell them if they did well on their report cards, she would stop drinking. They'd go to church and pray for that; they'd even dream about it. I would tell them, "Don't count on it. It's not that easy for your mom to stop drinking, even though she wants to." But they *wanted to believe it would happen.* They really tried to improve their grades, and they did, and she still didn't stop. They were heartbroken.
>
> Sometimes, she'd come to back-to-school night, and you could tell she'd been drinking. The boy would put his arm around her and try to keep her from making a scene. And then the next day, he'd come in to see me, all embarrassed, and apologize for her behavior. He'd say she wasn't feeling well, that she had the flu, even though he knew that I knew she was an alcoholic. He'd *participate in the secret,* he'd try to cover up, even as he confided in me. Children of substance abusers have such a tremendous need *to have things be normal.*

One of the most frustrating aspects of working with COAs is the realization that you do not have the power to change the child's home life. Instead, you must concentrate on what you *are* able to do during the six hours each day that the child is in school. Many of the strategies are not different from those we have espoused for all children. (See Table 13-2.) For example, it is essential that you establish clear, consistent rules and work to create a climate of trust and caring. It is also useful to focus attention directly and indirectly on topics related to addiction. In *Classrooms Under the Influence* (Powell, Zehm, and Kottler, 1995), Dennis Thompson, a seventh- and eighth-grade language arts teacher, describes the ways he teaches about addiction:

> When we first began to read and talk about the effects of addiction, I discovered that I could begin to help students from addicted families develop some of the important coping skills they needed to deal with the anger and shame they brought from home. I also

TABLE 13-2
WAYS OF HELPING CHILDREN OF ALCOHOLICS/ADDICTS (ADAPTED FROM POWELL,
ZEHM, AND KOTTLER, 1995)

1. **Be observant.** Watch your students not just for academic or behavior problems, but also for the more subtle signs of addiction and emotional distress. Remember that COAs can be over-achieving, cooperative, and quiet, as well as disruptive and angry.

2. **Set boundaries that are enforced consistently.** When chaos exists at home, some sense of order is crucial at school.

3. **Be flexible.** Although it is necessary to set boundaries, classroom rules that are too rigid and unyielding may invite students to act out.

4. **Make addiction a focus of discussion.** Find a way to deal with this subject. Incorporate addiction into literacy instruction (e.g., through children's literature, writing), science, social studies, etc.

5. **Make it clear you are available.** Communicate that you are eager and open to talk to children. Reach out to the troubled child in a gentle, caring way. "I notice you are having some difficulty. I just want you to know that I care about you. Call me any time you are ready to talk. And if you would rather speak to someone else, let me find you someone you can trust."

6. **Develop a referral network.** Find out what services are available to help and refer the child for appropriate professional care.

7. **Accept what you can do little about.** You can't make people stop drinking or taking drugs.

found that students from addicted families could begin to find the words they needed to describe and vent their anger and shame. They did this privately within the pages of their confidential journals. Later, they even began to do it publicly in the safety of role-playing and creative drama activities. . . . I'll never forget the day that Julie, one of my eighth graders, brought me her journal and said, "Mr. Thompson, please read page 31 of my journal, and *only* page 31." It was the beginning of her story about her alcoholic father. She trusted me enough to want me to know this about her.

[Another] strategy I use to reduce the negative effects students from addicted families bring into my classroom is to select and read adolescent literature to my students that focuses on the topic of healthy and unhealthy family living. . . . I am pleased to find lately that there are many new books of fiction for adolescents that focus on the topic of family addiction. My students enjoyed Elisa Carbone's *My Dad's Definitely Not a Drunk*, a short novel about the revelation of a family's secret and the eventual recovery of an alcoholic father. . . . I [also] use selections from children's literature like Judith Viorst's *Terrible, Horrible, No-Good, Very Bad Day,* and Bernard Waber's *Ira Sleeps Over* as examples of how kids learn to solve problems in healthy families. I then ask each of my students to use these stories as models for writing their own children's books about how their characters can solve problems at home in healthy ways. (Powell, Zehm, and Kottler, 1995, pp. 112-113)

In addition to using these strategies, you should find out if your school has Student Assistance Counselors or other special services personnel who can provide help. Find out if support groups for COAs are available. For example, Tonia runs groups at Barbara's school, sometimes alone and sometimes with the school's guidance counselor. Tonia speaks about the benefits that joining such a group can bring:

There's such a sense of relief. The comments are always the same: "I thought I was the only one." "I didn't know anyone else was going through this stuff." The shame is so great, even at a very young age, and the need to keep it all a secret is so hard. There's instant comaraderie.

We'll often start off by asking, "On a scale from one to ten, how are you feeling today?" That allows us to get a sense of the group and to learn quickly who's in the middle of a crisis. Then we'll ask them to share something positive that happened this week and something negative that happened. We'll ask who needs group time. We do activities that help to build self-esteem. We do role-playing to get at feelings—being disappointed, being unsafe, being embarrassed, being angry that you can never make plans, that you can never say, "My mother will be there," or even "I'll be there."

If there are no groups for COAs in your school, find out if your community has any support groups like *Alateen*, for children from eight to 19, and *Alatot*, for children under eight. These groups are part of the Al-Anon Family Groups and abide by the same "twelve steps" as Alcoholics Anonymous. (See Figure 13-2.)

In addition to having children in your classrooms who come from chemically dependent families, you may have youngsters who were *prenatally exposed to drugs and alcohol*. Prenatal substance exposure is increasing at an alarming rate, particularly since the "crack epidemic" of the mid-1980s, when crack, a cheaper, stronger form of cocaine, became readily available. Although the actual number of drug-exposed infants is unknown, some estimates of the number affected yearly *by crack alone* range from 48,000 to 400,000 (Grossman, 1995; Waller, 1993).

Prenatal substance exposure can cause a variety of learning and behavioral problems, but just how universal, permanent, and unique these problems are is still being debated. A few years ago, media accounts of "crack kids" led teachers to believe they were facing an onslaught of children who were uneducable, hyperactive, disorganized, aggressive, uncontrollable, and without a conscience. It now appears, how-

FIGURE 13-2
Suggested Preamble to the Twelve Steps (from *Alateen: Hope for Children of Alcoholics*, 1989)

Alateen, part of the Al-Anon Family Groups, is a fellowship of young people whose lives have been affected by alcoholism in a family member or close friend. We help each other by sharing our experience, strength and hope.

We believe alcoholism is a family disease, because it affects all the members emotionally and sometimes physically. Although we cannot change or control our parents, we can detach from their problems while continuing to love them.

We do not discuss religion or become involved with any outside organizations. Our sole topic is the solution of our problems. We are always careful to protect each other's anonymity as well as that of all Al-Anon and AA members.

By applying the Twelve Steps to ourselves, we begin to grow mentally, emotionally and spiritually. We will always be grateful to Alateen for giving us a wonderful, healthy program to live by and enjoy.

ever, that the situation is not quite so bleak. A large-scale, longitudinal study conducted by the National Association for Perinatal Addiction Research and Education
(NAPARE) has demonstrated that early intervention can overcome many
of the problems caused by prenatal exposure to cocaine (Griffith, 1992). The
NAPARE study tracked the development of 300 children whose mothers had used
cocaine. (Most had used a variety of other drugs as well.) Three major findings are
particularly encouraging. First, nearly all of the children in the study had normal intelligence; second, by the time they reached age three or four, their social, emotional,
and intellectual development was also in the normal range; and third, while 30 to
40 percent of the children displayed some problems with language development and
attention, only about five percent actually exhibited ADHD (Black, 1993). These
findings led Dan Griffith (1992), one of the NAPARE researchers, to conclude that

> "crack-babies" are not some new breed of children that we have never seen before;
> they are simply children. Some have behavioral and learning problems; some do not.
> To date, the problems that have been reported are problems that creative teachers have
> successfully handled for many years. (p. 34)

Although these findings are reassuring, there is still little cause for celebration.
The NAPARE study is clearly a "best-case scenario" (Griffith, 1992), making it difficult to generalize to the entire population of drug-exposed children. Mothers were
recruited into the project early in their pregnancies and received prenatal care, nu-
tritional counseling, and therapy for their addictions. The children themselves were
provided with good nutrition and health care, they received regular treatment for
any medical or developmental problems, and they were placed in stable caretaking
environments (Griffith, 1992). Obviously, most prenatally exposed children do not
have these advantages. Most cocaine-abusing women cannot break their addiction
when they become pregnant; nor do they receive adequate prenatal care or prenatal nutrition. Moreover, they may be unable or unwilling to care for their babies after they have been born—or they may abandon them in the hospital:

> Growing numbers of crack babies simply are being abandoned in hospitals by their
> crack-smoking mothers. As for those babies who are discharged, the vast majority go
> from the hospital nursery to chaotic home environments characterized by deep poverty
> and little physical or emotional nurturing. With one strike already against them, these
> babies are at high risk for the second strike—neglect and abuse by crack-using adults.
> (Rist, 1990, p. 19)

Furthermore, teachers who have had experience working with children who
have been prenatally exposed to crack take issue with Griffith's contention that
drug-exposed children are "simply children" with problems that teachers have successfully handled for many years. According to 123 teachers interviewed by Mary
Bellis Waller (1993), prenatally exposed children exhibit unique learning and behavior problems that set them apart from other "more typical" emotionally disturbed or hyperactive children. They may have normal intelligence, and may even
be gifted, but they manifest problems in attention, language, memory, and logic.
Table 13-3 summarizes the characteristics observed by these teachers.

TABLE 13-3
MAJOR OBSERVABLE CHARACTERISTICS OF CHILDREN PRENATALLY EXPOSED TO
CRACK (WALLER, 1993)

Unfocused, patternless activity	Unable to focus or give pattern to behavior, to "tell themselves a story" about what they're doing, or to recognize connections in what others are doing
No sense of cause and effect	Logical consequences of relationships of actions not understood
Lack of conscience	Problems with lying, stealing; unaware of others' feelings; no empathy
Attention problems	Unable to focus attention on anything for long, even if high interest
Poor language ability	Speech delayed, and then sloppy
Memory problems	Unable to remember reliably things learned; activity, skill, or fact seems to disappear, then can resurface days or weeks later
Hyperactivity	Unable to sit still or stay in one place; move around room, often at high speed
Impulsivity	Unable to control urges; this interferes with learning and with social interactions
Temper tantrums	Sudden and unpredictable tantrums or changes in mood; some children can scream for more than an hour without stopping
Violence	Impulses and mood swings can lead to violence; individuals unable to understand, recognize, or predict this behavior
Flat affect	Do not show sadness, anger, or joy in appropriate ways; apparently unaffected by normal emotions in others; often appear expressionless
Lack of body awareness	Late walking, and then awkward; sleep disorders; eating disorders, including eating 2 or 3 full meals within an hour, or going without food for a day; feel pain, but do not respond appropriately to it; may continue impulsive pain-producing actions; toilet training problems continuing into school age; impaired coordination
Low tolerance for stimulation	Unable to distinguish importance or strength among stimuli; respond to stimulus overload with hyperactivity or shutting down (losing consciousness); sensitive to changes of any kind
Social isolation	Self-absorbed; no bonding in infancy, few friends, no intimacy; resentment at isolation
Inappropriate social behavior	Unaware of boundaries of social behavior; unable to learn by watching or listening to others; may take teasing literally and act on it; often too loud or too active; often act out

Given the NAPARE study's lack of generalizability and the anecdotal reports of experienced teachers, the prognosis for drug-exposed children is still uncertain. What *is* certain is that children who have been exposed to cocaine have difficulty with *self-regulation,* the ability to control internal states of arousal and impulses (Griffith, 1992, p. 33). This means they have problems coping with transitions, frustration, and environmental stimulation—problems that are exacerbated in the complex, unpredictable, multidimensional environment of the classroom. (See

TABLE 13-4
STRATEGIES FOR WORKING WITH CRACK-AFFECTED CHILDREN
(ADAPTED FROM WALLER, 1993)

Simplify the classroom environment. Reduce all stimuli—visual, audio, physical. Children who have been prenatally exposed to crack are so sensitive to stimulation that a rich classroom environment would be overwhelming and might push them into withdrawal or hyperactivity.

Establish invariable routines. Create an atmosphere of safety and predictability. Since prenatally exposed children have difficulty self-regulating and making connections, their worlds are chaotic. They are constantly surprised by events. Setting routines in your classroom and sticking to them are vital. Minimize transitions, which are particularly difficult for crack-affected children.

Make the classroom safe. Check your classroom for objects that could become weapons in the hands of an out-of-control child; arrange the classroom so that you can see every part of it at all times.

Teach the child to attend. If necessary, focus attention on the task by using touch, by gently guiding the child's head down toward the paper or book, or by carefully moving the child's hand down over the page you are spotlighting. Use only one tactic at a time (e.g., if you are touching the child's hand, do not talk to the child at the same time; try to use as few stimuli as possible so that you don't overwhelm the child).

Simplify teaching techniques. Forget varying your teaching strategies; forget using varied materials; forget varying the format of lessons. Stick with one teaching approach.

Teach one thing at a time, and go slowly. Break down the learning task into a series of subtasks. Repeat lessons. Be prepared to teach the same thing next week or next month. Do not assume that ability to do something today means the child will be able to do it tomorrow.

Be specific; don't hint. Prenatally exposed children have difficulty picking up on social cues and nonverbal behavior. They seem not to understand what a smile or a frown means and therefore do not respond to them appropriately. (In other words, the "teacher look" will not work!) Spell out feelings. Tell the child exactly what you want and how the child must respond. Show what a smile looks like while describing it. Tell the child the occasions when people smile. Ask the child to demonstrate a smile.

Appeal to the intellect. Prenatally exposed children have problems with emotions, and they have specific learning problems (e.g., attention and memory problems), but they have the full normal range of intelligence. Use language precisely and frequently. Describe and explain everything. Remember that, on their own, they have difficulty making connections between experiences. You need to teach them cause and effect.

Teach social interactions and play. Prenatally exposed children may not learn how to play on their own, and they have difficulty learning from others. You must teach them to play directly, using words and demonstrations. Teach them to interact appropriately; practice common interactions (e.g., greeting another child; introducing yourself; asking for information). Use guided practice.

Help children control their behavior. Watch for early warning signs that children may be about to lose control. Intervene early, before they become hyperactive or aggressive. Learn how to restrain children safely so they do not get hurt or hurt others. With older and larger children, use time-outs. Restraint and time-outs are not meant as punishment; they are tools to allow children to regain control.

Chapter 1.) When they become overwhelmed, they either withdraw from the stressful situation, physically or emotionally, or they lose control.

Both the NAPARE researchers and the teachers interviewed by Waller emphasize that consistent, predictable environments help drug-exposed children to self-regulate. With stable routines and rules, and with caring, nurturing teachers, they can remain below the threshold of loss of control. Table 13-4 lists additional strategies that Waller's teachers have found helpful.

A third way substance abuse can affect elementary classrooms is when *children themselves abuse drugs and alcohol.* At the elementary level, the problems of COAs and prenatally exposed children are far more prevalent, but it would be naive to think there is no substance abuse among youngsters at the intermediate grade levels. The New Jersey Alcohol/Drug Resource Center and Clearinghouse, Center of Alcohol Studies (1994) reports that nearly 100,000 children aged 10 or 11 report getting drunk once a week. Significant alcohol, inhalant, and cigarette use is reported as early as fourth grade, and alcohol experimentation increases from 6 to 17 percent between fourth and sixth grades. Viviana even tells of a *first grader* whose mother not only taught him to use drugs, she also had him selling on street corners.

Although alcohol remains the number one drug of choice among adolescents, there has been a sharp rise in marijuana use (which ranks second), and an increase in the use of stimulants, LSD, and inhalants (New Jersey Alcohol/Drug Resource Center and Clearinghouse, Center of Alcohol Studies, 1994). (For a summary of the drugs most frequently used by adolescents, their street names, how they are taken, and their effects, see Table 13-5.)

To a large extent, SACs rely on teachers to refer students who might be having problems with alcohol and other drugs or who might be at risk for such problems. But teachers may be particularly reluctant to make referrals about suspected drug use because they are unsure about the indicators. Tonia Moore is very sensitive to this problem:

> Teachers tell me, "I have no idea what substance abuse looks like. It wasn't a part of my training. I wouldn't know when to refer a student." I tell them, that's okay. You can't tell substance abuse just by looking. There has to be a chemical screening. But you can see changes in behavior. You know enough about kids to know when somebody's behavior has changed, or if their behavior is different from all the other kids. You don't need to know the student is using; you just need to report that you've observed a change in behavior, and then those who are trained to identify drug and alcohol problems can check it out.

What are the behaviors that might lead you to suspect drug use and to make a referral? Figure 13-3 shows the behavior checklist used in South Brunswick. Many schools use forms that are very similar to this one. Keeping your school's behavior checklist handy can help you stay alert to the possibility that students are using drugs or living with addiction in their families.

It's important to distinguish between situations in which a pattern of behavior problems suggests possible *drug use outside of school* and situations in which a student appears to be *under the influence of drugs during school, at school functions, or on school property.* When you see students who might be "under the influence," you cannot wait to fill out a behavior checklist; you need to alert the appropriate personnel as soon as you possibly can. In New Jersey, teachers are legally required to report "as soon as possible" a student who appears to be under the influence of drugs. Tonia explains one of the reasons for mandating an immediate response:

TABLE 13-5
COMMONLY USED DRUGS

Category	Name	Street name	How it's taken	Effects
Depressants	Alcohol (beer, wine, "hard liquor")		Swallowed	Depresses the central nervous system (CNS), slowing down bodily functions; decreases pulse and breathing; affects motor coordination and speech; diminishes ability to concentrate and impairs judgment; lowers inhibitions; chronic, heavy use can damage nearly every organ and system in the body
	Barbiturates and tranquilizers	*Barbiturates:* barbs, barbies, blues, candy, courage pills, dolls, downers, goofballs, reds, sleepers, yellow jackets *Tranquilizers:* downers, sleepers, tranks	Swallowed, injected	Depress the CNS; relax muscles; slow breathing; lower blood pressure; produce drowsiness; may produce relaxation and feeling of well-being; may lead to poor judgment, lack of motivation, and concentration
	Inhalants (aerosols, gases, solvents, amyl and butyl nitrite)	gas, glue, poppers, rush, laughing gas	Inhaled	Depress the CNS; produce alcohol-like effects—a loss of inhibitions, slurred speech, lack of coordination, weakness, giddiness, and slowed reflexes; may cause confusion and mood swings; some inhalants cause delusions and hallucinations
Stimulants	Amphetamines and diet pills	Uppers, speed, crank, meth, crystal, glass, bennies, Black Beauties, pep pills	Swallowed or injected. "Ice," one of the strongest amphetamines, is smoked in a pipe.	Stimulate the nervous system; speed up heart and breathing rates; raise blood pressure; decrease appetite; increase alertness; may produce sleeplessness, dizziness, anxiety, excitability, hallucinations; interferes with vision, judgment, and coordination

TABLE 13-5
COMMONLY USED DRUGS

Category	Name	Street name	How it's taken	Effects
	Cocaine and crack (cocaine already in smokeable form)	"C," coke, cola, flake, gold dust, rock, snow, white; stardust	*Cocaine*—sniffed or snorted; can also be injected into veins Crack—smoked	Stimulate the primary central nervous system; similar to the effects of amphetamines; initially, can lead to feelings of euphoria, alertness, increased mental energy, and sense of well-being; dependence can lead to loss of energy, insomnia, sore throat, nosebleeds, headaches, sinus problems and runny nose, lost sex drive, trembling, nausea, constant licking of lips, sniffling of nose
Hallucinogens	LSD; psilocybin (found in mushrooms); PCP (synthetic); mescaline (found in peyote cactus buttons); LSA (found in some morning glory seeds)	LSD—acid, barrels, blotters, flats, Lucy in the sky with diamonds, mellow yellow, sugar cubes *Mescaline*—mesc, buttons, moon *PCP*—angel dust, cyclones, ozone *Psilocybin*—magic or sacred mushrooms	Usually swallowed, but can also be inhaled, smoked, and injected	Increase pulse and heart rate; increase blood pressure and temperature; may cause nausea, chills, convulsions; affect perceptions and judgment; may cause hallucinations; affect moods (may feel excited, peaceful, panicky)
	Marijuana (a very mild hallucinogen; the psychoactive ingredient in THC, tetrahydrocannabinal); hashish is a more potent form of marijuana	Pot, grass, tea, mary jane, weed; a marijuana or hashish cigarette—reefer, joint, roach (butt of a joint)	Typically smoked in cigarette form; can also be sprinkled in food and ingested	Increase in heart rate, reddening of eyes, dryness in mouth and throat; temporary impairment of short-term memory; alters sense of time, reduces ability to concentrate; feelings of euphoria and relaxation

343

STUDENT ASSISTANCE PROGRAM BEHAVIOR CHECKLIST

The goal of the Student Assistance Program is to help students who may be experiencing problems in their lives. These problems can be manifested in school through any combination of behaviors. The following is a list of typical behaviors students having problems may exhibit. While most students engage in many of the behaviors at one time or another, the student who may be having trouble will show a combination or pattern of these behaviors.

Student:_____Grade: _____

Staff
Member:_____Date: _____

Academic Performance
___Drop in grades
___Decrease in participation
___Inconsistent work
___Works below potential
___Compulsive overachievement
    + (preoccupied w/school
    success)

School Attendance
___Change in attendance
___Absenteeism
___Tardiness
___Class cutting
___Frequent visits to nurse
___Frequent visits to counselor
___Frequent restroom visit
___Frequent request for hall passes

Social Problems
___Family problems
___Run away
___Job problems
___Peer problems
___Constantly borrowing money
___Relationships problems

Physical Symptoms
___Staggering/stumbling
___Incoherent
___Smelling of alcohol/marijuana
___Vomiting/nausea
___Glassy, bloodshot eyes/dark
___Poor coordination
___Slurred speech

___Deteriorating physical appearance
___Sleeping in class
___Physical injuries
___Frequent physical complaints
___Dramatic change in musculature

Extracurricular Activities
___Lack of participation
___Possession of drugs/alcohol or other
    drugs
___Involvement in thefts and assaults
___Vandalism
___Talking about involvement in illegal
    activities
___Possession of paraphernalia
___Increasing noninvolvement
___Decrease in motivation
___Dropping out missing practice(s)
___Not fulfilling responsibilities
___Performance changes

Disruptive Behavior
___Defiance of rules
___Irresponsibility, blaming, lying,
    fighting
___Cheating
___Sudden outburst, verbal abuse
___Obscene language, gesture
___Attention-getting behavior
___Frequently in wrong area
___Extreme negativism
___Hyperactivity, nervousness
___Lack of motivation, apathy
___Problem with authority figures

FIGURE 13-3
The Referral Form Used in South Brunswick

Atypical Behavior
___Difficulty in accepting mistakes
___Boasts about alcohol/or drug use,
    "partying bravado"
___Erratic behavior
___Change of friends
___Overly sensitive
___Disoriented
___Inappropriate responses
___Depression
___Defensive
___Withdrawn/difficulty relating
___Unrealistic goals
___Sexual behavior in public

___Seeking adult advice without a
    specific problem
___Rigid obedience
___Constantly seeks approval

Other
___Students talking about alcohol or
    other drugs
___Having beeper
___Bragging about sexual exploits
___Mentions concerns about significant
    other's alcohol or other drug use,
    gambling
___Staff knowledge of addiction in family

FIGURE 13-3—cont'd
The Referral Form Used in South Brunswick

It used to be that teachers would come to me at the end of the day and say, "I was really worried about X today. I think he was really on something." That's no good. *I need to know at the time.* After all, that student could fall down the stairs, or the student could leave the building . . . and get killed crossing the street. *We have to deal with the problem immediately.* It can really be a matter of life and death.

Since you cannot be sure that a student is using drugs just by looking, it's important not to be accusatory when you talk with the student. Ken would ask, "Are you feeling okay? You don't look like yourself. Would you like to go to the nurse?" He would then alert the nurse that he was sending her a student whose behavior suggested possible drug or alcohol use. Making a referral like this is not easy, but you need to remember that turning away and remaining silent can send the message that you condone the behavior—or that you don't care enough to do anything.

Violence

Stories about kids shooting other kids, about stabbing incidents, and about teachers being killed in the crossfire are appearing in newspapers with increasing frequency—and the stories are supported by studies of school violence. In a study of 720 public school districts conducted by the National School Boards Association (1994; see Portner, 1994), 82 percent of the districts reported that school violence had increased in the past five years. Furthermore, the report indicated that violence is no longer confined to schools in inner cities, but affects rural and suburban districts as well. For many youngsters, schools are still the safest place in their lives, but "for many, the symbol of the little red schoolhouse as a safe haven has been replaced by the yellow and black sign, Danger Zone" (Curcio and First, 1993).

In response to the increasing violence, schools are installing metal detectors; having police and security guards patrol hallways; training faculty to intervene in violent situations; having guest speakers encourage students to refrain from violence; and establishing "weapons hotlines" that pay students for reporting weapons on school grounds. According to David and Roger Johnson (1995), these violence-prevention programs are a good beginning, but they do not go far enough. *Violence prevention must be coupled with conflict resolution*—programs that teach children to manage conflicts in nonviolent, constructive ways. Marilyn Green, director of New Brunswick's elementary "school-base" program, agrees. In the anger-management/conflict-resolution groups she runs, she tries to help children distinguish between feelings and behavior: While feeling angry is perfectly all right, expressing that anger in a violent way is *not.* Instead, children need to learn nonviolent alternatives to dealing with conflict.

Sometimes conflict-resolution programs focus on just a few students who are trained to mediate conflicts among their peers (Miller, 1994; Smith, 1993). Mediators do not hand down solutions; rather, they guide the parties to negotiate their own solutions. So far, anecdotal evidence suggests that peer-mediation programs can substantially reduce violent incidents, although peer mediation may actually have more impact on the *mediators* than on the antagonists (Miller, 1994). If this is so, it means that high-risk students—not just the "good kids"—must be trained and used as mediators.

Other conflict-resolution programs involve the whole student body, obviously a more costly, ambitious endeavor. David and Roger Johnson, for example, have developed "The Teaching Students to Be Peacemakers Program" (1991), in which students are taught how to negotiate a satisfactory resolution when they are involved in conflicts and how to mediate the conflicts of their peers. A recent study by the Johnsons and three of their students (Johnson, Johnson, Dudley, Ward, and Magnuson, 1995) demonstrated that the Peacemakers program can have a significant, positive impact on the strategies that elementary students use to resolve school conflicts. One very encouraging finding was that students also reported using the strategies to resolve conflicts at home.

Ken's school has tried to implement a broad-based program like this, although Leslie Lillian admits that an ever-increasing number of crises has begun to limit the time she has for preventive programs. Beginning with the kindergartners, Leslie teaches children to use "I messages"—much like those described in Chapter 6 ("When you . . . I feel . . ."). In fourth grade, she trains children in conflict-resolution and peer-mediation techniques. Once children are trained, they may sign up to be peer mediators.

Children in Barbara's school also participate in a broad-based program. Designed by psychologists Maurice Elias and John Clabby, the program focuses on social decision making and social problem solving (SDM/SPS) (Elias and Clabby, 1988, 1989). It is based on two premises: first, that a hierarchy of skills underlies competent interpersonal behavior—in particular, social-cognitive problem-solving skills; and second, that children can be taught these skills so that they can analyze, understand, and prepare to respond to everyday problems, decisions, and conflict.

Whereas traditional approaches to social decision-making have often been organized around a particular issue (drug and alcohol use, violence, nutrition), SDM/SPS believes that children need to learn social-cognitive skills that can be applied to a variety of decision-making situations. Figure 13-4 lists the sequence of skills that children are taught to use.

Vicki Pocdubicky, the health teacher at Bartle, has incorporated SDM/SPS into the health curriculum for all third and fourth graders. There, children are taught to deal with conflicts by using the problem-solving process and then to enact the process using their BEST skills: monitoring *Body* posture, making the appropriate *Eye* contact, *Saying* the appropriate words, and using the appropriate *Tone* of voice. In the classroom, teachers reinforce the SDM/SPS curriculum by having children complete "Hassle Logs" when they are having a problem. (Figure 13-5 shows a Hassle Log completed by a third-grade girl when her classmate started to "bug" her. Figure 13-6 shows a Hassle Log that uses a different format.) If, after three Hassle Logs, a problem still persists, a teacher can refer a child to the Social Problem-Solving Lab—not as a punishment, but as an opportunity to get special help. There, children can have a one-on-one conference with Vicki, role-play solutions to their problems, or use a software program, also developed by Elias and Clabby, to go through the problem-solving steps.

Another violence-prevention/conflict-resolution effort being tried in Highland Park, New Brunswick, and South Brunswick is SAVVY—Students Against

FIGURE 13-4
Steps in Thoughtful Problem Solving and Decision Making (Elias and Clabby, 1988)

1 Look for signs of different feelings.
Recognize your feelings of stress, anxiety, or uncertainty as a signal to begin problem solving, rather than a feeling to be eliminated or ignored; also recognize signs of others' feelings.
2 Tell yourself what the problem is.
"I feel nervous because I have a test tomorrow."
"I'm worried because those kids look really tough."
3 Decide on your goal.
"I want to do well on that test."
"I want to keep away from those tough kids."
4 Stop and think of as many solutions to the problem as you can.
"I'll study in the library tonight instead of staying home. That way I won't be able to talk on the phone."
5 For each solution, think of all the things that might happen next.
"Of course, if I meet friends in the library, I might waste time talking to them."
6 Choose your best solution.
7 Plan it and make a final check.
8 Try it and rethink it.

Hassle Log

Name: Madeleine   Date: Nov. 28, 1995

Time: 12:00

(1) I am feeling:

MAD!

My feeling looks like this: ►

(2) Tell the problem.

What did you say and do?

Lena Just startid buging me

Draw it.

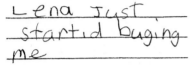

(3) Now what do you want to happen?

I want her to stop it!

Draw it.

(4) What could you do to have that happen?

I could have hit her but I rilised that shel wine about it, so I got a hassle log.

Draw it.

FIGURE 13-5
A hassle log completed by a third-grade girl

Hassle Log

Name _____Homeroom Teacher _____

Date _____Grade _____

Time of day: (Circle one)   morning   afternoon   evening

Where were you? _____

Who was involved? _____

What is the **problem?**_____

_____

What did you do? _____

_____

How did you **feel** before you did this? _____

_____

What was your **goal** (what were you trying to do)? _____

_____

How satisifed are you with the way(s) you have tried to solve the problem?

(Circle one)   not at all   only a little   okay   pretty satisfied   very satisifed

How easy or hard was it for you to keep calm and stay in control of yourself?

(Circle one)   very easy   pretty easy   okay   pretty hard   very hard

****************What else could you have done to be your **BEST?****************

Think of as many possible **solutions** as you can.

Solutions (what I could do)   **Consequences** (what could happen)

FIGURE 13-6
Another type of hassle log

Violence and Victimization of Youth. Since 1992, SAVVY has trained high school students in violence-prevention skills that they then teach to third, fourth, and fifth graders. One hope is that by the time these youngsters get to high school, they will have developed nonviolent ways of resolving their conflicts. Another hope is that the high school students involved with the program will also develop some new ways of thinking about and responding to violence.

Abuse and Neglect

During one meeting with our teachers, they related sad, frightening stories that illustrate the important role teachers serve in identifying victims of abuse. Listen to Garnetta:

TABLE 13-6
PHYSICAL AND BEHAVIORAL INDICATORS OF CHILD ABUSE AND NEGLECT

Type of child abuse or neglect	Physical indicators	Behavioral indicators
Physical abuse	Unexplained bruises and welts: —on face, lips, mouth —on torso, back, buttocks, thighs —in various stages of healing —clustered, forming regular patterns —reflecting shape of article used to inflict (electric cord, belt buckle) —on several different surface areas —regularly appear after absence, weekend or vacation Unexplained burns: —cigar, cigarette burns, especially on soles, palms, back or buttocks —immersion burns (sock-like, glove-like doughnut shaped on buttocks or genitalia) —patterned like electric burner, iron, etc. —rope burns on arms, legs, neck or torso Unexplained fractures: —to skull, nose, facial structure —in various stages of healing —multiple or spiral fractures Unexplained lacerations or abrasions: —to mouth, lips, gums, eyes —to external genitalia	Wary of adult contacts Apprehensive when other children cry Behavioral extremes: —aggressiveness —withdrawal Frightened of parents Afraid to go home Reports injury by parents
Physical neglect	Consistent hunger, poor hygiene, inappropriate dress Consistent lack of supervision, especially in dangerous activities or long periods Constant fatigue or listlessness Unattended physical problems or medical needs Abandonment	Begging, stealing food Extended stays at school (early arrival and late departure) Constantly falling alseep in class Alcohol or drug abuse Delinquency (e.g., thefts) States there is no caretaker
Sexual abuse	Difficulty in walking or sitting Torn, stained or bloody underclothing Pain or itching in genital area Bruises or bleeding in external genitalia, vaginal or anal areas Venereal disease, especially in preteens Pregnancy	Unwilling to change for gym or participate in PE Withdrawal, fantasy or infantile behavior Bizarre, sophisticated, or unusual sexual behavior or knowledge Poor peer relationships Delinquent or run away Reports sexual assault by caretaker

Source: Child Abuse and Neglect: A Professional's Guide to Identification, Reporting, Investigation and Treatment. Trenton, NJ: Governor's Task Force on Child Abuse and Neglect, October 1988.

TABLE 13-6
PHYSICAL AND BEHAVIORAL INDICATORS OF CHILD ABUSE AND NEGLECT

Type of child abuse or neglect	Physical indicators	Behavioral indicators
Emotional maltreatment	Habit disorders (sucking, biting, rocking, etc.) Conduct disorders (antisocial, destructive, etc.) Neurotic traits (sleep disorders, speech disorders, inhibition of play) Psychoneurotic reactions (hysteria, obsession, compulsion, phobias, hypochondria)	Behavior extremes: —compliant, passive —aggressive, demanding Overly adaptive behavior: —inappropriately adult —inappropriately infant Developmental lags (physical, mental, emotional) Attempted suicide

Libby had moved from another country with her mother and sisters, and they were living in her grandmother's house. Her father stayed back home, but within three or four years, he rejoined his family. Shortly after, I noticed physical bruises on Libby's arms and legs. I also noticed that her older brother had bruises, too. We reported the case to DYFS [Division of Youth and Family Services], and they sent a caseworker to the home to investigate. DYFS reported back to us that the father admitted he had hit the children because they hadn't gone to bed when he told them to. Apparently this wasn't the first time. According to the mother, when the children were very young, the father had been jailed for "hurting" the children. This time he agreed to counseling.

Libby and her brother are not alone. It has been estimated that one million children are victims of child abuse or neglect each year—and those are just the confirmed cases (Fossey, 1995). In order to protect these youth, most states have laws requiring educators to report suspected abuse to the state's "child protective service" or "child welfare agency." Garnetta, for example, contacted New Jersey's Division of Youth and Family Services, the agency charged with receiving and investigating all reports of suspected child abuse and neglect.

Amazingly, only 10 percent of abuse and neglect reports originate in schools, even though at least half of the nation's abused and neglected children are in school on any given day (McIntyre, 1990, cited in Fossey, 1995). One simple reason is teachers' lack of familiarity with the signs of abuse. Thomas McIntyre (1990) found that only 4 percent of the teachers he surveyed were "very aware" of the signs of sexual abuse; 17 percent could recognize obvious signs; and 75 percent could not recognize signs of sexual abuse at any point. These findings clearly underscore the need for teachers to become familiar with the physical and behavioral indicators of these problems. (See Table 13-6.)

Unfortunately, the signs of abuse can be difficult to detect. As Table 13-6 indicates, teachers need to watch not only for physical evidence, they must also be alert to behavioral indicators such as apprehension when other children are upset, reluctance to go home at the end of the school day, and wariness of adult contact. Children who give improbable explanations for their injuries, refuse to talk about them, or pretend they don't hurt may also be victims of physical abuse.

According to Leslie Lillian, the SAC at Ken's school, the teachers at Brunswick Acres see more neglect than abuse:

> We'll see parents who don't make sure that their kids get to school; parents who know that their first grader is lying and stealing but "don't want to hear"; parents who send their kid to school smelling of stale smoke—and won't do anything even when we tell them that the other kids tease him unmercifully. People tend to think that neglect occurs in poor families, but cases like this cross SES [socioeconomic lines] lines. I remember one girl in particular who would cry when she got sick and beg us not to send her home. She knew that her high-powered parents would be angry if their day was disrupted.

Teachers are often reluctant to file a report unless they have absolute proof of abuse or neglect. They worry about invading the family's privacy and causing unnecessary embarrassment to everyone involved. Nonetheless, it's important to keep in mind that *no state requires the reporter to have absolute proof* before reporting. What most states do require is reasonable "cause to suspect" or "believe" that abuse has occurred (Michaelis, 1993). If you are uncertain whether abuse is occurring, but have reasonable cause, you should err in favor of the youngster and file a report. Waiting for proof can be dangerous; it may also be illegal. If a child is later harmed, and it becomes clear that you failed to report suspected abuse, both you and your school district may be subject to both civil and criminal liability (Michaelis, 1993).

It's also important to learn about the reporting procedures in your state (*before* you are faced with a situation of suspected child abuse). Some states, like New Jersey, require teachers to file a report directly to the state's child protective service in order to avoid unnecessary delays. Other states allow teachers to report the suspected abuse to a school administrator or a nurse who then makes the actual call.

States also vary with respect to the form and content of reports required. Generally, however, you should be prepared to provide the student's name, age, address, and sex; the parents' names and addresses; the nature and extent of injury or condition observed; evidence of prior injuries; and your own name and telephone number (Tower, 1987).

This variation underscores the importance of becoming familiar with the procedures and resources in your own school. The best way to do this is to speak with people who can provide guidance and direction—experienced teachers, the principal, the school nurse, members of the core team, and the Student Assistance Counselor.

TALKING WITH STUDENTS WHO ARE TROUBLED

As we've stressed earlier, it is not your job to be a school counselor, therapist, or confidante for all your students. You have neither the time nor the training to serve in those roles. Nonetheless, there will be instances in which students will reach out to you for understanding. A student might confide her fears about her mother's boyfriend; another might tell you about his alcoholic father; still another might want to talk about her feelings of inadequacy and isolation. What will you do? As we've already indicated, in many cases, the appropriate response is to put the student in touch with a special service provider who has the expertise needed to intervene. But you can also be helpful by having some basic communication skills. These allow you to help students express their feelings, gain clarity, and reflect on ways to resolve their own problems.

Attending and Acknowledging

Giving a student your complete, undivided attention is the first and most basic task in being helpful (Kottler and Kottler, 1993). It is rare that individuals are fully attentive to one another. Have you ever tried to talk with someone who was simultaneously organizing papers, posting notices on the bulletin board, or straightening rows of desks? Divided attention like this communicates that the person doesn't really have time for you and is not fully paying attention.

Attending and acknowledging involve both verbal and nonverbal behaviors. Even without saying a word, you can convey that you are totally tuned in by orienting your body toward the student, establishing eye contact, nodding, leaning forward, smiling, or frowning. In addition, you can use verbal cues. Thomas Gordon (1974) recommends "empathic grunting"—the little "uh-huhs" and phrases (e.g., "Oh," "I see," "Mmmmm") that communicate "I'm really listening." Sometimes, when a student needs additional encouragement to talk more, you can use an explicit invitation, what Gordon calls a "door opener"—"Tell me more," "Would you like to say more about that?" "Do you want to talk about it?" "Want to go on?"

One of the hardest ideas for teachers to accept is that a person can help another simply by listening. But Kottler and Kottler (1993) remind us that attending can be a powerful helping tool:

> You would be truly amazed at how healing this simple act can be—giving another person your full attention. Children, in particular, are often so used to being devalued by adults that attending behaviors instantly tell them something is different about this interaction: "Here is a person who seems to care about me and what I have to say." (p. 40)

Active Listening

Attending and acknowledging communicate that you are totally engaged, but they do not convey if you really *understand*. Active listening takes the interaction one step further by having you reflect back what you think you heard. This feedback allows you to check out whether you are right or wrong. If you're right, the student knows that you have truly understood. If you're off target, the student can correct you, and the communication can continue. Examples of active listening appear in Figure 13-7.

If you're new to active listening, you may find it useful to use the phrase, "You feel . . ." when you reflect back what you heard. Sometimes, novices feel stupid, as if they're simply parroting back what the person just said. As you gain more skill, however, you are able to *paraphrase* what you hear, and the interaction becomes far more subtle.

STUDENT: Wait till my mom sees this test grade. She's gonna flip out.

TEACHER: You think she'll be really mad at you, huh?

STUDENT: Yeah, she expects me to come home with all A's.

TEACHER: Sounds like you're feeling really pressured.

STUDENT: Well, I am. You'd think that getting a B was like failing. My mom just doesn't understand how hard this is for me.

TEACHER: So you think a B is an okay grade in a tough course like this, but she thinks you can do better.

STUDENT: Yea, she has this thing that if I come home with a B, I'm just not working.

TEACHER: That's rough. I can see how that would make you feel like she doesn't appreciate the efforts you're making.

STUDENT: I can't believe I have to be home at 10:00! It's crazy! All my friends have a later curfew—or they don't have any curfew at all!

TEACHER: So you think your parents are a lot stricter than the other kids' parents.

STUDENT: Well, they are! I mean, I know it's 'cause they care about me, but it's really a pain to have to be home earlier than everyone else. I feel like a dork. And besides, I think I'm responsible enough to have a later curfew.

TEACHER: So you're not just embarrassed, you're mad because they don't realize how responsible you are.

STUDENT: All along she's been telling me how we'll be best friends forever, and then she goes and gets a best friend charm with Mira.

TEACHER: When something like that happens, you feel really abandoned.

STUDENT: I don't want to go to School-Base [for mental health counseling]. Only crazy kids go to School-Base!

TEACHER: Going to School-Base is kind of embarrassing. . . .

STUDENT: Yeah. My friends are gonna give me a really hard time.

TEACHER: You think they're going to say you're crazy.

STUDENT: Yeah. I wanna go, but I don't want people to make fun of me.

TEACHER: I can understand that. It's really rough when people make fun of you.

STUDENT: I had the worst nightmare last night! I mean, I know it was just a dream, but I just can't get it out of my head. This bloody guy with a knife was chasing me down this alley, and I couldn't get away.

TEACHER: Nightmares can be so scary.

STUDENT: Yeah, and I know it's babyish, but I just can't shake the feeling.

TEACHER: Sometimes a bad feeling from a nightmare stays with you a long time. . . .

FIGURE 13-7
Examples of Active Listening

Keep in mind that active listening is not easy. Student teachers with whom we work often want to reject it out of hand; they find it unnatural and awkward, and they would much prefer to give advice, not simply communicate that they understand. But knowing that someone really understands can be profoundly important, especially to children who so often feel misunderstood. In addition, active listening provides an opportunity for students to express their feelings and to clarify their problems. It can also help to defuse strong feelings without taking the responsibility away from the student for solving the problem.

Questioning

When people tell us their problems, we often want to ask them questions in order to find out more information. Kottler and Kottler (1993) caution teachers to be careful about this practice:

> The problem with questions, as natural as they may come to mind, is that they often put the child in a "one down" position in which you are the interrogator and expert problem solver. "Tell me what the situation is and I will fix it." For that reason, questions are used only when you can't get the student to reveal information in other ways. (p. 42)

If you must ask questions, they should be open-ended—requiring more than a one-word response. Like active listening, open-ended questions invite further exploration and communication, whereas close-ended questions cut off communication. Compare these questions:

What are you feeling right now? *v.* Are you feeling angry?
What do you want to do? *v.* Do you want to tell your mother?

Kottler and Kottler point out one notable exception to the rule of avoiding questions whenever possible: that is, when it is important to get very specific information in a potentially dangerous situation, such as when a student is discussing suicide. Then it would be appropriate to ask specific questions: Have you actually tried this? Will you promise not to do anything until we can get you some help?

Problem Solving

We have already discussed problem solving in Chapter 6, when we described Gordon's no-lose method of solving classroom conflicts. We also discussed the SDM/SPS program in use at Bartle (Elias and Clabby, 1988). But you can also use this approach when students have their own problems that they confide in you. A problem-solving approach helps students think about how they're feeling, define their problem, specify their goals, develop alternative solutions that might be constructive, narrow the choices to those that seem most realistic, and put the plan into action (Kottler and Kottler, 1993).

CONCLUDING THOUGHTS

As the number of children with special needs grows, the debate about how much schools can do becomes more heated. Free breakfast and lunch programs are now standard, but as we have seen, some districts are also providing mental health counseling, conflict-resolution programs, classes for teen parents, health and dental screenings, and child-care centers for the infants and toddlers of their students. In Philadelphia, Pennsylvania, principal Madeline Cartwright installed a washer and a dryer in the kitchen-cafeteria (Louv, 1990). Every morning she and members of her staff personally wash the clothing of many of the children. Cartwright maintains that this is the only way most of her schoolchildren will ever know what it's like to have clean clothes.

Even in less impoverished areas, the problems students bring to school can seem overwhelming, especially for beginning teachers who are coping with basic issues of survival. And, in fact, there may be students whose problems are so great, you really cannot help very much. That *doesn't* mean giving up. When students have serious problems, it's more important than ever to create a classroom that is safe, orderly, and humane. You may not be able to change youngsters' relationships with their families, but you can still work to establish positive teacher-student relationships and to create a climate of trust in your classroom. You may not be able to provide students with control over unstable, chaotic home lives, but you can create stable, predictable classrooms, and you can allow them some control over their time in school. You may not be able to do anything about the violence that permeates the neighborhoods in which they live, but you can structure classroom situations to foster cooperation and group cohesiveness. You may not be able to change students' lives, but you can try to make their time in school as productive and meaningful as possible.

SUMMARY

Because large numbers of America's youth are at risk for school failure, substance abuse, physical problems, psychological and emotional disorders, abuse and neglect, and violence, today's teachers have to deal with issues that require knowledge and skills beyond those needed to be an effective instructor. There are three primary ways teachers can help students with serious problems:

- Teachers need to be alert to the indicators of potential problems.
- Teachers need to be informed about the various special services that are available and to know how to obtain access to those services.
- Teachers need to develop communication skills that allow them to work more effectively with troubled or disaffected youngsters.

The chapter briefly discussed three serious problems teachers may encounter in today's elementary schools:

- Substance abuse
    Children from chemically dependent families
    Children who have been prenatally exposed to drugs and alcohol
    Children who are themselves substance abusers
- Violence
- Abuse and neglect

The chapter then outlined communication skills that can be helpful:

- Attending and acknowledging
- Active listening
- Asking open-ended questions
- Problem solving

Sometimes the problems students bring to school can be overwhelming, especially for beginning teachers who are coping with basic issues of survival. And, in fact, there may be students whose problems are so great, you just cannot help. Nonetheless, you can still try to create a classroom environment that is safe, orderly, and humane. You can show students you care by working to make their time in school as meaningful and productive as possible.

ACTIVITIES

1 In the school where you are observing or teaching, interview the Student Assistance Counselor, a guidance counselor, or the director of special services to determine what services are available for children who come from substance-abusing families.

2 Reporting suspected abuse and neglect varies from state to state. Find out the policies used in your state. Also find out if your school has particular policies and procedures you are to follow. In particular, get answers to the following questions:

Who is required to report abuse and neglect?
When should you report child abuse? (When you have reasonable cause to suspect? Reasonable cause to believe?)
To what state agency do you report?
What information must be included in the report?
Do you have to give your name when reporting?

3 In the following bits of conversation, students have confided in teachers about problems they are experiencing, and the teachers have responded in ways *not* suggested in this chapter. Provide a new response for each case, using the communication skills discussed in this chapter: acknowledging, active listening, asking open-ended questions, and problem-solving.

a STUDENT: My parents won't allow me to go out on weekends like the other kids. They say they trust me, but then they don't show it!

TEACHER: Well, I'm sure they have your best interests at heart. You know, you really shouldn't gripe. You're pretty young, and after all, a lot of kids don't have parents who care about them. I see a lot of kids whose parents let them do anything they want. Maybe you think you'd like that, but I'm sure you wouldn't. . . .

b STUDENT: I can't stand my stepmother. She's always criticizing me and making me come home right after school to watch my sister, and making me feel really stupid.

TEACHER: Oh, come on now, Cinderella. I'm sure it's not that bad.

c STUDENT: My sister told me she thinks she's pregnant. She made me promise not to tell our folks, but I'm really scared. I think they should know. I'm scared she's going to try to get rid of it by herself. What do you think I should do?

TEACHER: I think you should tell your parents.

REFERENCES

Alateen: Hope for children of alcoholics (1989). New York: Al-Anon Family Group Headquarters, Inc.

Black, S. (1993). Drug-exposed children. *The Executive Educator, 15*(5), 23–25. Reprinted in B. J. Seitz de Martinez (Ed.) (1995). *Teaching children affected by prenatal drug exposure.* Bloomington, IN: Phi Delta Kappa (Hot Topics Series).

Children's Defense Fund (1994). *The state of America's children yearbook 1994.* Washington, D.C.: Children's Defense Fund.

Curcio, J. L., and First, P. F. (1993). *Violence in the schools: How to proactively prevent and defuse it.* Newbury Park, CA: Corwin Press, Inc.

Elias, M. J., and Clabby, J. F. (1989). *SDM skills: A curriculum guide for the elementary grades.* Gaithersburg, MD: Aspen Publishers.

Elias, M. J., and Clabby, J. F. (1988). Teaching social decision making. *Educational Leadership, 45*(6), 52–55.

Fossey, R. (1995) The physically or sexually abused child: What teachers need to know. *The Harvard Education Letter, 11*(2), 4–7.

Gonet, M. M. (1994). *Counseling the adolescent substance abuser: School-based intervention and prevention.* Thousand Oaks, CA: Sage Publications.

Gordon, T. (1974). *Teacher Effectiveness Training (T.E.T.).* NY: Peter H. Wyden.

Griffith, D. R. (1992). Prenatal exposure to cocaine and other drugs: Developmental and educational prognoses. *Phi Delta Kappan, 74*(1), 30–34. Reprinted in B. J. Seitz de Martinez (Ed.) (1995). *Teaching children affected by prenatal drug exposure.* Bloomington, IN: Phi Delta Kappa (Hot Topics Series).

Grossman, H. (1995). *Classroom behavior management in a diverse society* (2nd edition). Mountain View, CA: Mayfield Publishing Company.

Johnson, D. W., and Johnson, R. T. (1995). *Reducing school violence through conflict resolution.* Alexandria, VA: ASCD.

Johnson, D. W., and Johnson, R. T. (1991). Teaching students to be peacemakers. Edina, MN: Interaction Book Company.

Johnson, D. W., Johnson, R., Dudley, B., Ward, M., and Magnuson, D. (1995). The impact of peer mediation training on the management of school and home conflicts. *AERJ, 32*(4), 829–844.

Kottler, J. A., and Kottler E. (1993). *Teacher as counselor: Developing the helping skills you need.* Newbury Park, CA: Corwin Press, Inc.

Louv, R. (1990) Hope in hell's classroom. *The New York Times Magazine,* November 25.

Michaelis, K. L. (1993). *Reporting child abuse: A guide to mandatory requirements for school personnel.* Newbury Park, CA: Corwin Press, Inc.

Miller, E. (1994). Peer mediation catches on, but some adults don't. *Harvard Education Letter, 10*(3), 8.

New Jersey Alcohol/Drug Resource Center and Clearinghouse, Center of Alcohol Studies, Rutgers University (1994). *Facts on adolescent substance abuse.* Clearinghouse Fact Sheet.

Newsam, B. S. (1992). *Complete student assistance program handbook.* West Nyack, NY: The Center for Applied Research in Education.

O'Neil, J. (1991). A generation adrift? *Educational Leadership, 49*(1), 4–10.

Portner, J. (January 12, 1994). School violence up over past 5 years, 82% in survey say. *Education Week,* p. 9.

Powell, R. R., Zehm, S. J., and Kottler, J. A. (1995). *Classrooms under the influence: Addicted families/addicted students.* Newbury Park, CA: Corwin Press, Inc.

Rist, M. C. (1990). The shadow children. *American School Board Journal, 177*(1), 19–24.

Smith, M. (1993). Some school-based violence prevention strategies. *NASSP Bulletin, 77*(557), 70–75.

Tower, C. C. (1987). *How schools can help combat child abuse and neglect* (2nd edition). Washington, D.C.: National Education Association.

Towers, R. L. (1989). *Children of alcoholics/addicts.* Washington, D.C.: National Education Association.

Walker, H. M., Colvin, G., and Ramsey E. (1995). *Antisocial behavior in school: Strategies and best practices.* Pacific Grove, CA: Brooks/Cole Publishing Company.

Waller, M. B. (1993). *Crack affected children: A teacher's guide.* Newbury Park, CA: Corwin Press, Inc.

FOR FURTHER READING

Gordon, T. (1974). *Teacher Effectiveness Training (T.E.T.).* New York: Peter H. Wyden.

Johnson, D. W., and Johnson, R. T. (1995). *Reducing school violence through conflict resolution.* Alexandria, VA: ASCD.

Katz, N. H., and Lawyer, J. W. (1993). *Conflict resolution: Building bridges.* Thousand Oaks, CA: Corwin Press, Inc.

Kottler, J. A., and Kottler, E. (1993). *Teacher as counselor: Developing the helping skills you need.* Newbury Park, CA: Corwin Press, Inc.

Michaelis, K. L. (1993). *Reporting child abuse: A guide to mandatory requirements for school personnel.* Newbury Park, CA: Corwin Press, Inc.

Powell, R. R., Zehm, S. J., and Kottler, J. A. (1995). *Classrooms under the influence: Addicted families/addicted students.* Newbury Park, CA: Corwin Press, Inc.

Seitz de Martinez, B. J. (Ed.) (1995). *Teaching children affected by prenatal drug exposure.* Bloomington, IN: Phi Delta Kappa (Hot Topics Series).

Tower, C. C. (1987). *How schools can help combat child abuse and neglect* (2nd edition). Washington, D.C.: National Education Association.

Towers, R. L. (1989). *Children of alcoholics/addicts.* Washington, D.C.: National Education Association.

Walker, H. M., Colvin G., and Ramsey E. (1995). *Antisocial behavior in school: Strategies and best practices.* Pacific Grove, CA: Brooks/Cole Publishing Company.

Waller, M. B. (1993). *Crack affected children: A teacher's guide.* Newbury Park, CA: Corwin Press, Inc.

In addition:

The National Clearinghouse for Alcohol and Drug Information (NCADI)—a communications service of the Office for Substance Abuse Prevention; the nation's primary source of information about alcohol and other drug abuse. *Address:* The National Clearinghouse for Alcohol and Drug Information, P.O. Box 2345, Rockville, MD 20852; (301) 468-2600.

THINGS TO DO . . .
. . . BEFORE THE FIRST DAY

ROOM/ENVIRONMENT/SUPPLIES

Bulletin boards
   welcome back sign
   posting of announcements:
    menus, calendar, etc.
   spaces for children's work
   subject matter

Student name tags
   personal name tags
   name tags for desks

Learning centers
   where to locate
   materials needed
   subject matter

Design classroom
   furniture arrangement
   storage of supplies
   access to materials for students

Obtain supplies
   art (paper, paint, brushes, crayons,
    markers, glue, scissors, etc.)
   office (staples, clips, plan book,
    folders, writing paper, tape, etc.)

CURRICULUM

Supplies
   texts
   workbooks
   manipulatives
   supplementary materials

Library books
   develop class library
   sign out books relevant to first units

Grouping
   tentatively group students based on
    recommended levels and records
   plan assessment tasks to refine levels

Lesson plans
   first week's tentative plans, materials,
   work sheets, etc., prepared

BUSINESS/ORGANIZATION

Prepare class lists, folders, bus lists, etc.

Prepare introductory letter to parents
   outlining program, requirements,
   and schedules

Organize schedules
   specials
   individual students
   whole-class/small-group times

AUTHOR INDEX

Adams, R.S., 33, 50
Ahlbrand, W.P., Jr., 229, 256
Anderson, L., 54-55, 62, 64, 74, 78, 88, 98-99,
   110, 119, 135-136, 171, 174-175, 179-180,
   196-197
Anderson, R., 171, 173, 186, 196
Arends, R.I., 241, 256
Arlin, M., 147-148, 150, 165
Aronson, E., 218, 224
Aussiker, A., 101, 136
Axelrod, D., 30, 50

Baird, J.H., 203, 225
Baker, K., 263, 294
Bassler, O.T., 264, 288-289, 293
Battistich, V., 57, 74, 88, 99
Baum, M., 88, 98
Becher, R.M., 262, 292
Becker, H.J., 263, 266, 286, 292
Bennett, N., 30, 50
Berla, N., 294
Berliner, D.C., 138, 141, 166, 196
Beyerbach, B., 234, 257
Biddle, B.J., 30, 50
Blaney, N., 218, 224
Bloome, D., 127, 135, 176, 196
Blundell, D., 30, 50
Brandt, R., 267, 286, 292
Brissie, J.S., 264, 293
Broden, M., 121, 135
Brophy, J., 7, 10, 77, 82, 88, 98-99, 107, 119,
   123, 132, 135-136, 144, 166, 198, 224, 232,
   234, 239, 245, 247, 256, 319, 326
Bruther, M., 48, 50

Cahen, L.S., 138, 141, 166, 196
Cairns, L.G., 101, 135
Cameron, J., 92, 98
Canter, L., 68, 74-75, 137
Canter, M., 68, 74-75, 137
Carlson, C.G., 266, 292

Carson, L., 215, 224
Carter, K., 7-8, 10, 169, 196, 200, 224, 234,
   256
Cazden, C.B., 74, 175, 196, 227, 251, 256-257,
   326
Charles, C.M., 126, 135, 137
Clark, C., 76, 79, 98
Clements, B.S., 75, 136, 151, 165-166, 183-
   184, 196
Cohen, E.G., 176, 196, 201-203, 208, 215, 224-
   226
Coles, R., 43, 50
Crawford, J., 88, 98
Curcio, J.L., 345, 358
Curwin, R.L., 102, 112, 114-115, 135, 137

Damon, W., 95, 98
Dauber, S.L., 266, 283, 286, 292
Delucchi, K.L., 57, 74, 88, 99
Davies, D., 266, 281, 292, 294
deVoss, G.G., 172, 196
Dishaw, M.M., 38, 51, 138, 141, 165, 196
Doyle, W., 4, 8, 76, 99, 100-101, 151, 240
Dreikurs, R., 112-113, 136-137

Edwards, C., 207, 210, 224
Elliott, S.N., 113, 137
Emmer, E., 54-57, 62, 64, 74-75, 78, 99, 101,
   110, 114, 136, 151, 165-166, 179, 183-184,
   196
Epstein, J.L., 216, 262-263, 266-267, 270, 283,
   286-287, 292, 294
Evans, S.S., 119, 124, 136
Evans, W.H., 119, 124, 136
Evertson, C.M., 7-8, 10, 54-57, 62, 64, 74-75,
   78, 88, 98-99, 110, 114, 119, 136, 151, 165-
   166, 179, 183-184, 196, 239, 256

Farrar, M.T., 236, 256
Feather, N., 82, 96, 99

SUBJECT INDEX

Abuse (*see* Child abuse, Substance abuse)
Academic learning time (ALT), 142-143, 162, 183
  (*See also* Time)
Accountability:
  individual, in groupwork, 211-213, 220, 222
  in learning centers, 154
  in recitation, 236
  of students, 151-158
Action zone, 33-34, 241
Active listening, 333, 353-355
Activity flow, 138, 144-145, 150, 161-163
Alateen (*see* Substance abuse)
Alcohol (*see* Substance abuse)
Allocated time, 139, 143, 161
  (*See also* Time)
Assertive Discipline, 68
Attending and acknowledging, 333, 353, 356
Attention Deficit Disorder (ADD), 29-30, 111, 147, 303-304
Attention Deficit Hyperactivity Disorder (ADHD), 29-30, 111, 147, 303-304
Available time, 139, 142
  (*See also* Time)

Back-to-school night, 276-278, 284, 291
Beginning Teacher Evaluation Study (BTES), 138-139, 141-143, 152-153, 157, 165
Behavior modification, 91, 116, 119-124, 134
  contingency contracting, 116, 119, 124, 134
  self-evaluation, 116, 119, 122-123, 134
  self-instruction, 116, 119, 123-124, 134
  self-monitoring, 116, 119-122, 134
Behavior problems, 100-136
  and drug-exposed children, 338-339
  and importance of context, 101-102
  kinds of, 100
    cheating, 126-127
    defiance, 129-131
    profanity, 126
    sexually related behavior, 131
    stealing, 127-128

    tattling, 126
  prevention of, 6-7, 10, 76-99
    (*See also* Activity flow)
  strategies for dealing with, 104-131, 340
    (*See also* Disciplinary interventions; Violence)
Beliefs:
  about efficacy, 264
  of families, 286
  about instruction, 193
  about management, 7, 65
Bilingual education (*see* Special needs, helping children with)

Chapter 1, 305-307, 315, 324
  (*See also* Compensatory education; Special needs, helping children with)
Child abuse and neglect, 9, 16, 133, 262, 295-296, 329, 333, 349-352, 357-359
  accusations of, teachers' fears of, 81
  difficulty of detecting, 351
  indicators of, 350
  reluctance to report, 352
  reporting procedures for, 352
  types of, 350
Children of alcoholics/addicts (*see* Substance abuse)
Class-running routines (*see* Routines)
Classroom environment, 3-6
  complexity of, 5
  and construction of history, 5, 10
  contradictions in, 3-4, 9-10
  and crack-affected children, 340
  crowdedness of, 3
  familiarity of, 3
  immediacy of, 5, 10
  lack of privacy in, 5
  mismatch of, with children's needs, 315-318, 324
  multidimensionality of, 4, 10
  physical design of (*see* Physical environment)